International Finance and Banking

International Finance and Banking

Edited by Rupert Fry

Clanrye International
www.clanryeinternational.com

Clanrye International,
750 Third Avenue, 9th Floor,
New York, NY 10017, USA

ISBN: 978-1-63240-621-7

Cataloging-in-Publication Data

International finance and banking / edited by Rupert Fry.
p. cm.
Includes bibliographical references and index.
ISBN 978-1-63240-621-7
1. International finance. 2. Banks and banking, International. 3. Finance. 4. Banks and banking.
I. Fry, Rupert.
HG3881 .I58 2017
332.042--dc23

For information on all Clanrye International publications visit our website at www.clanryeinternational.com

CLANRYE INTERNATIONAL

Printed in China.

Contents

Preface

As the field of banking and finance is emerging at a rapid pace, the contents of this book will help the readers understand the fundamental as well as modern concepts and applications of international finance and banking. The introduction of digital payment gateways, cashless transactions, etc. are some of the recent advancements in international finance and banking. The readers of this book would gain knowledge that would broaden their perspective about finance and banking. It also attempts to understand how the industry is evolving to keep up with the dynamics of monetary transactions. A number of latest researches have been included to keep the readers up-to-date with the global concepts in the area of finance and banking.

This book is a comprehensive compilation of works of different researchers from varied parts of the world. It includes valuable experiences of the researchers with the sole objective of providing the readers (learners) with a proper knowledge of the concerned field. This book will be beneficial in evoking inspiration and enhancing the knowledge of the interested readers.

In the end, I would like to extend my heartiest thanks to the authors who worked with great determination on their chapters. I also appreciate the publisher's support in the course of the book. I would also like to deeply acknowledge my family who stood by me as a source of inspiration during the project.

Editor

1

Audit reports timeliness: Empirical evidence from Tunisia

Imen Fakhfakh Sakka[1]* and Anis Jarboui[2]
*Corresponding author: Imen Fakhfakh Sakka, Faculty of Economics and Management of Sfax (FSEGS), Department of Finance and Accounting, Sfax, Tunisia
E-mail: imenfakhfakh.sakka@gmail.com
Reviewing editor: Marco Bisogno, University of Salerno, Italy

Abstract: Timeliness of corporate annual financial reports is considered to be a critical and important factor affecting the usefulness of information that is made available to external users. The purpose of this paper is to examine the relationship between corporate governance, external auditor's characteristics index, and timeliness in light of the recent amendments to the Financial Security Law (2005) in Tunisia. The paper uses panel data methodology of 28 Tunisian companies listed on the Tunisian Stock Exchange over the period 2006–2013. This study concludes that the good structures of corporate governance play a key role in improving the quality of timeliness of financial reports. As for the empirical tests, they appear to indicate that whenever the audit report publication date proves to be short, the external auditor's characteristics index is discovered to be high.

Subjects: Accounting; Business, Management and Accounting; Corporate Governance

Keywords: timeliness; corporate governance; external auditor's characteristics

1. Introduction

One of the important objectives of corporate reporting is to provide information that will assist external users in decision-making. This information, however, is required to be made available within a short period of time from the end of the reported period; otherwise, it loses some of its economic value (Al-Ajmi, 2008). Timeliness becomes one of the most important characteristics of financial accounting information for the accounting profession (Soltani, 2002). Timeliness can also be viewed as a way of reducing information asymmetry by improving pricing of securities, and by mitigating insider trading, leaks, and rumors in the market, and reducing the opportunity to spread rumors about the companies' financial health and performance. Audit report lag, which is the number of days from fiscal year end to audit report date, or inordinate audit lag, compromise the quality of financial

ABOUT THE AUTHORS

Imen Fakhfakh Sakka, PhD, is an associate researcher at LARTIGE (Laboratory of Research) in the University of Sfax, Tunisia. She is the corresponding author and her research interests are in audit risk, audit certification, and corporate governance.

Anis Jarboui, PhD, is a professor of finance and accounting at the University of Sfax, Tunisia. His research interests are in corporate governance, financial literacy, and behavioral finance.

PUBLIC INTEREST STATEMENT

An efficient and effective capital market needs a transparent financial reporting system to boost investors' confidence in making investment decisions. Given that the audit reports become the only reliable source available to investors and other external users, in a developing country like Tunisia, it will be interesting to identify all the factors that may influence audit certification (such as corporate governance and earning management). This identification can help guide the reforms to improve the functioning of the financial market, especially after the promulgation of the Financial Security Law (2005).

reporting by not providing timely information to investors. It's for these reasons that timeliness has long been recognized as one of the qualitative attributes of general purpose financial reports. The importance of timeliness in investors' decisions are reported in a number of studies in various countries' contexts. These studies have revealed the persistence of certain divergences with respect to measures, methodology, applied variables, as well as reached conclusions. Noteworthy, however, the auditing mission is usually carried out in a multi-stakeholder characterized environment. As a matter of fact, the auditor shall simultaneously stave to satisfy the audited firm's needs, respect the pertinent laws and regulations, and protect the public as well to ensure a certain proper profitability within a highly competitive market.

This research aims at studying the determinants of the timeliness of Tunisian annual reports during the period 2006–2013. Specifically, it tests the relationship between audit quality and auditees' specific characteristics, including corporate governance, with respect to both the timeliness of annual reports and the audit delay.

Indeed, corporate governance is maintained through diverse structures and mechanisms likely to help reconcile the executives and shareholders' divergent interests as well as a firm value (Wirtz, 2004), ensure a better performance or output limit wealth transfer among shareholders and the manager thus reducing shareholders risk of being dispossessed. Hence, the more effective these mechanisms prove to be in achieving their monitoring and cooperation role with the external auditor, the higher the audit mission quality will be.

Given, auditor's quality adds a significant value to investors in capital markets because they often use audited financial statements by auditors as the main basis for investment decisions (Sudsomboon & Ussahawanitchakit, 2009). It, therefore, seems well appropriate to understand the effect of control as provided by certain governance structures, and the requirement for a distinct external auditor's characteristics on timeliness. Our paper extends previous research by proposing an index to measure external auditor and using three proxies to explain timeliness. Our results add to the growing body of literature analyzing the relationship between corporate governance mechanisms and timeliness. They also offer a better understanding of the determinants of timeliness in the Tunisian context.

This present work is organized according to the following structure: Section 2 is devoted to presenting a theoretical framework and hypothesis development. As for, Section 3, it is designed to describe the applied methodology, the empirical model along with the variables' definitions. Finally, Section 4 involves the reached statistical results, summaries, and concluding remarks.

2. Theoretical framework

2.1. Agency theory

The agency relationship is a contract under which one party (the principal) engages another party (the agent) to perform some service on their behalf (Jensen & Meckling, 1976). As part of this, the principal will delegate some decision-making authority to the agent. This theory points out the role of certain corporate governance mechanisms' to decrease agency problems. In this context, Fama and Jensen (1983) have explained that outside board of directors could strengthen the firm value by lending experienced and monitoring services and supposed to be guardians of the shareholders' interests via monitoring and control.

According to Jensen and Meckling (1976), a component of the agency costs is represented by the monitoring costs supported by shareholders for the monitoring of the managers actions.

Since it is not acceptable to publish financial statements unless a certified public accountant (external and internal auditor) first audits them, the external audit effort is an important component of these costs, as long as auditors have to make sure that managers act according to the shareholders' interests, while also auditors have the required task to inspect the accounts of the company (Azubike & Aggreh, 2014). It may hence be supposed that auditors will spend more time inspecting the managers' activity and therefore increase timeliness if there are agency problems. In fact, the agency relationship between the managers and shareholders may cause the agency conflicts to occur, thus the corporate governance is assumed as the best monitoring and controlling mechanism to reduce such problems. In relation to financial reporting and audit timeliness, corporate governance mechanism may reduce the audit business risk of the company; hence reduce the audit work and hours taken by the auditor to complete their annual audit work.

2.2. External auditor's characteristics

According to DeAngelo (1981), the quality of the audit is composed of the joint probability that the auditor can detect and report material errors in the client's accounting system. Detection of material errors is related to technical competence, while the disclosure of these errors refers to the auditor's independence.

In addition, it is found that most literatures have been contented to approximate or even equate audit quality with the quality of auditors. However, there are some exceptions. Manita and Elommal (2010) claim that audit quality should be in terms of audit process quality and the studies on audit process should put emphasis on examining different stages of the audit process. In fact, in analyzing the audit quality impact on timeliness, previously conducted researchers have undertaken to distinguish the audit quality on the basis of external auditor's characteristics (independence, competence, Big N, industry specialization, audit fees, audit tenure, etc.).

In this context, some studies highlighting that Big N audit firms are more reliable and far highly qualified to minimize timeliness (Afify, 2009; Ahmed & Hossain Md, 2010; Lee & Jahng, 2008; Modugu, Eragbhe, & Ikhatua, 2012; Mohamad-Nor, Shafie, & Wan-Hussin, 2010; Owusu-Ansah & Leventis, 2006). In addition, several elaborated empirical studies are discovered to emphasize the prevalence of a significant relationship between timeliness and longer auditor–client tenure (Habib & Bhuiyan, 2011; Pizzini, Lin, Vargus, & Ziegenfuss, 2011; Wan-Hussin & Bamahros, 2013), since an auditor can save time by the experiment that obtained over this period. Other studies illustrate that audit report lag is shorter for firms audited by industry specialist auditors given that they are able to develop industry-specific knowledge and expertise and to familiarize themselves quickly with the clients' business operations and, therefore, are likely to complete the audit sooner than their non-specialist counterparts (Habib & Bhuiyan, 2011). It is clear that previous studies are interested in studying the effect of the external auditor on the audit period by choosing each time a different proxy to the external auditor. We suppose that, external auditor with high quality are more capable to complete the auditing mission and minimize timely disclosure. Thus, the following hypothesis can be formulated:

H1: There is a negative relationship between external auditor's characteristics and timeliness.

2.3. Corporate governance and timeliness

Corporate governance searches for more accuracy of disclosed information and organizes the relationship between the shareholders, board of directors, and management (Ezat & El-Masry, 2008). The variables, which will be used in this research work study, are directors' boards and ownership structure

2.3.1. Directors' boards and timeliness

The board constitutes a major control mechanism, exhaustively discussed on corporate governance-related research (Kachouri Ben Saad & Jarboui, 2015). In fact, the effectiveness of Directors' boards, as a control mechanism, is not very often guaranteed as it highly depends on the following main characteristics.

The number of directors on the company's board should play a critical role in monitoring of the board and in taking strategic decisions. One of the disadvantages associated with a large board is a communication/ coordination problem, which makes a large board a less efficient monitor than a small board. Some studies argue that a large board assists in performing more monitoring, providing companies with the diversity that help them in providing critical resources and eliminate environmental uncertainties, alleviating the dominance of the CEO, and increasing the pool of expertise that yields from the diversity of the board (Singh, Mathur, & Gleason, 2004; Yermack, 1996). Other studies find that a large board is likely to increase relevant experience, can assist with providing a greater deal of submitting greater deal of control, submitting greater critical resources, help greatly in avoiding uncertainties, and securing a promotional ground for enhancing skills and competences (Singh et al., 2004). In this respect, Ezat and El-Masry (2008) have indicated that listed Egyptian companies, involving a large number of directors within the board prove to be more updated with respect to websites. They find that as a result of the diversity of the board's membership and their desire to disclose more information on their company's website to attract more investors and satisfy the shareholders' needs. Consequently, the larger the number of the board's directors, the greater the desire for online disclosure. Thus, the following hypotheses sound worth reformulating:

H2: There is a negative relationship between board size and timeliness.

The board independence measured based on the proportion of non-executive directors to the total directors (Abdelsalam & Street, 2007). According to Jensen and Meckling (1976), external members' integration within the board helps increase the effectiveness of the board in the management and monitoring activities' effectiveness in order to prevent financial statement-related frauds. Stand as they are effective factors, should they represent more than 50% (Johari, Saleh, Jaffer, & Hassan, 2008). The results of previous studies which have examined the relationship between board composition and disclosure are mixed. Some studies show a significant relationship which is either positive (such as Abdelsalam & Street, 2007; Afify, 2009; Azubike & Aggreh, 2014), or negative (such as Eng & Mak, 2003). Nevertheless, Haniffa and Cooke (2002) did not find any significant relationship. Thus, the following hypotheses sound worth reformulating:

H3: There is a negative relationship between the board independence and timeliness.

Within the same context, the agency theory suggests that duality constitutes a major reason for the board's inefficiency (Jensen, 1993). Agency theory supports the separation of the two roles to provide for checks and balances over management's performance (Haniffa & Cooke, 2002). Combining both Chairmen and the CEO functions designates well the combination of two roles resulting in a high concentration of power likely to compromise the board's independence with a negative impact being engendered on shareholder's wealth. As a matter of fact, a structural unit helps prevent an effective disclosure of information (Gul & Leung, 2004; Haniffa & Cooke, 2002) from taking place, thus standing as a quality control endangering threat, a means of restraining unfavorable information to outsiders, and as a factor which increases timeliness (Afify, 2009). Consequently, the below may well be posed:

H4: There is a positive relationship between CEO duality and timeliness.

2.3.2. Ownership structure and timeliness

Ownership structure, as an internal control mechanism, has been discovered to be a crucial determinant of highly effective better governance practices, whose concentration and composition could strongly influence the power authority relationship between shareholders and managers and would influence the shareholders to invest in firm management control.

Concentration of ownership refers to the group who has the most influence among the equity owners, while dispersion of ownership looks only at the separation of ownership between managers and equity owners as a group (Haniffa & Cooke, 2002). When the property proves to be concentrated, a greater pressure is being placed on auditors to achieve elaborating the report within a very short time, for obtaining timely information. This finding is confirmed by the results reached by Al-Ajmi (2008) showing that the more concentrated the ownership structure is, the shorter the audit delay will be. In this context, two major studies elaborated by Ezat and El-Masry (2008), as well as Marston and Polei (2004) have stressed that the dispersion of the company ownership structure helps entice companies to disclose information and have more updated websites to reduce owners' information cost and help them monitor their manager's behavior. Consequently, this study investigates the relationship between ownership structure and timeliness. We suppose that companies whose ownership structure is concentrate tend to disclose less information. Thus, the following hypothesis seems worth testing:

H5: There is a negative relationship between ownership concentration and timeliness.

Given the considerable weight that have institutional investors enjoy within the company, they are liable to play an active role in monitoring and disciplining of manager discretionary powers as well as financial "reporting" process (Zureigat, 2011), this which might well help in minimizing financial statement-related fraud (Lajmi & Gana, 2011; Sharma, 2004). Previously conducted empirical studies dealing with the relationship between institutional ownership and audit reporting quality are not numerous. Indeed, Abdelsalam and Street (2007) along with Al-Ajmi (2008) have found that the increased institutional investors' ownership right help well in minimizing the audit achievement allocated time and reduce the likelihood of fraud (Lajmi & Gana, 2011). Consequently, institutional investors contribute to more efficient monitoring of management and that the benefits of better monitoring are shared by all stakeholders. Thus, the following hypotheses sound worth reformulating:

H6: There is a negative relationship between institutional ownership and timeliness.

3. Research design

3.1. Sample selection and data

The sample subject of study is composed of 28 Tunisian companies listed in the Tunisian Stock Exchange (TSE), over in eight-year period from the 2006 to 2013. It excludes companies from the finance-related sector as they operate under highly regulated regime. The listed companies' relevant data are collected from published financial statements as well as from official bulletins available from the prospectus found at the Financial Market Council of Tunis and on the BVMT websites. Our ultimate sample turns out to involve some 28 companies ensure achieving 224 observations (Table 1).

It is worth noting that we have considered opting for the balanced panel approach to ensure achieving consistent results.

3.2. Measures of external auditor's characteristics

People view external auditor's characteristics differently and sometimes they only focus on one or a bit more of the quite many attributes. Hence, a variety of audit quality proxies mushroomed

Table 1. Sample selection

Initial sample	**77**
Financial firms	(34)
Firms with insufficient data	(15)
Final sample	28
Study duration	8
Total observations	224

during the last years to help people assess the level of quality. Meanwhile, we have found that looking at single indicator alone would not provide a full image of audit quality. Relying on several previously conducted work studies, the present study attempts to devise a special EAI that rests on Bing, Xin Huang, Li, and Zhu's (2014) study, which includes different types of audit quality proxies (Table 2).

Five attributes are considered: auditor size, auditor industry specialization, independence, audit firm tenure et co-audit. EAI represents the index of external auditor's characteristics that takes the values 0, 1, 2, 3, 4, or 5.

For them, the index is calculated by simple summation of the notes obtained at the level of each single company (According, EAI = 5 denotes a higher quality external auditor). As a matter of fact, this particular type of additive and unweighted scoring approach has actually been applied and supported by several elaborated research studies.

3.3. Models and variables

The previously conducted studies have undertaken to apply calendar day timeliness starting from the fiscal year-end up until audit report achievement date. Noteworthy, however, according to Tunisian regulations highlights the distinction between two different dates namely a date corresponding to auditors' signature following achievement of the auditing mission, along with a date signifying publication at the CMF. For this reason three timeliness associated have been adopted measures (Al-Ajmi, 2008): They are: the intermediary period (INTERIM) the total period (TPERIOD) and the checking period (AUDITLAG). For our set research objective to be reached, the following regression is going to be estimated:

$$\text{Timeliness} = \beta_0 + \beta_1\ \text{BSIZE}_{i,t} + \beta_2\ \text{BIND}_{i,t} + \beta_3\ \text{CEO}_{i,t} + \beta_4\ \text{CONC}_{i,t} + \beta_5\ \text{INVES}_{i,t} + \beta_6\ \text{EAI}_{i,t} + \beta_7\ \text{SIZE}_{i,t} + \beta_8\ \text{LEV}_{i,t} + \varepsilon_{i,t}$$

where EAI = external auditor's characteristics index, BSIZE = the board size, BIND = the board independence, CEO = CEO duality, CONC = ownership concentration, INVES = institutional ownership, SIZE = firm size, LEV = debt level.[1]

Table 2. External auditor's characteristics index

Proxies	Sources	Measures
Auditor size/type	DeAngelo (1981), Francis (2004), Behn, Choi, and Kang (2008), Clinch, Stokes, and Zhu (2010), Kanagaretnam, Krishnan, Lobo, and Mathieu (2011), Chen, Chen, Lobo, and Wang (2011)	1: If a firm is audited by Big 4 audit firm
		0: Otherwise
Auditor industry specialization/ expertise	Carcello and Nagy (2004), Francis (2004), Watkins, Hillison, and Morecroft (2004), Mansouri, Pirayesh, and Salehi (2009), Li, Stokes, Taylor, and Wong (2009), Hakim and Omri (2010), Chen, Hsu, Huang, and Yang (2013)	1: If a firm is audited by industry specialist
		0: Otherwise
Independence: The likelihood of issuing going concern report	Carey and Simnett (2006), Jackson, Moldrich, and Roebuck (2008), Francis and Yu (2009), DeFond and Lennox (2011), Gunny and Zhang (2013)	1: If the opinion is unqualified
		0: Otherwise
Audit firm tenure	Hakim and Omri (2010)	1: For three years of audit tenure or more
		0: Otherwise
Co-audit	Gana and Krichen (2013)	1: If company is audited by second auditor or more

Table 3. Summary of variables definitions and measurements		
Variable names		**Measures**
Dependent variable: Timeliness		
Total period	TPERIOD	Number of days between the fiscal year-end and the publication date (log)
Interim period	INTERIM	Number of days from the external auditor's signature date on the audit report and publication date
Audit lag	AUDIT LAG	Number of days between the fiscal year-end and the external auditor's signature date (log)
Independent variables		
Board size	BSIZE	Number of directors on the board
Board independence	BIND	Number of outside directors to total of directors within the board
CEO duality	CEO	A dicothomous variable taking value "1" if there is duality function of the CEO, "0" otherwise
Ownership Concentration	CONC	A dicothomous variable taking value "1" if the proportions of shares held by the majority shareholder of the company >20%, "0" otherwise
Institutional Ownership	INVES	Proportions of equity held by institutional investors
External auditor's characteristics index	EAI	The summation of the notes obtained at the level of each single firm
Controls variable		
Firm size	SIZE	Log of firm's sales
Debt level	LEV	Total liabilities to total assets

The regression serves to determine the impact of internal governance mechanisms and external auditor's characteristics impact on timeliness. Table 3, below, depicts the entirety of the variables' pertaining measurements.

4. Empirical results

4.1. Descriptive analysis

Table 4 reports the descriptive statistics pertaining to the entirety of variables investigated in this study.

The descriptive statistics result indicates that the timeliness variable is an average rate of 155 days after closure of the fiscal year, ranging between 70 and 333 days. Actually this value highly exceeds greatly the regulatory ceiling (four months).[2] Still, delay witnessed audit report publication is highly dependent on the audit reporting signature by the external auditor which is equal to an average 129 days varying between 60 and 325 days. This finding might well have an explanation in the auditor's mal-conscience to respect the legal deadlines necessary for completing the auditing mission. As for the "INTERM" period, finding suggests that the mean period is 13 days, which may well extend up to 69 days at maximum. These findings suggest that the majority of Tunisian companies do not appear to respect the legal deadlines, despite the Tunisian legislator's efforts in this regard and adoption of the Financial Security Law (2005, Loi n° 2005-96 du 18 octobre 2005 relative au renforcement de la sécurité des relations financières).

The proportion tests of EAI variable highlights the following major results for the evolution of EAI, and shows that the average is of an order of 2.053, with a minimum rate (EAI = 0), and a maximum

Table 4. Variables' descriptive statistics

Numeric variables' descriptive statistics

Variables	Minimum	Maximum	Mean	Std. deviation
TPERIOD	70.00	333.00	154.54	40.17
INTERIM	1.00	69.00	12.72	11.42
AUDIT LAG	60.00	325.00	128.52	36.08
BSIZE	4	12	8.47	1.88
BIND	0	83	41.23	26.52
INVES	0	88.80	15.56	22.69
EAI	0	5	2.05	1.35
SIZE	13.70	20.12	17.39	1.31
LEV	8.00	97.00	47.43	19.98

Dichotomous variables' descriptive statistics

Variables	Frequency		Percentage (%)	
	Variable = 0	Variable = 1	Variable = 0	Variable = 1
CEO	82	142	36.61	63.39
CONC	153	71	68.30	31.70

Notes: TPERIOD = Number of days between the financial year-end and the publication date (log); AUDIT LAG = Number of days between the financial year-end and opinion signature date (log); INTERIM = Number of days from the opinion signature date on the auditors' reports and the publication date; BSIZE = Number of directors on the board; BIND = Number of outsiders directors to total of directors on the board; CEO = "1" if there is duality function of the CEO, "0" otherwise; CONC = "1" if the proportions of shares held by the majority shareholder of the company > 20%, "0" otherwise; INVES = Proportions of equity held by institutional investors; EAI = The summation of the notes obtained at the level of each single firm; SIZE = log of firm's sales; LEV = total Liabilities to Total Assets.

rate (EAI = 5). Hence, it appears clear that the EAI, relevant to the TSE (Tunisian Stock Exchange)-listed companies, is marked by noticeable significant variations. These remarkable shifts are actually reflected in the firms' audit nature, size, and characteristics.

This table indicates well that most Tunisian companies (63.39%) tend to be characterized with a president and the CEO respective roles. It is actually this combination of roles which leads to a high concentration of power likely to threaten the board's independence.

4.2. Correlation analysis

The correlation coefficients between independent variables are shown in Table 5. The Pearson correlation matrix demonstrates well that no correlation is discovered to be superior to "0.9," thus corroborating the reference work conducted by Tabachnick and Fidell (2007). Such a finding allows to accept the null hypothesis of no correlation between variables. In addition, the variance inflation factors (VIF) have computed the presence of collinearity phenomenon among the explanatory variables. Indeed, in all cases the VIF are discovered to be set at below two levels, a fact which confirms the absence of any multicollinearity problems.

The highest correlation is between the two variables, firm size and EAI at 0.5009, which suggests that multicollinearity is not a serious problem that would compromise the regression results.

4.3. Regression analysis

Based on panel data framework, our econometric estimates will be undertaken according to a panel cylinder capacity. Certain tests[3] seem well applicable to testifying the model's estimation via generalized least squares approach, by means of STATA 12 software. Table 6 depicts the regression

Table 5. Pearson correlations analysis

	BSIZE	BIND	CEO	CONC	INVES	EAI	SIZE	LEV	VIF
BSIZE	1								1.33
BIND	0.1432*	1							1.13
CEO	0.0169	0.0462	1						1.08
CONC	−0.1289	0.2198*	−0.0400	1					1.20
INVES	0.0004	0.1089	−0.1339*	0.2409*	1				1.23
EAI	0.0956	0.1669*	−0.0798	−0.1053	0.2824	1			153
SIZE	0.4378*	0.0645	−0.1751*	−0.1548*	0.2182	0.5009*	1		1.80
LEV	0.0879	0.0147	0.1278	−0.0706	−0.0528	0.1908*	0.1646*	1	1.09

Notes: TPERIOD = Number of days between the financial year-end and the publication date (log); AUDIT LAG = Number of days between the financial year-end and opinion signature date (log); INTERIM = Number of days from the opinion signature date on the auditors' reports and the publication date; BSIZE = Number of directors on the board; BIND = Number of outsiders directors to total of directors on the board; CEO = "1" if there is duality function of the CEO, "0" otherwise; CONC = "1" if the proportions of shares held by the majority shareholder of the company > 20%, "0" otherwise; INVES = Proportions of equity held by institutional investors; EAI = The summation of the notes obtained at the level of each single firm; SIZE = log of firm's sales; LEV = total Liabilities to Total Assets.

*Correlation is significant at the 0,05 level (2-tailed).

analysis relevant to this study. The three respective exhibit the figures of models 43.26, 14.13 and 48.60% which are actually highly significant.

The attained finding shows that corporate governance prove to have an important influence on timeliness. In fact, the attained results prove to reveal well the fact that the board size (BSIZE) sounds to exhibit a negative and significant effect (at 1% threshold) on timeliness as measured by TPERIOD and AUDIT LAG, along with a positive relationship and significant (at 10% level) with INTERIM. These results suggest well that a large board helps well implement greater more control, eliminate environmental uncertainties, and facilitate the external auditor's mission. This result proves to be highly consistent with that released by Ezat and El-Masry (2008). Nevertheless, this figures may well have a negative implication and could result in delaying the audit report release. Moreover, for the second variable, the obtained results are discovered to be inconclusive because the relationship between timeliness and the board independence is discovered to be non significant with TPERIOD, positive and significant within a 1% threshold with INTERIM, significantly negative at 10% with AUDIT LAG. It was thought that, the more independent the board is, the better the company in reducing their audit business risk because of less conflict between manager and shareholders; hence shorten the audit delay. This finding is inconsistent with agency theory and resource dependence theory, which suggests a non executive chair can play a more independent role in shaping disclosure due to influence and power.

Regarding CEO variable, a positive and significant relationship (at 1%) appears to prevail within the president's combined roles of president's board Chairman and CEO and timeliness as measured by total period (TPERIOD) and the audit review (AUDIT LAG) along with a negatively significant relationship with the interim period (INTERIM). This can be explained by the fact that when the personality is dominant, it is likely to render the taken decisions somewhat objective, which is likely to threaten the external auditor's mission, enticing the auditor to devote a greater deal of time to review the audit accounts. In fact, this result proves to be consistent with that present by Abdelsalam and Street (2007).

It is worth noting that our achieved results appear to be inconsistent with the studies conducted by Amari and Jarboui (2013), demonstrating that no significant relationship actually exist between the ownership structure and the interim period. Yet, this relationship proves to change with the two other remaining periods (TPERIOD and AUDIT LAG) by responding in a similar way. Indeed, ownership concentration (CONC) which is measured by a dummy variable tends to exhibit a

Table 6. Regression results

Variables	TPERIOD			INTERIM			AUDIT LAG		
	Coefficients	zStatistic	P > |z	Coefficients	z-Statistic	P > |z	Coefficients	z-Statistic	P > |z
BSIZE	−0.029***	−5.68	0.000	0.602*	1.84	0.066	−0.028***	−6.11	0.000
BIND	−0.062	−1.63	0.103	0.024***	2.68	0.007	−0.062*	−1.81	0.070
CEO	0.145**	7.71	0.000	−2.738**	−2.37	0.018	0.105***	5.78	0.000
CONC	0.057**	2.25	0.025	−2.588*	−1.93	0.053	0.099***	5.10	0.000
INVES	−0.130**	−2.49	0.013	5.755**	1.97	0.048	−0.206***	−4.28	0.000
EAI	0.008	0.90	0.366	−2.015***	−3.69.	0.000	0.043***	5.17	0.000
SIZE	−0.049***	−4.93	0.000	0.002	0.00	0.996	−0.032***	3.35	0.001
LEV	0.223***	6.34	0.000	2.252*	1.92	0.055	0.177***	5.08	0.000
N	224			224			224		
R^2	43.26%			14.13%			48.60%		
Prob. > Chi-2	0.0000			0.0001			0.0000		

Notes:TPERIOD = Numberofdaysbetweenthefinancialyear-endandthepublicationdate(log);AUDITLAG = Numberofdaysbetween the financial year-end and opinion signature date (log); INTERIM = Number of days from the opinion signature date on the auditors' reports and the publication date; BSIZE = Number of directors on the board; BIND = Number of outsiders directors to total of directors on the board; CEO = "1" if there is duality function of the CEO, "0" otherwise; CONC = "1" if the proportions of shares held by the majority shareholder of the company > 20%, "0" otherwise; INVES = Proportions of equity held by institutional investors; EAI = The summation of the notes obtained at the level of each single firm; SIZE = log of firm's sales; LEV = total Liabilities to Total Assets.

*Correlations significant at the 10% level.

**Correlations significant at the 5% level.

***Correlations significant at the 1% level.

simultaneously positive and significant relationship (at 1% level) with the audit review period and the total period. This finding helps us maintain that concentrated ownership (the proportions of shares held by the majority shareholder of the company > 20%) might lead the external auditors to further intensify the check and assessment tests extended and extend the audit period deadline, an idea that seems highly consistent with that advanced by Apadore and Mohd Noor (2013).

As a matter of fact, our regression results appear to reveal that institutional ownership (INVES) does prove to have a negative and significant relationship between and both audit period and audit lag at threshold of 1% level. Nevertheless, the estimated coefficient is discovered to be positive with INTERIM. Institutional investors prove to own significant proportion of shares, they apt to become active investors in firm management control and in monitoring the financial "reporting" process, thus facilitating speeding up the accounts of certification task (Abdelsalam & Street, 2007). With respect to the empirical results, they show that the variable external auditor's characteristics index (EAI) sounds to have no significant effect on TPERIOD. In reality, this result seems to be inconsistent with previous studies released results, highlighting the prevalence of a significantly relationship between timeliness and certain characteristics of external auditor (Afify, 2009; Ahmed & Hossain Md, 2010; Habib & Bhuiyan, 2011; Lee & Jahng, 2008; Modugu et al., 2012; Mohamad-Nor et al., 2010; Owusu-Ansah & Leventis, 2006; Wan-Hussin & Bamahros, 2013, etc.). These studies illustrate that timeliness is shorter for firms audited by industry specialist auditors or by Big N audit firms given that they are able to develop industry-specific knowledge and expertise and to familiarize themselves quickly with the clients' business operations. In turn, these studies illustrate that audit report lag is shorter for firms audited by industry specialist auditors and Big N audit firms, given that they are able to develop industry-specific knowledge and expertise and to familiarize themselves quickly with the clients' business operations.

With regard to the control variables, the results indicate the prevalence of a significantly negative relationship between firm size and timeliness. These findings are consistent with our predicted expectation and the already elaborated preceding empirical studies (Wan-Hussin & Bamahros, 2013). As for the second control variable, a positive relationship has been attained between leverage and timeliness, highlighting that the audit report delivery deadline of the mostly indebted companies discovered to be is higher than that of least indebted ones. This result proves to collaborate well with finding achieved by Cohen and Leventis (2013), Che-Ahmad and Abidin (2008) and Al-ghanem and Hegazy (2011). This implies that companies reporting more debt to equity in their capital structure are more likely to present their financial statements on time because of the need to provide the creditors with audited financial statements as at when due. Agency theory implies that the management would likely disclose the information on the Internet to voluntarily allow creditors to monitor the affairs of the firms as well as assessing the ability of firms to pay debts on time (Debrency et al., 2002).

From the above discussion, the findings suggest that timeliness can be shorten with board independence and high proportion of institutional investors. Those factors are able to mitigate the problem of long audit report lag, and thus able to improve the financial reporting quality.

5. Summary and conclusion

In this study, the relationship binding corporate governance, external auditor's characteristics and timeliness was examined with respect to a sample made up of 28 Tunisian companies observed over the period 2006–2013.

The results reached have revealed well that timely disclosure is on average some 155 days to be released highly exceeding regulatory ceiling limit. Moreover, the panel data regressions results have revealed that corporate governance significantly affects timeliness, turn out to be: The Board of Directors (board size and board composition, CEO duality) as well as ownership structure (capital concentration and institutional ownership), even though the significance signs prove to differ from one measure to another. The agency relationship between the managers and shareholders may cause agency conflicts, thus the corporate governance is assumed as the best monitoring and controlling mechanism to reduce such problems. This implies that corporate governance mechanism may reduce the audit business risk of the company; hence reduce the audit work and hours taken by the auditor to complete their annual audit work.

Besides, with respect to the relationship between timeliness and external auditor's characteristics, the reached results are discovered to be inconclusive. But a negative relationship turns out to match audit lag, which is the period between the financial year-end and opinion signature date, indicating that whenever the external auditor's characteristics proves to be high, the audit report publication date is discovered to be short.

Just like any other research work, the present study involves certain limitations. Firstly, the investigated sample size has been reduced to 28 companies owing to the unavailability of adequately necessary data relevant to the period under review (2006 and 2013). As for the second limitation, it relates to the neglect of certain items which may be included in calculating the external auditor's characteristics index (auditor change, auditor competence, audit fees, etc.). Hence, it would seem rather interesting to include, in a potential research work, the entirety of these factors for the sake of achieving results that would prove to be as realistic as possible.

Apart from contributing to the literature on corporate governance and audit timeliness, this study also falls under the strand of literature that examines the consequences of the regulatory changes introduced around the world to strengthen corporate governance and financial reporting transparency such as the Financial Security Law (2005) in Tunisia. Specifically, the study extend prior researches in emerging economies by providing important empirical evidence, on the role of corporate governance in financial reporting and auditing process.

Funding
The authors received no direct funding for this research.

Author details
Imen Fakhfakh Sakka[1]
E-mail: imenfakhfakh.sakka@gmail.com
Anis Jarboui[2]
E-mail: anisjarboui@yahoo.fr
[1] Faculty of Economics and Management of Sfax (FSEGS), Department of Finance and Accounting, Sfax, Tunisia.
[2] Department of Finance and Accounting, Higher Institute of Business Administration (ISAAS), Sfax, Tunisia.

Notes

1. Debt can be considered as a solution to the conflicts between managers and shareholders (Jensen & Meckling, 1976) thanks to its contractual obligations. The external auditor comes precisely to assert respect with the terms of the contract.
2. Article 3 CCC: "Companies lunching public offerings must publish the audit report in the Financial Market Council official newsletter as well as in Tunis published daily newspaper within four months following the financial year-end".
3. Tests of the individual effects (fixed and random), Hausman tests, and tests of heteroscedasticity.

References

Abdelsalam, O. H., & Street, D. L. (2007). Corporate governance and the timeliness of corporate internet reporting by U.K. listed companies. *Journal of International Accounting, Auditing & Taxation, 16*, 111.

Afify, H. A. E. (2009). Determinants of audit report lag. *Journal of Applied Accounting Research, 10*, 56–86. http://dx.doi.org/10.1108/09675420910963397

Ahmed, A., & Hossain Md, S. (2010). Audit report lag: A study of the Bangladeshi listed companies. *ASA University Review, 4*.

Al-Ajmi, J. (2008). Audit and reporting delays: Evidence from an emerging market. *Advances in Accounting, incorporating Advances in International Accounting, 24*, 217–226.

Al-ghanem, W., & Hegazy, M. (2011). An empirical analysis of audit delays and timeliness of corporate financial reporting in Kuwait. *Eurasian Business Review, 1*, 73–90.

Amari, M., & Jarboui, A. (2013). Financial reporting delay and investors behavior: Evidence from Tunisia. *International Journal Management Business Research, 3*, 57–67.

Apadore, K., & Mohd Noor, N. (2013). Determinants of audit report lag and corporate governance in Malaysia. *International Journal of Business and Management, 8*, 1833–8119.

Azubike, J., & Aggreh, M. (2014). Corporate governance and audit delay in Nigerian quoted companies. *European Journal of Accounting Auditing and Finance Research, 2*, 22–33.

Behn, B. K., Choi, J., & Kang, T. (2008). Audit quality and properties of analyst earnings forecasts. *The Accounting Review, 83*, 327–349. http://dx.doi.org/10.2308/accr.2008.83.2.327

Bing, J., Xin Huang, C., Li, A., & Zhu, X. (2014). Audit quality research report, Australian National Centre for Audit and Assurance Research, Canberra.

Carcello, J. V., & Nagy, A. L. (2004). Client size, auditor specialization and fraudulent financial reporting. *Managerial Auditing Journal, 19*, 651–668. http://dx.doi.org/10.1108/02686900410537775

Carey, P., & Simnett, R. (2006). Audit partner tenure and audit quality. *The Accounting Review, 81*, 653–676. http://dx.doi.org/10.2308/accr.2006.81.3.653

Che-Ahmad, A., & Abidin, S. (2008). Audit delay of listed companies: A case of Malaysia. *International Business Research, 1*, 32–39.

Chen, H., Chen, J. Z., Lobo, G. J., & Wang, Y. (2011). Effects of audit quality on earnings management and cost of equity capital: Evidence from China. *Contemporary Accounting Research, 28*, 892–925. http://dx.doi.org/10.1111/care.2011.28.issue-3

Chen, Y., Hsu, Y., Huang, M., & Yang, P. (2013). Quality, size and performance of Audi firms. *The International Journal of Business and Finance Research, 7*, 89–105.

Clinch, G., Stokes, D. J., & Zhu, T. (2010). *Audit quality and information asymmetry between traders.*

Cohen, S., & Leventis, S. (2013). Effects of municipal, auditing and political factors on audit delay. *Accounting Forum, 37*, 40–53. http://dx.doi.org/10.1016/j.accfor.2012.04.002

DeAngelo, L. E. (1981). Auditor size and audit quality. *Journal of Accounting and Economics, 3*, 183–199. http://dx.doi.org/10.1016/0165-4101(81)90002-1

Debrency, R., Gray, G., & Rahman, A. (2002). The determinant of Internet financial reporting. *Journal of accounting and Public Policy*, 21, 371–394.

DeFond, M. L., & Lennox, C. S. (2011). The effect of SOX on small auditor exits and audit quality. *Journal of Accounting and Economics, 52*, 21–40. http://dx.doi.org/10.1016/j.jacceco.2011.03.002

Eng, L. L., & Mak, Y. T. (2003). Corporate governance and voluntary disclosure. *Journal of Accounting and Public Policy, 22*, 325–345. http://dx.doi.org/10.1016/S0278-4254(03)00037-1

Ezat, A., & El-Masry, A. (2008). The impact of corporate governance on the timeliness of corporate internet reporting by Egyptian listed companies. *Managerial finance, 34*, 848 -1667.

Fama, E. F., & Jensen, M. C. (1983). Separation of ownership and control. *Journal of Law and Economics, 26*, 301–325.

Francis, J. R. (2004). What do we know about audit quality? *The British Accounting Review, 36*, 345–368. http://dx.doi.org/10.1016/j.bar.2004.09.003

Francis, J. R., & Yu, M. D. (2009). Big 4 office size and audit quality. *The Accounting Review, 84*, 1521–1552. http://dx.doi.org/10.2308/accr.2009.84.5.1521

Gana, M. R., & Krichen, A. L. (2013). Board characteristics and external audit quality: Complementary or substitute mechanisms? The Belgium case. *International Journal of Management Sciences and Business Research, 2*, 68–74.

Gul, F. A., & Leung, S. (2004). Board leadership, outside directors' expertise and voluntary corporate disclosures. *Journal of Accounting and Public Policy, 23*, 351–379. http://dx.doi.org/10.1016/j.jaccpubpol.2004.07.001

Gunny, K. A., & Zhang, T. C. (2013). PCAOB inspection reports and audit quality. *Journal of Accounting and Public Policy, 32*, 136–160. http://dx.doi.org/10.1016/j.jaccpubpol.2012.11.002

Habib, A., & Bhuiyan, B. (2011). Audit firm industry specialization and the audit report lag. *Journal of International Accounting, Auditing and Taxation, 20*, 32–44. http://dx.doi.org/10.1016/j.intaccaudtax.2010.12.004

Hakim, F., & Omri, A. (2010). Quality of the external auditor, information asymmetry, and bid-ask spread. *International Journal of Accounting and Information Management, 18*, 5–18. http://dx.doi.org/10.1108/18347641011023243

Haniffa, R. M., & Cooke, T. E. (2002). Culture, corporate governance and disclosure in Malaysian corporations. *Abacus, 38*, 317–349. http://dx.doi.org/10.1111/abac.2002.38.issue-3

Jackson, A. B., Moldrich, M., & Roebuck, P. (2008). Mandatory audit firm rotation and audit quality. *Managerial Auditing Journal, 23*, 420–437. http://dx.doi.org/10.1108/02686900810875271

Jensen, M. C. (1993). The modern industrial revolution, exit, and the failure of internal control systems. *The Journal of Finance, 48*, 831–880. http://dx.doi.org/10.1111/j.1540-6261.1993.tb04022.x

Jensen, M. C., & Meckling, W. (1976). Theory of the firm: Managerial behavior. *Agency Costs and Ownership Structure, Journal of Financial Economics, 3*, 305–360.

Johari, N., Saleh, N., Jaffer, R., & Hassan, M. (2008). The influence of board independence, competency and ownership on earnings management in Malaysia. *International Journal of Economics and Management, 2*, 281–306.

Kachouri Ben Saad, M., & Jarboui, A. (2015). Does corporate governance affect financial communication transparency? Empirical evidence in the Tunisian context. *Cogent Economics and Finance, 3*, 132–142.

Kanagaretnam, K., Krishnan, G. V., Lobo, G. J., & Mathieu, R. (2011). Audit quality and the market valuation of banks' allowance for loan losses*. *Accounting Perspectives, 10*, 161–193. http://dx.doi.org/10.1111/apr.2011.10.issue-3

Lajmi, A., & Gana, M. (2011). Director's board characteristics and audit quality: Evidence from Belgium. *Journal of Modern Accounting and Auditing, 7*, 668–679.

Lee, H.-Y., & Jahng, G-J. (2008). Determinants of audit report lag: Evidence from Korea—An examination of auditor-related factors. *The Journal of Applied Business Research, 24*, 27–44.

Li, Y., Stokes, D. J., Taylor, S. L., & Wong, L. (2009). *Audit quality, accounting attributes and the cost of equity capital* (Working Paper). Monash University.

Manita, R., & Elommal, N. (2010). The quality of audit process: An empirical study with audit committees. *International Journal of Business, 15*, 87–99.

Mansouri, A., Pirayesh, R., & Salehi, M. (2009). Audit competence and audit quality: Case in emerging economy. *International Journal of Business and Management, 4*, 17–25.

Marston, C., & Polei, A. (2004). Corporate reporting on the Internet by German companies. *International Journal of Accounting Information Systems, 5*, 285–311. http://dx.doi.org/10.1016/j.accinf.2004.02.009

Modugu, P. K., Eragbhe, E., & Ikhatua, O. J. (2012). Determinants of audit delay in Nigerian companies: Empirical evidence. *Research Journal of Finance and Accounting, 3*, 46–54.

Mohamad-Nor, M. N., Shafie, R., & Wan-Hussin, W. N. (2010). Corporate governance and audit report lag in Malaysia. *Asian Academy of Management Journal of Accounting and Finance, 6*, 57–84.

Owusu-Ansah, S., & Leventis, S. (2006). Timeliness of corporate annual financial reporting in Greece. *European Accounting Review, 15*, 273–287. http://dx.doi.org/10.1080/09638180500252078

Pizzini, M., Lin, S., Vargus, M. E., & Ziegenfuss, D. E. (2011). *The impact of internal audit function quality and contribution on audit delays*. Paper presented at the American Accounting Association Annual Meeting, Denver, CO.

Sharma, V. D. (2004). Board of directors' characteristics, institutional ownership, and fraud: Evidence from Australia. *Auditing: A Journal of Practice & Theory, 23*, 105–117.

Singh, M., Mathur, I., & Gleason, K. C. (2004). Governance and performance implications of diversification strategies: Evidence from large U.S. firms. *The Financial Review, 39*, 489–526. http://dx.doi.org/10.1111/fire.2004.39.issue-4

Soltani, B. (2002). Timeliness of corporate and audit reports. *The International Journal of Accounting, 37*, 215–246. http://dx.doi.org/10.1016/S0020-7063(02)00152-8

Sudsomboon, S., & Ussahawanitchakit, P. (2009). Professional audit competencies P: The effect on THAI'S CPAs Audit quality, reputation, and success. *Review of Business Research, 9*, 66–85.

Tabachnick, B. G., & Fidell, L. S. (2007). Using multivariate statistics. (5th ed.). Boston, MA: Allyn & Bacon.

Wan-Hussin, W. N., & Bamahros, H. M. (2013). Do investment in and the sourcing arrangement of the internal audit function affect audit delay? *Journal of Contemporary Accounting and Economics, 9*, 19–32. http://dx.doi.org/10.1016/j.jcae.2012.08.001

Watkins, A. L., Hillison, W., & Morecroft, S. E. (2004). Audit quality: A synthesis of theory and empirical evidence. *Journal of Accounting Literature, 23*, 153–193.

Wirtz, P. (2004). Meilleures pratiques de gouvernance, théorie de la firme et modèle de création de valeur: une appréciation critique des code de bonne conduite [Governance best practices, the firm theory and value creation model: a critical appraisal of the code of conduct]. *Cahier du FARGO*, (1051201).

Yermack, D. (1996). Higher market valuation of companies with a small board of directors. *Journal of Financial Economics, 40*, 185–221. http://dx.doi.org/10.1016/0304-405X(95)00844-5

Zureigat, Q. M. (2011). The effect of ownership structure on audit quality: Evidence from Jordan. *International Journal of Business and Social Science, 2*, 38–46.

2

Islamic and conventional bank market value: Manager behavior and investor sentiment

Mouna Abdelhedi-Zouch[1] and Achraf Ghorbel[1*]

*Corresponding author: Achraf Ghorbel, Laboratory URECA, Faculty of Economics and Management of Sfax, Université de Sfax, Sfax, Tunisia

E-mail: ghorbelachraf@yahoo.fr

Reviewing editor: David McMillan, University of Stirling, UK

Abstract: This paper studies the effect of bank manager behavior and investor behavior on market value of Islamic and conventional banks in the Middle East and North Africa region. Firstly, our analysis denoted the positive effect of discretionary behavior of manager on both types of banks on share prices since discretionary behavior transmits to investor a positive signal of future earnings' prospects. Also, we find that the conventional bank stock prices response is very high to negative signal compared with positive signal. This result is explained by prospect theory and loss aversion bias which specified that individuals are more sensitive to losses than gains of same magnitude. In particular, we discover that the negative effect of non-discretionary behavior is much lower on Islamic bank value since investors give more confidence to Islamic bank because they are motivated by the idea that Islamic banks are safer than conventional banks. Secondly, the results show that investor sentiment affects significantly both bank market prices. Thus, both Islamic and conventional banks' market value depends similarly on manager and investor behavior. The implication of this paper is that Islamic bank concentrations reveal a positive effect on their price values because of the recently increased investments in Islamic banks.

Subjects: Banking; Banking & Finance Law; International Finance

Keywords: Islamic and conventional banks; manager behavior; investor sentiment; bank concentration; performance

ABOUT THE AUTHORS

Mouna Abdelhedi-Zouch is an assistant professor at Higher School of Business of Sfax, University of Sfax, Tunisia. His research interests include Behavioral Finance, Financial Crises, Islamic Finance and Earnings Management. She has published articles, among others, in Research in *International Business and Finance*, *Journal of African Business*, *The Asian Academy of Management Journal of Accounting and Finance* and *International Journal of Monetary Economics and Finance*.

Achraf Ghorbel is an assistant professor at Higher School of Business of Gafsa, University of Gafsa, Tunisia. He is a member and Researcher at the Applied Economics Laboratory of Sfax, University of Sfax, Tunisia. Her topics of research activities deal with financial and commodity markets, Behavioral Finance, Financial Crises, Islamic Finance and Earnings Management.

PUBLIC INTEREST STATEMENT

The stock market value depends on various factors. This study investigates the effect of bank manager behavior and investor behavior on market value of Islamic and conventional banks in eight countries of the Middle East and North Africa region. The empirical findings of this paper show that the behavior of manager affects significantly the banks value. Indeed, discretionary behavior of manager transmits to investor a positive signal of future earnings' prospects. Moreover, conventional market bank value response is very high to negative signal compared with positive signal. Our results also indicate that the effect of investor sentiment on both bank market prices is also significant. Our paper highlights either an important implication that the limited number of Islamic banks presents a positive effect on Islamic market bank value.

1. Introduction

Banks as financial institutions play a crucial role to maintain financial stability in the stock financial markets. In this context, managers through their decisions and through the disclosures of provision are likely to have an effect on bank prices in financial markets. Indeed, bank managers transmit in the market positive and negative signals through Loan Loss Provision (LLP) which reflect the expected losses of portfolio lending affecting investors' perceptions of bank value. Therefore, LLP appears to reveal a signaling effect (Ahmed, Takeda, & Thomas, 1999; Grammatikos & Saunders, 1990; Hatfield & Lancaster, 2000) changing investor emotions and affecting their reactions toward bank stocks. Therefore, the effect of bank manager behavior and investor emotion on bank prices is an interesting issue worthy of investigation.

Bank manager transmitted positive and negative signals using bank accruals in financial markets which may affect prices since LLP comprises a discretionary (DLLP) and a non-discretionary (NLLP) component (Wahlen, 1994). In his paper, Wahlen (1994) has studied the effect of default risks on bank stock market values. He finds that the disclosures of discretionary component of unexpected provisions present a positive effect on investor despite that provisions is considered as a measure of expected losses. In the same context, Elnahass, Izzeldin, and Abdelsalam (2014) report a positive effect on share prices of an increase in provision due the discretion of bank manager. Beaver and Engel (1996) and Liu, Ryan, and Wahlen (1997) consider that investors positively appreciate an increase in Discretionary Loan Loss Provisions (DLLPs) since it is considered as a sign of strength. However, these authors find that the increased level of charge off and change in nonperforming loans (non-discretionary component) transmits a negative signal to the market since banks increase LLP to cover loan default. Consequently, each level of default risk increased may enlarge investor pessimism in financial market inducing them to sell bank stocks which may affect largely bank stock market values. Indeed, investor sentiment which can be defined as the feeling or the attitudes of investors toward a security or toward all financial markets can be transmitted to financial markets through its transactions and its choices.

In this context, the emotional psychology of investor represents an important factor which affects prices through optimistic or pessimistic vs. future market conditions. Indeed, when investors are optimistic due to the presence of positive returns, this reinforces investors to buy more equity increasing their prices. In contrast, investor pessimistic sentiment would generate the redemption of bank equity, which enforces investor to sell out stocks. Therefore, the discretionary and non-discretionary behaviors of the manager may affect the price and consequently affect the emotion of investor which is revealed in transaction volume, which may affect the confidence of investor in Islamic or conventional banks.

Therefore, it may be interesting to understand if bank value is driven mostly by bank characteristics and the discretionary behavior of managers or by external factors like investor sentiment and macroeconomic factors. In this context, it is important to indicate that a growing body of literature documents the single behavior for the discretionary behavior of manager. However, to our knowledge this is the first paper which investigates simultaneously the effect of manager behavior and the investor emotion on bank value.

Thus, this paper added multi to literature. First, it provides a refined analysis of the behavior of bank manger and the behavior of investor on financial markets by focusing on behavioral finance. Second, this study adds to the existing literature on Islamic finance because it analyzes the psychology of manager and investor and their behavior toward Islamic and conventional bank price. Third, it compares the effect of macroeconomic factors, specifically the effect of market concentration across Islamic and conventional banks' market value.

In this paper, firstly we study the effect of the behavior of bank manager on bank market value by focusing on the discretion of manager using LLP of 25 Islamic banks (IBs) and 45 conventional banks (CBs) during the period 2005–2013 by estimating Beaver and Engel (1996) and Ohlson (1995) models. Second, we examine simultaneously the effect of investor sentiment on Islamic and conventional banks' market price and the contribution of macroeconomic factors on bank value by estimating a model including lagged returns and trading volume as investor sentiment measures and Gross Domestic Product (GDP) and market concentration as macroeconomic factors.

This paper proceeds as follows. Section 2 presents the literature review and hypotheses. Section 3 contains the data and the methodology. The empirical results are discussed in Section 4. The final section is a conclusion.

2. Literature review and hypotheses

2.1. Manager behavior and Islamic and banks' market value

The field of behavioral finance is very relevant in a better study and understanding of human judgment and their effect in financial markets. The psychological parameters of the participants in the financial markets play a crucial role in the variation of bank market value. In this context, the discretionary behavior displayed by bank managers using LLPs may largely affect the investor sentiment and the bank market prices. This discretionary behavior is examined by several studies which indicate that bank managers by exercising discretionary behavior over LLP transmit in the market good news, about future prospects of banks. Beaver, Eger, Ryan, and Wolfson (1989) report that investors interpret the unexpected increases in LLP as a signal of a bank's financial strength. Scholes, Wilson, and Wolfson (1990) suggest that bank managers can lower their cost of capital by exercising discretion over LLP to convey their private information to investors. Shawtari, Saiti, Shaikh Hamzah, and Ariff (2015) find that the discretion magnitude is significantly lower in Islamic banks than conventional banks with some exceptions. Hansen and College (2015) have studied the managerial discretion during the financial crisis of 2007–2010. They find evidence that bank managers use loan reserve to improve the public's perception of bank performance.

Thus, the first and the second hypotheses to be tested are:

Hypothesis 1: Bank market value is positively related to loan loss provision.

Hypothesis 2: Bank market value is positively related to discretionary behavior of bank manager.

The LLP exhibit a discretionary behavior of bank manager. However, it also exhibits a non-discretionary behavior which is due to the increased level of charge off and changing in nonperforming loans. Elnahass et al. (2014) find that the increase of the non-discretionary component in Islamic and conventional banks is considered by investors as irrelevant valuation information.

The non-discretionary behavior due to default risk and bad debt information transmits negative signals in the market. Indeed, banks increase a Non discretionary Loan Loss Provision (NLLP) to cover loan. Consequently, each level's increase of default risk may enlarge investor pessimism in financial market which leads them to sell bank stocks which may affect largely bank stock market values.

Thus, the third hypothesis to be tested is:

Hypothesis 3: Bank market value is negatively related to non-discretionary behavior of bank manager.

The negative effect of non-discretionary component may exhibit a negative effect which can be higher in conventional banks compared to Islamic banks, since investors exhibit more confidence in Islamic banks which are considered stronger in facing risk than conventional banks especially during crisis period. Indeed, in the subprime financial crises, it has been proved that Islamic banks are weakly affected by this crisis compared with conventional banks. Zehri, Abdelbaki, and Bouabdellah

(2012) reports that during the 2007–2008 crisis, Islamic banks which adopted Sharia law are more stable than conventional banks. Bitar, Madiès, and Taramasco (2015) find that Islamic banks were more resilient in terms of capital and profitability than conventional banks during credit crisis of 2008. Beck, Demirgüç-Kunt, and Merrouche (2013) have compared the efficiency and the stability of Islamic and conventional banks during the subprime financial crisis. They note that Islamic banks perform better during crises in terms of capitalization and asset quality than conventional counterparts.

The fourth hypothesis to be tested is:

Hypothesis 4: The negative effect of non-discretionary behavior of manager is largely higher for conventional banks compared with Islamic banks.

2.2. Investor sentiment and banks' market value

The study of the impact of investor sentiment on price dynamics in financial markets is considered as a central focus in behavioral finance. The investor sentiment which can be defined by the feeling or attitudes of investors toward a security or toward all financial markets can be transmitted to financial markets through its transactions and its choices. Behavioral biases like loss aversion, pessimism, and herding can drive market during crisis period or tranquil period. The effect of investor sentiment on stock price in financial markets is well investigated. However, the question whether the sentiment or mood of investors has an impact especially on asset prices of banks has not been investigated to our knowledge.

A growing number of empirical studies (Baker & Wurgler, 2007; Fisher & Statman, 2000; Schmeling, 2009) mainly explore the relation between the investor sentiment and the returns. In fact, most studies suggest the existence of significant relation between the investor sentiment and the expected returns. Baker and Wurgler (2006) find evidence of significant effect of investor sentiment on the cross section returns. Quiang and Shu-e (2010) find that the fluctuation of investor sentiment asymmetrically affects the fluctuation of stock prices. Indeed, the change in stock prices depends on positive or negative investor sentiment changes. Kling and Gao (2008) find that the lagged positive returns lead optimism in the market. However, lagged negative returns lead pessimism in financial market.

Thus, lagged returns considered as investor sentiment measures may affect stock bank prices. Indeed, if the lagged return is positive we may anticipate that investor presents a certain level of optimism which may increase bank value. Benartzi and Thaler (1995) have found that the investor evaluates his portfolio annually based on prospect theory (behavioral theory). Thus, we suggest that the annual lagged return can affect the investment decision. If one year lagged return is positive, the investor will be optimistic about these stocks. However, if it is negative, he will be pessimistic about these stocks. Thus, we expect that lagged returns affect significantly the stock market prices.

The fifth hypothesis to be tested is:

Hypothesis 5: The investor sentiment measured by lagged returns significantly affects the bank market value.

In the same context, trading volume is considered as investor sentiment measure in many research papers (Baker & Wurgler, 2007; Karpoff, 1987; Rutledge, 1984; Scheinkman & Xiong, 2003; Westerfield, 1977; Ying, 1966). Al Samman and Al-Jafari (2015) find a significant positive effect of trading volume on stock returns.

We consider that when investor sentiment reveals optimism by a large trading volume, the price of bank value may increase. Thus, the increase in discretionary behavior of bank manager through

DLLP implies an increase in optimism of investor and thus an increase in market price of both Islamic and conventional banks.

The sixth hypothesis to be tested is:

Hypothesis 6: The investor sentiment measured by trading volume significantly affects the bank market value.

2.3. 3-GDP and market competitiveness conditions

Knowledge of external variables which significantly affect bank market value allows manager, investor and all other participants in financial market in taking the optimal decision. External variables like concentration and GDP are variables which are to be beyond the control of the management of a bank.

Clair (2004) finds that the increase in GDP is associated with an increase in higher returns earned by banks. Chun and Razak (2015) find that nominal GDP has significant impact on return on average asset, liquidity ratio, and equity to net loans. Moreover, several research papers report a positive relationship between GDP and profitability of the banks (Athanasoglou, Delis, & Staikouras, 2008; Kosmidau, Tanna, & Pasiours, 2008).

We consider that the positive conjuncture drives the investor to trade more and invest more in stocks which may imply an increase in stock market. However, if there is a negative conjuncture, this drives a decrease in prices in stock market.

Thus, the following hypothesis is:

Hypothesis 7: GDP positively affects bank market value.

The relation between market price variation and market concentration is an important point to investigate. Gallagher, Ignatieva, and McCulloch (2013) report that dominant companies operating in concentrated industries in Australia generate significant risk-adjusted excess stock returns and excess profits on sales (monopoly rents). However, Hou and Robinson (2006) find that firms in more concentrated industries experience lower returns. They explain this result by the fact these firms operated in concentrated industries are less risky because they engage less in innovation to the existence of barriers to entry in highly concentrated industries.

Generally, the relation between concentration and returns in financial markets is not well documented in previous research studies. Moreover, the relation between bank concentration and return has not been considered in previous studies, to our knowledge.

We consider that investors, and especially Islamic investors, desire more and more investing on Islamic banks which are actually limited in number. Thus, we can expect that the increase in Islamic stocks requested by investor drives an increase in stock market prices. However, conventional bank operates in markets because they exist in large number, thus their market value is independent of market condition.

The following hypotheses to be tested are:

Hypothesis 8: Market price of Islamic bank is significantly affected by market concentration.

Hypothesis 9: Market price of conventional bank is independent of market concentration.

3. Data and empirical models

3.1. Data

This study focuses on two panels of listed banks, Islamic and conventional banks from a group of eight countries in the MENA region (Saudi Arabia, Kuwait, Emirates, Qatar, Bahrain, Egypt, Jordan, and Turkey) for the sample period of 2005–2013.

The data used in this paper are extracted from balance-sheet and income statement data from Bankscope database. Market price, trading volume, and GDP come from Thomson database. Concentration data come from Bankscope database.

The full sample comprises 70 banks. Indeed, we select 25 Islamic banks (IBs) and 45 conventional banks (CBs). A balanced panel data-set is used. We excluded some countries in MENA region because of the unavailability of market data in Thomson and Bankscope database.

3.2. Empirical models

The identification of factors which mainly affect the bank market price is an important point to be considered since, the subprime crisis is due primarily to the dramatic decrease in bank market prices and which is transmitted to other stocks in US financial markets and to other financial markets around the world. In this paper, we focus on internal and external factors which may affect bank market prices by considering behavior finance.

Indeed, we firstly study the effect of the behavior of manager which exhibits a discretionary and a non-discretionary behavior using LLP on Islamic and conventional bank prices through estimating the following model (Beaver and Engel (1996) and Ohlson (1995) models):

$$P_{it} = \alpha_0 + \alpha_1 \mathrm{BV}_{it} + \alpha_2 \mathrm{ENI}_{it} + \alpha_3 \mathrm{TLLP}_{it} + \alpha_4 \mathrm{CO}_{it} + \alpha_5 \Delta\mathrm{NPL}_{it} + \alpha_6 \Delta\mathrm{LOAN}_{it} + \alpha_7 T_t + \alpha_7 C_j + \phi_{it} \quad (1)$$

where P_{it} represents the bank market value of bank *i* in financial markets measured three months after fiscal year-end *t*; BV_{it} represents the book value of bank *i* in year *t*; ENI_{it} represents the bank net income after excluding LLP of bank *i* in year *t*. TLLP represents total loan loss provision for bank *i* in year *t*. CO_{it} represents the net loan charge offs for bank *i* in time *t*. ΔNPL, the change in non-performing loans for bank *i* in time *t* measured by the difference between the bank's non-performing loans between year *t* and year $t - 1$. Non-performing loans and net loan charge offs reflect the probable loan losses. $\Delta\mathrm{LOAN}_{it}$ represents the change in outstanding loan for bank *i* in time *t*. T_t and C_j represent the country-year fixed effects. Equation (1) is estimated to test Hypotheses 1, 3, and 4.

In order, to test the effect of manager discretion (DLLP) on bank market value (Hypothesis 2), we should decompose TLLP into NLLP and DLLP.

Thus,

$$\mathrm{TLLP}_{it} = \mathrm{NLLP}_{it} + \mathrm{DLLP}_{it} \quad (2)$$

where DLLP_{it} is the discretionary component of LLP for bank_i in year *t* and NLLP_{it} is the non-discretionary component of LLP for bank_i in time *t*.

To estimate determinants of the unobservable NLLP, we should estimate LLP with charge offs (CO_{it}), Change in non-performing loans ($\Delta\mathrm{NPL}_{it}$), and the change in total loans ($\Delta\mathrm{LOAN}_{it}$).

Thus,

$$\mathrm{TLLP}_{it} = \beta_0 + \beta_1 \mathrm{CO}_{it} + \beta_2 \Delta\mathrm{NPL}_{it} + \beta_3 \Delta\mathrm{LOAN}_{it} + \beta_4 T_t + \beta_5 C_j + Z_{it} \quad (3)$$

where Z_{it}(composite term) $= \text{DLLP}_{it} + \varepsilon_{it}$ because ε_{it} is non-zero, this indicates that DLLP is measured with some error. Thus, in this paper, we consider that manager does not exhibit discretion when reporting these variables (Elnahass et al., 2014).

In order to assess the effect of manager's discretion on bank value, we insert DLLP determined from Equation (3) in the Equation number (4).

Thus, our value relevance model is defined as follows:

$$P_{it} = \lambda_0 + \lambda_1 \text{BV}_{it} + \lambda_2 \text{ENI}_{it} + \lambda_3 \text{DLLP}_{it} + \lambda_4 \text{CO}_{it} + \lambda_5 \Delta\text{NPL}_{it} + \lambda_6 \Delta\text{LOAN}_{it} + \lambda_7 T_t + \lambda_7 C_j + \phi_{it} \quad (4)$$

After testing the effect of manager behavior on bank market value, we focus on the behavior of investor against Islamic and conventional banks and its effect on bank market prices. Indeed, we test the effect of investor sentiment measured by one-year lagged returns and trading volume on bank value. In this model, we also added market condition variables (GDP, IHH) to this model. Thus, the value relevance model is as follows:

$$P_{it} = \delta_0 + \delta_1 \text{RT}_{it} + \delta_2 \text{VOL}_{it} + \delta_3 \text{IHH}_{it} + \delta_4 \text{GDP}_{it} + \varepsilon_{it} \quad (5)$$

where P_{it} represents the bank market value of bank *i* in financial markets measured three months after fiscal year-end *t*, RT_{it} represents the lagged one fiscal year equity returns. VOL_{it} represents the trading volume during lagged one fiscal year *t*. IHH represents the Index of Herfindahl–Hirshman measured as the sum of the squares of the market shares of bank_{it} competing in the market within the banks in the markets at the end of fiscal year, GDP represents the GDP at the end of fiscal year.

4. Results

Behavioral finance is relevant in explaining the trends and the variation of stock prices in financial markets based on the psychology of actors. In this paper, we study firstly the effect of manager discretion (internal factor) on bank market price using LLP. Secondly, we focus on the sentiment of investor (external factor) and its affect on both Islamic and conventional market prices. As external factors, we also study the effect of market conditions on bank prices and the difference of this effect between Islamic and conventional banks.

4.1. Internal factors: the effect of manager discretion non market value of Islamic and conventional Banks

In this part of study, we investigate the contribution of the behavior of bank manager using LLP on the bank market value. LLP is the amount of money reserved to offset future losses on bad loans. Bank manager exercises her discretionary behavior to estimate the necessary LLP. Firstly, we test the effect of bad debt levels which reflects the non-discretionary component of loss provision disclosures. Secondly, we test the effect of the discretion of manager on price market. Thus, we estimate Equation (1) which tests the effect of book bank value, net income, total LLP, net loans charge offs, Change in non-performing loans, and the change in outstanding loan. The net loan charge offs, Change in non-performing loans, and the change in outstanding loan represent the non-discretionary component of LLP. The results of the estimated Equation (1) are provided in Table 1.

The coefficients of all determinants exhibit the predicted signs. Total LLP has the predicted positive sign and is statistically significant, confirming Hypothesis 1 that manager increases TLLP in order to signal future prospect growth in both Islamic and conventional banks.

Manager uses LLP in many circumstances. One of these circumstances is that manager needs to revise upward the bank value when he considers that the bank value it is larger than value assessed in financial markets. So, he transmits in financial markets information that the bank is strong enough to absorb future potential losses through increasing the LLP. Increasing LLP is good news because

Table 1. Effect of manager behavior on bank market value

Model:

$$P_{it} = \alpha_0 + \alpha_1 BV_{it} + \alpha_2 ENI_{it} + \alpha_3 TLLP_{it} + \alpha_4 CO_{it} + \alpha_5 \Delta NPL_{it} + \alpha_6 \Delta LOAN_{it} + \alpha_7 T_t + \alpha_7 C_j + \phi_{it}$$

Variables	Islamic banks	Conventional banks
BV_{it}	0.21*	0.48*
	(2.17)	(31.71)
ENI_{it}	0.12*	0.058*
	(5.89)	(16.73)
$TLLP_{it}$	0.66*	0.16*
	(11.22)	(29.04)
CO_{it}	−0.16*	−0.98*
	(−3.79)	(−32.67)
ΔNPL_{it}	−0.02*	−0.09*
	(−13.43)	(−13.41)
$\Delta LOAN_{it}$	−0.42*	−0.66*
	(−13.04)	(−6.86)
Year-fixed effects	Yes	Yes
Country-fixed effects	Yes	Yes
No. of banks	25	45

*Significant at 1% level, *t*-statistic is reported in parenthesis.

the investor thinks that the prospects of future earnings are favorable, thus manager can take hits to current earnings. (Kanagaretnam, Lobo, & Yang, 2005; Skinner, 1994).

To study the effect of manager discretion on bank market price, we decompose total loan loss provision into DLLP and NLLP as explained in empirical models section. Estimation results of model 4 which comprise the DLLP and NLLP components are provided in Table 2.

Table 2. The effect of manager discretion on Islamic and conventional bank value

$$P_{it} = \lambda_0 + \lambda_1 BV_{it} + \lambda_2 ENI_{it} + \lambda_3 DLLP_{it} + \lambda_4 CO_{it} + \lambda_5 \Delta NPL_{it} + \lambda_6 \Delta LOAN_{it} + \lambda_7 T_t + \lambda_7 C_j + \phi_{it}$$

Variables	Islamic banks	Conventional banks
BV_{it}	0.21*	0.48*
	(4.17)	(17.21)
ENI_{it}	0.12*	0.08*
	(5.89)	(16.31)
$DLLP_{it}$	0.46*	0.68*
	(11.22)	(29.04)
CO_{it}	−0.25*	−0.93*
	(−3.79)	(−26.17)
ΔNPL_{it}	−0.21*	−0.83*
	(−13.43)	(−7.97)
$\Delta LOAN_{it}$	−0.19*	−0.20*
	(−10.77)	(−23.51)
Year-fixed effects	Yes	Yes
Country-fixed effects	Yes	Yes
No. of banks	25	45

*Significant at 1% level, *t*-statistic is reported in parenthesis.

The estimated regression coefficients of DLLP are positive and significant at 1% level. This result is consistent with the hypothesis that the discretionary behavior of bank managers exhibits a signaling effect, thus increasing bank market prices. Indeed, investor considers that both managers of Islamic and conventional banks increase LLP because they have a large margin to support future loss. So they disseminate favorable information that banks present a large capacity and future earning prospects. Therefore, investor positively appreciates the opportunistic increase in DLLP. Indeed, bank managers are well informed of loan portfolio default risk. Thus, they use this ability to exercise discretion and to transmit in the market positive signal.

Loan loss allowance has a negative significant association with the bank value at 1% level. Indeed, we find that variables like CO_{it} and ΔNPL_{it} used to proxy for NLLP are significantly negative indicating that investor negatively appreciates the increase in default credit risk. This result supports Hypothesis 3 that the increase in charge off and loan loss allowance transmits a negative signal to the markets and leads a decrease in market prices. This result confirms those obtained by Beaver and Engel (1996).

An important result found in this paper is that the conventional bank stock prices' response to negative signal (increase in charge off) is very high compared to the response to positive signal (increase in DLLP). This result confirms those obtained by Skinner (1994) in 93 NASDAQ firms. We can explain this result by prospect theory and behavioral bias. Prospect theory developed by Kahneman and Tversky (1979) suggests that the bias of loss aversion leads individuals to be more sensitive to losses than gains of the same magnitude. Thus, the price experiences a large decrease after bad news compared with the increase after good news. This result added to the literature of conventional banks. To our knowledge, this paper is the first that provides this result explained by behavioral finance theory.

We have found that coefficient for $DLLP_{it}$ is 0.6 and for NPL_{it} and CO_{it} is respectively −0.8 and −0.9 for conventional banks. However, for Islamic banks, DLLP is 0.4 and around −0.2 for negative news. Thus, the negative effect is higher on conventional stock market prices compared with Islamic stock market prices. This result is explained by the fact that investor has more confidence in Islamic banks than conventional banks because they consider that Islamic banks are safer than conventional banks, since subprime crisis has demonstrated that Islamic banks are less affected by this crisis compared with conventional banks which have experienced a dramatic decrease in market prices.

4.2. External factors: effect of investor sentiment and market conditions on Islamic and conventional bank market values

In the first part of this paper, we have tested the effect of manager behavior on bank market value. In this part, we study the effect of investor sentiment and macroeconomic conditions on bank value. Indeed, we estimate Equation (5) which includes proxies of investor sentiment like trading volume and lagged returns. Moreover, we have added the market condition variables of GDPs and bank competition variable of Index of Herfindahl-Hirshman.

Table 3 presents the estimated coefficients of Equation (5).

Results of Table 3 reveal that investor sentiment measured by one year lagged returns affect significantly the Islamic and conventional bank market values. Indeed, δ_1 is significant at 1% level for both bank types. This result can be explained by the fact that when lagged return is positive, investor presents a certain level of optimism which may increase bank value. However, the negative lagged return leads investor to be pessimistic about this stock. Thus, the sentiment of investor and their mood is considered as an important factor which affects significantly both types of bank market price.

Estimation results reveal that trading volume affects significantly the bank market value. Indeed, when investor sentiment reveals optimism associated with a large trading volume, the price of bank value experiences an increase. Thus, the increase in discretionary behavior of bank manager through

Table 3. The effect of investor sentiment and market condition variables on market bank value

$$P_{it} = \delta_0 + \delta_1 RT_{it} + \delta_2 VOL_{it} + \delta_3 IHH_{it} + \delta_4 GDP_{it} + \varepsilon_{it}$$

Variables	Islamic banks	Conventional banks
RT_{it}	0.45*	9.42*
	(2.59)	(16.31)
VOL_{it}	0.14*	0.07*
	(13.21)	(13.10)
IHH_{it}	0.07*	−12.60
	(12.66)	(−0.46)
GDP_{it}	0.301*	0.23*
	(15.81)	(2.76)
Year-fixed effects	Yes	Yes
Country-fixed effects	Yes	Yes
No. of banks	25	45

*Significant at 1% level, *t*-statistic is reported in parenthesis.

DLLP implies an increase in investor optimism and thus an increase in market price of both Islamic and conventional banks. Thus, banks' manager must carefully consider the effect of investor sentiment in order to maximize the value of the bank.

Other contribution of this paper is that it adds to the literature the contribution of external variables like GDP and market conditions in explaining bank price variation.

Table 3 reports the positive effect of GDP on bank price value. This result confirms previous results on conventional banks which report a positive relationship between GDP growth and banking efficiency (Awdeh & El Moussawi, 2009). Thus, favorable macroeconomic conditions drive an increase in stock market, confirming Hypothesis 7.

Up to date, to our knowledge we have not a research paper focusing on the effect of competitively on bank market price. Thus, we search to cover this lack by examining the impact of competition on Islamic and Conventional market prices (IHH). Results of the effect of market conditions that govern the two types of banks (IHH) estimated by model 5 are reported in Table 4.

We find that market structure affects the variation of Islamic bank market price. Indeed, we find that the effect of monopolistic Islamic market IHH_{it} (δ_3 significant at 1% level) can drive an increase in bank market price. Indeed, we find that Islamic banks in monopolistic market register an increase in prices compared with those which operate in a competitive market, confirming Hypothesis 8. This result can be explained by the fact that the number of Islamic banks is relatively very small compared to the number of shares requested by investors and especially by Islamic investors. Thus, the monopolistic market where Islamic banks operate contributes an increase in its prices. It is important to note that we have estimated model 5 by panel data. Therefore, this result may be changed if we estimate this model by taking the effect of concentration separately for each bank, especially for turkey since having numerous Islamic banks. So, it is an important point to investigate in future studies.

Table 4. The effect of market conditions on market banks value

Variables	Islamic banks	Conventional banks
IHH	0.07*	−12.60
	(12.66)	(−0.46)
No. of banks	25	45

*Significant at 1% level, *t*-statistic is reported into parenthesis.

No significant effect is detected of the effect of market condition on conventional bank prices, confirming Hypothesis 9.

5. Conclusion

This paper adds to the literature by exhibiting new evidence to the contribution of behavioral finance in explaining the variation of Islamic and conventional bank market price. In this paper, we have tested the effect of internal and external factors on the bank market price. Indeed, we have studied both the manager behavior and investor sentiment and their effects on prices. Moreover, we have examined the effect of market condition on Islamic and conventional market values for eight countries of MENA region.

Our empirical evidences show that the discretion of manager is good news and it is positively appreciated by investor and contributes an increase of market price. However, the non-discretionary behavior of bank manager due to the increase in credit risk transmits in the financial market bad information.

An important result found in this paper is that conventional bank stock prices response to negative signal (increase in charge off) is very high compared to the response to positive signal (increase in DLLP). This result is explained by prospect theory and loss aversion bias which suggest that the negative news induce a largely negative effect in financial markets (variation of market price) than the effect of positive news (increase in DLLP). This result added to the literature of conventional banks. Moreover, we have found that the negative effect of NLLP is higher on conventional stock market prices compared with Islamic stock market prices since investors are more confident in Islamic banks than conventional banks. Indeed, investors consider that Islamic banks are safer.

Our paper emphasizes the importance of investor sentiment and their mood as factors affecting significantly both types of bank market prices. Moreover, the analyses of the effect of market structure on bank stock reveals that monopolistic Islamic market drives an increase in Islamic bank market price.

Funding
This work was supported by Achraf Ghorbel.

Author details
Mouna Abdelhedi-Zouch[1]
E-mail: abdelhedimouuna@yahoo.fr
Achraf Ghorbel[1]
E-mail: ghorbelachraf@yahoo.fr
ORCID ID: http://orcid.org/0000-0001-6303-5612
[1] Laboratory URECA, Faculty of Economics and Management of Sfax, Université de Sfax, Sfax, Tunisia.

References

Al Samman, H., & Al-Jafari, M. K. (2015). Trading volume and stock returns volatility. Evidence from industrial firms of Oman. *Asian Social Science, 11,* 139–146.

Ahmed, A., Takeda, C., & Thomas, S. (1999). Bank loan loss provisions: A reexamination of capital management, earnings management and signaling effects. *Journal of Accounting and Economics, 28,* 1–25. http://dx.doi.org/10.1016/S0165-4101(99)00017-8

Athanasoglou, P., Delis, M., & Staikouras, C. (2008). Determinants of banking profitability in the south eastern European region. *Journal of Financial Decision Making, 2,* 1–17. Retrieved from http://ssrn.com/abstract=1146385

Awdeh, A., & El Moussawi, C. (2009). Bank efficiency and foreign ownership in the Lebanese banking sector. *Review of Middle East Economics and Finance, 5,* 66–87.

Baker, M., & Wurgler, J. (2006). Investor sentiment and the cross-section of stock returns. *The Journal of Finance, 61,* 1645–1680. http://dx.doi.org/10.1111/j.1540-6261.2006.00885.x

Baker, M., & Wurgler, J. (2007). Investor sentiment in the stock market. *Journal of Economic Perspectives, 21,* 129–151. http://dx.doi.org/10.1257/jep.21.2.129

Beaver, W., Eger, C., Ryan, S., & Wolfson, M. (1989). Financial reporting, supplemental disclosures, and bank share prices. *Journal of Accounting Research, 27,* 157–178. http://dx.doi.org/10.2307/2491230

Beaver, W., & Engel, E. E. (1996). Discretionary behavior with respect to allowances for loan losses and the behavior of security prices. *Journal of Accounting and Economics, 22,* 177–206. http://dx.doi.org/10.1016/S0165-4101(96)00428-4

Beck, T., Demirgüç-Kunt, A., & Merrouche, O. (2013). Islamic vs. conventional banking: Business model, efficiency and stability. *Journal of Banking and Finance, 37,* 433–447. http://dx.doi.org/10.1016/j.jbankfin.2012.09.016

Benartzi, S., & Thaler, R. H. (1995). Myopic loss aversion and the equity premium puzzle. *The Quarterly Journal of Economics, 110,* 73–92. http://dx.doi.org/10.2307/2118511

Bitar, M., Madiès, P., & Taramasco, O. (2015). Comparing Islamic and conventional banks' financial characteristics: A multivariate approach. Retrieved from SSRN. doi:10.2139/ssrn.2571631

Chun, H., & Razak, S. H. (2015). The impact of nominal GDP and inflation on the financial performance of Islamic banks in Malaysia. *Journal of Islamic Economics, Banking and Finance, 11,* 158–180.

Clair, R. S. T. (2004). *Macroeconomic determinants of banking financial performance and resilience in Singapore* (MAS Staff Paper, No. 38). Monetary Authority of Singapore. Retrieved from http://www.mas.gov.sg/~/media/resource/publications/staff_papers/MAS_Staff_Paper_No_38_RSTC_V3.pdf.

Elnahass, M., Izzeldin, M., & Abdelsalam, O. (2014). Loan loss provisions, bank valuations and discretion: A comparative study between conventional and Islamic banks. *Journal of Economic Behavior and Organization, 103*, S160–S173. http://dx.doi.org/10.1016/j.jebo.2013.08.018

Fisher, K. L., & Statman, M. (2000). Investor sentiment and stock returns. *Financial Analysts Journal, 56*, 16–23.

Gallagher, D., Ignatieva, K., & McCulloch, J. (2013). *Industry concentration, excess returns and innovation in Australia* (Quantitative Finance Research Centre, Research Paper 334). Retrieved from http://www.qfrc.uts.edu.au/research/research_papers/rp334.pdf

Grammatikos, T., & Saunders, A. (1990). Additions to bank loan-loss reserves. *Journal of Monetary Economics, 25*, 289–304. http://dx.doi.org/10.1016/0304-3932(90)90017-X

Hansen, G., & College, U. (2015). Manager discretion over loan loss reserves during the global financial crisis. *International Journal of Business and Finance Research, 9*, 51–61.

Hatfield, G., & Lancaster, C. (2000). The signaling effects of bank loan-loss reserve additions. *Journal of Financial and Strategic Decisions, 13*, 57–73.

Hou, K., & Robinson, D. T. (2006). Industry concentration and average stock returns. *The Journal of Finance, 61*, 1927–1956. http://dx.doi.org/10.1111/j.1540-6261.2006.00893.x

Kahneman, D., & Tversky, A. (1979). Prospect theory: An analysis of decision under risk. *Econometrica, 47*, 263–291. http://dx.doi.org/10.2307/1914185

Kanagaretnam, K., Lobo, G., & Yang, D. H. (2005). Determinants of signaling by banks through loan loss provisions. *Journal of Business Research, 58*, 312–320. http://dx.doi.org/10.1016/j.jbusres.2003.06.002

Karpoff, J. M. (1987). The relation between price changes and trading volume: A survey. *The Journal of Financial and Quantitative Analysis, 22*, 109–126. http://dx.doi.org/10.2307/2330874

Kling, G., Gao, L. (2008). Chinese institutional investors' sentiment. *Journal of International Financial Markets, Institutions and Money, 18*, 374–387. http://dx.doi.org/10.1016/j.intfin.2007.04.002

Kosmidau, K., Tanna, S., Pasiours, & F. (2008). *Determinants of profitability of domestic UK commercial banks: Panel evidence from the period of 1995–2002.* (Economics, finance and accounting applied research working paper series no. RP08-4). Coventry University. Retrieved from http://wwwm.coventry.ac.uk/bes/cubs/aboutthebusinessschool/Economicsfinanceandaccounting/Pages/AppliedResearchWorkingPapers.aspx .

Liu, C., Ryan, S. G., & Wahlen, J. (1997). Differential valuation implications of loan loss provisions across banks and fiscal quarters. *The Accounting Review, 72*, 133–146.

Ohlson, J. A. (1995). Earnings, book values, and dividends in equity valuation. *Contemporary Accounting Research, 11*, 661–687. http://dx.doi.org/10.1111/care.1995.11.issue-2

Quiang, Z., & Shu-e, Y. (2010). Noise trading, investor sentiment, volatility, and stock returns. *Systems Engineering-Theory and Practice, 29*, 40–47.

Rutledge., D. J .S. (1984). Trading volume and price variability: New evidence on the price effects of speculation. In A. E. Peck (Ed.), *Selected writings on futures markets: Research directions in commodity markets* (pp. 237–251). Chicago, IL: Chicago Board of Trade.

Scheinkman, A., & Xiong, W. (2003). Overconfidence and speculative bubbles. *Journal of Political Economy, 111*, 1183–1220.

Schmeling, M. (2009). Investor sentiment and stock returns: Some international evidence. *Journal of Empirical Finance, 16*, 394–408. http://dx.doi.org/10.1016/j.jempfin.2009.01.002

Scholes, M., Wilson, G., & Wolfson, M. (1990). Tax planning, capital planning, and financial reporting strategy for commercial banks. *Review of Financial Studies, 3*, 625–650. http://dx.doi.org/10.1093/rfs/3.4.625

Shawtari, F. A., Saiti, B., Shaikh Hamzah, A. R., & Ariff, M. (2015). The impact of efficiency on discretionary loans/finance loss provision: A comparative study of Islamic and conventional banks. *Borsa Istanbul Review, 15*, 272–282.

Skinner, D. J. (1994). Why firms voluntarily disclose bad news? *Journal of Accounting Research, 32*, 38–60. http://dx.doi.org/10.2307/2491386

Wahlen, J. M. (1994). The nature of information in commercial bank loan loss disclosures. *The Accounting Review, 69*, 455–478.

Westerfield, R. (1977). The distribution of common stock price changes: An application of transactions time and subordinated stochastic models. *The Journal of Financial and Quantitative Analysis, 12*, 743–765. http://dx.doi.org/10.2307/2330254

Ying, C. C. (1966). Stock market prices and volumes of sales. *Econometrica, 34*, 676–686. http://dx.doi.org/10.2307/1909776

Zehri, C., Abdelbaki, A., & Bouabdellah, N. (2012). Effects of the current financial crisis on Islamic banks compared to conventional banks. *Banks and Bank Systems, 7*, 83–93.

Cross-border mergers and acquisitions: Mature markets vs. emerging markets—with special reference to the USA and India

Geeta Rani Duppati[1] and Narendar V. Rao[2]*

*Corresponding author: Narendar V. Rao, College of Business and Management, Northeastern Illinois University, Chicago, IL, USA

E-mails: N-Rao@neiu.edu, nvrao13@gmail.com

Reviewing editor: Len Tiu Wright, University of Huddersfield, UK

Abstract: Due to the differences in the merger waves across markets, the market for cross-border mergers and acquisitions by Indian companies differs in context and situations from those of the mature markets. Post-acquisition performance is critical to the success of companies involved in overseas investments. This paper uses event study methodology to analyse the long-term performance of Indian-acquiring companies by undertaking 30 outward foreign direct investment (OFDI)-related deals, during 2000–2008 period. Further, it compares the empirical findings from India with the prior findings from the USA. It is evident from the empirical results that the stock markets reacted positively in the short run following the announcements of the OFDI-related mergers and acquisitions by Indian companies. The empirical findings also showed positive results in the post-acquisition period following the overseas deals.

Subjects: Business, Management and Accounting; Corporate Finance; International Business; Organizational Studies; Strategic Management

Keywords: cross-border mergers and acquisitions; emerging markets; mature markets; India; event study; internationalisation; post-acquisition performance

JEL classification: G34

ABOUT THE AUTHORS

Geeta Rani Duppati is a senior lecturer in the Department of Finance, The University of Waikato, Hamilton, New Zealand. She had several years of teaching experience in India and Ethiopia, before moving to Auckland University of Technology in New Zealand. Her research interests include corporate governance, asset pricing, corporate social responsibility, foreign investment and mergers and acquisitions. She has several publications and presentations in these areas.

Narendar V. Rao is a tenured professor of Finance at Northeastern Illinois University (NEIU) in Chicago, USA. He obtained his master's and doctorate from the University of Cincinnati. He has been the external examiner for PhD dissertations for several universities in India as well as The University of Waikato, Hamilton, New Zealand. His research interests are primarily in the areas of mergers and acquisitions, Islamic finance, and diversification strategy. He also has an impressive list of scholarly publications.

PUBLIC INTEREST STATEMENT

The phenomenon of cross-border mergers and acquisitions has been significant in the USA since 1950. Emerging markets vary widely in terms of how developed their economies and capital markets are. In the case of India, overseas acquisitions by Indian companies have been evident since 2000. This paper discusses the reasons for the variations in the outcomes of cross-border deals based on empirical findings from the USA and India. The findings of this study would provide significant insight into various elements of the deal mechanism including asset exploitation, mode of settlement, ownership control and regulatory issues. This could assist emerging-market investment bankers and corporate executives to design appropriate strategies for lasting shareholders value creation.

1. Introduction

During the last two decades, businesses have become increasingly global. The quest to gain competitive leverage has led companies to look at opportunities globally. Multinational corporations have played a major role in this process of globalisation (Das, 1997; Pandya & Rao, 1998). The globalisation of business has initiated a search for worldwide competitive advantage through economies of scale and scope. The growth in foreign direct investment (FDI) has been particularly marked since the mid-1980s, with the world economy witnessing a surge due to which FDI has become the most common means of gaining competitive advantage, particularly after the raising participation by firms from emerging economies (Amighini, Cozza, Giuliani, Rabellotti, & Scalera, 2015). Thus, FDI can take a variety of forms including the establishment of "green-field" sites and joint ventures. However, the most prevalent form of FDI is via cross-border mergers and acquisitions (Gregory & McCorriston, 2005; UNCTAD, 2013).

Following the liberalisation of the policy regime by the Indian Government beginning in the early 1990s, the country experienced a rapid growth in outward FDIs, particularly between 2000 and 2007. Encouraged by the financial reforms unleashed by the Indian Government, an increase in large-scale mergers and acquisitions (M&A) by Indian companies occurred. This was primarily because the shackles that prevented Indian firms from acquiring firms abroad were removed. The socialist dogma of quixotic self-reliance was cast aside and Indian firms were given the freedom to grow and fulfil their international aspirations (e.g. Ahluwalia, 2002; Dongre, 2012). This enabled Indian companies to pursue cross-border acquisitions in order to become globally competitive. Unfortunately, the economic effects of these overseas ventures have received little evaluation by academic researchers so far. The Indian companies' acquisitions were large-scale ventures involving billions of dollars of investment in a bid to gain a global presence and achieve competitiveness.

Recently, cross-border acquisitions by Indian companies has been aimed at accessing high-growth markets, buying prestigious brands, acquiring advanced technology, processes, management expertise, marketing and distribution networks, as well as consolidating existing markets while seeking new ones (Bhagat, Malhotra, & Zhu, 2011; Kohli & Mann, 2012; Nagano & Yuan, 2013). Building scale to enhance global competitiveness has been the mantra followed by many Indian firms. They seem to have concluded that overseas expansion is the panacea for the stifling competition that they face in the domestic market. Their outward push has been facilitated by prudent and timely policy reforms by the Indian Government that has taken a much more positive attitude towards this internationalisation trend. The liberalised foreign exchange policies, increase in foreign ownership ceilings, access to international capital markets and other changes in rules and regulations—all of these have been undertaken with the aim of facilitating outward investments by Indian companies. The first wave of Indian outward FDI in the pre-liberalisation period by firms was concentrated largely in Asian and African developing countries. However, the second wave of outward FDI by Indian corporates, especially since 2000, has been focused on developed countries, primarily in the form of CB-M&A, as opposed to greenfield ventures (Rajan, 2009).

1.1. Indian Government policy relating to outward foreign direct investment

The new economic policy adopted by the government of India in mid-1991, after a severe economic crisis, was based on the twin principles: first, deregulation of the government's economic interventionist functions and second, encouraging competition (Das, 1997). The main thrust of this policy was to ensure free flow of investment, products, technology and managerial personnel across national borders, leading to greater integration of the Indian economy with the rest of the world. Various Indian regulations have already been changed extensively to facilitate liberalisation and deregulation of key sectors. The areas in which change has been made effective include industrial licensing, monopoly and restrictive trade practices, foreign exchange regulations, import and export rules, capital markets, external commercial borrowing, the Companies Act and convertibility of rupee in current accounts.

The most recent phase (2000–2008) of fast economic growth saw an expansion of Indian enterprises in domestic and international markets while competing with the global brands and multinational enterprises. In the years 2000 and 2002, the upper limit for automatic overseas investment approval was raised to US$100 million. The requirement to obtain prior approval from the Reserve Bank of India (RBI) was dispensed with and firms were allowed to obtain the remittances through any authorised foreign exchange dealer. In 2005, banks were permitted to lend money to Indian companies for acquisitions of equity in overseas joint ventures or other overseas companies as strategic investment. The limit of overseas investment of Indian companies was increased to 300% of net worth in June 2007, and further raised to 400% in September 2007. The policy changes with regard to Indian overseas investment from the year 2004 onwards have been described as liberal (Nayyar, 2008).

1.2. Global expansion by Indian corporates

Encouraged by the financial and structural reforms, an increase in large-scale M&A by Indian corporations occurred. Owing to the changes in the global investment landscape and the deregulatory FDI policy of the government of India, the Indian companies had to position themselves to face the challenges on the domestic as well as the international fronts (Kohli & Mann, 2012; Nicholson & Salaber, 2013). The majority of the Indian companies that were hitherto protected and limited to their domestic environment were now exposed to the vagaries of the international markets. The key issue to examine is whether the changes in approach of Indian companies are likely to create value for the shareholders of the acquiring firm by enhancing the stock price in the long run.

Motivated by these factors, this paper aims to examine long-term consequences of the cross-border acquisitions by Indian companies. It also analyses whether the experiences of the Indian-acquiring companies involved in cross-border mergers are in any way different from those of the mature markets because of the changes in the time period and regulatory environment in the post-acquisition period. The findings of this paper eventually contribute to the growing literature on emerging market firm strategies in international business.

The remaining paper is organised as follows. Section 2 presents an overview of findings reported in previous studies, Section 3 depicts the methodology, Section 4 discusses the findings and Section 5 concludes.

2. Related literature

There is extensive literature on CB-M&A that has studied both mature and emerging markets' deals. For example, a number of recent studies in emerging markets have focused on the motives and determinants of cross-border mergers and acquisitions (CB-M&A), performance of acquiring firms, corporate governance and overall experience of acquisitions (e.g. Anderson, Sutherland, & Severe, 2015; Aybar & Thanakijsombat, 2015; Bhagat et al., 2011; Buckley, Elia, & Kafouros,2014; Chittoor, Aulakh, & Ray, 2015; Deng & Yang, 2015; Du & Boateng, 2012; Kim & Lu, 2013; Lebedev, Peng, Xie, & Stevens, in press; Malatesta, 1983; Nagano & Yuan, 2013; Rani, Yadav, & Jain, 2015; Reddy, 2015; Sinkovics, Sinkovics, Lew, Jedin, & Zagelmeyer, 2015).

In terms of the experiences of mature markets, for instance, Langetieg (1978) re-examined the pre-merger and post-merger stock performance from the perspective of a three-factor performance index. The sample was drawn from NYSE for a period of 72 days before the event and 72 days following the mergers during 1929 and 1969. The study concluded that the post-merger excess returns are found not to be significantly different from zero, thus providing no support for merger benefits. Malatesta (1983) examined the net effects of the long-run sequence of events leading to merger, and of merger per se, on shareholder wealth. The period of study was from 1969 to 1974. The sample size comprised 256 acquiring firms and 85 acquired firms. The evidence also revealed that measured abnormal rates of return to acquiring firms are sensitive to a slight variation in model specification and dependent on firm size, with smaller firms earning significantly negative post-merger returns. Weidenbaum and Sheldon (1987) concluded, based on an analysis of 10 studies, that the historical data revealed that negative returns to shareholders for acquisitions are more prevalent. Singh and Montgomery (1987) investigated the conceptual argument that acquisitions, which are related in product/market or technological terms, create higher value than unrelated acquisitions. Related acquisitions are found to have greater total dollar gains for acquired firms than those in unrelated acquisitions. These findings indicate that related target firms benefit more from acquisitions than unrelated target firms do.

In case of emerging markets experience, according to Makino, Lau, and Yeh (2002), the asset exploration perspective of outward foreign direct investment (OFDI) is viewed as a means to acquire strategic assets (i.e. technology, marketing and management expertise) available in a host country. The asset exploitation perspective of FDI is viewed as the transfer of a firm's proprietary assets across borders. The asset exploitation perspective of FDI commonly posits that firms that possess firm-specific advantages utilise these advantages to operate abroad in order to seek markets or low-cost natural resources or labour force. In a similar study, Rasiah, Gammeltoft, and Jiang (2010) mention that the main drivers of OFDI include market seeking, labour seeking, natural resource seeking, value chain control seeking, financial incentive seeking and technology seeking. More specifically, Contractor (2013) reports various possible location-specific competencies of firms in emerging markets, which include the mindset of top management (e.g. long-term orientation and tolerance of ambiguity), home-country cultural traits (e.g. family ownership and private equity control), technically talented pool, cheap labour and the common language.

In the recent past, for 698 deals made by emerging market firms during 1991–2008, Bhagat et al. (2011) report that acquiring firms obtained a positive mean market return of about 1.09% on the announcement day. These returns may explain the better corporate governance mechanisms in the given target nation. In case of Indian acquirers, Kohli and Mann (2012) examine 202 overseas deals and find that cross-border acquisitions produce superior wealth gains compared to domestic deals. In a cross-country study, Nicholson and Salaber (2013) conduct an empirical survey on 203 Indian and 63 Chinese cross-border deals during 2000–2010, and report that location is one of the key factors affecting acquirers' performance. For example, Indian-acquiring firms have benefited from deals in proximate, culturally similar countries. In addition, acquiring firms enjoy higher shareholder returns when the deal occurs in mature markets. In case of inward cross-border acquisitions, Nagano and Yuan (2013) discover that both Chinese and Indian firms are being targeted because of their higher cash-reserve ratio, and further suggest that overseas acquisitions produce higher shareholders' returns compared to domestic deals. This result is similar to Kohli and Mann (2012). In a few recent studies, for example, Buckley et al. (2014) test the framework describing resource and context specificity of prior experience in acquisitions by emerging market firms and its impact on the performance of target firms. They find mixed results on resource and investment experiences. In case of overseas acquisitions by Indian firms, Chittoor et al. (2015) analyse the impact of ownership characteristics on the propensity of firms to make outbound deals for a sample of BSE-500 list during 2002–2011 period, using behavioural risk-taking approach. They suggest that promoter shareholding pattern, international experience of CEO and ownership share of foreign institutional investors positively influence the propensity of firms making acquisitions in overseas markets, and it will be stronger for stand-alone ones than that of firms affiliated to business groups. In case of comparative studies, for instance, Deng and Yang (2015) examine foreign acquisitions by firms from nine emerging markets for the period 2000–2012, testing the resource dependence theory. They report differences in the factors affecting CB-M&A by emerging market firms in developed and developing countries. Hence, institutional environment of host country plays a vital role in acquisitions marked by Chinese firms, which is different from other emerging countries.

The above studies seem to indicate that emerging market firms participate in cross-border acquisitions for two important reasons: resource advantage (e.g. financial, technological, managerial and ownership) and fast entry into global market (e.g. geographical diversification and international competitive share). On the other hand, it is also important to note that there is a great deal of academic interest shown in this area with reference to emerging markets such as India since the recent global financial crisis (Reddy, Nangia, & Agrawal, 2014). Therefore, this paper aims to shed light on comparative empirical findings of Indian and USA enterprises following CB-M&A.

3. Research method and data

The present study compares the empirical findings of Indian companies following CB-M&A with the prior findings of USA companies. This paper explains the reasons for differing outcomes of the findings of USA and Indian companies. A number of comparisons are being exhibited between mature and emerging markets, but not a probable group between mature market parent and mature market target due to limited sample. The study also examines internationalisation theories and other relevant prior findings (Reddy, in press).

The present study measures the short-run performance of 30 OFDI-related M&A by Indian companies. The study considers a three-day short-event window surrounding the acquisition announcement period. It includes a day prior to the announcement, the event day (announcement day) and a day following the announcement. The study concentrates only on a short-run event study method, restricting analysis to a short-event window (closely surrounding the announcement day). The event date for the study is set to be the date of announcement of the respective M&A event. This provides the best comparison of the various methods because the shorter the event window, the more precise the tests. The coefficients of the market model (MM) are estimated using the data for 100 days of stock return data on each security in the sample firms involving in acquisitions from the BSE Index (Bombay Stock Exchange).

It also measures the long-run performance of Indian companies involved in OFDI-related M&A. The study considers a maximum of 36 months following the acquisition event month. The period of the study signifies acquisition activity and covers selected Indian firms involved in OFDI-related M&A during the 2000–2008 period. The coefficients of the MM are estimated using 24 months prior to the acquisition event month. The monthly stock return data for each security in the sample and the monthly market returns from the BSE Index are used to estimate the expected returns. The α_i and β_i are the OLS parameter estimates obtained by regressing the firm returns with the market returns. Returns are calculated as the difference in natural logarithm of two consecutive monthly stock prices. It estimates each security's systematic risk relative to the market portfolio. It controls for market-wide variations through the independent variable R_{mt}. Any variation that is due to factors not present in the market portfolio will be captured in the disturbance term ε_{it}. The event period is 36 months following the acquisition month. The excess of firm returns over the estimated returns is abnormal returns. The study tests the null hypothesis relating to the long-term performance of CB-M&A by Indian M&A firms:

Ho: There are no long-run abnormal returns to the Indian acquiring firms following acquisition activity.

3.1. Market model

The abnormal return using the MM is

$$R_{it} = \alpha_i + \beta_i R_{mt} + \varepsilon_{it}$$

where α_i and β_i are MM parameter estimates obtained by regressing monthly returns for security "*i*" on the equally weighted market returns over the estimation period.

3.2. Cumulative abnormal returns

The monthly abnormal returns are summed up over the event period to derive the cumulative abnormal returns (CAR)

$$\mathrm{CAR}_{it} = \sum_{t=1}^{n} \mathrm{AR}_{it}$$

4. Empirical findings and discussion

From the short-term perspective, this paper presents the empirical findings of the stock market reactions in terms of returns following the announcements of cross-border mergers and acquisitions by Indian companies. From the long-term perspective, this paper presents the empirical findings relating to the stock market performance of the Indian corporates involved in cross-border mergers and acquisitions in the post-acquisition period. The sample considered is 30 CB-M&A by Indian-acquiring firms.

The CAR and standard cumulative abnormal returns (SCAR) over the event window (−1, 0, +1) are statistically significant at 1% level. The results support the rejection of the null hypothesis at 1% level of significance. The empirical results provide good evidence of value addition to the stockholders of the bidding firms following the announcements of cross-border mergers and acquisitions by the Indian corporations. The results indicate that the stockholders remained positive to the announcements relating to cross-border mergers and acquisitions by Indian companies. It is evident from Table 1 that cross-border mergers and acquisitions' announcements had a positive effect on the Indian stock market.

The empirical findings presented in Table 2 show that the parametric and non-parametric test results are significant at 1% level of significance. The results indicate positive wealth effects to the stockholders of the Indian-acquiring companies involved in CB-M&A in the post-acquisition period. The empirical results therefore support the rejection of the null hypothesis at 1% level of significance.

4.1. Comparison of empirical findings with prior findings from mature markets

It is evident from the empirical findings presented in Tables 1 and 2 that the present study has shown positive and significant long-term stock price performance of Indian-acquiring companies involved in CB-M&A. In contrast, the prior findings from the mature markets show negative wealth effects to the stockholders of the acquiring firms. The global landscape changed over the period, the phenomenon identified in mature markets relating to the short term, and long-term performance following M&A activity differs from the Indian context. The following comparison is undertaken to show how the context, situation and environment in which the CB-M&A by Indian corporates differ from those of the mature markets. Hence, there are possibilities of variations in the findings.

Table 1. Cumulative abnormal returns (CAR) and standard cumulative abnormal returns (SCAR)

Event window (−1, 0, +1)		
CAR	0.0147	0.01*
SCAR	0.6982	0.01*

*Significant at 1% level.

Table 2. Parametric and non-parametric tests

	CAR-market model			
Parametric tests	***t*-Value**	***P*-value**	***F*-value**	***P*-value**
	2.22	0.02	4.96	0.029
t-Test: *P*-value				
ANOVA *F*-test: *P*-value		2.03		
Non-parametric tests	Value		Probability	
Wilcoxon/Mann–Whitney	2.03		0.0421	

4.2. Ownership structure

The institutional environment in Asian countries is different from the USA; various researchers have suggested that agency problems may be less severe in Asian countries, partly because they have a more concentrated ownership structure (i.e. wealth controlled by a few family groups or by the federal government). Some studies also suggested that agency theory and other management theories are not suitable to explain M&A activities in Asian emerging markets because of the differences in ownership structures and institutional causes between developed and developing countries (e.g. Reddy, 2015). For instance, in case of India, the majority of companies that have opted for overseas investments have been family owned.

There are two differences in M&A deals documented in the literature between the USA and other developed countries with M&A deals of Asian emerging economies. First, the USA has a well-developed legal and regulatory system to protect the interests of shareholders and the welfare of consumers that differs from that of many emerging economies that suffer from a poor legal and regulatory environment as well as weak enforcement of existing laws (La Porta, Lopez-De-Silanes, & Shleifer, 1999). Second, the cultural and governance differences between developing and developed markets lead to differences in the organisational structure of firms (Dennis & McConnell, 1986).

Regarding conglomerate mergers, it is evident from the literature that conglomerate mergers were central from the period of 1960 onwards. The distinguishing feature of the mergers occurring in the 1960s was to diversify or extend the acquiring companies' product mix (Mueller, 1977). Unlike the above, in case of India, all the cross-border mergers and acquisitions by Indian corporates belong to the same sector and fall in the category of non-diversifying M&A. This difference could add to the variations in the results.

4.3. Mode of settlement

Most of the research focuses on whether cash offers or equity offers are value maximising from the perspective of shareholders. There is reasonably consistent evidence that cash bids are associated with better performance in both the short run (Dong, Hirshleifer, Richardson, & Teoh, 2005) and the long run. The prior findings provide evidence that stock-based deals are associated with significantly negative returns at deal announcements, whereas cash deals are zero or slightly positive (Asquith, 1983).

One reason for these results may be that acquirers decide on their payment method, depending on whether they expect higher or lower performance in the forthcoming periods. Hence, acquirers will pay in cash if they believe their shares are undervalued, and they will choose equity if they think their shares are overvalued. Cash payments might serve as a signal to the market that acquiring firm management expects an increase in firm value over the post-acquisition period. Transactions paid with equity will result in a dilution of the share price, as the number of outstanding shares increases, while the value of the firm remains the same until expected synergies take effect.

As documented in the literature, the mode of settlement for majority of the companies involved in M&A activity in the mature markets was equity settlement. On the contrary, it is evident from Table 2 that all Indian companies involved in 30 OFDI-related M&A settled their M&A transactions in cash.

4.4. Regulatory issues

Empirical findings from the USA suggest that M&A regulation is costly to investors. Weir (1983) finds evidence suggesting that Federal Trade Commission antitrust actions benefit competitive rivals of both the buyer and the target. Jarrell and Bradley (1980) and Asquith (1983) find that returns to merging firms were significantly higher before than after implementation of the Williams Act in October 1969. Likewise, Schipper and Thompson (1983) consider four regulatory changes between 1968 and 1970 and found wealth-reducing effects associated with increased regulation.

More recently, the rules and regulations governing the international firms have been dramatically altered to facilitate operations of the foreign firms (UNCTAD, 2008, 2013). Opening up of capital markets has been made easier than before for emerging multinational enterprises from developing countries to raise equity capital and debt besides facilitating their listing of shares on foreign stock exchanges. These firms have been encouraged by emerging developing countries as well as they (home countries) have made suitable policy changes to enable their firms raise equity capital and debt from foreign markets (Ramamurti, 2008; RBI, 2009). However, in some of the cross-border deals, the Indian Government failed to offer policy recommendations relating to dual listing norms (e.g. the proposed Bharti Airtel—MTN telecom deal had broken up in 2008).

4.5. Asset exploitation

It is evident from the literature that firms are driven by asset exploitation perspective when they possess firm-specific advantages. They tend to expand, internationalise and use their scale of operations to a fuller extent. These corporates are those which possess firm-specific advantages (FSAs) in the form of superior technology, brands and extensive networks of channels of distributions in the mature markets and they try to expand the horizons of their markets. This is relevant to the mature markets. According to Mathews (2006), asset exploitation is not appropriate to companies from emerging markets because they often seek to invest abroad to secure a competitive advantage they do not possess at home. It is true in the Indian context and evident from acquisitions by Tata Steel and Hindalco. By combining their firm-specific skills with the competitive skills acquired through cross-border mergers and acquisitions, Indian companies are able to compete in the international markets. They also draw synergies through complementary fit occurring due to the de-integrated model of operations subsequent to the acquisitions.

For instance, from the Indian context, the case of Tata-Corus steel is the good example of Indian companies with asset exploitation perspective. For instance, by acquiring Corus, Tata Steel gained access to an established and well-recognised brand name, superior technology and an extensive distribution network in the Western markets. The empirical findings showing positive stock price performance in the post-acquisition period indicate that Tata-Corus obtained the expected synergies by making primary metal in markets close to raw materials (India) and establishing finishing (value-adding) facilities in the end-user markets (Athukorala, 2009). In other words, the acquisition of Corus enabled Tata Steel to link their FSA-like labour-intensive production, access to raw materials, accumulated managerial skills with the advantages of access to the high-margin markets and high technology in the West through Corus. It could therefore leverage in the Western markets the cost advantage of operating from India and product differentiation based on better technology from Corus in Asian markets. This acquisition enabled Tata Steel to acquire a competitive advantage in terms of local presence in high-growth markets. It was able to compete with the international players with the synergies drawn from cost-efficiency due to the de-integrated operations. It was also able to leverage the cost advantages in the mature markets. In the emerging markets, it had the advantage of product differentiation occurring due to superior technology.

It is understood from the above case that asset-exploitation to the Indian companies is possible only through acquiring firms in the mature markets, unlike the firms from mature markets which is not necessarily because they have the firm-specific advantages in terms of established brands and technology.

The asset exploration perspective of outward FDIs is appropriate to the emerging markets because they try to expand into the high-growth markets by acquiring strategic assets (i.e. technology, marketing and management expertise), which are available in the mature markets. The companies from mature markets are not driven by asset exploration perspective because they already possess the required infrastructure for innovation and further development of new products. This perspective has more relevance to the companies from emerging economies. For instance, the case of Dr. Reddy's Laboratories (DRL) is a good example of Indian companies with asset exploration perspective. Indian firms are moving up the value chain by acquiring specific skills and technologies in advanced markets.

Table 3. Comparison between mature market and emerging market studies

Details	Mature market studies	Indian studies
Settlement of M&A transaction	Equity settlements	Cash settlements
Asset exploitation	Corporates are driven by asset exploitation because they possess firm-specific advantages which enables them to compete in international markets	Asset exploitation is possible only when the corporates acquire the competitive advantages and combine them to their firm-specific advantages so that they can compete in the global markets
Motive	Asset exploitation	Asset exploration and asset exploitation
Performance of bidding and target firm	Acquiring firm's Tobin's Q > target firm's Tobin's Q	Acquiring firm's Tobin's Q < target firm's Tobin's Q
Agency problems	More severe because of the diffused ownership structures	Less severe because the ownership structures are concentrated and majority of them are either family owned or government owned
Regulations	Increased regulations	Liberalised/unregulated
Legal systems	Well developed	Not well developed
Diversification	Conglomerate mergers	Non-diversifying acquisitions
Acquired and target group—Geography	Developed to developed countries	Emerging to developed countries

In the high-volume low-cost active pharmaceutical ingredient market, Indian firms are now facing competition from Chinese firms, which can manufacture bulk drugs at a cheaper cost than Indian firms. Indian firms are using access to technology as a differentiating factor, where competition based on cost has limitations (Kale, 2007). DRL's acquisition of Trigeneis shows Indian firm's efforts to move up the value chain by augmenting existing capabilities through acquisition. DRL's acquisition of Trigeneis gives the company access to certain products and proprietary drug delivery technology platforms to develop a pipeline of drugs in the dermatology segment. One of Trigeneis's proprietary technologies takes care of major challenges faced in the formulation and delivery of drugs in the areas of oral, injectables, inhaled and topical deliveries. The above empirical findings show the motive of asset exploration by the Indian pharmaceutical companies.

Table 3 presents the possibilities for differences in the outcomes of the studies from mature markets and Indian context due to underlying differences behind initiating the M&A transaction. Therefore, it is evident from above that the context and the situation in which the CB-M&A were initiated by mature markets differ from that of the emerging market and in specific from the Indian context. This explains the differing outcomes.

5. Concluding remarks

The motive for mergers and acquisitions and the market's perception of these deals has received attention from researchers in the Western countries. However, the motives and market reaction to the announcements of OFDI by companies in mature markets have not been contrasted with those in emerging markets until now.

Contrary to the findings of studies, using USA data that have showed negative wealth effects to shareholders in the short as well as long term, this study indicates that the Indian stock market reacted positively in the short term following the announcement of OFDI by Indian companies. This indicates that Indian corporations should consider OFDI as a viable means of creating lasting value for their shareholders. The findings of this study will not only benefit the managers participating in overseas deals, but will also benefit the government in emerging markets in formulating policy with regard to the OFDI limit and tax provisions. The variation in the market reaction to the OFDI announcements in the USA and India could be due to the differences in the motives as well as market characteristics.

Extending this study to other emerging markets would shed further light on this issue and provide guidance to senior executives of companies in emerging markets in their quest to become globally competitive and create lasting value for their shareholders. Yet, this paper is restricted to the sample of Indian multinational firms and comparison with domestic firms. Indeed, comparative analysis of cross-border acquirer performance following the acquisitions in developed and developing markets, post-merger integration issues facing by emerging market acquirers and institutional issues in deal mechanism deserve future research. In particular, critical research on probable groups in cross-border acquisitions such as emerging market parent/mature market target, emerging market parent/emerging market target, mature market parent/emerging market target and mature market parent/mature market target would enhance the understanding of institutional settings.

Acknowledgements

Authors have equally contributed to this article. Authors thank the section editor and anonymous reviewers for their helpful comments on earlier versions of this paper. Authors also thank Dr. K.S. Reddy for his research assistance. The usual disclaimer applies.

Funding

The authors received no direct funding for this research.

Author details

Geeta Rani Duppati[1]

E-mail: geetad@waikato.ac.nz, nvrao13@gmail.com

ORCID ID: http://orcid.org/0000-0002-7429-6057

Narendar V. Rao[2]

E-mail: N-Rao@neiu.edu

[1] Department of Finance, Waikato Management School, University of Waikato, Hamilton, New Zealand.

[2] Department of Finance, College of Business and Management, Northeastern Illinois University, Chicago, IL, USA.

References

Ahluwalia, M. S. (2002). Economic reforms in India since 1991: Has gradualism worked? *Journal of Economic Perspectives, 16*, 67–88. http://dx.doi.org/10.1257/089533002760278721

Amighini, A., Cozza, C., Giuliani, E., Rabellotti, R., & Scalera, V. G. (2015). Multinational enterprises from emerging economies: What theories suggest, what evidence shows. A literature review. *Economia E Politica Industriale, 42*, 343–370.

Anderson, J., Sutherland, D., & Severe, S. (2015). An event study of home and host country patent generation in Chinese MNEs undertaking strategic asset acquisitions in developed markets. *International Business Review, 24*, 758–771.

Asquith, P. (1983). Merger bids, uncertainty, and stockholder returns. *Journal of Financial Economics, 11*, 51–83. http://dx.doi.org/10.1016/0304-405X(83)90005-3

Athukorala, P. C. (2009). Outward foreign direct investment from India. *Asian Development Review, 26*, 125–153.

Aybar, B., & Thanakijsombat, T. (2015). Financing decisions and gains from cross-border acquisitions by emerging-market acquirers. *Emerging Markets Review, 24*, 69–80. http://dx.doi.org/10.1016/j.ememar.2015.05.008

Bhagat, S., Malhotra, S., & Zhu, P. (2011). Emerging country cross-border acquisitions: Characteristics, acquirer returns and cross-sectional determinants. *Emerging Markets Review, 12*, 250–271. http://dx.doi.org/10.1016/j.ememar.2011.04.001

Buckley, P. J., Elia, S., & Kafouros, M. (2014). Acquisitions by emerging market multinationals: Implications for firm performance. *Journal of World Business, 49*, 611–632. http://dx.doi.org/10.1016/j.jwb.2013.12.013

Chittoor, R., Aulakh, P. S., & Ray, S. (2015). What drives overseas acquisitions by Indian firms? A behavioral risk-taking perspective. *Management International Review, 55*, 255–275. http://dx.doi.org/10.1007/s11575-015-0238-7

Contractor, F. J. (2013). Punching above their weight: The sources of competitive advantage for emerging market multinationals. *International Journal of Emerging Markets, 8*, 304–328. http://dx.doi.org/10.1108/IJoEM-06-2013-0102

Das, R. (1997). Defending against MNC offensives: Strategy of the large domestic firm in a newly liberalizing economy. *Management Decision, 35*, 605–618. http://dx.doi.org/10.1108/00251749710176118

Deng, P., & Yang, M. (2015). Cross-border mergers and acquisitions by emerging market firms: A comparative investigation. *International Business Review, 24*, 157–172. http://dx.doi.org/10.1016/j.ibusrev.2014.07.005

Dennis, D. K., & McConnell, J. J. (1986). Corporate mergers and security returns. *Journal of Financial Economics, 16*, 143–187. http://dx.doi.org/10.1016/0304-405X(86)90059-0

Dong, M., Hirshleifer, D., Richardson, S., & Teoh, S. H. (2005). Does investor misvaluation drive the takeover market? *Journal of Finance, 61*, 725–762.

Dongre, A. P. (2012). Policy changes in the wake of globalization and its impact on Indian industries. *Journal of Policy Modeling, 34*, 476–496. http://dx.doi.org/10.1016/j.jpolmod.2011.10.004

Du, M., & Boateng, A. (2012). Cross-border mergers & acquisitions by emerging market firms: A review and future direction. *ACRN Journal of Entrepreneurship Perspectives, 1*, 24–54.

Gregory, A., & McCorriston, S. (2005). Foreign acquisitions by UK limited companies: Short- and long-run performance. *Journal of Empirical Finance, 12*, 99–125. http://dx.doi.org/10.1016/j.jempfin.2003.10.003

Jarrell, G. A., & Bradley, M. (1980). The economic effects of federal and state regulations of cash tender offers. *The Journal of Law and Economics, 23*, 371–407. http://dx.doi.org/10.1086/jle.1980.23.issue-2

Kale, D. (2007). *Internationalisation strategies of Indian pharmaceutical firms* (IKD Working Paper No. 23). Milton Keynes: Open University Research Centre on Innovation, Knowledge & Development, The Open University.

Kim, E. H., & Lu, Y. (2013). Corporate governance reforms around the world and cross-border acquisitions. *Journal of Corporate Finance, 22*, 236–253. http://dx.doi.org/10.1016/j.jcorpfin.2013.05.005

Kohli, R., & Mann, B. J. S. (2012). Analyzing determinants of value creation in domestic and cross border acquisitions in India. *International Business Review, 21*, 998–1016. http://dx.doi.org/10.1016/j.ibusrev.2011.11.006

La Porta, R., Lopez-De-Silanes, F., & Shleifer, A. (1999). Corporate ownership around the world. *The Journal of Finance, 54*, 471–517. http://dx.doi.org/10.1111/0022-1082.00115

Langetieg, T. C. (1978). An application of a three-factor performance index to measure stockholder gains from merger. *Journal of Financial Economics, 6*, 365–383. http://dx.doi.org/10.1016/0304-405X(78)90010-7

Lebedev, S., Peng, M. W., Xie, E., & Stevens, C. E. (in press). Mergers and acquisitions in and out of emerging economies. *Journal of World Business.*

Makino, S., Lau, C.-M., & Yeh, R.-S. (2002). Asset-exploitation versus asset-seeking: Implications for location choice of foreign direct investment from newly industrialized economies. *Journal of International Business Studies, 33*, 403–421. http://dx.doi.org/10.1057/palgrave.jibs.8491024

Malatesta, P. H. (1983). The wealth effect of merger activity and the objective functions of merging firms. *Journal of Financial Economics, 11*, 155–181. http://dx.doi.org/10.1016/0304-405X(83)90009-0

Mathews, J. A. (2006). Dragon multinationals: New players in 21st century globalization. *Asia Pacific Journal of Management, 23*, 5–27. http://dx.doi.org/10.1007/s10490-006-6113-0

Mueller, D. C. (1977). The effects of conglomerate mergers. *Journal of Banking and Finance, 1*, 315–347. http://dx.doi.org/10.1016/0378-4266(77)90008-5

Nagano, M., & Yuan, Y. (2013). Cross-border acquisitions in a transition economy: The recent experiences of China and India. *Journal of Asian Economics, 24*, 66–79. http://dx.doi.org/10.1016/j.asieco.2012.08.003

Nayyar, D. (2008). The internationalization of firms from India: Investment, mergers and acquisitions. *Oxford Development Studies, 36*, 111–131. http://dx.doi.org/10.1080/13600810701848219

Nicholson, R. R., & Salaber, J. (2013). The motives and performance of cross-border acquirers from emerging economies: Comparison between Chinese and Indian firms. *International Business Review, 22*, 963–980. http://dx.doi.org/10.1016/j.ibusrev.2013.02.003

Pandya, A. M., & Rao, N. V. (1998). Diversification and firm performance: An empirical evaluation. *Journal of Financial and Strategic Decisions, 11*, 67–81.

Rajan, R. S. (2009). *Outward foreign direct investment from India: Trends, determinants and implications* (ISAS Working Paper). Singapore: Institute of South Asian Studies, National University of Singapore.

Ramamurti, R. (2008). *What have we learned about emerging-market MNES? Insights from a multi-country research project, emerging multinationals: Outward FDI from emerging and developing economies.* Copenhagen: Copenhagen Business School.

Rani, N., Yadav, S. S., & Jain, P. K. (2015). Market response to internationalization strategies: Evidence from Indian cross-border acquisitions. *IIMB Management Review, 27*, 80–91. http://dx.doi.org/10.1016/j.iimb.2015.03.002

Rasiah, R., Gammeltoft, P., & Jiang, Y. (2010). Home government policies for outward FDI from emerging economies: Lessons from Asia. *International Journal of Emerging Markets, 5*, 333–357. http://dx.doi.org/10.1108/17468801011058415

Reserve Bank of India. (2009, January). *Indian investment abroad in joint ventures and wholly owned subsidiaries: 2008–09.* Monthly Bulletin.

Reddy, K. S. (2015). Beating the odds! Build theory from emerging markets phenomenon and the emergence of case study research—A "test-tube" typology. *Cogent Business & Management, 2*, 1–25.

Reddy, K. S. (in press). Extant reviews on entry-mode/internationalization, mergers & acquisitions, and diversification: Understanding theories and establishing interdisciplinary research. *Pacific Science Review.*

Reddy, K. S., Nangia, V. K., & Agrawal, R. (2014). The 2007–2008 global financial crisis, and cross-border mergers and acquisitions: A 26-nation exploratory study. *Global Journal of Emerging Market Economies, 6*, 257–281. http://dx.doi.org/10.1177/0974910114540720

Schipper, K., & Thompson, R. (1983). Evidence on the capitalized value of merger activity for acquiring firms. *Journal of Financial Economics, 11*, 85–119. http://dx.doi.org/10.1016/0304-405X(83)90006-5

Singh, H., & Montgomery, C. A. (1987). Corporate acquisition strategies and economic performance. *Strategic Management Journal, 8*, 377–386. http://dx.doi.org/10.1002/(ISSN)1097-0266

Sinkovics, R. R., Sinkovics, N., Lew, Y. K., Jedin, M. H., & Zagelmeyer, S. (2015). Antecedents of marketing integration in cross-border mergers and acquisitions: Evidence from Malaysia and Indonesia. *International Marketing Review, 32*, 2–28. http://dx.doi.org/10.1108/IMR-07-2014-0211

UNCTAD. (2008). *World investment report: Transnational corporations and the infrastructure challenge.* New York, NY: United Nations Publications.

UNCTAD. (2013). *World investment report: Global value chains—Investment and trade for development.* New York, NY: United Nations Publications.

Weidenbaum, M., & Sheldon, V. (1987). Takeovers and stockholders: Winners and losers. *California Management Review, 29*, 57–168.

Weir, P. (1983). The costs of antimerger lawsuits: Evidence from the stock market. *Journal of Financial Economics, 11*, 207–224.

4

Determinants of bank technical efficiency: Evidence from rural and community banks in Ghana

Michael Adusei[1]*
*Corresponding author: Michael Adusei, Department of Accounting and Finance, Kwame Nkrumah University of Science and Technology, Kumasi, Ghana
E-mail: madusei10@yahoo.com
Reviewing editor: David McMillan, University of Stirling, UK

Abstract: What are the determinants of the technical efficiency of rural and community banks in Ghana? This paper addresses this question with data from 101 rural and community banks in Ghana. Data envelopment analysis based on the variable return to scale assumption and binary logistic regression technique has been used for analysis. The results show that only 20 rural and community banks are technically efficient. The binary logistic regression analysis provides evidence that size, profitability, and bank funding quality are significant determinants of technical efficiency in the rural banking industry in Ghana. Whereas an increase in the size and funding quality of a rural bank results in a decrease in its technical efficiency, an increase in the profitability of a rural bank improves its technical efficiency. It can be inferred from these results that the resource utilization of many rural and community banks in Ghana is weak and that the resource utilization performance of a rural bank can be assessed by considering its size, profitability, and funding quality.

Subjects: Area Studies; Economics, Finance, Business & Industry; Social Sciences

Keywords: rural and community banks; technical efficiency; data envelopment analysis; Ghana

JEL classifications: G20; G21

ABOUT THE AUTHOR

Michael Adusei is a senior lecturer of banking and finance in the service of Kwame Nkrumah University of Science and Technology, Ghana. His research interests include financial intermediation, corporate governance, entrepreneurship, and microfinance. He has published in international peer-reviewed journals including *Cogent Economics and Finance, Journal of International Development and Journal of African Business.*

PUBLIC INTEREST STATEMENT

Technical efficiency (TE) of financial institutions including rural and community banks (RCBs) is increasingly gaining popularity in bank regulation and supervision in recent times. This paper explores the factors that explain the variations in the TE of RCBs in Ghana using data envelopment analysis as well as binary logistic regression technique. The paper shows that only 20 out of the 101 RCBs used for the study are technically efficient and that the TE of a rural bank in Ghana is influenced by its size, funding quality, and profitability. When the size of a rural bank increases, its TE deteriorates. Similarly, when the funding quality of a rural bank improves, its TE suffers. On the other hand, when the profitability of a rural bank improves, its TE also improves. Apparently, these factors should be of immense importance to policy-makers as well as RCBs in Ghana.

1. Introduction

There is no doubt that the instability of the banking sector poses a serious threat to the foundations of every economy. This is because when a lot of banks become distressed in the banking industry resources are misallocated, overall return on capital drops and high transaction costs are incurred in the industry. The cumulative effect is that the growth of the sector in particular as well as the growth of the economy in general is undermined (Kumar, 2008). It is for this reason that bank performance measurement is at the heart of bank regulation in every economy.

One measure of bank performance which could indicate the vulnerability of a bank to financial distress is technical efficiency (TE). TE measures the distance of a firm's performance from the best-practice frontier that represents the optimal use of resources (Yin, Yang, & Mehran, 2013). It indicates the resource utilization performance of a firm relative to its peers.

The TE measurement of banks is of paramount importance to central banks in assessing the effects of policy interventions such as deregulation in the banking industry. Besides, in a vibrant and competitive banking system, only strong technically efficient and profitable banks can promise a realistic return to their stakeholders and reduce the probability of bankruptcy. Consistent with this postulation, the banking literature is flooded with studies on the TE of commercial banks (Fujii, Managi, & Matousek, 2014; Homma, Tsutsui, & Uchida, 2014; Hou, Wang, & Zhang, 2014; Rosman, Wahab, & Zainol, 2014; Shyu & Chiang, 2012; Sufian, 2009; Tecles & Tabak, 2010; Yin et al., 2013). However, what is observable about these studies is that most of them truncate their investigations at assessing only the TE of the financial institutions they investigate. They fail to extend their investigations to identify the factors that predict TE. Only few of these studies have explored the factors that account for TE (e.g. Al-Gasaymeh, 2016; Řepková, 2015; Rosman et al., 2014; Singh & Fida, 2015; Sufian, 2009).

The purpose of this paper, therefore, is to expand the frontiers of the empirical literature on the determinants of bank TE with data from the rural banking industry in Ghana. The paper shows that only 20 out of the 101 rural and community banks (RCBs) used for the study are technically efficient and that the TE of a rural bank in Ghana is influenced by its size, funding quality, and profitability. When the size of a rural bank increases, its TE deteriorates. Similarly, when the funding quality of a rural bank improves, its TE suffers. On the other hand, when the profitability of a rural bank improves, its TE also improves.

The current study is different from a recent one on RCBs in Ghana done by Iddrisu, Aboagye, and Osei (2014) in that it employs current data, utilizes a larger sample size, and transcends the borders of hackneyed mere analysis of TE to explore the factors that account for RCBs' TE. Consequently, it should offer a better understanding of the TE of RCBs in Ghana than the previous study.

The value of this paper is founded on the following reasons. First, the paper contributes to the ongoing debate on the effect of size on bank TE with evidence from the rural banking industry that bank size hurts bank TE. This contribution is especially significant because, over the years, the debate on the size-TE hypothesis has revolved around commercial banks. Thus, the current evidence represents a new perspective on the size-TE hypothesis. Second, to the extent apparently that studies on the determinants of bank TE have not considered the effect of funding quality on bank TE, its inclusion in the current study represents an extension of the frontiers of the bank TE literature. Third, the finding that bank profitability supports bank TE reinforces the theoretical and empirical position that there is an inextricable link between bank profitability and bank TE. Fourth, in terms of policy significance, the study provides a hint to policy-makers in Ghana that most RCBs are technically inefficient which calls for efficiency-enhancing interventions.

2. Overview of rural banking in Ghana

Largely, the rural banking model was integrated into the banking system in Ghana in the early 1970s to address two obstacles to rural financial intermediation (collateral and current accounts requirements of commercial banks) that had made access to credit in the rural areas very difficult (Asiedu-Mante, 2011). Before the advent of the model, a special development bank called agricultural development bank (ADB) had been set up to promote rural financial intermediation as part of efforts to accelerate the growth of agriculture in Ghana. However, with time it became apparent that the demand for financial services in the rural areas had outgrown the capacity of ADB. This led to the introduction of the rural banking model with the establishment of Nyakrom Rural Bank in 1976. This was done at the recommendation of the two-man team sent by the Bank of Ghana to understudy the rural banking model of Philippines.

Rural banks are also called RCBs.[1] They are special banks established to carry on the business of unit banking in the rural communities in Ghana. As unit banks, RCBs are not mandated to have branches; their operations are restricted to geographically defined locations. They are limited liability companies whose shares are owned by residents of the localities where they are set up with limits placed on the number of shares an individual can acquire. These limits are placed as a control mechanism to avoid concentrated ownership structure of the banks.

The highest decision-making body in the governance system of a rural bank is the board of directors. The board of a rural bank is formed with the approval of the Bank of Ghana after the prospective directors have completed and submitted the director's questionnaire accompanied by the statement of affairs of their financial positions to the Bank of Ghana for review. The board of directors of a new rural bank becomes extinct at the first annual general meeting of the bank but the directors are eligible to seek re-election. Subsequently, one-third of the directors of the bank are to step down by rotation but shall be allowed to seek re-election pursuant to section 298 of the Companies Code of Ghana 1963 (ACT 179).

There are four major services offered by RCBs. These are microfinance loans, susu loans, salary loans, and commercial loans (Nair & Fissha, 2010). Table 1 provides details of major products marketed by RCBs.

As at January 2013, when this study commenced there were 137 RCBs (www.bog.gov.gh) with the regional distribution provided in Table 2. As the table shows, in terms of absolute figures, Ashanti region has the highest number of RCBs followed by Eastern region. The region with the lowest number is Upper West, accounting for only four out of the 137 RCBs in Ghana. However, in terms of rural population served by the RCBs in their regions, Central region leads with each rural bank in the region serving 55,428 rural dwellers. The region with the poorest ratio is Northern region. A rural bank in the Northern region serves 246,964 dwellers.

Figure 1 shows the regional distribution of RCBs in terms of percentages. It can be observed that Ashanti commands the highest percentage of 18 followed by Eastern region which holds 16. Upper West region has the lowest percentage of 3.

Figure 2 depicts the regional distribution of RCBs relative to regional rural population. It is observable that Greater Accra region has the lowest ratio followed by Central region. The region with the highest ratio is the Northern region. Apparently, Northern region needs more RCBs for efficient and effective rural financial intermediation.

3. Review of theoretical and empirical studies

There is no doubt that the search for factors that significantly explain bank TE is increasingly gathering momentum in recent times (Al-Gasaymeh, 2016; Řepková, 2015; See & He, 2015; Singh & Fida, 2015). However, consensus as to the variables that significantly explain bank TE appears elusive.

The efficient structure hypothesis, the structure-conduct-performance hypothesis, and the quiet-life hypothesis provide an explanation for the effect of firm size on firm TE. Credited to Demsetz (1973), the *efficient structure hypothesis* suggests that under market competition efficient firms outwit the competition and grow larger, gain greater market share, and chalk higher profits. It postulates that a market becomes more efficient as it becomes more concentrated. On the other hand,

Table 1. Major rural bank credit products

Loan type	Description
Microfinance loans	These are four-to-six month loans with interest rate ranging between 30 and 36% offered to groups of individuals to fund micro and small income-generating activities. In some rural banks, the group is the borrower, in others each member of the group is the borrower. However, in both cases, the group assumes a joint liability for the loan. A microfinance loan usually does not exceed GH¢ 1000[a]. Mostly, the size falls between GH¢ 100 and GH¢ 500
Susu loans	These are deposit-driven loans offered to individuals. The loans are offered after the client has saved with the bank (mostly daily and weekly deposits) for three months. The size of a ***susu*** loan is similar to that of a microfinance loan. The difference between a ***susu*** loan and microfinance loan is that whereas the former is given to individuals the latter is offered to groups
Salary loans	These are salary-secured loans offered to workers whose salaries pass through the bank. The loans have maximum term of 48 months with interest rate ranging between 30 and 33%. Consumption, investment, and social purposes usually trigger salary loans. The size of a salary loan depends on the salary of the borrower
Commercial loans	These are loans given to companies and individual entrepreneurs for working capital or fixed capital. The maximum size of a commercial loan is GH¢ 100,000, with the maximum term of 36 months and interest rate falling between 28 and 35%

Source: Nair and Fissha (2010).

[a]GH¢1 = US$4.

the *structure-conduct-performance hypothesis* posits that market concentration promotes low degree of competition culminating in market inefficiency. The *quiet-life hypothesis* argues that firms in a concentrated market hardly reduce costs because of unproductive expenditures to increase and keep monopoly power, deficient managerial effort, lack of profit-maximizing behavior, and/or survival of inefficient managers (Berger & Hannan, 1998).

Homma et al. (2014) use data from Japan to test the above hypotheses and report that, consistent with the efficient structure hypothesis, Japanese banks grow larger. They also report that, in line with the quite-life hypothesis, market concentration diminishes bank efficiency (Homma et al., 2014). However, Yin et al. (2013) find that bank size is negatively related to efficiency to some point (at the lower end) and that as bank size grows larger efficiency is hurt. According to Rosman et al. (2014), larger banks spend less on their inputs because of their perceived market power. Increasing returns to scale obtained from the spread of fixed costs over a large volume of services as well as increasing returns to scale gained from a specialized workforce has been cited to explain the positive relationship between size and efficiency (Hauner, 2005). On the other hand, as postulated by the quiet-life hypothesis, a negative relationship between size and efficiency is also predictable. Recent studies by Al-Gasaymeh (2016), Řepková (2015), and Singh and Fida (2015), find no significant effect of bank size on bank TE. In effect, it can be argued that the debate on the relationship between size and TE is inconclusive.

Developed by Berger and DeYoung (1997), the skimping hypothesis suggests that a bank that seeks to enhance cost efficiency as a way of maximizing long run profits may decide to cut down cost of operations in order to be cost-efficient in the short run by skimping on the resources allocated to loan screening and monitoring (underwriting cost). This may result in adverse selection with dire consequences for credit quality of the bank. In other words, the skimping strategy may result in the bank experiencing greater loan performance problems in the long run. The hypothesis points to a negative relationship between efficiency and credit risk. Sufian (2009) provides evidence in support of the skimping hypothesis with a study that reports a negative statistically significant relationship between credit risk and bank TE. Some studies have also reported that banks that are approaching failure tend to have low-cost efficiency and record high ratios of problem loans. Additionally, distressed banks tend to deviate significantly from the best-practice frontiers (Wheelock & Wilson, 1995). However, Řepková (2015) finds no significant relationship between credit risk and TE.

Table 2. Regional distribution of rural banks in Ghana

Region	Number of rural/community banks	Rural population per rural bank[a]
Ashanti	25	75,324
Central	21	55,428
Eastern	22	67,693
Brong Ahafo	20	64,126
Western	14	97,718
Volta	12	117,043
Greater Accra	7	54,157
Upper East	5	165,380
Upper West	4	146,864
Northern	7	246,964
Total	137	88,420

Source: Bank of Ghana Website.

[a]This has been calculated by dividing the total rural population in each region obtained from 2010 Population Census in Ghana by the number of rural banks in each region.

Apparently, there is room to further explore the relationship between credit risk and TE since the extant literature is inconclusive.

Diversification of activities is one of the factors that explain TE. Jeon and Miller (2005) and Sufian (2009) find that diversification positively impacts TE. The implication is that as banks generate more income from non-interest sources their TE improves (Sufian, 2009). Thus, there is a positive relationship between firm diversification and firm efficiency.

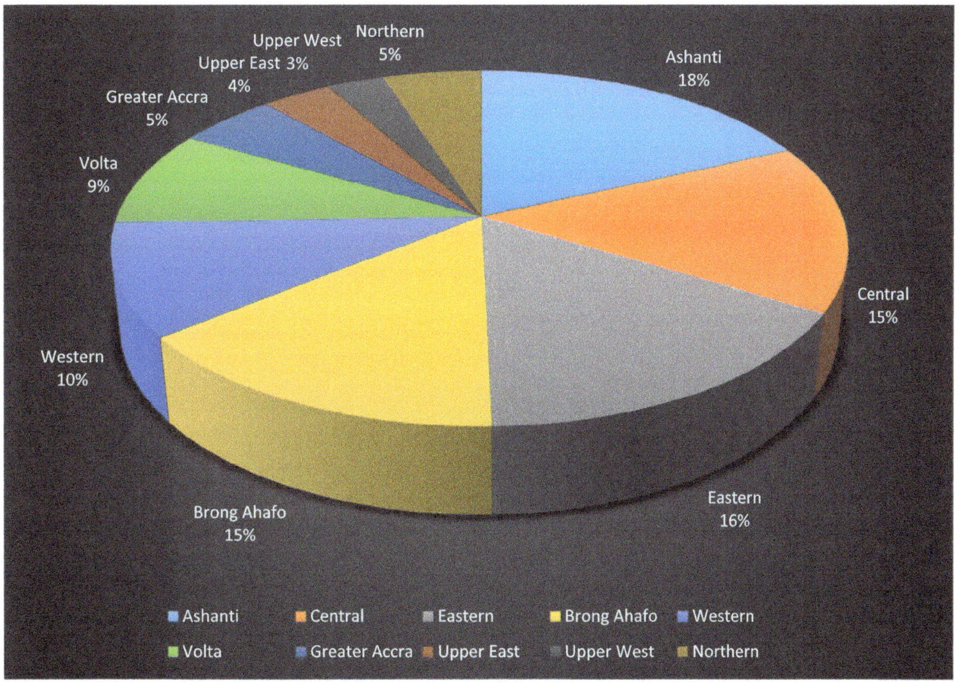

Figure 1. Regional distribution of RCBs.

Source: Author's construction.

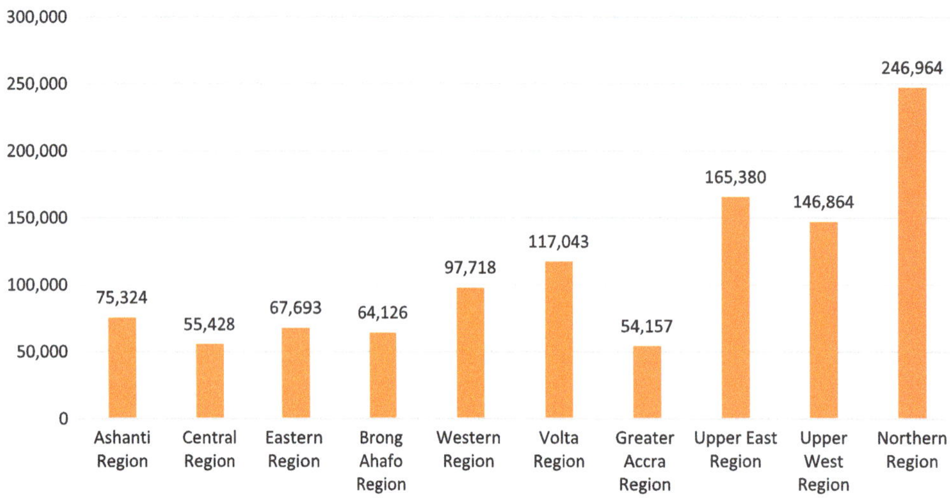

Figure 2. Rural population per rural bank per region.

Source: Author's construction.

Profitability as measured by ROA has a positive, statistically significant relationship with TE (Hasan & Marton, 2003; Rosman et al., 2014; Sufian, 2009). Banks that have higher profitability ratios are usually preferred by clients. As a result, such banks are able to gather the biggest share of deposits as well as the best potential creditworthy borrowers. From the point of view of intermediation activities, such conditions create a favorable environment for profitable banks to be more efficient (Sufian, 2009). A recent paper by Singh and Fida (2015) find profitability as the most important parameter of bank efficiency in Oman. However, contrary evidence exists that profitability measured in terms of ROA hurts bank TE (Řepková, 2015). Does profitability as measured by ROA promote or hurt rural bank TE in Ghana?

The debate on the equity capitalization–efficiency relationship generally concludes that capital positively influences efficiency (Řepková, 2015; Rosman et al., 2014; Singh & Fida, 2015; Tecles & Tabak, 2010). García-Herrero, Gavilá, and Santabárbara (2009), Goddard, Molyneux, and Wilson (2004), and Pasiouras and Kosmidou (2007) provide evidence that banks that record higher level of equity relative to assets are best-performing banks because they tend to have lower costs of funding owing to lower bankruptcy costs. However, Akhigbe and McNulty (2005) and Sufian (2009) find that capitalization is negatively related to TE. The implication is that more efficient banks use more leverage (less equity). It is obvious from the above that consensus does not exist in the literature on the relationship between equity capital and TE.

Developed by Berger and DeYoung (1997), the bad management hypothesis postulates that management quality/efficiency should negatively affect TE. Bad managers are unable to sufficiently monitor and control their operating expenses. When a bank records low TE, it indicates poor senior management practices in terms of input-usage, day-to-day operations, and management of loan portfolio (Sufian, 2009). Evidence from Sufian (2009) shows that management quality/efficiency has a negative, statistically significant relationship with TE. Is this hypothesis sustainable in the rural banking context?

Köhler (2015) posits that retail banks fund their activities with customer deposits. RCBs are retail banks that rely largely on customer deposits. Their ability to raise more deposits may promote managerial laxity leading to technical inefficiency. Thus, it is plausible to argue that there should be an inverse relationship between funding quality and TE. Does funding quality promote or hurt the TE of a rural bank?

4. Methodology

4.1. Analytical framework

The study adopts a two-stage approach to data analysis. The first stage involves the measurement of the TE of RCBs. The second stage involves the use of the TE scores of RCBs to explore the determinants of TE.

4.2. Technical efficiency analysis

Data envelopment analysis (DEA) is used to determine the TE scores of RCBs based on constant-return-to-scale technique (Banker, Charnes, & Cooper, 1984). It performs multiple comparisons between a set of homogeneous units (Gutiérrez-Nieto, Serrano-Cinca, & Mar Molinero, 2007). The choice of the DEA methodology is informed by its acclaimed superiority to the conventional parametric techniques. For instance, whereas the conventional parametric techniques require prior assumptions about the distributions of the observations, DEA does not (LaPlante & Paradi, 2015). According to Berger and Humphrey (1997), DEA is appropriate when there is no justification for conventional cost and profit functions.

When DEA is applied to multiple outputs and inputs, efficiency is defined as the ratio of weighted sum of outputs to weighted sum of inputs. The weights for the ratio are calculated by the constraint that each DMU's ratio must be less than or equal to one, thus condensing multiple inputs and outputs into a single "virtual" input and single "virtual" output without providing pre-assigned weights. Having done this, the efficiency score is calculated by dividing weighted outputs by the weighted inputs. The weighted efficiency scores are then used to determine the TE scores of the DMUs by solving the following efficiency-maximizing problem with variable return to scale technology assumption:

$$\text{Max}\, hc = \sum_{r=1}^{s} u_r y_r c / \sum_{i=1}^{m} v_i X_i c$$

Subject to:

$$\sum_{r=1}^{s} u_r y_{ri} / \sum_{i=1}^{m} v_i X_{ij} \quad \leq 1; u_r, v_i \geq 0 \quad r = 1, \ldots, S; i = 1, \ldots, m \text{ and } j = 1, \ldots, n \tag{1}$$

where c = a specific rural bank to be evaluated, y_{rj} = the amount of output r from rural bank, X_{ij} = the amount of input i to rural bank j, u_r = weight chosen for output r, v_i = weight chosen for input i, n = number of rural banks, s = number of outputs, and m = number of inputs.

The above equation suggests that a bank in the sample seeks to maximize the ratio of weighted outputs to weighted inputs subject to the constraint that none of the banks in the sample should have an efficiency score of more than unitary using the weights. The weights are, however, assumed to be unknown but obtained through optimization.

Variable selection (inputs and outputs selection) is one of the important requirements for DEA. Two approaches are used to select inputs and outputs for DEA: production and intermediation approaches. The production approach views bank as providing services to its clients in the form of transactions with the objective of either minimizing the amount of resources it consumes in providing various products and services or maximizing products and services for given levels of resources (Avkiran, 2006). The intermediation approach, on the other hand, views bank as channels of wealth transfer. Banks take funds from the saving surplus units in the form of deposits and other funds such as insurance policyholder liabilities, transform them, and give them out to the savings deficit units in the form of loans and other assets such as investments to generate income. Following the example of previous studies on the TE of banks (Mostafa, 2007; Rosman et al., 2014), we favor the intermediation approach. It is, thus, used to select the variables listed in Table 3.

Table 3. Selected inputs and outputs in bank technical efficiency model based on intermediation approach

Inputs	Outputs
Deposits (GH¢)	Loans (GH¢)
Shareholders' equity (GH¢)	Investments (GH¢)
	Profit before interest and tax (PBIT) (GH¢)

Notes: This table lists it the inputs and outputs selected for the study. They are all measured in the Ghana cedi (GH¢ 4.2 = US$1).

Source: Author.

Table 4. Variables, definitions, notations and expected signs

Variable	Definition	Notation	Expected Sign
Dependent variables			
Technical Efficiency	Dummy variable: = 1 if bank has a technical efficiency score of 1; = 0 if otherwise	TE	
Independent variables			
Bank size	Natural logarithm of total assets	SIZE	?
Credit risk	Total loans divided by total assets	CRISK	–
Return on assets	Profit before interest and tax divided by total assets (%)	ROA	+
Capitalization	Equity divided by total assets	CAP	+
Bank funding quality	Natural logarithm of total customer deposits	FUNDQUAL	–

Source: Author.

Another important issue in DEA is isotonicity test (Avkiran, 1999). The test is performed to ensure the validity of DEA model specification. It involves the determination of all inter-correlations between inputs and outputs to identify whether increasing amounts of inputs should result in greater outputs, implying that there should be positive correlations between inputs and outputs.

4.3. Hypothesized determinants of technical efficiency of rural and community banks

The TE scores obtained from stage one are coded into binary data. Following the work of Rosman et al. (2014), the factors that account for rural bank TE are explored. Since the coded efficiency scores from the DEA provide a dependent variable bounded by 0 and 1, it is appropriate to opt for binary logistic regression technique to perform the multivariate analysis. Interest lies in whether five variables (size, credit risk, profitability, equity capitalization and funding quality) of RCBs significantly predict their TE. The relationships between these explanatory variables and TE are provided in Table 4.

4.4. The model

Based on the above analytical framework, the model adopted for this study is stated as:

$$\mathrm{TE}_{it} = \beta_1 + \beta_2 \ln \mathrm{BSIZE}_{i,t} + \beta_3 \ln \mathrm{CRISK}_{i,t} + \beta_4 \ln \mathrm{ROA}_{i,t} + \beta_5 \ln \mathrm{CAP}_{i,t} + \beta_6 \ln \mathrm{FUNDQUAL}_{i,t} + \mu_i \quad (2)$$

where TE refers to bank TE score obtained from the coded DEA scores, *i* denotes the bank being evaluated, *t* examines time period, ln denotes natural logarithm, β is the parameter estimated, μ is the stochastic error term, SIZE denotes size of bank, CRISK denotes credit risk, ROA denotes bank profitability, CAP denotes equity capitalization, and FUNDQUAL denotes bank funding quality.

4.5. Data sources

Quantitative data have been extracted from the reports of all RCBs in Ghana compiled by the Apex Bank (the supervisory body of RCBs in Ghana). Inclusion of a rural bank in the sample is based on availability of complete data needed for the study. Thus, all RCBs with requisite data needed for the study have been included in the study.

5. Empirical results

The analysis is in two parts. In the first part, the TE of 101 RCBs is measured using the DEA methodology. The second part of the analysis uses the results from the first part (TE scores) to run binary logistic regression.

5.1. Technical efficiency analysis

TE analysis requires that isotonicity test is performed on the data to ascertain the validity of the DEA model specification. It involves the determination of all inter-correlations between inputs and outputs to identify whether increasing amounts of inputs should result in greater outputs, implying that there should be positive statistically significant correlations between inputs and outputs. The results of the isotonicity test are presented in Table 5.

The results confirm the validity of the inputs and outputs selected for the DEA. This is because there are positive correlations between inputs and outputs implying that increasing amounts of inputs result in greater outputs. The results of the DEA model show that of the 101 RCBs only 20 have TE scores of 1. This means that only 20 out of 101 RCBs are technically efficient. The remaining 81 RCBs are technically inefficient. Each of the 20 technically efficient RCBs is given the code of 1, while each of the 81 technically inefficient RCBs is given the code of 0 to create binary data for the next stage of the analysis. Details of the DEA results are attached as Appendix A.

5.2. Logistic regression analysis of determinants of RCB technical efficiency

We start off the analysis by assessing the correlations among the explanatory variables. As can be observed in Table 6, the correlation between size and bank funding quality is almost 100%, suggesting that it is not advisable to combine the two in one model since doing so creates multicollinearity problem in the model. Thus, two models are estimated with bank size and bank funding quality. Apart from this, the correlations among the rest of the explanatory variables are in line with the acceptable limits of the extant literature (Bryman & Cramer, 1997).

The predictive power of the models as measured by Cox and Snell and Nagelkerke R^2 lies between 43 and 58%. This suggests that between 43 and 58% of variations in the TE of rural banks is

Table 5. Results of isotonicity test–Pearson's correlation matrix

Variable	Equity	Deposits	Loans	Investment	PBIT
Equity	1				
Deposits	0.641***	1			
Loans	0.707***	0.916***	1		
Investment	0.510***	0.870***	0.641***	1	
PBIT	0.583***	0.901***	0.766***	0.917***	1

Note: PBIT = Profit before interest and tax.

***Significance at 1%.

Table 6. Correlation matrix					
Variable	**CRISK**	**ROA**	**CAP**	**SIZE**	**FUNDQUAL**
CRISK	1				
ROA	0.274	1			
CAP	−0.223	−0.414	1		
SIZE	0.314	0.475	−0.259	1	
FUNDQUAL	−0.353	−0.503	0.258	−0.999	1

Notes: This table presents the correlations among the independent variables. CRISK = credit risk. ROA = return on assets, CAP = equity capitalization, SIZE = bank size and FUNDQUAL = funding quality.

explained by the models. It is obvious that the predictive power of the models is high. Table 7 reports the results of the logistic regression without bank funding quality and Table 8 reports the results of the logistic regression without bank size.

The effect of size on TE is inconclusive in the extant literature. For instance, whereas Rosman et al. (2014) report a positive relationship between the size of a bank and its TE, Homma et al. (2014) report a negative relationship between size and TE. Some studies have also reported no significant impact of size on TE (Al-Gasaymeh, 2016; Řepková, 2015; Singh & Fida, 2015). The results in Table 7 indicate that the size of a rural bank has a negative statistically significant effect on TE, implying that larger RCBs are more likely to be technically inefficient than smaller RCBs. This smacks of diseconomies of scale where increasing size of a rural bank comes with inefficient utilization of scarce resources of the bank. The quiet-life hypothesis argues that firms in a concentrated market hardly minimize their costs because of unproductive expenditures to gain and maintain monopoly power, insufficient managerial effort, lack of profit-maximizing behavior, and/or survival of inefficient managers (Berger & Hannan, 1998). The rural banking model promotes monopoly. This is because RCBs are unit banks with geographically demarcated area of operation for each of them. This arrangement is such that hardly will one find two rural banks in one locality fiercely competing with each other for deposits and other financial contracts. Thus, it is highly probable for a rural bank to gain and keep monopoly power over its catchment area, experience insufficient managerial effort coupled with lack of profit-maximizing behavior and tolerate inefficient managers (Berger & Hannan, 1998).

Sufian (2009) reports that credit risk has a negative statistically significant relationship with bank TE. Some studies have also reported that banks that are approaching failure tend to have low-cost efficiency and record high ratios of problem loans and that distressed banks tend to deviate significantly from the best-practice frontiers (Wheelock & Wilson, 1995). Consequently, the a priori expectation of the study was that credit risk should be negatively related to TE. Evidence in Table 7 confirms this expectation. However, this is statistically insignificant.

Table 7. Results of logistic regression analysis without FUNDQUAL		
Variable	**Coefficient**	***p*-value**
SIZE	−0.434	0.023**
CRISK	−0.284	0.905
ROA	80.97	0.000***
CAP	−25.39	0.110
Cox & Snell $R^2 = 0.43$; Nagelkerke $R^2 = 0.58$; $N = 101$		

Notes: This table presents the logistic regression results when funding quality (FUNDQUAL) is dropped. SIZE = bank size, CRISK = credit risk, ROA = return on assets, and CAP = equity capitalization.

**Significance at 5% level.

***Significance at 1% level.

Table 8. Results of logistic regression analysis without SIZE

Variable	Coefficient	*p*-value
CRISK	0.116	0.961
ROA	83.96	0.000***
CAP	−25.47	0.108
FUNDQUAL	−0.482	0.015**
Cox & Snell R^2 = 0 .44; Nagelkerke R^2 = 0.58; *N* = 101		

Notes: This table presents the logistic regression results when size is dropped. CRISK = credit risk, ROA = return on assets, CAP = equity capitalization, and FUNDQUAL = funding quality.

**Significance at 5% level.

***Significance at 1% level.

Hasan and Marton (2003), Rosman et al. (2014), Singh and Fida (2015), and Sufian (2009), and have reported a positive relationship between bank profitability as measured by ROA and bank TE. The explanation is that banks that have higher profitability ratios are usually preferred by clients and, therefore, gather the biggest share of deposits as well as the best potential creditworthy borrowers. The a priori prediction of the study was that profitability should be positively related to TE. The results in Tables 7 and 8 confirm this prediction. Succinctly, the results Tables 7 and 8 demonstrate that higher profitability of a rural bank signals higher TE.

Evidence on the relationship between bank capitalization and bank TE is inconclusive. Whereas Rosman et al. (2014) and Tecles and Tabak (2010) report a positive relationship between bank capital and bank TE, Akhigbe and McNulty (2005) and Sufian (2009) find that capital is negatively related to TE. In Tables 7 and 8, the coefficient of equity capitalization (CAP) is negative, suggesting that it has a negative but statistically insignificant effect on rural bank TE. The implication is that contrary to the position of the extant literature that equity capitalization is a significant predictor of bank TE; the data in this study fail to provide support for this.

The a priori expectation of the study has been that the funding quality of a rural bank should be negatively related to its TE. The intuition is that RCBs that map out effective deposit-mobilization strategies are able to gather more customer deposits. Having more customer deposits may promote managerial laxity leading to technical inefficiency. The results in Table 8 show a negative statistically significant relationship between FUNDQUAL and TE, suggesting that RCBs with higher funding quality are less likely to be technically efficient than their counterparts. This smacks of managerial laxity in RCBs that are able to mobilize more deposits. All things being equal, a rural bank that is sited in a community where income levels of dwellers are high is likely to mobilize more deposits. Mobilizing more deposits may trigger technical inefficiency in that managerial laxity may be created by abundance of deposits leading to the creation of more bad loans as well as unproductive investments. In a nutshell, evidence from the data support the assertion that a rural bank that has better funding is less likely to be technically efficient.

6. Conclusion and recommendations

Predictors of TE in the rural banking industry in Ghana have been investigated with 2013 data from 101 RCBs. Inclusion of a rural bank in the sample has been informed by the availability and completeness of its data needed for analysis. The study first uses the BCC DEA model to determine the TE of each bank in the sample. The TE scores of the rural banks have been used to create binary data by assigning to each technically efficient rural bank the value of 1 and 0 to each technically inefficient rural bank. The study then uses binary logistic regression technique to explore the determinants of the TE of RCBs. The results show that only 20 RCBs are technically efficient and that size, profitability, and funding quality are significant predictors of TE in the rural banking industry in Ghana. It can be inferred from these results that the resource utilization of many RCBs in Ghana is weak.

The results of the study suggest that RCBs in Ghana need efficiency-improvement interventions. Considering the strategic importance of RCBs as agents of rural financial deepening in Ghana, allowing the status to remain may not augur well for agriculture as well as rural development in Ghana. It is, thus, recommended that the Bank of Ghana, in collaboration with the ARB Apex Bank, should organize regular efficiency training programs and workshops for boards of directors and managers of RCBs. It is envisaged that the adoption and implementation of this initiative are likely to promote the sustainability of RCBs as well as deepen financial inclusion with incalculable economic benefits for Ghana's economy.

The observation that size hurts the TE of RCBs points to the need for the Bank of Ghana to intensify its regulation on the growth of RCBs. To the extent that growth in size implies a dip in the TE of RCBs tactfully constraining their growth may be instrumental to improving their TE. Apparently, this is not going to be smooth judging from that, in recent times, managers of RCBs have been making frantic efforts to expand as a way of maximizing shareholder value. That notwithstanding, allowing them to grow without controls may spell doom for the entire financial system in the near future.

The negative statistically significant relationship between funding quality and TE points to poor utilization of customer deposits which may be due to ineffective lending standards. It is recommended that RCBs should strengthen their lending standards so that deposits mobilized from customers will be given to credit-worthy customers for maximization of shareholders' wealth. Putting in place effective lending standards and ensuring strict adherence to them will go a long way to improve RCBs' TE.

The literature identifies diversification and management efficiency as significant predictors of TE. However, due to data constraints the current study has not been able to investigate whether these variables have significant effects on the TE of RCBs. This serves as one of the areas where future studies can explore.

Funding
The author received no direct funding for this research.

Author details
Michael Adusei[1]
E-mail: madusei10@yahoo.com
[1] Department of Accounting and Finance, Kwame Nkrumah University of Science and Technology, Kumasi, Ghana.

Note
1. In this paper, rural banks and rural and community banks are used interchangeably.

References
Akhigbe, A., & McNulty, J. E. (2005). Profit efficiency sources and differences among small and large U.S. commercial banks. *Journal of Economics and Finance, 29*, 289–299. http://dx.doi.org/10.1007/BF02761575
Al-Gasaymeh, A. (2016). Bank efficiency determinant: Evidence from the gulf cooperation council countries. *Research in International Business and Finance, 38*, 214–223. http://dx.doi.org/10.1016/j.ribaf.2016.04.018
Asiedu-Mante, E. (2011). *Rural Banking in Ghana*. Ghana: Combert Impressions.
Avkiran, N. (1999). An application reference for data envelopment analysis in branch banking: Helping the novice researcher. *International Journal of Bank Marketing, 17*, 206–220. http://dx.doi.org/10.1108/02652329910292675
Avkiran, N. K. (2006). Developing foreign bank efficiency models for DEA grounded in finance theory. *Socio-Economic Planning Sciences, 40*, 275–296. http://dx.doi.org/10.1016/j.seps.2004.10.006
Banker, R. D., Charnes, A., & Cooper, W. W. (1984). Some models for estimating technical and scale inefficiencies in data envelopment analysis. *Management Science, 30*, 1078–1092. http://dx.doi.org/10.1287/mnsc.30.9.1078
Berger, A. N., & DeYoung, R. (1997). Problem loans and cost efficiency in commercial banks. *Journal of Banking and Finance, 21*, 849–870. http://dx.doi.org/10.1016/S0378-4266(97)00003-4
Berger, A. N., & Hannan, T. H. (1998). The efficiency cost of market power in the banking industry: A test of the "quiet life" and related hypotheses. *Review of Economics and Statistics, 80*, 454–465. http://dx.doi.org/10.1162/003465398557555
Berger, A. N., & Humphrey, D. B. (1997). Efficiency of financial institutions: International survey and directions for future research. *European Journal of Operational Research, 98*, 175–212. http://dx.doi.org/10.1016/S0377-2217(96)00342-6
Bryman, A., & Cramer, D. (1997). *Quantitative data analysis with SPSS for windows: A guide for social scientists*. London: Routledge.
Demsetz, H. (1973). Industry structure, market rivalry, and public policy. *The Journal of Law and Economics, 16*, 1–9. http://dx.doi.org/10.1086/466752
Fujii, H., Managi, S., & Matousek, R. (2014). Indian bank efficiency and productivity changes with undesirable outputs: A disaggregated approach. *Journal of Banking and Finance, 38*, 41–50. http://dx.doi.org/10.1016/j.jbankfin.2013.09.022
García-Herrero, A., Gavilá, S., & Santabárbara, D. (2009). What explains the low profitability of Chinese banks? *Journal of Banking and Finance, 33*, 2080–2092. http://dx.doi.org/10.1016/j.jbankfin.2009.05.005

Goddard, J., Molyneux, P., & Wilson, J. (2004). The profitability of european banks: A cross-sectional and dynamic panel analysis. *The Manchester School, 72*, 363–381. http://dx.doi.org/10.1111/manc.2004.72.issue-3

Gutiérrez-Nieto, B., Serrano-Cinca, C., & Mar Molinero, C. (2007). Microfinance institutions and efficiency. *Omega, 35*, 131–142. http://dx.doi.org/10.1016/j.omega.2005.04.001

Hasan, I., & Marton, K. (2003). Development and efficiency of the banking sector in a transitional economy: Hungarian experience. *Journal of Banking and Finance, 27*, 2249–2271. http://dx.doi.org/10.1016/S0378-4266(02)00328-X

Hauner, D. (2005). Explaining efficiency differences among large German and Austrian banks. *Applied Economics, 37*, 969–980. http://dx.doi.org/10.1080/00036840500081820

Homma, T., Tsutsui, Y., & Uchida, H. (2014). Firm growth and efficiency in the banking industry: A new test of the efficient structure hypothesis. *Journal of Banking and Finance, 40*, 143–153. http://dx.doi.org/10.1016/j.jbankfin.2013.11.031

Hou, X., Wang, Q., & Zhang, Q. (2014). Market structure, risk taking, and the efficiency of Chinese commercial banks. *Emerging Markets Review, 20*, 75–88. http://dx.doi.org/10.1016/j.ememar.2014.06.001

Iddrisu, A., Aboagye, A. Q. Q., & Osei, K. (2014). Measuring rural bank efficiency in Ghana: An application of the data envelopment analysis (DEA) approach. *Journal of Human and Social Science Research, 3*, 41–59.

Jeon, Y., & Miller, S. M. (2005). Performance of domestic and foreign banks: The case of Korea and the Asian financial crisis. *Global Economic Review, 34*, 145–165. http://dx.doi.org/10.1080/12265080500117491

Köhler, M. (2015). Which banks are more risky? The impact of business models on bank stability. *Journal of Financial Stability, 16*, 195–212. http://dx.doi.org/10.1016/j.jfs.2014.02.005

Kumar, S. (2008). An analysis of efficiency-profitability relationship in Indian public sector banks. *Global Business Review, 9*, 115–129. http://dx.doi.org/10.1177/097215090700900108

LaPlante, A. E., & Paradi, J. C. (2015). Evaluation of bank branch growth potential using data envelopment analysis. *Omega, 52*, 33–41. http://dx.doi.org/10.1016/j.omega.2014.10.009

Mostafa, M. (2007). Modeling the efficiency of GCC banks: A data envelopment analysis approach. *International Journal of Productivity and Performance Management, 56*, 623–643. http://dx.doi.org/10.1108/17410400710823651

Nair, A., & Fissha, A. (2010). *Rural banking: The case of rural and community banks in Ghana, agriculture and rural development* (Discussion Paper No. 48). Washington, DC: The World Bank.

Pasiouras, F., & Kosmidou, K. (2007). Factors influencing the profitability of domestic and foreign commercial banks in the European Union. *Research in International Business and Finance, 21*, 222–237. http://dx.doi.org/10.1016/j.ribaf.2006.03.007

Řepková, I. (2015). Banking efficiency determinants in the Czech banking sector. *Procedia Economics and Finance, 23*, 191–196.

Rosman, R., Wahab, N. A., & Zainol, Z. (2014). Efficiency of Islamic banks during the financial crisis: An analysis of Middle Eastern and Asian countries. *Pacific-Basin Finance Journal, 28*, 76–90. http://dx.doi.org/10.1016/j.pacfin.2013.11.001

See, K. F., & He, Y. (2015). Determinants of technical efficiency in Chinese banking: A double bootstrap data envelopment analysis approach. *Global Economic Review, 44*, 286–307. http://dx.doi.org/10.1080/1226508X.2015.1014392

Shyu, J., & Chiang, T. (2012). Measuring the true managerial efficiency of bank branches in Taiwan: A three-stage DEA analysis. *Expert Systems with Applications, 39*, 11494–11502. http://dx.doi.org/10.1016/j.eswa.2012.04.005

Singh, D., & Fida, A. B. (2015). Technical efficiency and its determinants: An empirical study on banking sector of Oman. *Problems and Perspectives in Management, 13*, 168–175.

Sufian, F. (2009). Determinants of bank efficiency during unstable macroeconomic environment: Empirical evidence from Malaysia. *Research in International Business and Finance, 23*, 54–77. http://dx.doi.org/10.1016/j.ribaf.2008.07.002

Tecles, P. L., & Tabak, B. M. (2010). Determinants of bank efficiency: The case of Brazil. *European Journal of Operational Research, 207*, 1587–1598. http://dx.doi.org/10.1016/j.ejor.2010.06.007

Wheelock, D. C., & Wilson, P. W. (1995). Explaining bank failures: Deposit insurance, regulation and efficiency. *The Review of Economics and Statistics, 77*, 689–700. http://dx.doi.org/10.2307/2109816

Yin, H., Yang, J., & Mehran, J. (2013). An empirical study of bank efficiency in China after WTO accession. *Global Finance Journal, 24*, 153–170. http://dx.doi.org/10.1016/j.gfj.2013.07.001

Appendix A. Technical efficiency scores, technical inefficiency and reference set for rural banks in Ghana (2013)

		Technical efficiency	Technical inefficiency	Bank	Technical efficiency	Technical inefficiency
ANLO	1.00000	0.00000	BRAKWA BRE-MAN	0.96914	0.03086	
GOMOA	1.00000	0.00000	AKIM BOSOME	0.96364	0.03636	
ODUPONGKPEHE	1.00000	0.00000	WAMFIE	0.96203	0.03797	
NANDOM	1.00000	0.00000	KWAHU	0.94732	0.05268	
SONZELE	1.00000	0.00000	ADANSI	0.94705	0.05295	
KINTAMPO	1.00000	0.00000	FIAGYA	0.94378	0.05622	
MEPE AREA	1.00000	0.00000	NZEMA MANLE	0.94267	0.05733	
ATWIMA MPONUA	1.00000	0.00000	SEKYERE	0.93371	0.06629	
FIASEMAN	1.00000	0.00000	ASUTIFI	0.92941	0.07059	
ATWIMA KWAN-WOMA	1.00000	0.00000	ENYAN DEN-KYIRA	0.92833	0.07167	
AMENFIMAN	1.00000	0.00000	LA COMM.	0.92028	0.07972	
UNION	1.00000	0.00000	BIA TORYA COMM	0.91981	0.08019	
AFRAM	1.00000	0.00000	SEKYEDUMASE	0.91805	0.08195	
AMANTIN & KASEI	1.00000	0.00000	SOUTH BIRIM	0.91765	0.08235	
TIZAA	1.00000	0.00000	BONZALI	0.91555	0.08445	
NAARA	1.00000	0.00000	SISSALA	0.91425	0.08575	
BUILSA COMM	1.00000	0.00000	ODWEN ANOMA	0.91351	0.08649	
YAPRA	1.00000	0.00000	ASANTE AKYEM	0.91064	0.08936	
NORTH TONGU	1.00000	0.00000	JUABEN	0.90657	0.09343	
OKOMFO ANOKYE	1.00000	0.00000	OTUASEKAN	0.90316	0.09684	
KWAMAMAN	0.98824	0.01176	NWABIAGYA	0.89687	0.10313	
KAASEMAN	0.98502	0.01498	DERMA AREA	0.89478	0.10522	
BAWJIASE AREA	0.97895	0.02105	AKUAPEM	0.89230	0.10770	
ASOKORE	0.97607	0.02393	AVENOR	0.89163	0.10837	
ANUM	0.97099	0.02901	AMANSIE WEST	0.88921	0.11079	
ODOTOBRI	0.97026	0.02974	AGONA	0.88538	0.11462	
EAST MAMPRUSI	0.88146	0.11854	AKOTI	0.80316	0.19684	
DANGME	0.87690	0.12310	ADA	0.79889	0.20111	
TOENDE	0.86343	0.13657	MPONUA	0.79406	0.20594	
BOSOMTWE	0.86163	0.13837	AGAVE	0.79167	0.20833	
SEFWIMAN	0.86115	0.13885	SHAI	0.79139	0.20861	
MUMUADU	0.86096	0.13904	AWUTU EMASA	0.79003	0.20997	
ANKOBRA WEST	0.86090	0.13910	UPPER MANYA KRO	0.77795	0.22205	
WETO	0.85272	0.14728	AHANTAMAN	0.77781	0.22219	
AMANANO	0.85253	0.14747	UNITY	0.77599	0.22401	
ADONTEN	0.85028	0.14972	NYAKROM	0.77290	0.22710	
AKATAKYIMAN	0.84887	0.15113	NYANKUMASI AHENKRO	0.77282	0.22718	

(Continued)

Appendix A. *(Continued)*

		Technical efficiency	Technical inefficiency	Bank	Technical efficiency	Technical inefficiency
ABOKOBI AREA	0.84625	0.15375	CAPITAL	0.76724	0.23276	
AKYEM MANSA	0.84621	0.15379	TWIFU	0.75191	0.24809	
SUMA	0.84403	0.15597	ATWIMA	0.74835	0.25165	
ASSINMAN	0.84342	0.15658	ATIWA	0.74590	0.25410	
SOUTH AKIM	0.84132	0.15868	KWAHU PRASO	0.73655	0.26345	
UPPER AMENFI	0.84082	0.15918	DROBO COMM	0.72863	0.27137	
MFANTESMAN COMM	0.83860	0.16140	KAKUM	0.71891	0.28109	
NSUTAMAN	0.83547	0.16453	NORTH VOLTA	0.71491	0.28509	
BADUMAN	0.83402	0.16598	NSOATREMAN	0.70908	0.29092	
AHAFO COMM	0.81816	0.18184	AKYEMPIM	0.68483	0.31517	
GA	0.80706	0.19294	NKORANZA KWABRE	0.68173	0.31827	
LOWER PRA	0.80613	0.19387	KWABIBIREM	0.62812	0.37188	
MANYA KROBO	0.80573	0.19427	AKROFUOM	0.61660	0.38340	
KUMAWUMAN	0.80399	0.19601				

5

Investigating impact of financial stress on FII flows in Indian equity market

Amanjot Singh[1]* and Manjit Singh[1]

*Corresponding author: Amanjot Singh, University School of Applied Management, Punjabi University, Patiala 147002, Punjab, India

E-mail: amanjot_42@yahoo.com

Reviewing editor: David McMillan, University of Stirling, UK

Abstract: The present study attempts to capture the impact of financial stress prevailing in the Indian as well as US financial system on FII flows in the Indian equity market by employing logistic regression model. The span of monthly data ranges from 2004 to 2014. Owing to non-existence of any standardized index, the study firstly constructs Indian Financial Stress Index. The empirical results have established that with an increase in financial stress in the Indian and US financial system, probability of positive FII flows reduces and consequently the probability of negative flows increases. The results are critically important for the international as well as Indian investors.

Subjects: Business, Management and Accounting; Economics; Finance

Keywords: financial stress; FII; India; logit; logistic regression; US

1. Introduction

With the onset of globalization and financial integration among the international economies, the domestic stock markets are prone to both internal as well as external financial shocks. The adverse events taking place in one economy like the "US sub-prime crisis (2007–2009)" have a "contagion or ripple effect" on other international economies through trade as well as financial linkages shared between the said economies. Above all, irrational behavior and investors' sentiments also play pivotal role in directing international financial flows across foreign boundaries. Seemingly, there are

ABOUT THE AUTHORS

Amanjot Singh is a senior research fellow at University School of Applied Management, Punjabi University, Patiala (India). He specializes in the area of personal financial planning and financial economics. To date, he has 15 research publications to his credit in various national as well as international journals of Emerald Group Publishing, Sage Publications, Institutional Investor Journals, etc. He is also one of the ad hoc reviewers of three reputed journals namely, *International Journal of Emerging Markets* (Emerald Group Publishing), *International Journal of Management Practice* (Inderscience Publishers), and *Cogent Economics and Finance* (Taylor and Francis Group).

Manjit Singh is working as a professor and head in the University School of Applied Management, Punjabi University, Patiala (India) and has 21 years of teaching experience in the field of Management and Commerce education at the university level. He has 65 research publications to his credit in various national and international journals.

PUBLIC INTEREST STATEMENT

Owing to liberalization, volatile FII flows in the emerging equity markets are a matter of concern to the domestic financial market investors and policy-makers. There are numerous factors accounting for FII flows in the latter equity markets. Out of these factors, the present study attempts to capture the impact of financial stress prevailing in the Indian and US financial system on FII flows in the Indian equity market making the study first of its kind. The logistic regression model is used to account for the said relationship. Interestingly, with an increase in financial stress in the Indian and US financial system, probability of positive FII flows reduces. These results are critically important for the policy-makers as well as equity investors in their act of managing portfolio risk and contagion phenomenon.

wide variety of factors ranging from fundamental-based to sentimental-based that guide the behavior of international financial flows or more specifically Foreign Institutional Investors (FII hereafter) in channelizing their funds.

According to SEBI (Foreign Institutional Investors) regulations (1995), a Foreign Institutional Investor means "an institution established or incorporated outside India and proposing to make investment in Indian securities." Over a period of 14 years, non-resident portfolio investment liabilities have registered a compounded annual growth rate of around 90% in India, thereby indicating substantially increasing foreign portfolio investments in the Indian financial market. Accordingly, volatility in these international financial flows makes the domestic or recipient markets to witness huge swings in asset prices causing transmission of financial shocks across foreign boundaries (Frank & Hesse, 2009). The authors argued that during a crisis or financial stress, international investors prefer relatively safer asset classes like developed equity markets pushing sell button in the emerging equity markets like India. Consequently, the emerging equity markets witness a downward phase in their respective markets owing to unwinding of long positions and reversing of capital flows having a magnified impact on the shareholders' wealth.

In today's scenario, the Central Bankers around the world are not independent in the context of their monetary policy initiatives. The US dollar has effectively become the global reserve currency for the emerging markets underpinning implied dependence of the latter markets on direction of global capital flows and US monetary policy actions (Sheel, 2016). Moreover, there is "Impossible Trinity" of the Mundell–Fleming framework, whereby it is impossible to follow three objectives of fixed exchange rate, monetary policy independence, and free capital flows simultaneously by a domestic economy. So, it is quite pertinent to account for various factors that direct and channelize these foreign financial flows or "Hot Money flows" in a domestic economy. In this regard, voluminous literature has examined various factors channelizing foreign flows in the emerging equity markets. For instance, according to Rai and Bhanumurthy (2004), FII flows to the Indian equity market are strongly dependent on stock market returns, inflation rates, and ex-ante risk. On a similar note, Kaur and Dhillon (2010) and Srinivasan and Kalaivani (2013) examined various determinants ranging from stock market returns, P/E ratios, conditional volatility, etc. causing FII flows to the Indian equity market. These studies have tried to establish number of factors driving financial flows to the Indian equity market.

Out of "*n*" number of factors, one of the factors that the present study attempts to report is the "Financial Stress" prevailing in an economy. A priori one would expect an inverse relationship between the respective financial stress episodes and FII inflows to the Indian equity market due to risk aversion attitude of the investors. In the present study, we have made an attempt to empirically capture the impact of financial stress prevailing in the US (being economically dominant) and Indian financial system on FII flows to the Indian equity market. The term financial stress can be regarded as disturbance or uncertainty in an economy's financial system. A financial system further comprises different subsystems in the form of equity, debt, money, and foreign exchange markets. Our objective is to encapsulate overall stress in the US and Indian financial system in the form of an index and then analyzing its impact on FII flows to the Indian equity market by employing logistic regression model across the years 2004–2014. The study adds empirical evidence to the literature by measuring concomitant relationship shared between Indian–US financial stress episodes and FIIs' Indian equity market flows.

The results report statistically significant impact of the said financial stress indices on FII flows in the Indian equity market. The study is the first of its kind, empirically capturing impact of the Indian as well as US financial stress on FII flows in the Indian equity market. A case of one emerging market and one developed market has been considered to analyze the impact of the same. These results are critically important for the policy-makers as well as equity investors in their act of managing portfolio risk and contagion phenomenon as a response to financial stress. Moreover, FIIs' equity investment behavior also act as financial contagion medium, transmitting financial shocks from one economy to another and further directing investment strategies of the domestic institutional investors. So, it becomes an imperative task to account for the impact of financial stress episodes on FIIs' equity investment behavior. The rest of the paper is divided as follows: Sections 2 and 3 explains empirical framework and findings respectively. Section 4 concludes the paper.

2. Empirical framework

To account for the impact of financial stress on FII flows in the Indian equity market, we have considered Kansas City Financial Stress Index (KCFSI) reflecting stress in the US financial system and constructed Indian Financial Stress Index (IFSI) across the monthly sample period: January 2004–October 2014. The monthly data reduce sensitivity and increase reliability of the analysis comparing to daily or weekly data. The KCFSI is a monthly measure of stress in the US financial system based on 11 financial market variables.[1] On a similar note and following the studies like, Balakrishnan, Danninger, Elekdag, and Tytell (2011), Park and Mercado (2013) and Yiu, Ho, and Jin (2010), the study initially develops IFSI by considering four different sectors of the Indian financial system, namely, equity, debt, foreign exchange, and money market owing to non-existence of a standardized index.

$$\begin{aligned} \text{FSI} = &\ \text{Equity Market Return} + \text{Equity Market Volatility} + \text{Debt Market}(\text{Spread}) \\ &+ \text{Banking Sector}(\text{Spread}) + \text{Exchange Rate Volatility} \end{aligned} \quad (1)$$

To capture stress in the Indian equity market, the NIFTY 50 (Indian equity market benchmark index) monthly continuously compounding gross index returns and conditional volatility are taken. The NIFTY monthly continuously compounding gross index returns are computed as follows:

$$R_t = \log\left(P_t/P_{t-1}\right) \times 100 \quad (2)$$

where R_t is the monthly return, P_t is the current month closing price, and P_{t-1} is the previous month closing price. To model conditional volatility of NIFTY index, GARCH (1,1) model has been employed. The conditional volatility also captures an implied impact of negative equity market returns because higher volatility is generally backed by negative returns. To capture stress in the banking sector/money market, spread between MIBOR (Inter-bank rate) 3 monthly rate and Treasury Bill 3 monthly yield is taken. The spread captures inter-bank lending risks. For an emerging market like India, major worry with regard to the foreign exchange market is volatility in the exchange rate owing to its dependence on export-import led policies. So, the study employs GARCH (1,1) model to account for volatility in the real time Dollar/Rupee exchange rate. Furthermore, to capture stress in the sovereign debt market, spread between the India Government securities 10-year yield and US Government securities 10-year yield is taken. All of the five variables are firstly converted into their standardized form.[2] The study employs principal component analysis (PCA) for the purpose of creating an aggregative index encapsulating overall stress in the Indian financial system across the sample period from 2004 to 2014 through standardized weights (Hakkio & Keeton, 2009).

While constructing a financial stress index, other indicators like, GDP growth rate, unemployment levels, inflation index, etc. can also be considered but these variables capture overall financial condition of an economy. Contrary to this, our objective is to capture core and overall financial stress irrespective of overall financial condition.[3] Finally, to capture the impact of the US and Indian financial stress on FII flows to the Indian equity market, logistic regression model has been employed. We have considered net FII flows on a monthly basis. A positive flow indicates buying behavior of the international investors, whereas a negative flow denotes selling behavior of the investors. The main benefit of employing a logistic-based regression model is that the model helps in computing probabilities for the existence of a particular condition, for instance, probability of a positive flow with a corresponding increase in financial stress.

Under logistic regression model, a dependent variable is a non-linear function of the independent variables and a binomial probability distribution as it has only two values either 0 or 1 (Chauhan, 2015). The value 1 denotes the existence of a condition (P), whereas the value 0 denotes absence of a condition$(1 - P)$. In the present study, the probability distribution is expressed as follows: Net Positive flows = 1 and Net Negative flows = 0. So, the value 1 indicates FII inflows in the Indian equity market and the value 0 denotes FII outflows from the Indian equity market. The whole model is estimated using Maximum Likelihood Estimation method and further Wald test statistic captures the impact of an independent variable on the dependent one. The logistic regression equation is expressed as follows:

$$\log\left(\frac{P_i}{1-P_i}\right) = a_0 + \beta_1 \text{ US or Indian Financial Stress index} + \varepsilon_t \quad (3)$$

where a_0 is the constant term and β_1 is the slope coefficient of respective financial stress indices. Technically, (P_i), the probability of existence of a condition is regarded as $\left(P_i = \frac{e^z}{1+e^z}\right)$: logit model and $(1 - P_i)$, the probability of absence of a condition is regarded as $\left(\frac{1}{1+e^z}\right)$. e^z is the exponential function of the regression equation. So, $\log\left(\frac{P_i}{1-P_i}\right)$ is the odd ratio and hence its quite complicated to comprehend the impact of independent variables. However, exponential betas are computed which can be defined as rate of change in odd ratio relating to per unit change in independent variable. If exponential beta is greater than 1, then the independent variable has a positive impact on the existence of a condition or an increasing impact on the probability of existence of a condition and if it is less than 1, then the independent variable has a negative impact on the existence of a condition.

The overall analysis has been done taking respective financial stress indices as separate independent variables and binomial probability distribution as a dependent variable. Lastly, to capture the impact of respective indices on FII flows in a graphical format, the ex-ante probabilities $\left(P_i = \frac{e^z}{1+e^z}\right)$ are computed out of the regression model results. The overall data have been collected from the Bloomberg terminal, Yahoo finance database, and moneycontrol real-time financial database as per availability.

3. Empirical findings

For the construction of IFSI, second component of the PCA model explains around 66% of the total variations in five variables. So, normalized component loadings of the second component are used for constructing IFSI across the period 2004–2014.[4] Figure 1 is the graphical presentation of Indian as well as US financial stress index.

Both of the indices have fairly captured the Global Financial Crisis period that got triggered at a full force aftermath the Lehman Brothers' episode (shaded area) thereby confirming accuracy of the indices thereon. It is quite apparent from the movement of IFSI that the US sub-prime crisis had a financial contagion impact on the Indian financial system during the years 2007–2009.

3.1. Indian financial stress and FII flows in the Indian equity market

Now we move on to the logistic regression model results taking probability distribution of FII flows and IFSI as dependent and independent variables respectively. Table 1 reports R-square (R^2) values

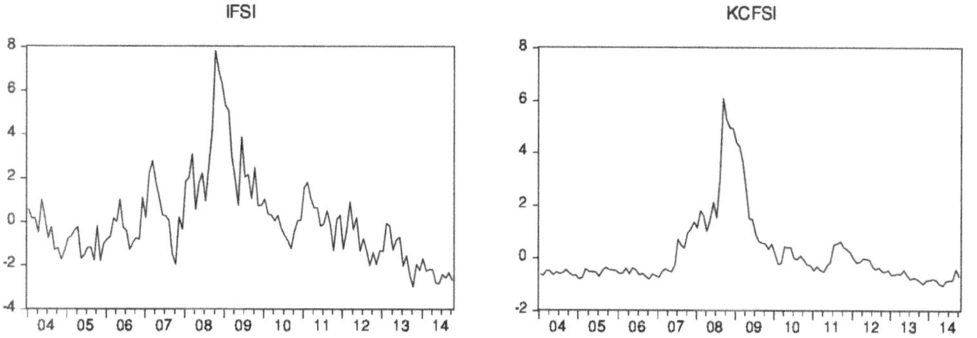

Figure 1. Graphical presentation of Indian and US financial stress.

Table 1. R^2 values

Step	−2 log likelihood	Cox and Snell R^2	Nagelkerke R^2
1	134.725[a]	.107	.156

[a]Estimation terminated at iteration number 4 because parameter estimates changed by less than .001.

Source: Authors.

of the model employed or explanatory power of IFSI in explaining FII flows. The values are quite reasonable because FII flows in the Indian equity market are not only a function of Indian financial stress alone, but it also depends on so many other factors as well.

The R^2 value ranges from 10 to 15%. Table 2 is classification table which indicates percentage of correctness or correct predictions of the model employed. In technical terms, percentage of correct predictions is regarded as "HIT" ratio. The hit ratio is around 74.6, which is quite adequate and more than the cut-off value of 50. For instance, both the observed and predicted values report positive FII flows in 92 of the cases.

Table 3 reports logistic regression equation results. The stress in the Indian financial system has a statistically significant impact on FII flows in the Indian equity market. The coefficient is found to be significant at 5% significance level. However, the exponential beta value is less than 1, thereby indicating a decreasing impact of IFSI on the probability of positive FII flows in the Indian equity market. In other words, with an increase in overall stress in the Indian financial system, probability of positive FII flows reduces and probability of outflows increases in the economy. The results support strong implications for the domestic investors in the Indian equity market.

It is well documented that both foreign as well as domestic flows to equity markets share a feedback relationship with each other. Subsequently, the present study contributes to the literature by quantifying the impact of financial stress episodes on FII flows in the Indian equity market and thereby on the domestic equity flows. As mentioned earlier, explanatory power of the IFSI in explaining FII flows in the Indian equity market ranges from only 10 to 15%, however, still the results are quite effective in directing the impact of the same.

Table 2. Classification table[a]

	Observed		Predicted		
			Probability		Percentage correct
			0	1	
Step 1	Probability	0	5	29	14.7
		1	4	92	95.8
	Overall percentage				74.6

[a]The cut value is .500.

Source: Authors.

Table 3. Variables in the equation

		Coefficient	SE	Wald	df	Sig.	exp (B)
Step 1[a]	IFSI	−.405	.117	12.041	1	.001*	.667
	Constant	1.142	.217	27.624	1	.000*	3.132

[a]Variable(s) entered on step 1: IFSI.

*Reject null hypothesis of no significant relationship at 5% significance level.

Source: Authors.

Table 4. R^2 values

Step	−2 log likelihood	Cox and Snell R^2	Nagelkerke R^2
1	137.290[a]	.089	.130

[a]Estimation terminated at iteration number 4 because parameter estimates changed by less than .001.

Source: Authors.

3.2. US financial stress and FII flows in the Indian equity market

The R^2 value ranges from 8 to 13% (Table 4), again quite reasonable. The hit ratio is 76.2 (Table 5) stating that approximately 76% of the predictions are correct.

On a similar note, financial stress in the US financial system has a statistically significant impact on FII flows in the Indian equity market (Table 6). The coefficient is found to be significant at 5% significance level. The exponential beta value is less than 1 signifying a reducing impact of the US financial stress on probability of positive FII flows in the Indian equity market. Lastly, we have tried to report expected probabilities of positive FII flows in relation to both of the financial stress indices.

For this, the financial stress index values are firstly arranged in an increasing order with an interval of 0.5, respectively. After this, the ex-ante probabilities are computed out of the results generated from logistic regression model. Graphically, the results support "flight to safe haven" concerns of the foreign institutional investors (Figure 2.). Hence, with an increase in financial stress in the Indian as well as US financial system, the probability of positive FII flows decreases in the Indian equity market. The impact of Indian financial stress on FII flows in the Indian equity market is quite obvious. However, on a very interesting note, the stress in the US financial system also leads to reversal of FII flows in the Indian equity market. Consequently, the foreign institutional investors switch to other safer asset classes during stressful episodes.

Overall, the results accentuate significant role of the financial stress episodes in directing FII flows in the Indian equity market. A decrease in probability of positive FII flows may further magnify financial stress in the overall Indian financial system through propagation of shocks via equity market.

Table 5. Classification table[a]

	Observed		Predicted		
			Probability		Percentage correct
			0	1	
Step 1	Probability	0	6	28	17.6
		1	3	93	96.9
	Overall percentage				76.2

[a]The cut value is .500.

Source: Authors.

Table 6. Variables in the equation

		Coefficient	SE	Wald	df	Sig.	exp (B)
Step 1[a]	KCFSI	−.495	.155	10.138	1	.001*	.610
	Constant	1.159	.214	29.199	1	.000*	3.187

[a]Variable(s) entered on step 1: KCFSI.

*Reject null hypothesis of no significant relationship at 5% significance level.

Source: Authors.

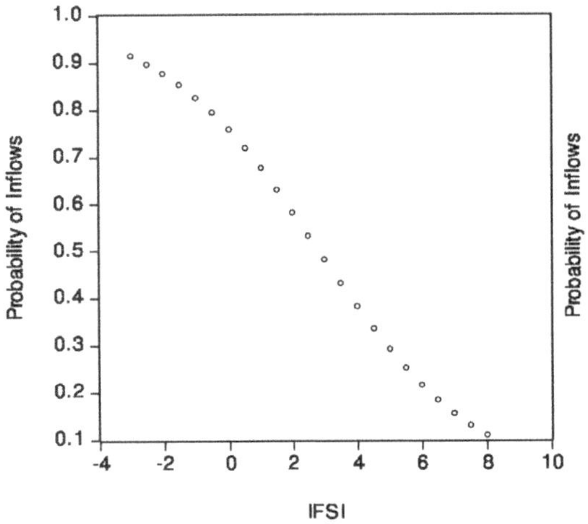

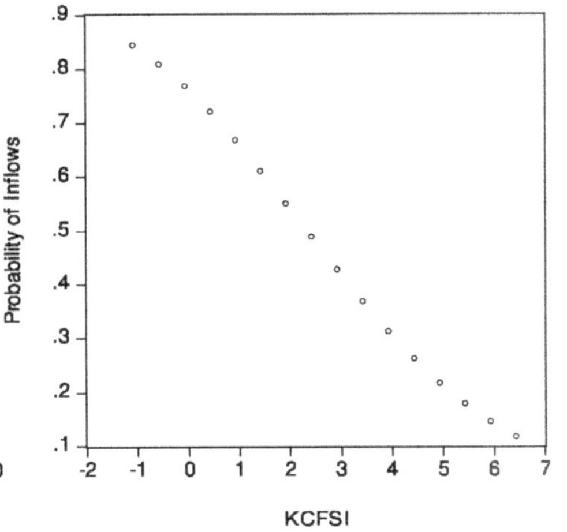

Figure 2. Ex-ante probabilities vis-à-vis financial stress.

The crux of the whole study is that the emerging markets like India are considered to be riskier and relatively volatile in comparison to the developed equity markets like the US, Europe, Japan, etc. owing to greater degree of information asymmetry present in the former markets; evidenced from Celık (2012) and Lhost (2004). So, with an increase in financial stress, either in the Indian or US financial system, foreign investors switch to "withdrawal of funds" strategy from the Indian equity market which may augment already existing stress in the overall Indian financial system.

4. Concluding remarks

The present study attempts to capture the impact of financial stress prevailing in the Indian as well as US financial system on FII flows in the Indian equity market by employing logistic regression model across the sample period 2004–2014. The results exhibit that with an increase in financial stress in the Indian and US financial system, probability of positive FII flows reduces and consequently the probability of negative flows increases. The study provides an insight regarding possible future FII flows against stressful episodes in the domestic and foreign markets, thereby spotlighting different possible actions that may be undertaken in combating negative impact of the same.

On the whole, the results are important for both the international as well as Indian investors. They should discount in advance these probable FII flows and undertake positions in derivative market so as to hedge themselves from adverse market scenarios. At the same time, the findings are also important for policy-makers in their attempt to channelize overall Indian financial system. According to IMF (April, 2014), the emerging markets with higher volatility in the capital flows and current account deficit or fiscal imbalances are likely to be more vulnerable to global financial shocks. So, the impact of the US and Indian financial stress on FII flows in the Indian equity market significantly matter for the equity investors. Furthermore, FII flows in an emerging market, like India, direct investment positions of domestic equity market investors. Eventually, volatility and factors affecting FII flows should be accounted by the market participants on regular basis. As a future scope of study, other factors responsible for directing FII flows in the Indian equity market can also be considered and factored into the logistic regression framework.

Acknowledgments
We would like to express our sincere gratitude to the Editor and Reviewer of the journal for their insightful suggestions and comments. We are also highly grateful to Dr. Navneet Kaur for assisting in data collection.

Funding
The authors received no direct funding for this research.

Author details
Amanjot Singh[1]
E-mail: amanjot_42@yahoo.com
ORCID ID: http://orcid.org/0000-0002-0828-2749
Manjit Singh[1]
E-mail: amanjot288@gmail.com
[1] University School of Applied Management, Punjabi University, Patiala 147002, Punjab, India.

Notes

1. Collected from the website of the Federal Reserve Bank of Kansas City.
2. $Y_t = \frac{(X_t - \text{Mean Value})}{\text{Standard Deviation}}$
3. For further details on Indian Financial Stress Index (see Singh & Singh, 2016).
4. The respective standardized weights are .97, .23, −.29,0.94, and −.65 for bank spread, exchange rate volatility, debt spread, equity market volatility ,and equity market returns. A negative weight highlights an increasing impact of the respective variable during negative phases, for instance, negative equity market returns enhance financial stress.

References

Balakrishnan, R., Danninger, S., Elekdag, S., & Tytell, I. (2011). The transmission of financial stress from advanced to emerging economies. *Emerging Markets Finance and Trade, 47*, 40–68. http://dx.doi.org/10.2753/REE1540-496X4703S203

Celık, S. (2012). The more contagion effect on emerging markets: The evidence of DCC-GARCH model. *Economic Modelling, 29*, 1946–1959. http://dx.doi.org/10.1016/j.econmod.2012.06.011

Chauhan, A. K. (2015). *Research analytics: A practical approach to data analysis*. New Delhi: Dreamtech Press.

Frank, N., & Hesse, H. (2009). Financial spillovers to emerging markets during the global financial crisis. *Finance a uver - Czech Journal of Economics and Finance, 59*, 507–521.

Hakkio, C. S., & Keeton, W. R. (2009). Financial stress: What is it, How can it be measured, and Why does it matter? *Economic Review, Q*, 5–50.

Kaur, M., & Dhillon, S. S. (2010). Determinants of foreign institutional investors investment in India. *Eurasian Journal of Business and Economics, 3*, 57–70.

Lhost, J. (2004). *The cause, effects, and implications of financial contagion*. Retrieved from http://economics.about.com/cs/moffattentries/a/contagion_3.htm

Park, C., & Mercado, R. V. (2013). *Determinants of financial stress in emerging market economies*. Retrieved from http://www10.iadb.org/intal/intalcdi/PE/2013/12502.pdf

Rai, K., & Bhanumurthy, N. R. (2004). Determinants of foreign institutional investment in India: The role of risk return and inflation. *The Developing Economies, XLII*, 479–493.

Singh, A., & Singh, M. (2016). Investigating impact of US, Europe, frontier and BRIC stock markets on Indian Financial Stress Index. *Journal of Banking and Financial Economics, 2*, 23–44.

Sheel, A. (2016). Monetary policy dilemmas at the current juncture. *Economic and Political Weekly, LI*, 46–55.

Srinivasan, P., & Kalaivani, M. (2013). *Determinants of foreign institutional investment in India: An empirical analysis*. Retrieved from https://mpra.ub.uni-muenchen.de/43778/

Yiu, M. S., Ho, W. Y. A., & Jin, L. (2010). *A measure of financial stress in Hong Kong financial market - the financial stress index*. Retrieved from www.hkma.gov.hk/media/eng/publication-and-research/research/research-notes/RN-02-2010.pdf

6

Consumers' responses to CSR in a cross-cultural setting

Hakan Karaosman[1]*, Gustavo Morales-Alonso[1] and Mercedes Grijalvo[1]

*Corresponding author: Hakan Karaosman, Department of Industrial Management, Business Administration and Statistics; School of Industrial Engineering, Universidad Politécnica de Madrid (UPM), Calle de José Gutiérrez Abascal, 2, 28006 Madrid, Spain

E-mail: Hakan.karaosman@upm.es

Reviewing editor: Collins Gyakari Ntim, University of Huddersfield, UK

Abstract: The paper aims to clarify the relationship between corporate social responsibility (CSR) and consumer behaviour in an international setting. Consumers' responses to CSR activities and the impact on the purchase decision are limited discourses. CSR-based studies in the fashion and apparel industry are also scarce. Therefore, this study attempts to enlighten the subject of how consumers from different countries respond to CSR adopted in the fashion and apparel industry. This study is based on an exploratory qualitative research for which focus group interviews, including six group discussions with Spanish and Turkish consumers, have been used. The fundamental dimension for sampling was consumers' interest and knowledge of CSR-related issues. The data were examined by constant comparison analysis. The paper provides empirical insights that suggest that these consumers, regardless of their country of origin, perceive CSR actions as part of companies' marketing strategies, while overall consumer awareness to CSR is low. Moreover, the criteria, which determine the purchase decision is to be governed by self-interest. A difference between participants from both countries has been found with regard to their demand for more regulation towards CSR. An identified research need in international marketing discipline, is fulfilled in this study.

ABOUT THE AUTHOR

Hakan Karaosman is a research assistant and sustainability management professional with international experience in sustainability reporting, business process improvement and sustainability strategy in various industries. Previously, he worked as a consultant to companies in various industries for their Carbon Disclosure Project, and corporate social responsibility reports by assisting clients to identify, measure, manage and communicate their performance in sustainability management. He holds BSc in Environmental Engineering; MBA and MSc in Management in Engineering of Energy and Environment; a joint master degree funded by the EU, and hosted by KTH (Sweden), EMN (France) and UPM (Spain). He is currently pursuing his PhD studies in European Doctorate in Industrial Management, a double-degree programme funded by the EU, and hosted by KTH (Sweden), POLIMI (Italy) and UPM (Spain). His specific focus is on sustainability management in the fashion industry.

PUBLIC INTEREST STATEMENT

Sustainability was developed to respect people, preserve the planet, and generate profits without mishandling societal and environmental conditions. In this vein, corporate social responsibility (CSR) focuses on the social aspects to leverage responsibilities while making profit. The global fashion industry experiences an exceptional growth, and is expected to account for €1,512 billion by 2018. The fashion and apparel industry appears to have a high social impact due to multinational sourcing, and labour conditions. Marketing literature also stresses that CSR is a dynamic process, which involves interrelated market variables. Considering the high impact of fashion industry, and changing consumer behaviour; this paper explores how consumers from Spain and Turkey perceive CSR, how CSR awareness is influenced by cultural values, how actual purchase behaviour is influenced by CSR, and how CSR communication is received by the end-consumers in these highly growing fashion markets.

Subjects: Consumer Behaviour; Corporate Social Responsibility & Business Ethics; Marketing; Marketing Management; Marketing Research; Relationship Marketing; Sustainable Development

Keywords: corporate social responsibility; consumer behaviour; qualitative research; fashion industry; cultural differences

1. Introduction

Sustainability was developed to respect *people*; preserve the *planet*; and generate *profits* without mishandling societal and environmental conditions (Joy, Sherry, Venkatesh, Wang, & Chan, 2012). Corporate social responsibility (CSR) specifically focuses on the social aspects to leverage responsibilities while making profit. CSR has become highly critical in many consumer goods industries, and researchers as well as practitioners pay a significant attention to the topic since the balance must be reached between social needs and corporate objectives. The fashion and apparel industry emerges as a significant industry with a high impact, considering vertical disintegration of production networks, physically distributed business environment and growing consumerism (Ageron, Gunasekaran, & Spalanzani, 2012; McKinnon & Edwards, 2014), Hence, it could be stated that social impact is highly critical in the fashion and apparel industry due to multinational sourcing, and labour conditions (Perry, Fernie, & Wood, 2014).

In addition to operations, CSR is also closely linked to marketing. Consumer attitude can be influenced and this could lead to purchase behaviour. Marketing literature further stresses that CSR is a dynamic process, which involves interrelated market variables (Becker-Olsen, Cudmore, & Hill, 2006). Consumers' attitudinal and behavioural outcomes are influenced by many factors such as corporation identification, product attributes, brand reputation and social records. In this vein, there are some other important parameters to take into account. For instance, cultural differences and political, economical and legal factors must be carefully incorporated to examine consumer responses to CSR (Beckmann, 2007). Therefore, an international setting in marketing literature is needed to understand how consumers from different countries pose to CSR adopted by multinational fashion brands across the world.

The fashion and apparel industry is devoted to production, distribution, sales and promotion of apparels worldwide. The fashion industry has been experiencing an exceptional growth in recent years, and is expected to account for €1,512 billion by 2018 (MarketLine, 2014). Although the fashion and apparel industry receives attention (Ageron et al., 2012; Azevedo, Carvalho, Duarte, & Cruz-Machado, 2012; Bray, Johns, & Kilburn, 2010; Caniato, Caridi, Crippa, & Moretto, 2012), few contributions analysed the relevance in social or environmental responsibility (Achabou & Dekhili, 2013; Caniato, Caridi, Castelli, & Golini, 2011; Joy et al., 2012; Nagurney & Yu, 2012). Thus far, the majority of the organizational theory literature has analysed CSR by focusing on its financial aspects. Some studies investigated the impact of CSR on marketing (Caniëls, Gehrsitz, & Semeijn, 2013), and firms' economic performance (Gualandris, Golini, & Kalchschmidt, 2014); however, consumer perspective and the perception of CSR demonstrated by an empirical evidence is scarce. Regular monitoring of the relationship between society and corporate strategies is thus required.

Surprisingly, less often, studies tend to point out what consumers from different countries think about CSR. "What are the consumers' perceptions of CSR", and "how can these perceptions affect consumers' behavioural responses?" are limited discourses that need to be further explored in cross-cultural settings (Abreu, Castro, Soares, & Silva Filho, 2012). Particularly, even though CSR is a fast-growing trend worldwide, very few studies have been conducted specifically for the fashion and apparel industry. On the whole, despite the growing CSR trend in academia, the literature indicates that a majority of studies focus on domestic markets or consumer outcomes in local settings. This finding suggests that CSR disclosure in international marketing is highly needed. This paper thus aims to present the results of a qualitative research conducted with real consumers from two different countries, namely Spain and Turkey, and more precisely, on their cities Madrid and Istanbul. It is essential to emphasize the motive behind this selection. Both Madrid and Istanbul are significant given their high growth rate in the fashion and apparel market. Istanbul emerges as a metropolitan city where global fashion brands have numerous displays just to attract highly growing and equally trend-driven society, while Madrid has been the capital of some significant mainstream brands that rule the street style. Given both cities' inevitable influence on street style, utilizing consumers from these markets would make a significant contribution to the course where corporate behaviours of these fashion brands are questioned. Another important reason could be highlighted from a rather regulatory perspective. CSR emerges as an essential topic at the European Level. "Europe 2020" is the European Union's growth strategy (European Commission, 2011), and within this strategy, not only member states but also candidate countries are asked to comply with laws, reach sustainability based objectives, and integrate social and environmental concerns into their agendas. Spain is a member country, and with Turkey is a candidate; so that focusing on these cities could bring valuable contributions to check how end-consumers perceive, understand and react to CSR strategies.

This paper is thus set to explore (1) how consumers from both Spain and Turkey perceive CSR, (2) how CSR awareness is influenced by cultural values, (3) how attitude and actual purchase behaviour are influenced by CSR and (4) how CSR communication is received by the end-consumers in these highly growing fashion markets.

The paper is organized as follows. Section 2 provides a theoretical background of the topics under study. In Section 3, the research framework, gaps and research questions are presented. Then, the methodological approach is described in Section 4. In Section 5, the results obtained are presented and discussed. Lastly, conclusions of the study are provided in Section 6.

2. Theoretical background

The past decades have witnessed an increased flow of academic research in the area of CSR. However, considering the aforementioned theoretical gaps, this study was conducted to contribute to the understanding of CSR and its effects on consumers' perceptions, attitudes and behaviours in the international marketing. Hence, theoretical background encompasses four main areas: (1) The concept of CSR, (2) The influence of cultural values on CSR, (3) CSR impact on consumer behaviour and (4) CSR in the fashion and apparel industry.

2.1. The concept of CSR

United Nations defined sustainability as a development to meet the needs of present without compromising future generations' ability to meet their own (United Nations, 1987). The principle of sustainable development is an unavoidable association among economical, environmental and social dynamics (Karaosman, Mermod, & Yuksel, 2015). CSR, in particular, implies doing business right by respecting societal needs. Due to a widespread attention that has been paid to CSR, the formal acceptance of CSR practices and strategies has become roughly universal (Oh, Park, & Ghauri, 2013). Bhattacharya and Sen (2004) have found that corporations have a significant impact on society and the environment. In order to reduce these impacts for a sustainable future, not only are corporations required to have a greater sensitivity to today's changing values, but they are also required to incorporate CSR standpoints into strategic decisions (Werther & Chandler, 2005). Over decades, the definitions and the phases of social responsibility have evolved. In the 1950s, the definition of CSR in corporate policy was associated with management ethics. During the 1960s and early 1970s, CSR was showcased as responsiveness. According to the "Iron Law of Responsibility" theory from the early 1960s, corporations that had big social power also had big social responsibilities (Mercer, 2003). During the 1970s, Friedman's theory was discussed. He argued that a corporation's sole responsibility was to make profit for its shareholders (Wang & Juslin, 2009). However, starting from the 1980s, stakeholder groups (i.e. consumers, local communities and employees) were also introduced in the CSR concept. That decade fostered an ethical culture in corporations, when a code of ethics became an important aspect in corporate culture and various levels of stakeholders were recognized within common CSR principles. From the 1990s onward, CSR has been associated with Corporate Citizenship, which is formed by economic, legal, ethical and philanthropic constituents (Beckmann, 2007; Oh et al., 2013).

More recently, CSR has emerged as a fundamental topic at the European Level. "Europe 2020" is the European Union's growth strategy (European Commission, 2011). Within this strategy, five fundamental objectives have been set for 2020. Areas list employment, innovation, education, social inclusion and climate/energy. Each of these categories has been adopted for member states (Europe 2020, 2011). In 2006, the European Commission defined CSR as a concept whereby corporations voluntarily integrate social and environmental concerns into their business operations and into their interaction with their stakeholders. As mentioned, until now CSR actions taken by corporations have been strictly on a voluntary basis. There is an increasing pressure and demand in the EU to develop legislation that will make CSR activities mandatory. The European Commission has been working on redefining CSR to emphasize this necessity. "Should" has been added to the definition in order to shift away from the voluntary approach (Kaufmann & Olaru, 2012). However, since each corporation has its own corporate culture, set of values, industrial challenges and various stakeholder groups, it is almost impossible to generate one general standard or ethical code. Given these industrial diversities, CSR should be utilized as a guideline to generate a corporate language to assess specific actions and improve social conditions. According to Porter and Kramer (2006), corporations should incorporate social responsibility into their business strategy instead of having it done as a separate project. Podnar and Golob (2007) also suggested that ethical and philanthropic responsibilities could lead to a competitive advantage based on desired consumer response. So as to reach this, a right balance among strategy, brand management and CSR should be established. Short-term and transactional outcomes were investigated in earlier research in past decades. Nevertheless, recent academic attempts have mostly been grounded in long-term and relational outcomes (Bhattacharya & Sen, 2004). Researchers seek further demonstrations to channel sector-specific relational outcomes such as loyalty, trust and brand ambassador type of behaviours.

2.2. The influence of cultural values on CSR

Since the scope of present study is to shed light on the CSR perception of consumers from different international settings, reference must be given to the expected cultural values of individuals from different cultural origins. When mentioning cultural values across different countries, the cultural dimensions of Geert Hofstede are an inevitable reference and source of information. His study was based on a sample of IBM employees across different countries, obtained between 1967 and 1973 from more than 117,000 respondents. The findings of his research were four statistically independent dimensions that explained the cross-country cultural variations. Later on, he added a fifth dimension, which has been recently substituted by two new dimensions, obtained with more recent data. Regarding the setting of the four original dimensions, Hofstede admits that using data from a single organization can limit the generalization of the data (Hofstede, Pedersen, & Hofstede, 2002). This is the most common criticism received from his results, as stated by Schwartz (1994, p. 91), "highly educated well-paid IBM employees' ability to represent the general population likely differs from country to country, with the discrepancy probably being greater, for example, in the Third World nations ... than in industrialized Western nations". In spite of the criticism received, Hofstede's results proved their validity in a wide range of organizational and national issues (Taras, Steel, & Kirkman, 2012).

The six cultural dimensions gathered by Hofstede by the time of writing this paper are (1) power distance (PDI), (2) individualism (IDV), (3) masculinity (MAS), (4) uncertainty avoidance (UAI), (5) pragmatism (PRA) and (6) indulgence (IND) (Hofstede, 2014). The Power Distance dimension can be defined as the extent to which the less powerful individuals in a society consider normal the unequal distribution of power. In the second dimension, Individualism describes the degree to which people look preferably after themselves and their closest relatives, while Collectivism stands for societies where belonging to a group is believed to be of great importance. The Masculinity–Femininity dimension juxtaposes some masculine values such as competitiveness and success against so-called feminine values by Hofstede, like maintaining quality of life or solidarity. The fourth classical dimension is the

Uncertainty Avoidance index, which rates the level of anxiety that unpredictable, risky situations cause people. Pragmatic versus Normative is the dimension that expresses if the individual requires concrete explanations for the complexity of life. A pragmatic orientation in life allows for adaptation to a variety of situations and a propensity to save money for the future, while normative cultures give great importance to social traditions and the feeling of saving for the future is much smaller. Last, the Indulgence versus Restraint dimension terms a culture indulgent if control of leisure and one's own life is given a certain importance, and if freedom of expression is valued.

The marketing literature highlighted the role of national culture, cultural distance and similarity between the countries. It was argued that a firm's competitive performance within world markets is influenced by a variety of home country factors (Rugman, Oh, & Kim, 2011). Therefore, it could be stressed that country and national environment have a noteworthy effect on consumer behaviour and marketing. Particularly, the extent to which a society can be considered collectivist or individualist determines the moral behaviour of its individuals. In collectivist cultures, individuals tend to behave as expected by the group, even when these individuals disagree with the group norm (Triandis & Gelfand, 1998). That is, an inconsistency appears between personal belief and behaviour. On the contrary, in individualist cultures, decisions are driven by the personal thoughts of the people (Radhakrishnan & Chan, 1997), avoiding the mentioned inconsistency, as the people are more likely to behave according to their moral decisions. While several researchers found that CSR adoption is positively linked with collectivism, power distance has a negative correlation. Matten and Moon (2008) articulated that individualistic cultures tend to value "explicit CSR" by which corporations address social issues through their CSR actions. Contrarily, collectivist cultures tend to adopt and value "implicit CSR" by which corporations address social issues through some other voluntary actions in a much wider scope. In summary, CSR reflects societies' expectations. Cultural values and tendencies shape a country's identity and its people's behaviour. Therefore, cultural movements, values and attributes are extremely important when examining consumers' responses to CSR. Even though CSR studies have previously incorporated the cultural effect, a limited number of studies were conducted to compare different countries and their priorities in response to CSR.

2.3. CSR impact on consumer behaviour

CSR is a multifaceted topic to be interpreted from various standpoints. In stakeholder theory, Freeman, Velamuri, and Moriarty (2006) indicates that corporations are part of a bigger society, and possessing responsibilities for different groups of people (Beckmann, 2007; Freeman et al., 2006). In this vein, marketing concept could also be defined as a distinct organizational culture to meet demands of numerous actors. Corporate marketing is a fundamental shared set of beliefs and values that put the consumer in the centre of the corporation's strategies and operations (Cadogan, Souchon, & Procter, 2008).

Hence, it is possible to link CSR with expectation relationship (Podnar & Golob, 2007) to go beyond profit maximization by meeting societal needs and expectations. Consumers, on the other hand, are perceived as the most influential stakeholder group due to their inevitable impact on corporations' financial success. Nevertheless, marketing scholars investigated CSR by focusing on very limited dimensions. Despite its importance, when it comes to consumers' responses to CSR, limited scopes have been taken into account. This leads to the scarcity of comprehensive theoretical frameworks deriving from the marketing discipline (Maignan & Ferrell, 1997). Previous researches declare that while CSR might entail short-term costs, it pays off for the corporation in the long term as a source of competitive advantage (Branco & Rodrigues, 2007; Burke & Logsdon, 1996; Porter & Kramer, 2006). Similarly, Wang and Juslin (2009) addressed the positive and cognitive effect of CSR on consumer behaviour. Besides, Maignan and Ferrell (1997) observed that consumers would engage in positive word of mouth about corporations, which demonstrated devotion to institutional standards. Nevertheless, CSR could also bring negative exposure. In their study, Porter and Kramer (2006) argued that due to social scandals some corporations could be in danger of losing their consumers' trust.

When engaging in a specific social issue, a corporation should clearly acknowledge the mission of its strategy and potential consequences (Maignan & Ferrell, 1997). Öberseder, Schlegelmilch, and Murphy (2013) suggested that proactive communication strategies could affect consumers positively while reactive communication strategies could create a negative effect. This theory was contributed by further arguing that consumers might respond negatively when a corporation was not perceived sincere and honest (Park, Lee, & Kim, 2014). Multinational corporations that target different markets are often accused of utilizing CSR to empower their brand image and increase their profits (Torres, Bijmolt, Tribó, & Verhoef, 2012). Marketing managers thus must choose their multinational strategies and communication tools carefully in order to establish a connection between long-term benefits and short-term outcomes (Cheung, Jiang, & Tan, 2012). Previous studies on CSR demonstrated that many consumers were relatively uninformed regarding responsible corporate behaviour and activities (Boulstridge & Carrigan, 2000). It could be suggested that low-fit initiatives are likely to diminish overall attitude as well as perceptions of corporate credibility, corporate position and purchase intention (Becker-Olsen et al., 2006). It is very important to monitor consumers' perceptions since they affect attitude. Consumer attitude is likewise significant due to its influence on consumers' behavioural intentions. In this sense, intentions have been pointed out as the determinant of the actual behaviour (Bygrave, 1989) and of actual purchasing choice (Keh & Xie, 2009). Consumer identification is an important but slightly underused concept. It could exert influence on purchase behaviours. Previous academic attempts suggested that, based on social identity and organizational identification theories, some of the strongest consumer-corporation relationships occur when consumers identify with the corporations that satisfy their self-interest (Maignan & Ferrell, 1997). A corporation with high consumer identification could benefit through loyalty, willingness to try new products, spreading positive word of mouth and tolerance for negative information. Recent investigations also suggest that organizational misidentification may occur when individuals perceive a conflict between their defining attributes and the attributes characterizing the organization (i.e. strategies and corporate actions). These findings support Boulstridge and Carrigan's (2000) theory in which individualism and self-interest emerged as powerful consumer trends. Furthermore, price and quality have been pointed out as major factors that affect purchase decisions (Rizkallah, 2012). Therefore, corporations in today's multinational competitive environment should maintain their commitment to quality and reasonable prices, while putting CSR into their strategic planning (Castaldo, Perrini, Misani, & Tencati, 2008). On the whole, it can be stressed that self-interest is an important indicator, and consumers are mostly influenced by CSR initiatives when the results benefit them. Price, design and other product attributes go beyond social awareness during the purchase decision-making process, yet it is still important to comprehend how consumers with different cultural mind-sets would conceptualize CSR.

CSR has a big influence on marketing, ethics and different groups of consumers worldwide. Despite this importance, CSR in international marketing literature has only recently received significant attention. One of the biggest limitations of current literature is that consumer perspective, (from a cross-cultural point of view) has been neglected. Over the previous decades, it was seen that during the purchase decision-making process, consumers attached importance to product quality, value for money and brand name over social problems. However, recent studies have shown a change in this tendency. Cultural differences and personal values could be variables that alter this consensus. Conversely, despite earlier research attempts, a clear understanding of responses of consumers (from different countries with different backgrounds) still remains inconclusive and mixed. There is a lack of conceptual understanding surrounding what consumers from different corporations expect from a corporation and how this multinational corporation responds based on varying expectations. In summary, this paper seeks to address some of the academic limitations that could be highlighted as follows: (1) business ethics were mostly studied as a single issue rather than a strategy and (2) only a few selected stakeholder groups have widely been investigated. The latter shows that a clear understanding of consumer perception in cross-country settings is lacking (Öberseder et al., 2013), and it is equally important to understand how consumers with different cultural backgrounds perceive and react to CSR endorsed by multinational corporations.

2.4. CSR in the fashion and apparel industry

Fashion encompasses numerous commodities including apparel, footwear, jewellery and cosmetics (Joy et al., 2012). Furthermore, it embodies products in which style is relevant as an essential critical success factor, and product shelf life is relatively short (Choi, 2014; Fionda & Moore, 2009). The fashion and apparel industry is a multinational sector devoted to manufacturing, distribution, sales and promotion of apparels. Buckley and Ghauri (2004) address that globalization is a process driven by economic forces, which encompasses manufacturing, international trade and the integration of financial markets. Especially, manufacturing is an important parameter for globalization (World Economic Forum, 2012). In the fashion and apparel sector, manufacturing processes are divided into multiple partial operations and separate stages that are held in different locations; consequently, the globalization and multinational fashion brands' strategies leave a significant impact on sustainability (Buckley & Ghauri, 2004). In a fast fashion environment, time and cost are the key parameters dominating buyer and manufacturer negotiations (Bruce & Daly, 2006). Thus, fashion and apparel industry incorporates quick yet dynamic response processes to reduce lead time (Caro & Martínez de Albéniz Margalef, 2014). To do so, various activities are coordinated within supply chains, since fashion and apparel industry is transformed from manufacturer-push to the consumer-pull era. Fernie and Sparks (2014) issued that, a fashion company, is indeed responsible for all activities performed in its entire value chain.

Requirements for a successful fashion management include organizational culture, communication strategy, risk management and transparency to meet sustainability needs (Alexander, Walker, & Naim, 2014; Chan, He, & Wang, 2012; Ciliberti, Pontrandolfo, & Scozzi, 2008; Mentzer et al., 2001). Ageron et al. (2012) further highlighted the importance CSR in supply chain management. From this perspective, a need becomes visible to incorporate social sustainability in fashion talks. As challenging as it sounds, sustainability of any fashion brand cannot be achieved without integrating social dimensions into their corporate strategies. This could only be accomplished when companies step beyond own boundaries; hence, supplier and consumer association plays a significant role. Sustainability cannot be accomplished unless consumers are not involved into their corporate strategies (Grimm, Hofstetter, & Sarkis, 2014). A poor sustainability management of any fashion company could jeopardize a high level of consumer loyalty. Statistics show that more than 70% of EU member states' apparel imports come from developing and low labour cost countries to minimize the production and distribution costs (World Bank, 2007). By taking all of these factors into account, it may be concluded that global economy, unequal conditions and interactive dynamics make the fashion and apparel industry an interesting sector to examine through a CSR perspective. Due to globalization and industrial characteristics, the fashion and apparel industry features six aspects linked with CSR (Laudal, 2011; Woo, 2013). Table 1 shows CSR-related characteristics of the industry.

Up until now, business and academic literature have lacked an international analysis of how CSR could influence consumer behaviour in the fashion and apparel industry. Many studies agreed that CSR could enhance consumer equity (Kim, Ko, Xu, & Han, 2012). However, few studies have examined the relationship between consumer-related outcomes and CSR for this specific sector. Specifically,

Table 1. CSR-related characteristic of the fashion and apparel industry
Labour intensity—Directly linked to human rights and labour issues
Global sourcing—Labour and social issues are related since international retailers choose less developed countries to minimize the production costs
Market structure—To serve global-scale consumers quickly, buyers dominate suppliers
Short deadlines in production—Unpredictable orders and demands lead to mass production in a limited time
Low transparency—Product responsibility, environmental issues and supply chain are related
Lack of communication—Communication barriers between suppliers and buyers affect labour issues

Source: Own development based on Laudal (2011) and Woo (2013).

for the fashion and apparel industry, for which CSR is an essential topic, empirical examination is scarce and needed. The fashion and apparel brands are in need of determining under what conditions consumers respond positively to CSR, and how their perceptions differ from one country to another. Identifying consumer insights will likely have practical implications regarding operational and communication strategies.

3. Research framework

In the previous section, the absence of concrete results regarding the influence of different cultural values on consumer perception of CSR has been stated. The scope of the present research is to shed light on this issue, by means of a close analysis of the consumer behaviour of two different countries. The central research question that leads this research is set to explore to what extend consumer's perception and response to CSR differ between Spanish and Turkish individuals. These two countries, Spain and Turkey, were chosen since they have similar cultural values yet they are very different in history and cultural inheritance. Both countries share the particularity of having a unique cultural and historical background. Being the biggest part of the Iberian Peninsula under Muslim governance for eight centuries has shaped Spanish cultural identity in a different way from that of its neighbouring countries. Moreover, the discovery and conquest of the American continent, the establishment of a worldwide empire and its later fall has limited the historical economic development of the country (Acemoglu & Robinson, 2012), which has led to the particular idiosyncrasy of Spanish temper. On the other hand, Turkey is a democratic and secular country where the population is mainly from the Muslim religion. Subsequent to the foundation of the Turkish Republic in 1923, Turkey was turned into a modern nation-state in the Western style, with the adoption of the Latin script, among other measures to limit the influence of religion in civil life.

Spain and Turkey are also interesting places to investigate CSR agendas. In the context of CSR, the European Commission set some significant targets in the "Europe 2020: European Union's Growth Strategy", and its corresponding directives related to CSR as well as their national frameworks to foster social responsibility. To this end, the Member States of the EU are requested to comply with the regulations, and laws, while the candidate countries are also expected to improve their sustainability performances (Karaosman et al., 2015). Spain as a member state, and Turkey as a candidate country are important places to investigate to what extend societies perceive and communicate with CSR, which is widely endorsed at the governmental level. While global corporations reinforce their priorities to develop economies based on innovation, investigating consumer insights would be highly significant to show how CSR could be further embarked. More sustainable economies could be achieved only when consumer perceptions are positively linked with real purchase behaviour. The dimensions of Hofstede could be utilized to approach to the cultural values of Spain and Turkey. For each country, an index scale from 0 to 100 is used to measure each dimension and justify the cultural difference. The score of 100 is the highest level of power distance, while in the case of individualism and collectivism, "100" refers to the most individual country. For masculinity-femininity, higher ranks emphasize a culture's masculinity and uncertainty avoidance regards a high level of anxiety under unexpected situations. Last, for pragmatism and indulgence higher ranks call for high levels of each topic, respectively. A closer look must be given to the values given to each dimension. Table 2 shows the cultural dimensions as of Hofstede for both countries under study. It is believed that CSR perception and consumer behavioural outcomes are mostly shaped by these differences.

Table 2. Cultural dimensions as of Hofstede (2014)

	PDI	IDV	MAS	UAI	PRA	IND
Spain	57	51	42	86	48	44
Turkey	66	37	45	85	46	49

The Turkish score of 66 in power distance dimension indicates a hierarchical culture both at family and work level. Nevertheless, the score of Spain is slightly lower but also above the mean, which means that it should not be expected to find differences between consumers from both countries associated with this dimension. Due to power distance's negative relationship with CSR (Woo, 2013), the following question could be formulized.

RQ1: How do consumers in both countries perceive CSR?

Contrarily, Spain has a higher value on individualism compared to Turkey. This suggests that Spanish individuals are seen more as individualists with regard to their Turkish counterparts. However, when compared to other European countries Spain could be regarded as collectivist. For instance, the values of individualism for France (71), Italy (76), Germany (67) or Sweden (71) contrast with the value obtained for Spain. In collectivist societies, people have a shared group feeling, which could bring some interesting insights regarding consumer behaviour. Particularly, in collectivist cultures, the communication that surrounds CSR is more indirect and loyalty is seen to be higher than in individualist cultures. This leads us to the second question to be answered in this study.

RQ2: How could cultural values affect CSR awareness in both countries?

Regarding the femininity dimension, both countries score similar values, 45 for Spain and 42 for Turkey. They are on the feminine side of the scale, which calls for a sympathy for the weak, poor and needy members of society. Therefore, it could be expected that, CSR awareness is high. Nevertheless, since the collectivist index is of a higher value than the femininity dimension, in the opinion of the authors the former would override the latter. For this reason, consumers say they care for sustainable products, although their actual purchase decision will be based on different, more practical criteria. Hence, the following question arises.

RQ3: How is purchase decision influenced by CSR awareness?

Both countries' scores in uncertainty avoidance are rather high, 86 for Spain and 85 for Turkey. In both countries, there is a strong feeling of having the need for rules. At the same time, citizens of these countries are famous for their ways of feeling rather comfortable in the grey zone of dishonesty. Therefore, it could be logical to ask to what extend global corporations are expected to channel their performance by showing results of their actions.

According to these results in uncertainty avoidance, it is foreseen that both Spaniards and Turks could demand that corporations communicate their CSR efforts and expect fashion brands to control their performance while maximizing profit. However, it is equally important to measure how CSR communication of multinational fashion brands is really received by locals.

RQ4: How is CSR communication received by the end-consumers in both countries?

The following section is dedicated to methodology to explain how aforementioned research questions were investigated.

4. Methodology

The research strategy in international marketing research is determined by the current information in the field (Sinkovics, Penz, & Ghauri, 2005). Due to the limited understanding provided by existing literature into consumer responses to CSR in an international setting, an exploratory qualitative study has been undertaken. In order to obtain in-depth knowledge, an inductive and exploratory approach is recommended as the most appropriate (Elg, Ghauri, & Tarnovskaya, 2008). This research utilized focus group interviews to acquire input from Spanish and Turkish consumers. Focus groups are considered to be an effective means of exploratory data collection, as they are defined as "a way of collecting qualitative data by attracting a small number of people in group discussions, 'focused' around a particular set of issues" (Onwuegbuzie, Dickinson, Leech, & Zoran, 2009). This suggests that, compared to other forms of group interviews, participants' reactions, responses and interactions are encouraged and monitored to sustain the topic's focus (Saunders, Lewis, & Thornhill, 2009). This methodology is particularly appropriate when insights surrounding a subject are limited and context is relatively unresearched (Pookulangara & Shephard, 2013), as in this case. Focus group data were analysed in order to develop an inductively derived theory emerging from them. The methodology used in this research is consistent with procedures recommended for marketing theory development (Parasuraman, Zeithami, & Berry, 1986).

4.1. Sample and data collection

Academic literature suggests conducting one focus group interview by gathering four to eight participants (Saunders et al., 2009). The more complex the subject under study is, the smaller the number of members recommended in the focus group. In this case, based on the subject's complexity and the need for further discussions, the chosen number of participants in each interview is six. The rationale for this precise number was to promote diversity and generate a comfortable environment to enable participants to exchange ideas, thoughts and experiences. Focus group data were gathered through multiple sources including a moderator, an assistant moderator and observer. These three individuals composed the moderator team. This team worked closely to obtain, verify and interpret the data. For the purposes and intentions of this research, multiple focus groups were conducted to achieve saturation of both data and theory. In order to undertake sufficient focus groups, it is suggested conducting three or four group interviews with any one type of participant or group (Saunders et al., 2009). After the third or fourth group, if a moderator team can no longer receive new information, it is believed that saturation has been reached. A total of six focus group interviews were conducted in the two countries under study. Three focus groups, six participants per group, were held in Madrid, Spain. The remaining three, six participants per group, were conducted in Istanbul, Turkey. It is important to highlight the reason behind the selection of sample cities. Madrid and Istanbul are two important cities in the fashion and apparel industry considering the high growth in the fashion market. Istanbul emerges as an important metropolitan city where global fashion brands have numerous displays just to attract highly growing and equally trend driven society, while Madrid has been the capital of some significant mainstream brands that rule the street style such as Zara, Mango and Desiqual. Given both cities inevitable influence on street style, utilizing consumers from these markets would make a significant contribution to the course where CSR applications of said brands are explored. Furthermore, due to Europe 2020 addressed previously, both markets have a significant importance to put CSR in corporate agendas.

All focus groups took place in February 2014, during a short period of time in which there were no scandals in the media that could bias the participants' opinions. The focus groups were structured in accordance with standards conventionally applied in marketing literature (Parasuraman et al., 1986). Participants were selected due to their common characteristics and relation to the topic discussed, with the aim at achieving a consensus. Respondents were assessed to ensure that they were active consumers and interested in the fashion industry. To maintain homogeneity and assure maximum participation, individuals were chosen based on demographic areas including age, marital status, occupation, gender and education. Table 3 shows the main characteristics of the participants.

Consistency in age was ensured within groups; however, age diversity across groups was also provided to have different standpoints. With regard to the consumer participants, the fundamental dimension for sampling was consumers' interest and knowledge about CSR-related issues.

The researchers established one set of questions to utilize during the focus group interviews. The questions asked in the discussions were based on current literature and were open-ended to let participants actively participate. At the beginning of each group discussion, a brief definition of CSR was given to initiate the discussion. In order to maximize individuals' participation in the discussion, the focus groups in Spain were held in Spanish while the focus groups in Turkey were held in Turkish. Each discussion was recorded with the participants' permission, and then the transcript of these

Table 3. Focus group participants' characteristics

Group	Spain 1	Spain 2	Spain 3	Turkey 1	Turkey 2	Turkey 3
Number of participants	6	6	6	6	6	6
Age average	25–30	20–25	25–30	25–30	35–40	25–30
Education	Doctoral	University	Masters	Doctoral	University	Masters
Female/male distribution	4 F, 2 M	3 F, 3 M	4 F, 2 M	3 F, 3 M	2 F, 4 M	4 F, 2 M
Annual income	€30,000–€35,000	€35,000 and more	€30,000–€35,000	20,000–24,999 TL	35,000 TL or more	30,000–34,999 TL
CSR knowledge	Basic	High	High	Basic	Basic	High
Purchase frequency	Not often	Often	Not often	Quite often	Quite often	Often
Segment	Mainstream	Mainstream	Mainstream	Mainstream	Luxury	Mainstream

Notes: Minimum wage in Spain: €752.85 per month in 12 payments, €645.30 per month in 14 payments.
Minimum wage in Turkey: 1,071.00 YTL per month in 12 payments.

group discussions was translated into English. The method used to analyse each of these six focus groups' transcripts is described in the next section. The questions asked during the discussions were primarily aimed at gaining new insights into the following research areas, which are in accordance with the objectives presented in the previous section, (1) the concept of CSR; (2) cultural differences in consumer perception and CSR awareness; (3) CSR impact on consumer purchase decision and (4) CSR and its communication in the fashion and apparel industry.

4.2. Data analyses

As previously indicated, focus group interviews were recorded while the moderator and assistant moderator took notes. In order to establish a careful investigation, a tape-based analysis was conducted for this research. The tape-based analysis is a widely used method in which the researcher listens to the recordings and creates a transcript by organizing the ideas (Onwuegbuzie et al., 2009). This technique was pursued so as to focus on the research question and transcribe the sections that could fit in with a better understanding of the research interest. Analysing and interpreting the data from different groups' interactions, especially from dissenters, allowed researchers to determine to what extent the data achieved saturation. More specifically, constant comparison analysis was applied. Various scholars suggest that using this technique to analyse data could generate valid contextual implications. Constant comparison analysis covers three major stages; open coding, axial coding and selective coding (Onwuegbuzie et al., 2009). During the first stage, (open coding) the data are sorted into small units by assigning codes. Then during the second stage (axial coding) these initial codes are grouped into categories. In the final stage (selective coding), themes are developed to channel the content of focus group data. In this research, 110 codes were assigned, 12 categories were created and accordingly four themes emerged. During open and axial coding processes, online qualitative data analysis software was used (Saturate, 2013). Constant comparison analysis was used since multiple focus groups were conducted in this research. The purpose of using constant comparison analysis was to assess saturation in and across groups. One focus group's data are analysed at a time; therefore, multiple focus groups' analyses could serve as a substitution for theoretical sampling in order to assess the relevance of the themes. After analysis, the themes emerged showed a consistency with research questions, and could be listed in four categories, (1) *consumers' perception of CSR* to explain how consumers in both countries perceive CSR, (2) *the influence of cultural values on CSR awareness* to explain how cultural values affect CSR awareness, (3) *CSR impact on consumer behaviour* via *exemplification* to explain how purchase decision is influenced by CSR and (4) *transparency of CSR communication* to explain how CSR communication is received by the end-consumer in both countries. The findings associated with these categories are described in the next section.

5. Results and discussion

In this section, the findings of this exploratory study are presented.

5.1. Consumers' perceptions of CSR

In both Spain and Turkey, CSR embraces activities associated with consumers, local communities, workplace and environment. When participants were asked to define the concept of CSR, a consensus was recorded across groups; however, some differences emerged across countries. Spanish consumers defined responsibility as required corporate actions towards employees. In spite of being aware of the fact that a corporation seeks to maximize profits, participants in Spanish focus groups are nevertheless concerned with how those profits are made. The consumers identify the corporation as being responsible when it treats its employees in a fair manner and when consumers are asked to pay a reasonable price for good quality. Turkish consumers, on the other hand, indicated that corporations' biggest responsibility is satisfying consumers. Corporations' consumer-related responsibilities consist of a wide range of attributes including quality, product durability, after sales support and service quality. Some participants also stressed that corporations should be environmentally responsible. Recycling, waste reduction and renewable energy are some aspects that corporations are expected to further implement.

It is worth noting that consumers from both countries felt that CSR is part of a marketing strategy. According to the opinion of the focus groups, regardless of the country, CSR should be employed at corporate level rather than being held as a separate strategy for a marketing purpose. Turkish and Spanish participants stressed that, in their opinion, CSR can be considered not part of such marketing strategies only when the corporation integrates it into the business model. This result allows us to conclude that consumer perception of CSR is similar in both countries, as no differences in power distance have been encountered. That is, there is empirical evidence of a reasonable similarity in the perception of CSR among participant from both countries. This finding is in line with Öberseder et al. (2013) who stated that corporations were expected to be more credible, and with the fact that there are two types of corporations involved in sustainable actions. A first group involves multinational corporations that want to break into "green" actions to gain market share, while the second is composed of smaller corporations that adapted their business models to establish their own brand associated with these positive environmental attributes. The focus groups with Turkish participants revealed that multinational corporations were expected to encourage governments to improve the regulations. Due to its multinational nature, the fashion and apparel industry involves different countries, facilities, groups or individuals. Turkish consumers argued that frameworks and regulations had some legal holes in some countries. Therefore, multinational fashion enterprises are strongly expected to improve legal conditions and have local standards improved rather than taking advantage of them. This supports the ideology that CSR should be held at a governmental level. Turkish consumers emphasized that governments were also responsible for social welfare; CSR-related activities should thus be strictly monitored.

5.2. The influence of cultural values on CSR awareness

The majority of the participants from both countries stressed that they did not check or ask where fashion garments came from. This finding suggests that, in both countries, CSR awareness does not intervene while purchasing. Although, Spanish participants indicated that social awareness in society was growing, it is still not seen as a direct enabler to respond positively. During the interviews, there was a common theme that CSR-related problems or social scandals would be forgotten fast. Several of the participants agree that since those incidents happen far away from Spain, consumers do not feel affected in person. This finding suggests an interesting perspective: when a Spanish person or group is affected directly, other Spaniards would consider punishing the corporation that causes the incident, in the so-called "My People" approach. Even though Spanish participants do not punish the corporations due to previous social records, they would respond negatively when their local communities are in danger. When Turkish participants were inquired, the majority of participants agreed that corporations would be punished if their local communities were to encounter a social scandal. Though, Turkish participants also indicated that under normal circumstances, they would not consider what happened in other countries or what previous social records were. That is, for both countries a change of mentality, which involves thinking about punishing the corporation, could be observed when their local communities encounter a social challenge or scandal. The consistency in Spanish and Turkish consumers' perceptions of how to respond to a social scandal suggests that CSR awareness is low and similar for both countries, as their cultures are of a collectivist nature. It can be termed "low" as no influence of geographically far scandals affect them as consumers. But at the same time, the worry for the well-being of local communities is present in both countries. This is attributed to the dominance in both Turkish and Spanish culture of the collectivist dimension over the individualist. While people in individualist societies look after themselves and their immediate nuclear families, in collectivist cultures children are taught to think in terms of "we" rather than "I", which justifies the mentioned result. Moreover, it was articulated that individualistic cultures would value "explicit CSR" by which corporations address social issues through their CSR actions (Matten & Moon, 2008). Contrarily, collectivist cultures tend to value "implicit CSR" by which corporations address social issues through some other voluntary actions in a much wider scope. Apart from the abovementioned issues, other issues arose as findings of this research. Participants from both countries expect fashion corporations to hold explicit CSR strategies by which consumers could be well informed and convinced, and conditions would be precisely improved. Furthermore, participants from both countries stated that education would be an important indicator to assess and respond to CSR. In that sense, Northern European countries were believed to be more aware and conscious regarding CSR due to their socio-economic situation than Spain and Turkey.

5.3. CSR impact on consumer behaviour via exemplification

During the interviews, the participants were inquired to prioritize their purchase criteria. Participants of both countries claimed that self-interest and personal values were the biggest influences. Particularly, Spanish consumers indicated that price and product attributes (i.e. design and quality) were their main criteria. Similarly, Turkish respondents indicated that price, product durability and quality were their main criteria to purchase. This stresses that both Spanish and Turkish consumers would choose products with responsible attributes when explicitly asked. However, their actual purchase decision is based on other practical criteria, regarding the purchase criteria. These findings show that CSR is not the most dominant criteria within the purchase decision-making process. Price, quality, branding and other product attributes are considered relevant and decisive factors in the purchase decision. An evidence of the validity of the result is Pookulangara and Shephard's (2013) theory, which argues that regardless of the awareness level, price, design and quality have greater impacts on purchase behaviour. In order to find out if the participants would choose products with responsible attributes when explicitly inquired, an exemplification was employed, through the depiction of two products A and B.

- Product A: One garment that is desired to be possessed by the consumers. It is unique, cheap and accessible. However, the fashion brand is associated with social scandals and it was exposed to the media.

- Product B: One garment with standard attributes, nothing is original. It is accessible and affordable. However, the fashion brand is investing in improving the social conditions of workers.

When participants were explicitly asked which one they would choose, the majority of both Spanish and Turkish consumers answered that, even though price would be the essential purchase criteria, they would rather buy Product B, the socially responsible one than buy Product A, associated with social scandals. When asked to elaborate, participants stated that they would not support bad working conditions. This is a contradiction, as participants had previously declared that social records did not affect their purchase criteria. Therefore, this could be attributed to the emergence of some traces of feminine values present in both Spanish and Turkish cultures, that show social awareness when inquired about it, but that is surpassed and smoothed by the actual strong collectivist values that drive the overall national culture of participants. This was proved with a further brainstorming on this issue, in which all participants agreed that after a certain time, social scandals in distant countries would not be remembered and most likely, consumers would keep purchasing the brand. Another interesting theme emerged during the interviews with Spanish consumers. The majority of the participants argued that fast fashion products were not of quality, irrespective of the brand or the category, meaning that consumers spent money on a brand name rather than quality. Contrarily, the majority of Spanish participants agreed that local manufacturers had better quality than fast fashion retailers. However, since international fashion retailers' products are relatively affordable and names are more known, people keep purchasing in spite of knowing that regular merchandize would not last long.

5.4. Transparency of CSR communication

The findings revealed that in order for consumers to respond to CSR, they should be fully informed. Transparency is an important indicator for the communication of CSR (Pookulangara & Shephard, 2013). Both Spanish and Turkish responders indicated that the communication of CSR was not sufficient and consumers could not comprehend the intentions, purposes and CSR reality. Due to this communication lack, consumers are not aware of the corporations' entire CSR missions. There is a general consensus arguing that corporations should deploy CSR into their business models; yet consumers react sceptically since the majority perceives fashion retailers' CSR actions as marketing tactics. The main idea all respondents agreed upon was that transparent disclosure was needed. Turkish participants argued that in order to prevent them from being suspicious, fashion retailers should answer what, why and how questions regarding their CSR strategies. Spanish consumers claimed not to be aware of Spanish fast fashion retailers' CSR actions. Some Turkish participants suggested that if multinational fashion retailers would allow consumers to engage in social actions, these would be more easily perceived, and would contribute to the corporation's reputation. This shows that consumers respond to CSR actions when they are appropriately disclosed. The implication is clear; corporations should examine their strategies and channels of CSR for a better communication.

6. Conclusions and implications

In this paper, exploratory research was conducted by utilizing the focus group methodology. The influence of CSR actions adopted by global fashion and apparel brands on consumer behaviour, and an intermediate effect of cultural differences on consumer perception were investigated by comparing two important yet culturally different fashion markets, Spain and Turkey. Based on our findings, some important insights could be derived in terms of academic as well as managerial implications. The subject of this study was raised due to a lack of research in existing literature dealing with the relationship between CSR and consumers' behavioural outcomes in a cross-cultural setting.

In particular, consumer background, and the intermediate effect of culture were neglected while studying ethical standpoints in marketing literature. Having obtained a sufficient base of information - from six focus groups featuring 36 end-consumers—the extent to which (1) CSR is perceived, (2) cultural values affect CSR awareness and (3) CSR awareness could influence purchase decision of global end-consumers' were identified.

Results demonstrated that two countries under study could be regarded as sharing many of their cultural values, despite their geographical distance and historical background differences. Both countries can be identified with collectivist culture, although Turkey scores higher in the rank. The importance of the collectivist dimension in the culture of both countries has proved to be determinant in the development of consumer awareness towards CSR. While participants of both countries show concern about the well-being of local communities, a lack of interest in the manufacturing conditions of fast fashion retailers in distant countries has been encountered. Moreover, CSR awareness of consumers from both countries has been found to be low. Regarding the credibility of multinational fashion brands' CSR actions, it can be concluded that consumers, regardless of the country, perceive CSR actions as part of the marketing strategies. This brings a negative influence on consumer perception. Contrarily, when corporations integrate CSR actions into their business models, consumers' perceptions are positively affected. Furthermore, multinational fashion corporations are expected to become change agents towards enhancing local regulations. Another finding is that the criteria that determine the purchase decision is governed by self-interest, mainly price, design and product durability. However, a contradiction has been detected between attitudes and behaviours. Even though the intention is to avoid purchasing from brands that have bad social records, people actually do not avoid doing so. Therefore, it can be stressed that practical issues mainly motivate purchase decisions. This is attributed to the fact that both countries' collectivist dimension prevails over their femininity dimension. A difference between participants from both countries has been found with regard to their demand for more regulation towards CSR in their local setting. While this was an important issue for Turkish interviewees, the Spaniards did not mention it. This difference is attributed to the only noticeable dissimilarity in cultural dimensions between these countries, the higher Turkish score in collectivism. Finally, transparency in CSR disclosure is not sufficient in the opinion of participants from both countries. Therefore, appropriate communication of CSR is required for a positive consumer response.

Results suggest that, the level of awareness is often low among consumers, regardless of their country. This could imply that such fashion brands must leverage their communication strategies to increase the awareness. Pressure to adopt CSR practices is expected to come from brand-owning fashion companies in order to lead to a proactive approach in the industry. Nevertheless, end-consumers stress that CSR has been acknowledged as a part of marketing campaigns, hence a positive association among consumers and CSR is hard to obtain. In this vein, fashion companies must implement strategies with a clear message of what is intended and what has been and not been accomplished. Providing clearer information, disclosing performance results, and giving real-life examples could improve consumer interest in CSR. Even though, CSR perception is low and consumers were not found so eager to change their behavioural outcomes, there is an inclination in society to support business models aiming at meeting societal needs. It could be depicted that CSR knowledge is like water in a pot, which requires time to boil. Once the water starts boiling, the pot would not resist the pressure, and the boiling water would overflow. CSR takes time to be well perceived and get boiled. The message thus should be clear, real and more transparent. End-consumers are in need of affordable yet healthier business practices. Nevertheless, to boil the water of CSR, companies must invest in communication to leverage the process. Self-interest is an important parameter to take into account, for both consumers and companies. Thus, legislative compliance should intervene to move CSR beyond voluntary boundaries. Practical criteria, such as price and design, were observed dominating the purchase decision-making process. Nevertheless, once CSR is integrated into business models rather than being sold as a separate project in bespoke collections, consumers could feel the need in changing their behaviours toward supporting CSR. Monitoring suppliers, distributors and consumers is as equally important as implementing CSR practices along the value chain. Consumer awareness must aim to be increased by taking into account cultural values. Thus, companies are suggested to provide "easy-to-understand and easy-to-reach" information to increase knowledge among consumers across countries in terms of materials, performance measures, and social conditions behind the showcases. Lack of commitment was observed, and its negative effect on consumer identification was also noticed. To positively change this, communication must be improved. There is an increase in sustainability disclosure among fashion companies. Nonetheless, this proliferation could not be considered well received and understood. It is suggested that information should be better channelled on what companies are doing and aiming at. This study provides important academic contributions. A significant research gap, which is CSR impact on consumer behaviour in a cross-cultural setting, was contributed with a clear understanding of how CSR influenced purchase behaviour in two different yet significant countries for mainstream fashion market. In this vein, a contribution was made to consumer behaviour literature by showing how cultural values could change CSR perception, and how this perception could lead to purchase behaviour. Suggestions provided could extend the knowledge on how to balance CSR agendas, consumer expectations, and company objectives. Collaboration between societal and organizational theories, and a clear understanding of what could be done to make CSR become more understandable, and communicative must be the standpoint of any kind of CSR research, which was delivered as a key message of this study.

7. Avenue for future research

Given that the results for two countries could not take us to the saturation point, which is Spain and Turkey within this study, further research, which may help make more generalizable and comparable conclusions, is required. To achieve saturation of CSR impact on consumer behaviour in fashion and apparel industry, other countries could be studied and future research could deliver more comprehensive results out of cross-cultural settings. Afterwards, through comparison, it could even be useful to verify global results to enhance communication as well as the marketing strategies of fast fashion retailers.

Acknowledgement
This research was conducted within the framework of the European Doctorate in Industrial Management (EDIM).

Funding
This doctorate programme is funded by European Commission's the Education, Audio-visual and Culture Executive Agency (EACEA), under Erasmus Mundus Action 1 programs.

Author details
Hakan Karaosman[1]
E-mail: Hakan.karaosman@upm.es
Gustavo Morales-Alonso[1]
E-mail: gustavo.morales@upm.es
Mercedes Grijalvo[1]
E-mail: mercedes.grijalvo@upm.es
[1] Department of Industrial Management, Business Administration and Statistics; School of Industrial Engineering, Universidad Politécnica de Madrid (UPM), Calle de José Gutiérrez Abascal, 2, 28006 Madrid, Spain.

References

Abreu, M. C. S. D, Castro, F. D, Soares, F. D. A., & Silva Filho, J. C. L. D (2012). A comparative understanding of corporate social responsibility of textile firms in Brazil and China. *Journal of Cleaner Production, 20*, 119–126. doi:10.1016/j.jclepro.2011.08.010

Acemoglu, D., & Robinson, J. (2012). *Why nations fail: The origins of power, prosperity, and poverty*. New York, NY: Crown Publishers.

Achabou, M. A., & Dekhili, S. (2013). Luxury and sustainable development: Is there a match? *Journal of Business Research, 66*, 1896–1903. doi:10.1016/j.jbusres.2013.02.011

Ageron, B., Gunasekaran, A., & Spalanzani, A. (2012). Sustainable supply management: An empirical study. *International Journal of Production Economics, 140*, 168–182. doi:10.1016/j.ijpe.2011.04.007

Alexander, A., Walker, H., & Naim, M. (2014). Decision theory in sustainable supply chain management: A literature review. *Supply Chain Management: An International Journal, 19*, 504–522. doi:10.1108/SCM-01-2014-0007

Azevedo, S. G., Carvalho, H., Duarte, S., & Cruz-Machado, V. (2012). Influence of green and lean upstream supply chain management practices on business sustainability. *IEEE Transactions on Engineering Management, 59*, 753–765. doi:10.1109/TEM.2012.2189108

Becker-Olsen, K. L., Cudmore, B. A., & Hill, R. (2006). The impact of perceived corporate social responsibility on consumer behavior. *Journal of Business Research, 59*, 46–53. doi:10.1016/j.jbusres.2005.01.001

Beckmann, S. C. (2007). Consumers and corporate social responsibility: Matching the unmatchable? *Australasian Marketing Journal (AMJ), 15*, 27–36. doi:10.1016/S1441-3582(07)70026-5

Bhattacharya, C. B., & Sen, S. (2004). Doing better at doing good: When, why, and how consumers respond to corporate social initiatives. *California Management Review, 47*, 9–24. http://dx.doi.org/10.2307/41166284

Boulstridge, E., & Carrigan, M. (2000). Do consumers really care about corporate responsibility? Highlighting the attitude–behaviour gap. *Journal of Communication Management, 4*, 355–368. doi:10.1108/eb023532

Branco, M. C., & Rodrigues, L. L. (2007). Positioning stakeholder theory within the debate on corporate social responsibility. *Electronic Journal of Business Ethics and Organization Studies, 12*, 5–15.

Bray, J., Johns, N., & Kilburn, D. (2010). An exploratory study into the factors impeding ethical consumption. *Journal of Business Ethics, 98*, 597–608. doi:10.1007/s10551-010-0640-9

Bruce, M., & Daly, L. (2006). Buyer behaviour for fast fashion. *Journal of Fashion Marketing and Management, 10*, 329–344. doi:10.1108/13612020610679303

Buckley, P. J., & Ghauri, P. N. (2004). Globalisation, economic geography and the strategy of multinational enterprises. *Journal of International Business Studies, 35*, 81–98. doi:10.1057/palgrave.jibs.8400076

Burke, L., & Logsdon, J. M. (1996). How corporate social responsibility pays off. *Long Range Planning, 29*, 495–502. doi:10.1016/0024-6301(96)00041-6

Bygrave, W. D. (1989). The entrepreneurship paradigm (1): A philosophical look at its research methodologies. *Entrepreneurship Theory and Practice, 14*, 7–26.

Cadogan, J. W., Souchon, A. L., & Procter, D. B. (2008). The quality of market-oriented behaviors: Formative index construction. *Journal of Business Research, 61*, 1263–1277. doi:10.1016/j.jbusres.2008.01.014

Caniato, F., Caridi, M., Castelli, C., & Golini, R. (2011). Supply chain management in the luxury industry: A first classification of companies and their strategies. *International Journal of Production Economics, 133*, 622–633. doi:10.1016/j.ijpe.2011.04.030

Caniato, F., Caridi, M., Crippa, L., & Moretto, A. (2012). Environmental sustainability in fashion supply chains: An exploratory case based research. *International Journal of Production Economics, 135*, 659–670. doi:10.1016/j.ijpe.2011.06.001

Caniëls, M. C. J., Gehrsitz, M. H., & Semeijn, J. (2013). Participation of suppliers in greening supply chains: An empirical analysis of German automotive suppliers. *Journal of Purchasing and Supply Management, 19*, 134–143. doi:10.1016/j.pursup.2013.02.005

Caro, F., & Martínez de Albéniz Margalef, V. (2014). How fast fashion works: Can it work for you, too? Operational innovation. *IESE Insight*, 58–65. Retrieved from http://www.ieseinsight.com/review/articulo.aspx?doc=114445&seccion=6 http://dx.doi.org/10.15581/002.ART-2565

Castaldo, S., Perrini, F., Misani, N., & Tencati, A. (2008). The missing link between corporate social responsibility and consumer trust: The case of fair trade products.

Journal of Business Ethics, 84(1), 1–15. doi:10.1007/s10551-008-9669-4

Chan, H. K., He, H., & Wang, W. Y. C. (2012). Green marketing and its impact on supply chain management in industrial markets. *Industrial Marketing Management, 41*, 557–562. doi:10.1016/j.indmarman.2012.04.002

Cheung, Y.-L., Jiang, K., & Tan, W. (2012). "Doing-good" and "doing-well" in Chinese publicly listed firms. *China Economic Review, 23*, 776–785. doi:10.1016/j.chieco.2012.03.013

Choi, T.-M. (2014). Luxury fashion branding: Literature review, research trends, and research agenda. In T. M. Choi (Ed.), *Fashion branding and consumer behaviors* (pp. 7–27). New York, NY: Springer Science+Business Media. doi:10.1007/978-1-4939-0277-4

Ciliberti, F., Pontrandolfo, P., & Scozzi, B. (2008). Investigating corporate social responsibility in supply chains: A SME perspective. *Journal of Cleaner Production, 16*, 1579–1588. doi:10.1016/j.jclepro.2008.04.016

Elg, U., Ghauri, P. N., & Tarnovskaya, V. (2008). The role of networks and matching in market entry to emerging retail markets. *International Marketing Review, 25*, 674–699. doi:10.1108/02651330810915583

Europe 2020. (2011). *Europe 2020 targets*. Retrieved March 16, 2014, from http://ec.europa.eu/europe2020/pdf/targets_en.pdf

European Commission. (2011). *Europe 2020—EU-wide headline targets for economic growth*. Europe 2020. Retrieved March 15, 2014, from http://ec.europa.eu/europe2020/europe-2020-in-a-nutshell/targets/index_en.htm

Fernie, J., & Sparks, L. (2014). Retail logistics: Changes and challenges. In J. Fernie & L. Sparks (Eds.), *Logistics and retail management: Emerging issues and new challenges* (4th ed., pp. 1–28). London: Kogan Page.

Fionda, A. M., & Moore, C. M. (2009). The anatomy of the luxury fashion brand. *Journal of Brand Management, 16*, 347–363. doi:10.1057/bm.2008.45

Freeman, E., Velamuri, R., & Moriarty, B. (2006). *Company stakeholder responsibility: A new approach to CSR*. Virginia, VA: Business Roundtable.

Grimm, J. H., Hofstetter, J. S., & Sarkis, J. (2014). Critical factors for sub-supplier management: A sustainable food supply chains perspective. *International Journal of Production Economics, 152*, 159–173. doi:10.1016/j.ijpe.2013.12.011

Gualandris, J., Golini, R., & Kalchschmidt, M. (2014). Do supply management and global sourcing matter for firm sustainability performance? *Supply Chain Management: An International Journal, 19*, 258–274. doi:10.1108/SCM-11-2013-0430

Hofstede, G. (2014). *Cultural dimensions*. Retrieved March 26, 2014, from http://geert-hofstede.com/dimensions.html

Hofstede, G. J., Pedersen, P., & Hofstede, G. (2002). *Exploring culture: Exercises, stories and synthetic cultures* (2nd ed.). Intercultural Press. Retrieved from http://marte.biblioteca.upm.es/uhtbin/cgisirsi/UPM/SIRSI/0/5?searchdata1=%5EC431031

Joy, A., Sherry, J. F., Venkatesh, A., Wang, J., & Chan, R. (2012). Fast fashion, sustainability, and the ethical appeal of luxury brands. *Fashion Theory: The Journal of Dress, Body & Culture, 16*, 273–296. doi:10.2752/175174112X13340749707123

Karaosman, H., Mermod, A. Y., & Yuksel, U. (2015). Corporate social responsibility in the European Union: An assessment of CSR strategy. In S. O. Idowu, C. S. Frederiksen, A. Y. Mermod, & M. E. J. Nielsen (Eds.), *Corporate social responsibility and governance: Practice & theory* (1st ed., pp. 317–337). Berlin: Springer.

Kaufmann, M., & Olaru, M. (2012). The impact of corporate social responsibility on business performance—Can it be measured, and if so, how? In C. Vivas & F. Lucas (Eds.), *7th European Conference on innovation and entrepreneurship* (pp. 818–826). Portugal: Academic Publishing International Limited Reading.

Keh, H. T., & Xie, Y. (2009). Corporate reputation and customer behavioral intentions: The roles of trust, identification and commitment. *Industrial Marketing Management, 38*, 732–742. doi:10.1016/j.indmarman.2008.02.005

Kim, K. H., Ko, E., Xu, B., & Han, Y. (2012). Increasing customer equity of luxury fashion brands through nurturing consumer attitude. *Journal of Business Research, 65*, 1495–1499. doi:10.1016/j.jbusres.2011.10.016

Laudal, T. (2011). *Determinants and impacts of corporate social responsibility: A market centric approach*. University of Stavanger, Stavanger.

Maignan, I., & Ferrell, O. C. (1997). Corporate social responsibility and marketing: An integrative framework. *Journal of Academy of Marketing Science, 32*, 3–19. doi:10.1177/0092070303258971

MarketLine. (2014). *Industry guides: Apparel retail in Spain*. Dublin. Retrieved from http://www.researchandmarkets.com/reports/2093798/apparel_retail_in_spain

Matten, D., & Moon, J. (2008). "Implicit" and "explicit" CSR: A conceptual framework for a comparative understanding of corporate social responsibility. *Academy of Management Journal, 33*, 404–424.

McKinnon, A., & Edwards, J. (2014). The greening of retail logistics. In J. Fernie & L. Sparks (Eds.), *Logistics and retail management: Emerging issues and new challenges* (4th ed., pp. 237–257). London: Kogan Page.

Mentzer, J. T., DeWitt, W., Keebler, J. S., Min, S., Nix, N. W., Smith, C. D., & Zacharia, Z. G. (2001). Defining supply chain management. *Journal of Business Logistics, 22*(2), 1–25. http://dx.doi.org/10.1002/jbl.2001.22.issue-2

Mercer, J. J. (2003). *Corporate social responsibility and its importance to customers*. Claremont, CA: Claremont Graduate University.

Nagurney, A., & Yu, M. (2012). Sustainable fashion supply chain management under oligopolistic competition and brand differentiation. *International Journal of Production Economics, 135*, 532–540. doi:10.1016/j.ijpe.2011.02.015

Öberseder, M., Schlegelmilch, B. B., & Murphy, P. E. (2013). CSR practices and consumer perceptions. *Journal of Business Research, 66*, 1839–1851. doi:10.1016/j.jbusres.2013.02.005

Oh, C. H., Park, J.-H., & Ghauri, P. N. (2013). Doing right, investing right: Socially responsible investing and shareholder activism in the financial sector. *Business Horizons, 56*, 703–714. doi:10.1016/j.bushor.2013.07.006

Onwuegbuzie, A. J., Dickinson, W. B., Leech, N. L., & Zoran, A. G. (2009). A qualitative framework for collecting and analyzing data in focus group research. *International Journal of Qualitative Methods, 8*, 1–21.

Parasuraman, A., Zeithami, V. A., & Berry, L. L. (1986). A conceptual model of service quality and its Implications for future research. *Journal of Marketing, 49*, 41–50.

Park, J., Lee, H., & Kim, C. (2014). Corporate social responsibilities, consumer trust and corporate reputation: South Korean consumers' perspectives. *Journal of Business Research, 67*, 295–302. doi:10.1016/j.jbusres.2013.05.016

Perry, P., Fernie, J., & Wood, S. (2014). The international fashion supply chain and corporate social responsibility. In J. Ferrie & L. Sparks (Eds.), *Logistics and retail management: Emerging issues and new challenges* (4th ed., pp. 77–100). London: Kogan Page.

Podnar, K., & Golob, U. (2007). CSR expectations: The focus of corporate marketing. *Corporate Communications: An International Journal, 12*, 326–340. doi:10.1108/13563280710832498

Pookulangara, S., & Shephard, A. (2013). Slow fashion movement: Understanding consumer perceptions—An exploratory study. *Journal of Retailing and*

Consumer Services, 20, 200–206. doi:10.1016/j.jretconser.2012.12.002
Porter, M., & Kramer, M. (2006). Strategy and society: The link between competitive advantage and CSR. *Harvard Business Review, 84*, 78–94.
Radhakrishnan, P., & Chan, D. K. S. (1997). Cultural differences in the relation between self-discrepancy and life satisfaction. *International Journal of Psychology, 32*, 387–398.
Rizkallah, E. G. (2012). Brand-consumer relationship and corporate social responsibility: Myth or reality & do consumers really care? *Journal of Business & Economics Research, 10*, 333–344.
Rugman, A., Oh, C. H., & Kim, D. S. K. (2011). *The regional and global competitiveness of multinational firms* (No. 2011-003, Discussion Paper Series). Oxfordshire: John H Dunning Centre for International Business.
Saturate. (2013). *Saturate*. Retrieved March 13, 2014, from http://www.saturateapp.com/
Saunders, M., Lewis, P., & Thornhill, A. (2009). *Research methods for business students* (5th ed.). Harlow: Pearson Education.
Schwartz, S. H. (1994). Beyond individualism/collectivism: New cultural dimensions of values. In U. Kim, H. C. Triandis, C. Kagitcibasi, S. C. Choi, & G. Yoon (Eds.), *Individualism and collectivism: Theory, methods and applications* (pp. 85–119). London: Sage.
Sinkovics, R. R., Penz, E., & Ghauri, P. N. (2005). Analysing textual data in international marketing research. *Qualitative Market Research: An International Journal, 8*, 9–38. doi:10.1108/13522750510575426
Taras, V., Steel, P., & Kirkman, B. L. (2012). Improving national cultural indices using a longitudinal meta-analysis of Hofstede's dimensions. *Journal of World Business, 47*, 329–341. doi:10.1016/j.jwb.2011.05.001
Torres, A., Bijmolt, T. H.a. Tribó, J. A., & Verhoef, P. (2012). Generating global brand equity through corporate social responsibility to key stakeholders. *International Journal of Research in Marketing, 29*, 13–24. doi:10.1016/j.ijresmar.2011.10.002
Triandis, H. C., & Gelfand, M. J. (1998). Converging measurement of horizontal and vertical individualism and collectivism. *Journal of Personality and Social Psychology, 74*, 118–128. doi:10.1037//0022-3514.74.1.118
United Nations. (1987). *Report of the World Commission on environment and development: Our common future*. Retrieved from http://conspect.nl/pdf/Our_Common_Future-Brundtland_Report_1987.pdf
Wang, L., & Juslin, H. (2009). The impact of chinese culture on corporate social responsibility: The harmony approach. *Journal of Business Ethics, 88*, 433–451. doi:10.1007/s10551-009-0306-7
Werther, W. B., & Chandler, D. (2005). Strategic corporate social responsibility as global brand insurance. *Business Horizons, 48*, 317–324. doi:10.1016/j.bushor.2004.11.009
Woo, H. (2013). *Do consumers want a "Good" apparel brand? The effects of apparel brands' corporate social responsibility (CSR) practices on brand equity moderated by culture*. Greensboro: University of North Carolina.
World Bank. (2007). *Vertical and regional integration to promote African textiles and clothing exports a close knit family?* Washington, DC: Author. Retrieved from http://documents.worldbank.org/curated/en/2007/07/8508182/vertical-regional-integration-promote-african-textiles-clothing-exports-close-knit-family
World Economic Forum. (2012). *The future of manufacturing opportunities to drive economic growth*. Cologny/Geneva: Author.

7

Macroeconomic policy interaction: State dependency and implications for financial stability in UK: A systemic review

Muhammad Ali Nasir[1]*, Junjie Wu[1], Milton Yago[1] and Alaa M. Soliman[1]

*Corresponding author: Muhammad Ali Nasir, Faculty of Business & Law, Leeds Beckett University, Leeds, UK

E-mail: m.a.nasir@leedsbeckett.ac.uk

Reviewing editor: David McMillan, University of Stirling, UK

Abstract: The association between economic and financial stabilities and influence of macroeconomic policies on the financial sector creates scope of active policy role in financial stability. As a contribution to the existing body of knowledge, this study has analysed the implications of macroeconomic policy interaction/coordination for financial stability, proxied by financial assets, i.e. equity and bonds price oscillation. The critical review and analysis of the existing literature on the subject suggests that there is also ample evidence of interdependence between monetary and fiscal policies and this interrelation necessitates coordination between them for the sake of financial stability. There is also a case for analysing the symmetry of financial markets responses to macroeconomic policy interaction. On methodological and empirical grounds, it is vital to test the robustness of policy recommendations to overcome the limitation of a single empirical approach (Jeffrey–Lindley's paradox). Hence, the Frequentist and Bayesian approaches should be used in commentary manner. The policy interaction and optimal policy combination should also be analysed in the context of institutional design and major financial events to gain insight into the implications of policy interaction in the periods of stable economic and financial environments as well as period of financial and economic distress.

ABOUT THE AUTHORS

Muhammad Ali Nasir is a senior lecturer in Leeds Beckett University, UK. His main areas of research interest are macroeconomics, financial economics, labour markets, international trade and macroeconomic modelling. Nasir also has a great interest in the history of economic thought, European integration and more recently, European financial crises, with which the article was inspired from. He is the corresponding author of this paper.

Milton Yago is a senior lecturer in Leeds Beckett University, UK. His main areas of research interest are macroeconomics, international trade, microeconomics and DSGE modelling.

Junjie Wu is a senior lecturer in Leeds Beckett University, UK. Her wide research interests include accounting, finance and economics. She is particularly interested in SME and CSR-related issues.

Alaa M. Soliman is a senior lecturer in Leeds Beckett University, UK. His main areas of research interest are macroeconomics, financial economics, econometrics and macroeconomic modelling.

PUBLIC INTEREST STATEMENT

The stability of the financial sector is very important for both the economy and society. This importance creates scope of active policy role in financial stability. However, relying on a single policy measure is not the best scheme to achieve neither economic nor financial stability. This study has analysed the implications of macroeconomic policy coordination for financial stability and is particularly focused on stock and bond markets. The critical review and analysis of the existing literature on the subject suggest that there is also ample evidence of interdependence between monetary and fiscal policies and this interrelation necessitates coordination between them for the sake of financial stability. There is also a case for analysing the symmetry of financial markets' responses to macroeconomic policy interaction. This study also suggests that it is vital to test the robustness of policy recommendations using alternative empirical approaches. Furthermore, the institutional design and major financial events are important factors in coordination of policies.

Subjects: Banking; Investment & Securities; Macroeconomics; Monetary Economics

Keywords: macroeconomic policy interaction/coordination; symmetry of financial markets responses; financial stability; Bayesian estimation; Jeffrey–Lindley's paradox; institutional design

JEL Classifications: C11; E02; E44; E52; E58; E61; E63; G12; G18

1. Introduction/background and contemporary research issues' role of economic policies

Fiscal and monetary policies are the most prominent and widely used macroeconomic policies in addressing many economic issues by policy-makers. The basic function of macroeconomic policy is to contribute towards the achievement of economic objectives, e.g. price stability and economic growth (Bank of England, 1997). Hence, as defined by the US Federal Reserve (2011), monetary policy is referred to the actions taken by monetary authority (Central Bank) to control the availability and cost of monetary instruments for national economic goals. Correspondingly, fiscal policy can be described as government's policies of, e.g., revenue collection and spending to accomplish its financial obligations. Particular to the UK economy, Her Majesty's Treasury (HMT) is responsible for the formulation and implementation of fiscal policy, whereas monetary policy is autonomously formulated by the Bank of England (hereafter BoE; official abbreviation[1]). The stance of a macroeconomic policy can be either categorized as contractionary or expansionary, depending upon its effects on the supply of money in the economy. Macroeconomic policy which leads to the expansion of money supply, for instance, through tax or interest rate cuts would be called expansionary macroeconomic policy and vice versa (Sullivan & Sheffrin, 2003).

The effects of macroeconomic policies are not limited to the real economy[2] as various studies, for instance Bredin, Hyde, and Reilly (2005), Ardagna (2009) and Arnold and Vrugt (2010), reported significant impacts of macroeconomic policies on the financial sector. In practise, the responses of stock and bond markets to monetary policy are acknowledged by the Bank of England (2011), stating that bonds and equities are inversely related to interest rates due to the high rates on which future income is discounted.

1.1. State dependency

The associations between macroeconomic policies, the real economy as well as the financial sector are not consistent and have shown some dynamics with respect to the state of the economy. Putting it simply, the impact of a macroeconomic policy may vary under different circumstances. In support of this, Lippi and Trachter (2012) and Chen (2012) showed that monetary policy effects on output and US stock market vary according to the state of economy. It implies that the scope of monetary or fiscal policy for achievement of any objective could be influenced by other factors, often prevailing macroeconomic conditions. This dynamic behaviour of macroeconomic policy impact is called *State Dependency*. It also raises the question about the implications which business cycles or any other macroeconomic factors could have for effectiveness of a single or both macroeconomic policies.

In addition to business cycles, the impacts of monetary policy could be influenced by the institutional framework for policy-making and major macroeconomic events impacting the economy. The macroeconomic events and or institutional changes in policy frameworks could result in paradigm shifts which in turn influence the impacts of monetary policy (see Kontonikas, MacDonald, & Saggu, 2012; Wong, Khan, & Du, 2006). Similarly, an important aspect of macroeconomic policies is the structure and design of their parental institutions. Any change in the framework of policy-making intuitions could affect the effectiveness of monetary policy (see Lu & In, 2006; Osborn & Sensier, 2009; Semiromi & Reza, 2010). Specific to institutional framework in the UK, some major changes in the past few decades can be noted, particularly the independence of the Bank of England (1997) which resulted in a big shift in institutional design. Certain responsibilities related to financial stability, e.g. banking sector supervision and management of sovereign debt were transferred to the

Financial Services Authority (FSA) and Debt Management Office (DMO). We will have a detailed discussion on intuitional framework in the later sections. However, the point to be made here is that state dependency and institutional design are important aspects to be considered in a study on the subject of macroeconomic policies.

Most studies on this subject have been either focused on the Econometric or General Equilibrium approaches to gauge the impacts of macroeconomic policies on the economy. In this regard, Bhattarai (2011) strongly emphasized that DSGE and Econometric models should be considered complementary techniques rather than competitive. Apart from separate empirical frameworks, we also have separate approaches to estimations in this study, i.e. Traditional or Frequentist approach and Bayesian techniques. These are based on different theorems (Gauss–Markov theorem and Bayes theorem), and both approaches are fundamentally different in various contexts. The Frequentist approach is deterministic in approach, whereas the Bayesian approach is stochastic in nature. Nevertheless, these differences in empirical approaches may show different impacts of macroeconomic policies. In this aspect, Robert (2013) cautioned that each estimation approach may lead to a different conclusion and we could end up with a situation called Jeffreys–Lindley's paradox. Thus, an analysis of the role of macroeconomic policies and resulting policy decisions might be influenced by the choice of empirical approach employed to perform the policy analysis.

1.2. Significance of the financial sector

Despite their influences on the financial sector, it could be legitimately questioned why macroeconomic policies should consider financial market dynamics when financial stability has not been the mandate of macroeconomic policy-makers and institutions so far. Minsky (1974) reported the significance of the financial sector for the real economy quite a while ago, yet the behaviour of financial markets has not been incorporated into macroeconomic policy formulation hitherto. On this issue, by criticizing monetary policy stance in the real world, Mishkin (2011) argued that "although central bankers were aware that the financial sector has an important effect on economic activity, financial frictions were not an element of the pre-crisis monetary policy".[3] Hence, the defence of our intention to consider the financial sector within the macroeconomic policy mix is due to its importance for the real economy. In a recent post-financial crisis study, Borio (2011, p. 33) argued that "financial and macroeconomic stabilities are two sides of the same coin and monetary policy plays a critical role in both". Similarly, Tsouma (2009), Funke, Paetz, and Pytlarczyk (2010) and most recently Airaudo, Cardani, and Lansing (2015) declared that financial market performance itself is important for economic stability. It was also suggested that monetary policy by incorporating stock market prices in its formulation (Taylor type rules) could help reduce economic fluctuations, which could not be done solely focusing on the real economy only.

1.3. Scope of macroeconomic policies in financial stability

The frequent argument in favour of monetary policy role in financial stability documented in previous paragraphs does not imply that there is consensus among academics and economists and policy-makers on this subject. For instance, by rejecting the aspect of monetary policy role in financial stability, Nakov and Thomas (2011) argued that the optimal monetary policy should only be strict inflation targeting. This rejection was also revealed by Albulescu (2011) that monetary policy role in financial stability has not been appreciated by the Austrian school of thought. In a rather recent study, Williams (2012) showed that optimal monetary policy should be able to react to financial crises. Similarly, Blanchard, Dell'Ariccia, and Mauro (2010) argued that in the post-crises scenario, despite the fact that there is no change in ultimate goals of output and inflation stability, asset prices and leverage of agents should also be in the sight of macroeconomic policy makers. Mishkin (2011) argued that as price and output stability do not ensure financial stability, therefore, macroeconomic policy solely based on these objectives may not be enough to produce good economic outcomes. It is therefore unambiguous that there is an important role for macroeconomic policies in financial stability worth serious consideration. This is one of the considerations we are taking in this study.

1.4. *Macro-prudential policies*

Financial stability[4] and growth have been the remit of macro-prudential policies formulated by different regulatory bodies, for instance, by the FSA in the case of the UK. In addition, there is also an unconventional instrument of asset purchases called Quantitative Easing (Q.E) which has been used by the BoE and could be considered a policy tool for achieving financial stability. Some studies, for instance Benigno, Chen, Otrok, Rebucci, and Young (2013), argued that macro-prudential policies are welfare reducing and should not be used to avoid financial crises. In addition, Agenor and Silva (2012) and Borio (2011) claimed that prudential policies are insufficient for financial stability and urged monetary actions instead. Whereas accepting the limitations of prudential policies, Svensson (2012) and Collard, Dellas, Diba, and Loisel (2012) cautioned that monetary policy (interest rates cut) should only be used as a "Last Line of Defence" in financial crises when prudential polices are insufficient. Their caution also raises concerns as monetary policy can only take us so far due to the limitation of the liquidity trap (zero bound or nominal interest rates cannot be cut further below zero). This limitation was acknowledged by Mishkin (2011) and could be witnessed in the present economic scenario.[5] Cúrdia and Woodford (2011) assert that QEs are not very effective in addressing financial crisis since they depress the returns (yield) on financial assets.

Coupling the macro-prudential policies with monetary policy has been suggested as a solution to financial and economic crises. Angelini, Neri, and Panetta (2010) found that active macro-prudential policies coupled with macroeconomic policies have the potential to reduce economic volatility, though the benefits might be trivial. There is also the risk of failure of policy coordination which could bring adverse outcomes for the economy. Looking at the functioning of macro-prudential policies and macroeconomic policies, macro-prudential policies could be considered preventative, whereas macroeconomic policies work as preventative as well as reactive measures. These features of monetary and fiscal policies (macroeconomic policy) make them stand apart. A recent study on the role of fiscal policy by Benigno, Chen, Otrok, Rebucci, and Young (2012) showed that fiscal policy was an affective pre- as well as post-financial crises policy instrument. Similarly, Mishkin (2011) argued that "Leaning against financial instability is better than cleaning up after the crises". It has been widely acknowledged that the current global financial and economic crises were so severe that they overwhelmed the ability of conventional monetary policy to counteract it. This sentiment also indicates the limitation of monetary policy and potential scope of fiscal policy as a complimentary tool for more effective macroeconomic policy interventions.

1.5. *Fiscal–monetary policy combination*

In comparison with monetary policy, lesser attention has been paid to analyse the association between fiscal policy and the financial sector (Ardagna, 2009). The phenomenon behind this discrimination against fiscal policy for its potential role in economic and financial stabilities was explained by Blanchard et al. (2010). These authors argued that in the past two decades, fiscal policy took a backseat to monetary policy in the practise of macroeconomic policy implementations. The reason for this seemed to be the wide scepticism about the effects of fiscal policy, largely based on the *Ricardian Equivalence*.[6] Hence, if monetary policy could maintain stable output and price, there was then little reason to use another instrument. A distinctive aspect of this study is the use of macroeconomic policy combinations for financial stability as there is evidence of a consensus emerging in recent studies that considers it preferable to use both policies simultaneously (see Gomis-Porqueras & Peralta-Alva, 2010; Sims, 2011).

The notion of using more than one policy instrument is half a century old due to what is called Tinbergen's Principle. This principle itself is not a policy guideline. Agenor and Silva (2012, p. 6) argued that "Tinbergen's does not assert that any given set of policy responses will, in fact, lead to that solution. To assert this, it is necessary to investigate the stability properties of a dynamic system". In simple words, one policy combination does not fit all and *Tinbergen does not suggest any policy combination either*. Most importantly, in the context of financial (government debt) stability, Hughes Hallett, Libich, and Stehlík (2011, p. 2) argued that "let us note that there will be no additional policy instrument to achieve the financial stability goal (in the spirit of Tinbergen, 1952) and it is never socially optimal for monetary policy to do the job on its own".

Despite the acknowledged importance of joint policy analysis, most studies in the existing literature have only focused on a single policy. Even the studies which incorporated policy combinations into their analyses mainly focused on the EU and the real economy (see Jansen, Li, Wang, & Yang, 2008; Semmler & Zhang, 2003). A point to note here which is interesting and which will also be relevant in this study is Auerbach and Gorodnichenko (2012) who found heterogeneity in impacts of fiscal policy on different sectors of the economy. In relation to this finding and due to country-wise heterogeneity, Baum, Poplawski-Ribeiro, and Weber (2012) called for a tailored use of fiscal policy and a country-by-country assessment of their effects. Thus, sectoral and country-wise heterogeneity in impacts of monetary and fiscal policies imply that we may have a very unique optimal macroeconomic policy combination for a specific context of the financial sector's stability. Hence, it may not be appropriate to generalize the existing evidence of policy combinations on the real economy to the financial sector's stability everywhere. On top of this, UK financial markets have several unique features which make them stand apart (see Yang, Zhou, & Wang, 2009). In other words, the policy guidelines drawn on the basis of a particular sector of the real economy of any country should not be generalized to the financial sector's stability in the UK, unless and until a comprehensive analysis is performed.

1.6. Indistinct key concepts

It is essential that a few indistinct and elusive yet quite important concepts are defined and explained for the convenience of the reader. First is *Financial Stability* which has no single generally agreed definition, and therefore it is not as explicit as price stability, for example, which could be quantified as 2% inflation target by the BoE. On this same subject, according to Foot (2003) there is "no particular definition of financial stability". However, it could be defined in the context of *financial assets price volatility and generality of financial markets and institutions.* An interesting and rather bold argument was made by Goodhart (2004, p. 2) that "Indeed there is currently no good way to define, nor certainly to give a quantitative measurement of financial stability". Fortunately, the answer to the question about how financial stability could be defined in an appropriate way came out in a recent study by Khorasgani (2010, pp. 20–21). Taking a line, somewhat similar to Foot (2003, p. 3), it was argued that "There is no consensus on a definition of financial instability. However oscillation of some variables is often considered. House and stock prices, exchange rate and the prices of some other financial assets, on the one hand, and household debt growth and debt accumulation, on the other hand, are some of the main variables which are used to investigate the financial imbalances issue." Hence, considering these arguments, our definition of financial stability is simply about the price behaviour of financial assets, i.e. stock (equities) and government bonds.

Now, a legitimate question could be posed about why the *particular segments of the financial market* on which this study is focused are only the *stock and bond markets?* A simple answer and reason for this choice could be to a small extent the limited scope of this research as we are unable to consider all segments of the financial market. However, it is particularly because of the "*wealth effects of stock and bond markets* on the real economy" (see Airaudo et al., 2015; Funke et al., 2010; Malikane & Semmler, 2008). In addition to those authors, Broome and Morley (2004) also found that stock prices are a significant *indicator of financial crises*. Similarly, Campbell (1995) and David Gulley and Sultan (2003) gave a comprehensive account of the importance of bond market for governments as well as for private sector investors. Third and final reason for this choice is our *definition of financial stability*. Following the footsteps of Foot (2003) and Khorasgani (2010), it can be defined as financial assets price oscillation and financial market *generality of financial markets and institutions.*

1.7. Optimality

The second term on which there is some consensus, yet requires some explanation, is our definition of *Optimal Policy*. In this context, we refer to Mishkin's (2011) argument that the theory of optimal monetary policy starts by specifying an objective function that represents economic welfare, and then maximizes this objective function subject to a set of constraints. The existing evidence on the definitions of *Optimal Policies* shows that various studies use this term in a range of contexts. For instance, Bénassy (2003) declared the optimal combination of monetary and fiscal policies as the one which leads to maximization of household utility and firm profits, whereas Nakov and Thomas (2011) categorized a monetary policy as optimal which curtails inflation.

A fascinating point to note here is that apart from the different contexts in which optimality of a policy has been seen by various studies, it is also interesting to recognize that for the same context, the parameter of optimality has been different. Ferrero (2009) showed that optimal monetary policy should be flexible inflation targeting, while taking an opposite line, Nakov and Thomas (2011) argued that optimal monetary policy should only be strict inflation targeting. Hence, in these two examples, there is a difference of opinion on the optimality of monetary policy for achieving the same objective, i.e. price stability. One reason for this difference could be the constraints which should also be satisfied. In this study, we are analysing the optimality of macroeconomic policies in the context of financial stability. There is very few, yet sufficient evidence to support the importance of analysing optimality of policy combination for financial stability. For example, a recent study by Benigno et al. (2012) showed that optimal fiscal policy (taxes) is effective in restoring financial stability. This study used *capital flows* as the measure of financial stability. However, this study measures financial stability using stock and bond markets. In this regard, this is associated with Kontonikas and Montagnoli (2006) who argued that optimal monetary policy should positively affect stock market and house prices due to the wealth effects of these assets. In other words, this study considers a macroeconomic policy combination as *optimal* which positively influences our objective function, e.g. stock prices without negatively affecting the bond market (constraint) and vice versa. The optimal policy combination for financial stability is to some degree unique as mostly optimal policy has been seen as a single policy in context of the real economy. The difference of this study from any other is to take it further by taking fiscal policy and bond markets on board. Furthermore, this study also tests the optimality of our policy mix in various contexts (discussion on policy combinations and state dependencies in separate section) as a robustness measure.

1.8. Estimation of optimal policy

At this point, a methodological question may arise about how this study would measure the impact of optimal macroeconomic policies on financial stability. More specifically, how long the positive effects of macroeconomic policies on stock and bond markets should persist to make a contribution to financial stability? To provide an adequately satisfying answer, this study looks into the theoretical as well as philosophical backgrounds of these questions and the answers appropriate to them. "The stock and bond markets are used as proxies for financial markets and we specifically consider the wealth effects of these markets." In other words, the increase in value of assets leads to increase in wealth of their holders, resulting in increased consumption and economic growth (see Airaudo et al., 2015; Caporale & Soliman, 2013; Case, Quigley, & Shiller, 2012). At this point, it's worth mentioning that Altissimo et al. (2005) comparing various European economies argued that the wealth effects are rather more important for the British economy due to the high degree of financialization than in other European countries. Figure 1 best illustrates their argument, clearly depicting the relatively gigantic size of the British financial sector in comparison to its national income relative to other countries.

The wealth affects are instantaneously created with the increase in value of financial assets. A study by Carroll, Otsuka, and Slacalek (2011) found that the *wealth effects are immediate and persist for several quarters before completely being defused.* Similarly, an earlier study by Carroll (2004) compared various studies and argued that although there is mixed evidence, mostly the *wealth effects* persist into the medium term (3 years).

"The full effect happens asymptotically as time reaches infinity." Despite the fact that the wealth effects are instant, instead of looking at the short term (news effects), this study will consider the

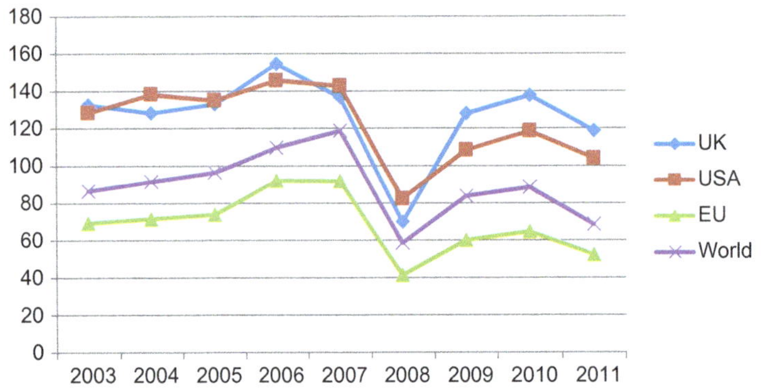

Figure 1. Market capitalization in comparison with national income (% of GDP).
Source: World Bank's World Development Indicators (2013).

long-term behaviour of financial markets in response to macroeconomic policies combinations. The rationale is that a positive response from financial markets which persists over several periods may result in enduring wealth affects.

The philosophical foundation of this study is derived from positivism, which suggests this study will urge on adopting the scientific approach, objective measures and systematic statistical analysis to better understand how an interaction of monetary and fiscal policies could influence financial stability. Hence, this study intends to provide a comprehensive theoretical framework which provides theoretical rationale to include the most appropriate data. Having access to two policies means there could be four possible policy combinations.[7] As explained earlier, a policy combination which maximizes the objective function (*Bliss Point*) while satisfying the constraints would be the most appropriate or *Pareto Optimal*[8] *policy combination*. Putting it more simply, an optimal policy combination would lead to relatively long-lasting positive impacts on stock and bond markets, which also significantly contributes to financial stability through the *wealth effects/real economy* dynamics.

Considering the pragmatic aspect of this study, an insight into the current outlook of the financial sector in the UK is essential. It would shed some light on the scope of macroeconomic policies in the light of theories as well as contemporary macroeconomic and institutional environments in which financial markets exist.

2. Current financial outlook and policy measures

The current state of affairs in the financial sector shows a gloomy picture. Exceptional and to a degree unprecedented events in the last few years, specifically the aftermath of Lehman Brothers collapse, led to both monetary and fiscal authorities to adopt unconventional and aggressive approaches to address the effects of the financial and economic repercussions of the crises. The BoE launched an asset purchase programme referred to as quantitative easing (QE) and the HM Treasury bailed out financial institutions including notably the Royal Bank of Scotland (RBS) and Northern Rock building society. Money was pumped into the financial sector through QE to try to solve the liquidity problems. The BoE introduced the so-called Special Liquidity Scheme*[9] in 2008 to improve the liquidity position in the UK economic system. Similar practices were implemented by other countries like the USA, China and Euro zone countries, etc. However, the focus of this study is on the British economy and its relatively large financial sector. Figure 2 represents the stance of the Bank of England in response to the financial and economic crises and post-Lehman Brother's bankruptcy episode.

It is evident from the diagram that in addition to the very active expansionary stance by dropping interest rates, the BoE has also used the unconventional instrument of Quantitative Easing by purchasing financial assets on a large scale. There is some evidence in the macroeconomic literature on the intensity of the response by the BoE to the crises. Study by Landolfo (2004) showed that among

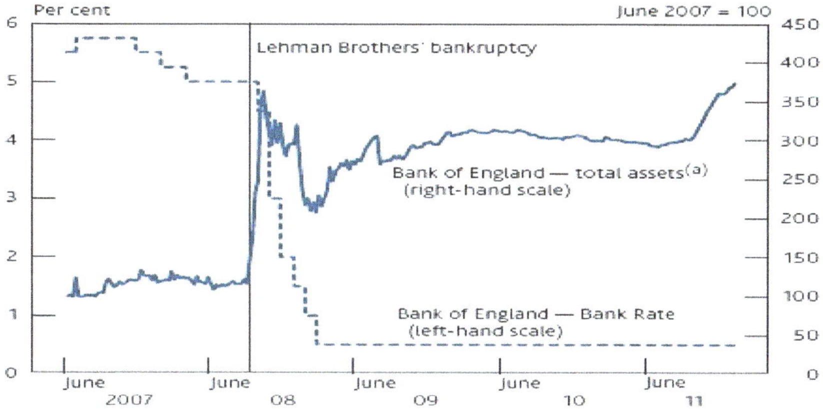

Figure 2. Bank of England, monetary policy (rates) and balance sheet.
Note: Assets in Billions GBP. Source: Bank of England Quarterly Bulletin (2012, p. 1).

the world major central banks, i.e. the US Fed, European Central Bank (ECB) and the Bank of England (BoE), the latter showed the most aggressive behaviour in response to adverse economic conditions. The current state of affairs represented in the above diagram clearly has two implications. Firstly, it indicates the severity of the financial and economic crises and their implications for the real economy which led the BoE to adopt an additional unconventional instrument of QE. Secondly, it also indicates the limitation of interest rates as an instrument in this particular case because of the so-called liquidity trap when rates are so low that they cannot drop much further. There is lack of sufficient evidence on the success of the Quantitative Easing measures in the existing literature due to the unprecedented nature of these strategies. However, there is some evidence in a recent contribution by Cúrdia and Woodford (2011), showing that QE may not be very useful, and it may even depress the returns (yield) on financial assets, even though asset purchases could be fruitful when there is turmoil in the financial markets. Hence, despite the fact that these measures of low interest rates and asset purchases were important to support the financial sector by providing liquidity, there may be some downsides of these measures reflected in depressed yield on assets, specifically government bonds or gilts.

Figure 3 represents these effects on the most current outlook in this study of real yield curves of gilts. The outlook is very discouraging in real terms, as it is evident that in real terms, the yield curve indicates a negative return in the short term as well as falling returns in the long term (negative risk premium), i.e. between 10 and 25 years to maturity.

In such a situation, the government and financial institutions might be beneficiaries of low cost borrowing and high prices of asset holdings. However, the household constituting pensioners and

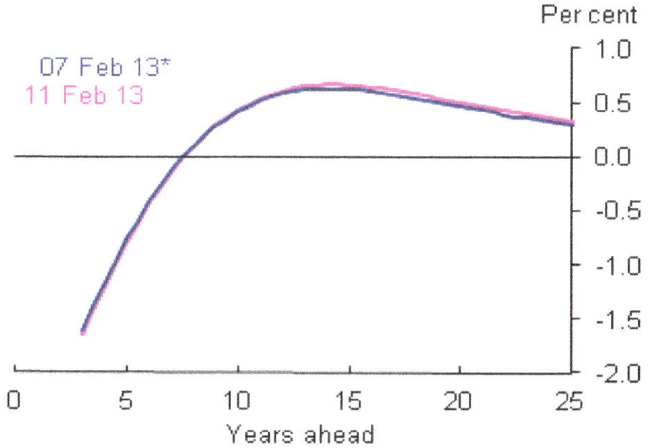

Figure 3. Real yield curve for UK government bonds (Gilts).
Source: Bank of England (2013, February).

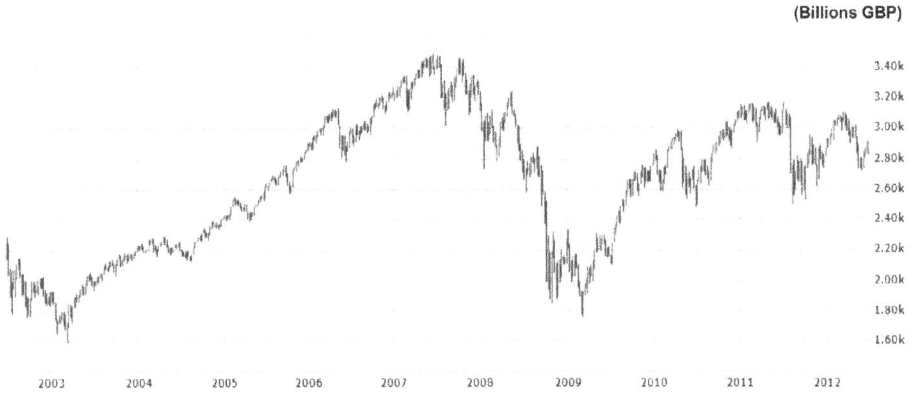

Figure 4. Performance of London Stock Exchange (FTSE All) July 2002–July 2012.

Source: London Stock Exchange (2012).

savers might be on the losing end. Some studies, for instance Moosa (1998), argued that the cyclical relationship of economy and financial markets had been weakened in the post-war period (1946–1991). However, the financial and economic crises which started in 2007–08 proved otherwise. This scenario provides some support for the notion that using fiscal policy as a complementary instrument due to the adverse effects of QEs may be beneficial. A discussion on this perspective will be provided in detail in a later section.

Similar to the bond market, the stock markets have been adversely affected by the financial and economic crises as shown in Figure 4, where we have value of stock index (FTSE-All) on X-axis and Y-axis representing the timeline. The London Stock Exchange (LSE) has faced a series of adverse shocks from the 4th Quarter of 2008 to 1st Quarter of 2009 before settling on a slow and long route to recovery. Perhaps it was the worst performance of the LSE during the last decade and since the technology bubble of (2002–2003).

A visual comparison of Figures 3 and 4 shows that in contrast to the bond market, the stock market comparatively presents a better outlook after the implementations of the policy measures discussed. This contrast indicates an asymmetry to policy responses between the two markets, an aspect of policy that this study is considering.

In the context of recent developments to restore financial stability, it is important to mention here that the BoE has recently set up a Financial Policy Committee (FPC).[10] As cited earlier, there is a major change in the functioning of the BoE since May 1997 when various responsibilities including sovereign debt management and banking supervision were transferred to the FSA and the DMO. Since then, the official mandate of the BoE has been price stability by targeting inflation at 2% of the consumer price index. However, in the context of these changes, it could be well anticipated that in future, the financial sector would also be considered in macroeconomic policy formulation, even though this has not been a normal practice before the crises.

In terms of the financial sector, the role of fiscal policy has not been investigated to the same extent as monetary policy (Jansen et al., 2008) has been. Recent studies have considered it more preferable to use both macroeconomics policies simultaneously while analysing their impacts on the real economy (Gomis-Porqueras & Peralta-Alva, 2010; Sims, 2011). Despite the acknowledged importance of joint macroeconomic policy analyses, most studies in the existing literature have been focused on single policy implementation. The limited number of studies which investigated the effects of macroeconomic policy interactions or combination has only considered impacts on the real economy, and the financial sector has not been a priority concern (Jansen et al., 2008).

As acknowledged in previous paragraphs, the impacts of monetary and fiscal policies are state dependent. This implies that there is a prospect that optimal combination of macroeconomic policies may also be influenced by the underlying state of the economy. Therefore, the optimality of macroeconomic policy combinations for financial stability in various contexts (the underlying states) should be analysed. There are three interesting aspects of state dependency this study is intending to consider: (1) analysis of intuitional arrangements, (2) alternative empirical approaches/frameworks and (3) major macroeconomic events. There are three reasons for enriching our state dependency with these aspects. First, the literature on the subject has shown a shift in effectiveness of macroeconomic policies followed by structural changes in their formulating institutions (see Lu & In, 2006; Osborn & Sensier, 2009; Semiromi & Reza, 2010), for example, institutional changes in the BoE. Those studies indicated variability in effectiveness of monetary policy post-changes in its intuitional framework. There have been some changes in the structure and arrangements of institutions responsible for design and implementation of macroeconomic policies, for instance, the operational independence of the BoE in 1997. Hence, it is imperative to analyse the dynamics of macroeconomic policy interactions in the light of intuitional changes during the period of the study. Second, the macroeconomic policy literature also shows that either General Equilibrium modelling or Econometrics techniques have been used for empirical analyses. In this regard, Bhattarai (2011) and latter Consolo, Favero, and Paccagnini (2009) highlighted the weakness of a single framework and urged that the DSGE (dynamic stochastic general equilibrium) and Econometrics should be considered complementary techniques rather than competitive ones. Nevertheless, it is not a matter of empirical frameworks only, but the important point is that the Frequentist approach (Econometrics) and Bayesian approach (DSGE) are based on different theorems and could lead to different empirical results and conclusions, a situation called Jeffreys-Lindley's paradox (Robert, 2013). Hence, differences in the fundamental principles of estimation could also have implications for optimality of our policy combinations. Third and lastly, the reason for including the contexts of macroeconomic events is due to the shifts of stock markets' response to monetary policy after an episode of crisis (see Kontonikas et al., 2012; Wong et al., 2006), which is associated with change in market efficiency. This could also have important implications for the optimality of macroeconomic policy combinations.

In the next section, the discussion of some research gaps in the existing body of literature on macroeconomic policy interactions, particularly in the context of state dependency and the effects on the financial sector, will be provided.

3. Research gaps in the existing literature on policy interaction/optimal*[11] combination

Earlier studies have shown that financial markets have substantial effects on the real economy. Therefore, this association creates scope for active monetary response to financial market dynamics. However, a major limitation of these studies was their focus on monetary policy only, even though recent studies have strongly emphasized joint fiscal-monetary policy analyses (Gomis-Porqueras & Peralta-Alva, 2010; Sims, 2011). Macro-prudential policy combinations have also been suggested as an alternative policy combination, but have been heavily criticized for their failure, unlikely beneficial effects and potential risk of coordination failure (Angelini et al., 2010).

Other than urging for monetary response to ensure financial stability, existing studies do not suggest any particular monetary stance in this regard. To support this position, Borio (2011, p. 15) states that "no such agreement as yet exists concerning whether, and if so how, monetary policy frameworks should be adjusted to better support financial and macroeconomic stability. The crisis has generated much soul-searching, but as yet no clear answers". It is worth mentioning that various researchers have also cautioned about aggressive use of expansionary monetary policy for financial market stability as it could adversely affect the real economy (see Airaudo, Nistico, & Zanna, 2008; Bernanke & Gertler, 2001; Giorgio & Nistico, 2007).

This discussion seems to suggest optimally combining macroeconomic policies as supported by Gomis-Porqueras and Peralta-Alva (2010) and Sims (2011) to achieve more effective outcomes for real economy. Despite the acknowledged importance of fiscal policy[12] on the economy, reviewed literature on macroeconomic policies to the best of our knowledge, we could not find a study which has addressed the issue that fiscal policy could realize the financial sector's stability in the context of its importance for economic stability. Jansen et al. (2008) on the notion of optimal macroeconomic policy combinations reported that the relationship between monetary policy and the US stock market might be influenced by fiscal policy. The study does not suggest any optimal policy combination neither does it give any insight into the effects of policy interactions on the stock or bond markets. This study, however, will take the opportunity to address the subject of optimal policy combinations for the financial sector's stability. The study will also analyse the *symmetry* (homogenous or heterogeneous) of the responses of both markets, i.e. bonds and stocks to macroeconomic policy interactions for the reasons discussed before. In keeping with our earlier mentioned definition of optimal policy combination, we can remind ourselves that a policy combination could only be considered as optimal if it positively contributes to one market, e.g. stock or bond, provided no adverse effects are imposed on the other and vice versa.

As discussed and cited earlier, it is evident that the impacts of fiscal and monetary policies on the bond and stock markets are not consistent and subject to change, often led by business cycle dynamics. In addition, the structure and design of their parental institutions (see Lu & In, 2006; Osborn & Sensier, 2009) and major macroeconomic events (see Kontonikas et al., 2012; Wong et al., 2006) also result in shifts in the impacts of monetary policy. This implies that optimal policy combinations of macroeconomic policies may also vary in their compositions under the influence of business cycles, intuitional designs and macroeconomic events. Therefore, this research takes these factors into account. However, in the existing body of literature on the subject, there is a lack of studies which have analysed the impacts of these factors on macroeconomic policy interactions, for the financial sector's stability and for the real economy.

Lastly, an important context in our consideration of optimal policy combinations is the role of alternative empirical frameworks, i.e. Econometric as well as General Equilibrium frameworks. It is worth mentioning that the Econometric framework would be based on the so-called *Frequentist Approach*, while estimation of the DSGE model would be carried out using *Bayesian techniques*. Apparently, it not just a matter of choosing an empirical approach because more importantly, both approaches have fundamental differences as the Frequentist is deterministic while the Bayesians is a stochastic approach. To accommodate the aforementioned research gaps, this study intends to achieve the following research aims and objectives as stated in the next section.

4. Aim and objectives of the study

The main aim of this research is to theoretically derive, evaluate and recommend an optimal policy framework for financial stability. Hence, the achievement of the main research objective would lead to a recommendation of an empirical framework which further based on macroeconomic policy combination could facilitate the financial sector's stability in various contexts (empirical framework/approaches, institutional framework and macroeconomic events). As the bases for reasoning, the study raises the following research questions:

(1) What are the effects of macroeconomic policy interactions on financial stability?
(2) What is the symmetry (homogenous or heterogeneous) of stock and bond markets' responses to macroeconomic policy interactions?
(3) How do the empirical frameworks, intuitional designs and macroeconomic events influence the composition of optimal macroeconomic policy combinations?

However, critical analysis and reasoning which could lead to answering the research questions could also help to attainment the following specific objectives, which would pave the way to the achievement of the main objective:

(1) To evaluate the impacts of macroeconomic policy combinations/interactions on the financial sector's stability.

(2) To appraise the symmetry of bond and stock markets' responses to optimal macroeconomic policy combinations.

(3) To evaluate the implications of the empirical frameworks, intuitional designs and major macroeconomic events on the optimality of macroeconomic policy combinations.

The first and second specific objectives are limited to the overall impacts of macroeconomic policies on the financial sector's stability. The rationale behind this exercise is that: (1) it would help understand the symmetry of stock and bond markets' responses to a particular macroeconomic policy combination, (2) it would also help analyse how the impacts and composition of "optimal policy mix" change when analysis is limited to one sector, i.e. equity (stocks) markets or bond markets, and vice versa. However, in the third specific objective, we would analyse the robustness of our optimal policy mix in the light of alternative empirical approaches, institutional changes and major macroeconomic events. The achievement of the third objective would help us understand the influences of intuitional designs, macroeconomic events and empirical approach/framework choices on the optimality of the suggested policy combinations.

5. Rationale and contributions of research

Major factors which provide grounds for this research include the significance of financial stability for real economy's stability and scope of policy combination in this context. Certainly, in the light of research gaps acknowledged in the previous section, there is a need for the formulation of macroeconomic policies which could assist in the financial sector's stability due to its importance for the real economy. The *particular segments of financial market* on which this study is focused are the *stock and bond markets*. One reason for this choice is the limited scope of this research but also particularly because of the *wealth effects of stock and bond markets* on the economy (see Airaudo et al., 2015; Funke et al., 2010; Malikane & Semmler, 2008). In addition, Broome and Morley (2004) found that stock prices are significant *indicators of financial crises*. Third and finally, the reason for this choice is due to our *definition of financial stability*, which follows Foot (2003) and Khorasgani (2010), as financial assets price volatility. There are several reasons for the choice of UK as the financial sector rather than any other: including, (1) the relative *size and significance of the financial sector for the British economy as well as international financial system*, (2) the availability of reliable data from credible sources and (3) how well established the macroeconomic policy-making intuitions and financial markets are.

This study is to (1) address the problem of future policy formulation, also in case of conflicting stances of monetary and fiscal authorities, e.g. non-coordinating monetary and fiscal policy-makers. It is to take it further by, (2) bringing fiscal policy on board and finding optimal combination of monetary and fiscal policies which could facilitate stock as well as bond markets, (3) it will also test the optimality of our policy mix in various contexts to understand the dynamics of policy interactions in different circumstances and their implications for the financial sector's stability. Hence, the contributions made by this study would have three remarkable aspects, i.e. pragmatism, theoretical context and its innovation to the application of methodology. The details are explained in the following sections.

5.1. Pragmatism

A significant, perhaps most important aspect of this study is its practicability and pragmatism. Though the coordination among macroeconomic policies has been widely perceived as beneficial, this may not be the case in practise as Niemann and Hagen (2008) accused independent central banks of being reluctant to coordinate with fiscal authorities. In particular to the analysis of the UK economy, Fragetta and Kirsanova (2010) also showed that fiscal and monetary policies act in a non-cooperative manner. They did not however mention the cause of non-cooperation, its implications for the financial sector or the economy and neither gave any recommendations for future policy formulation.

In the context of the present economic scenario, this study provides new perspectives for future policy formulation. An important practical contribution is the incorporation of the financial sector in macroeconomic policy formulation. The rationale to bring financial (stock and bond) markets analysis to the fore is strengthened by the BoE's recent efforts to ensure financial stability and the launch of the FPC. This research also considers state-dependent impacts of policy combinations in the presence of various institutional arrangements and macroeconomic events. This particular feature of the study makes it very pragmatic as we would be able to see how intuitional designs and macroeconomic events define the ability of policies and the contexts in which they are formulated.

5.2. Theoretical context

On the theoretical context, we may not be able to come up with a unified theory on macroeconomic policy interactions, financial sector's stability and state dependency as it is a nexus of theories. To some extent, we can associate this study as mentioned earlier with Minsky (1974) and his recently well-publicized theory of Financial Instability Hypothesis. Despite being limited to private sector debt, this theory would still be categorized as pioneering in highlighting the financial sector's importance for the real economy. Secondly, with regard to the policy interactions, it might be observed that this study in the light of the FTPL emphasized fiscal policy as complimentary to monetary policy. It stemmed from the empirical work of Sargent and Wallace (1981) and their remarkable arguments that the *Friedman's list of the things that monetary policy cannot permanently control may have to be expanded to include inflation*. This theory refutes the concept of the Ricardian Equivalence according to which fiscal policy has no real impact on the economy.

Further to these interesting economic theories, a well-known study by Dixit and Lambertini (2003) also emphasized the importance of cooperation between fiscal and monetary authorities in order to achieve a desirable outcome, for that they coined the term "Symbiosis". To add values to these cited theories, our study is to take it further and bring the financial sector stability into consideration. We would analyse the effectiveness of fiscal policy by the FTPL and Dixit and Lambertini's (2003) strategy of symbiosis could be helpful in the formulation of an optimal macroeconomic policy combination for financial stability due to its importance for economy *as acknowledged by* Minsky (1974).

5.3. Methodological innovations

This study makes a significant addition to the existing literature on the subject area. This study critically reasons the option of alternative empirical frameworks, i.e. DSGE and Econometric frameworks, *for comparison, robustness and overcoming limitations of a particular framework*. Furthermore, it gives a detailed insight into the estimation of the empirical models which could also be carried out using alternative approaches, i.e. the Econometric model by traditional or Frequentist and the DSGE model by Bayesian estimation approach. We would have detailed discussion on both approaches in the next section. The methodological contribution also has a practical aspect as it would elaborate how the choice of empirical framework affects the outcome and resulting policy formulation.

6. Structure of the study

The study consists of three sections which includes the introduction as the first section. The second section will comprehensively review the existing literature on macroeconomic policies, their impact on financial markets and evidence on policy interaction. It will also provide in-depth discussion and insight into the Bayesian approach (based on Bayes' theorem) and Frequentist approach (Gauss Theorem). It would give readers insights into our methodological choices and their impacts on optimal policy mixes, i.e. whether our optimal policy combination is robust against the Jeffreys–Lindley's paradox. Moreover, we will also look at two important elements: firstly, the implications of institutional arrangements and design of macroeconomic policy-making intuitions and secondly, shedding some light on the impact of macroeconomic events for the dynamics of the relationship between the financial sector and macroeconomic policy combinations.

Third, section three would give us an insight into the financial sector (bond and equity markets) of the UK economy. In this regard, some descriptive historical statistics would also be provided to give the reader a flavour of the subject of the financial sector and its background. Furthermore, the macroeconomic policy framework, its performance in the last few decades and evidence on its relationship with the financial sector would also be acknowledged. Conclusions will be drawn on the basis of in-depth and critical discussion and logical reasoning, and critical review of existing and prevailing wisdom. Moreover, the implications and contributions to macroeconomic policy formulation would also be described. In the last section, some indication towards potential extensions for future research will be suggested.

7. Review of existing evidence on macroeconomic policy's role in the financial sector

In this section, we will comprehensively review the existing literature on macroeconomic policies, their impact on financial markets and evidence on policy interaction.

7.1. Macroeconomic policy interaction

Despite ample effort, we could not evident ample evidence on the impact of macroeconomic policy interaction on the financial sector; however, its influence on real economy would be acknowledged to highlight and establish its importance. Regardless of the limited attention paid to the joint analysis of macroeconomic policies and their interaction, its significance has been frequently acknowledged and increasingly emphasized in recent past. There are a number of current studies we would review, yet the comments by Leeper (1993, p. 3) are very important in this context that ...

> Analysing one policy is like dancing a tango solo: it's a lot easier, but it is incomplete and ultimately unfulfilling.

Indeed, analysing one policy is quite easy; however, it neither shows the complete picture nor leads to a desired outcome. Nevertheless, the arguments by Isaac (2009) are also very interesting on the issue of macroeconomic policy mix. Analysing the interaction between monetary and fiscal policies in the long and short run, it was argued that ...

> The macroeconomic stability does not depend on particular fiscal or monetary policy but on a mix of these policies.

It was also showed that the monetary policy could also overcome the inflationary effects of expansionary fiscal policy, for instance, by influencing inflation expectation by changing its targets. We should also acknowledge the arguments Hughes Hallett and Libich (2007) made, that "it is important to take the government's intentions into account, as well as those of the central bank, if we are to get a realistic picture of the effectiveness of the policies and policy institutions in any economy." The comparative analysis of fiscal and monetary policies' effects on economy by Dungey and Fry (2009) showed that the overall impact of fiscal policy shocks has been larger than monetary policy shocks. In addition, among fiscal instruments, taxation and debt policy shocks have been more significant than government expenditure shocks. Nevertheless, they compare the magnitude of the policy effects, however, as the both fiscal and monetary policies operate simultaneously and there is substantial evidence of interaction in this section; analysing effects of only one policy exclusively may conceal the effects of policy interaction.

In particular to the UK, the monetary and fiscal policies are formulated by separate institutions. The interaction is important as it may influence the real economy as well as financial sector's stability; moreover, the conflicting and coordinating policies may have various implications for economy. The interaction is also important as macroeconomic policies may influence actions of each other; in this context, Neri (2003) observed that as fiscal policy was introduced in the VAR model, the effect of monetary policy decreased to almost half. In a study with similar outcome, where fiscal policy acts as a stabilizer of government debt under various forms of monetary policy, von Thadden (2004) found that the monetary policy may restrict fiscal policy as additional fiscal restraint may be needed under strict inflation targeting which was not required under a constant money growth rule. Similarly, analysing coordination of economic policies and its effects on economy, Barnett (2005) urged that the fiscal and monetary authorities should coordinate with each other as the fiscal policy often puts some constraints on monetary policy. Moreover, the central bank inflation targeting should be coupled with fiscal constraints. In recent cases of reporting inter-dependence between macroeconomic policies, Zubairy (2009) and rather later Davig and Leeper (2011) also showed that the strong action of monetary policy can restrain the effects of fiscal policy. Consequently, policies influence the role of each other; therefore, their interaction cannot be overlooked.

7.2. Coordinating macroeconomic policies' "symbiosis"

In their study, Dixit and Lambertini (2001) argued that the interaction of the both fiscal and monetary is a recent phenomenon and it has gained importance in the field of economic policy formulation as several studies have considered the interaction of monetary and fiscal policies. They emphasized the coordination between monetary and fiscal policies and cautioned that the non-cooperative behaviour can cause low output growth and high rate of inflation, but if the authorities' preferences coincide, the ideal growth and inflation is attainable. In case of disagreement, the outcome can be influenced by institution design; therefore, it was recommended that giving a leadership role to either monetary of fiscal authority can be fruitful. Latter investigation by Dixit and Lambertini (2003) showed almost similar findings that the optimal results are achieved by consensus of fiscal and monetary authorities on the desirable level of output and inflation, for which they coined the, later became famous, term "*Symbiosis*". Similar and recent study on European Monetary Union (EMU) where monetary policy is formulated at union level (European Central Bank) but fiscal policy is formulated at country level, Ferré (2008) also emphasized that EMU should adopt coordination and exchange of information in fiscal policies as it affects economies in EMU.

In the context of "Symbiosis" discussed in previous paragraphs, a recent study by Di Bartolomeo and Giuli (2011) on macroeconomic policy interaction showed that the symbiosis suggested by Dixit and Lambertini (2003) does not hold under uncertainty effects on monetary policy. They argued that macroeconomic policy uncertainties are not symmetric and could affect economy. Moreover, the role of monetary policy under uncertainty could be affected by fiscal stance. However, in the context of coordination, they unanimously supported the theme; they cautioned on viewing monetary and fiscal institutions as separate entities and urged for coordination in uncertain economic scenario.

For the achievement of economic objectives, Bénassy (2003) emphasized that the optimal combination (household utility and firm profit maximized) of monetary and fiscal policies leads to better outcomes, even when information available to the policy-makers is constrained. In a recent study on dimension of information, the coordination among macroeconomic policies was investigated by Nasir, Ahmad, Ali, and Rehman (2010). Although they reported that there had been very week coordination between macroeconomic policies, yet they emphasized on more coordination and exchange of information among policy-makers for economic stabilization. Similarly, seeing coordination in the light of openness and integration of financial markets, empirical results by Pierdzioch (2004) showed that the higher capital mobility does not reduce the effectiveness of fiscal policy and it is important to consider the interaction of fiscal and monetary policies while considering the integration of financial markets as the fiscal policy shocks propagate through an open economy.

Macroeconomic policy coordination is also important due to the inter-dependence between macroeconomic policies as reported in a recent study by Andrew, Libich, and Stehlik (2011). They found that the macroeconomic policies have spill-over effects on each other, and therefore even formulated independently, they are interdependent. In the medium term, coordination is more important in the context of ambition than conservatism. The coordination is important even when the policies have different objectives, as in non-coordination (Nash Equilibrium) they fall in "tug-of-war". They suggested that the coordination should not be limited to exchange of information but extended to details of each policy. However, they did not provide empirical support to their arguments nor any framework on policy coordination.

7.3. Absence of policy coordination and consequence

Macroeconomic policy interaction is also important for the reason that the conflicting and coordinating policies could have different implications for economy. In this context, Hughes Hallett and Libich (2007) showed that the absence of coordination is damaging for policies' credibility; moreover, it leads towards economic instability. They also declared it necessary to take fiscal and monetary policies' intentions into account to get a realistic picture of the effectiveness of the policies and policy institutions. Similarly, Chadha and Nolan (2007) investigated monetary and fiscal interaction and found that the design of optimal stabilization policy requires consideration of both monetary and fiscal plans. Moreover, "passive" fiscal policy necessitates large long run responses to inflation from monetary policy and aggressive monetary policy may result in an aggressive set of fiscal plans. Similarly, analysing the macroeconomic policy interaction in Romania, Talvan and Lupu (2010) argued that for economic and price stabilities, the monetary policy needs to be supplemented by fiscal policy. However, they went further and also cautioned that the non-coordination between policies could not only lead to economic instability but also social unrest.

A major factor leading to popularity of coordination between fiscal and monetary policies was adverse outcome in the case of conflict between policies, supported by the work of Leitemo (2004), as they cautioned that the Nash game between an inflation-targeting central bank and the fiscal policy authorities may lead to strong interest rate and exchange rate fluctuations due to a conflict over the output gap. Economic fluctuations can be harmful to the financial stability of an open economy; therefore, fiscal policy should support the monetary policy objective to a greater extent. Similarly, the study by Lombardo and Sutherland (2004) also supported the view that the fiscal and monetary policies should be coordinated for welfare gains in monetary union. Passive fiscal policy would be better than non-cooperative fiscal policy; however, non-cooperative fiscal policy can be a better choice if monetary policy is non-cooperative. Most of these studies had been on European Union economy which has its idiosyncratic policy framework, whereas in the UK, both monetary and fiscal policies are formulated at country level.

Analysing macroeconomic policy interaction in Croatian economy in an Econometric framework (Structural VECM model) empirical analysis by Rukelj (2009) showed that the fiscal policy and monetary policy showed negative impacts on each other, which showed that they moved in opposite directions; therefore, they were categorized as substitutes. However, they did not incorporate the outcome of conflicting stance, which might be due to the limited empirical framework.

Specific to an aspect of the financial sector (Forex markets), study by Giorgio and Nistico (2008) showed that in the case of counter cyclical fiscal policy, fiscal discipline plays an important role in the movement of exchange rates and Net Foreign Assets. "Most importantly, they cautioned that monetary authority's solo efforts to stabilize the financial sector (Net foreign Assets) fluctuation may results in high volatility of Forex." Similarly, appreciating the macroeconomic policy coordination, Hanif and Arby (2009) argued that the monetary and fiscal measures may conflict with each other; *poor coordination could lead to financial instability (interest rates and Forex volatility) high inflation and instable growth.* In their economy analysis of Pakistan, the Monetary and Fiscal Policy Coordination Board had been established for the purpose. However, in their later study, Arby and Hanif (2010) showed that the monetary policy stance has shown a poor coordination with fiscal policy in Pakistan. The institutional arrangements, i.e. establishment of Monetary and Fiscal Policies Coordination Board, could not contribute towards coordination. This finding would be interesting in the UK context as the Monetary Policy Committee (MPC) of the BoE responsible for formulation of monetary policy has representation of fiscal authority (HM Treasury); our empirical findings in this study would give us further insight if this arrangement had been successful for policy coordination.

7.4. Fiscal coordination for monetary policy objectives

The prime objective of a monetary authority is price stability; however, it may not be achievable by monetary policy on its own as a study by Beetsma and Jensen (2005) found that a negative supply shock raises the inflation and requires fiscal contraction. They also urged that there is more fiscal coordination needed in Europe as the fiscal policies are formulated in national interest. Similar study by Eichengreen (2005) criticized monetary and fiscal policy framework and SGP poor performance as the European Commission cannot fully enforce fiscal policy matters. They also urged for cooperation from fiscal authorities.

Analysing the influence of fiscal policy on monetary policy role, Doughty (1991) argued that the fiscal policy stance influences the role of monetary policy and inflation at two levels: (a) in the short term, fiscal policy affects the transmission of monetary policy (b) while in the long term, it affects the sustainability of monetary policy. The channels through which it influences monetary policy are domestic demand, interest rates, capital market effects and inflation effects. In practice, fiscal policy affects the monetary policy inflation-targeting strategy. Moreover, the sustainability of fiscal policy (debt stabilization) also affects monetary policy objective achievements in the long term. Therefore, it was urged that the fiscal stance should be considered for monetary policy price stability objective and overall policy framework. In a later study, investigating importance of fiscal cooperation for monetary policy, Forlati (2006) argued that in an open economy scenario, there is incentive for fiscal policy to use the tax instrument. Therefore, it was argued the fiscal policy cooperation is important for monetary policy. Later study with similar outcome by Schabert (2006) showed that the monetary policy objective of price stability relies on fiscal policy stance. The monetary policy should not behave aggressively towards achievement of its object, yet fiscal policy should also support (balanced budget) monetary policy objective.

In recent evidence, analysing the effects of monetary and fiscal policies' interaction in the context of fiscal policy effect on monetary role in price stability, investigation by Libich et al. (2011) showed that the effects of undisciplined fiscal policy can spill over to monetary policy role in price stability. It was suggested that the monetary policy should be made more explicit (inflation targeting) and show commitment (transparency and accountability) towards price stability. Their argument was that this mechanism would work as a partial substitute of monetary independence and coordination from the fiscal authority. However, their arguments require empirical validations as absence of coordination could bring sub-optimal results as acknowledged in a previous section. In the context of allocating leadership to a policy, analysing macroeconomic policy interaction in the EMU under three scenarios (Fiscal Lead, Monetary Lead and simultaneous policy formation), the study by Hallett (2008) concluded that the fiscal leadership along with instrument independence and central bank independence results in a better outcome for output, inflation and fiscal balances. Furthermore, it provides fiscal stability without engaging into fiscal rules. The results were robust against fiscal override, market reforms, globalization and changes in savings. However, it was cautioned that in case monetary authority gets leadership, target and instrument setting could cause adverse effects. Their suggestion to allocate leadership to fiscal policy supported its role even for price stability, a basic objective of monetary policy.

As briefly discussed earlier, a prominent limitation of monetary policy is the zero-bond or so-called liquidity trap. In practice, the BoE has set interest rates at an all time low (0.5%) since March 2009, which is almost zero-bonds. This limitation of monetary policy in the light of macroeconomic policy interaction was investigated by Dhami and Al-Nowaihi (2009). They showed that a target (inflation or output) for one policy-maker that ignores the incentives and constraints faced by the other policy-makers can lead to extremely poor outcomes. They argue that the fiscal policy expansion is fruitful in the liquidity trap when an independent central bank is not very effective. They also urged to avoid giving monetary and fiscal authorities high targets and suggested some dependence on costly fiscal policy in a liquidity trap. However, their arguments were based on a theoretical model without substantial empirical support.

7.5. Monetary coordination for fiscal objectives

Fiscal policy is often the mandate of a political administration which also has responsibility of economic growth, perhaps a superior and politically profitable objective. Analysing the economic and political aspects of macroeconomic policy interaction, Nordhaus (1994) argued that the deficit reduction can result in an electoral cycle (political effects) if monetary policy is non-cooperative and monetary authority may not offset the contractionary effects of fiscal policy. It was cautioned that the poorly timid deficit reduction can have adverse effects of real economy for a decade or longer; this deficit reduction can increase domestic and foreign investments, but if the monetary policy is non-cooperative (contractionary), there can be an adverse impact on economy. However, in case of monetary cooperation with simultaneous and sufficient monetary expansions (rate cuts), the gains are very high.

In a later study, Shively (2004) empirically showed that the monetary and fiscal policies' shocks dominate output fluctuations in the contractionary regime. It was urged that the policy-makers should focus on macroeconomic policy which minimizes the fluctuation of economy as well as policies which maximize the level of aggregate supply. Their findings supported the Keynesian view of stimulating aggregate demand by fiscal policy. Interestingly, they urged monetary policy cooperation for this purpose. Analogously, analysing effects of fiscal policy on output growth in the US economy, Zubairy (2009) showed the fiscal policy (Spending) effects economic growth. Most importantly, it was showed that the strong action of monetary policy can restrain the effects of fiscal policy. Therefore, these findings have important implications for simulation of economy and the financial sector by fiscal expansions and influence of monetary on their association.

The scope of monetary policy in fiscal efforts to stabilize economy was brought into analysis by Leith and Wren-Lewis (2006). Focusing on EU, they found that if the monetary authority does not adopt active inflation-targeting policy, it helps the fiscal authority to stabilize government debt and has a strong impact on output and inflation. Otherwise, conflicting policies can cause macroeconomic instability. They further emphasized that restriction on fiscal policy requires supporting active monetary policy. In EU if a fiscal authority cannot meet fiscal requirements, monetary authority has to adopt a passive stance to stabilize debt equilibrium by reducing debt cost. Seeing this complementarity of monetary policy for fiscal policy in the context of fiscal measures in post-financial crises (2008–09), Midthjell (2011) argued that the outcome of fiscal measures is not certain as it depends on choice of instruments and monetary stance. Moreover, there is limited space for fiscal policy to manoeuver due to the limits of public debt and deficit. On the same dimensions, investigating design of optimal monetary and fiscal stabilization policies, Ferrero (2009) showed that the optimal monetary policy takes the form of a flexible inflation targeting, while the optimal fiscal rule prevents national governments from creating inflationary expectations at the union level. Strict inflation targeting by the monetary authority in a currency union level and fiscal flexibility were recommended, as flexible debt targeting improves welfare. Although findings and recommendations may vary from a non-monetary union country like Britain with particularly economic environment, most importantly, fiscal flexibility may lead to excessive sovereign debt issues, e.g. Greek and Ireland cases as mentioned earlier.

The role of monetary and fiscal policies in the light of Consensus Assignment (monetary policy look after inflation and output, while fiscal does debt stabilization) was analysed by Kirsanova, Leith, and Lewis (2010). It was argued that in New Keynesian framework, monetary policy dominates fiscal policy for inflation and output stabilization, also in a situation when monetary policy cannot control inflation; therefore, it was suggested that this aspect focusing on monetary policy only should not be overstated. Moreover, they also supported the role of monetary policy in debt stabilization as it costs less than in the general perception and is effective in swift stabilization. Hence, fiscal policy does not dominate in debt stabilization. Though their analysis lacked empirical support, however, based on theoretical model, their augments established the importance of monetary policy in a fiscal role.

In the context of this study, the prime focus is on the financial sector rather than real economy, although the financial sector's stability is not a formal objective of fiscal authority; the unconventional steps (bailouts) taken by various fiscal authorities mentioned earlier could associate financial stability as an implicit object of fiscal authority.

7.6. Macroeconomic policy formulation: discretion vs. commitment

Policy formulation can be either by discretion of policy-makers or by following predetermined policy rules. There are mix arguments on the choice of discretion or commitment. In the critical analysis of the US macroeconomic policy, Tager and Van Lear (2001) urged that the fiscal and monetary policies' rules may not be as successful as there can be the problem of rigidity with policy rules. Policy rules do not help the people and organization left behind the market. There was no analytical model or data used in their research; therefore, their arguments were not supported by empirical evidences. More recent analysis by Adam and Billi (2011) showed that the discretionary macroeconomic policies cause high economic volatility and fiscal imbalance. To deal with this situation, they suggested a conservative monetary authority completely focused on inflation and determined after fiscal policy. However, if monetary policy is formulated before fiscal policy or simultaneously, it loses optimality, even in the case when fiscal policy overlooks its impact on a monetary policy role. Nevertheless, their assertion on non-cooperating monetary policy rules raises concerns about the adverse outcome in case of policy conflict as mentioned earlier.

Contrarily, we can also acknowledge some evidence in favour of commitment of macroeconomic policies; for instance, a study by Pappa and Vassilatos (2007) claimed that in a monetary union, constrained fiscal policy with clear rules and active monetary policy for inflation control is necessary for macroeconomic stability. Strict fiscal rules are effective in price stability and are also not that much unbearable as they have been thought. However, their arguments were opposing to the idea that the aggressive policy actions could hamper economic and financial stabilities.

7.7. Popularity of policy interaction in euro zone

Most of the study considering policy interaction had been focused on EMU; hence, Semmler and Zhang (2003) associated a whole aspect of literature on policy interaction to the Euro Zone. Prominent studies on the Euro zone, for instance Lombardo and Sutherland (2004), Beetsma and Jensen (2005), Leith and Wren-Lewis (2006) and Ferré (2008), have urged for coordination between macroeconomic policies as it positively affects real economy. They also cautioned that the conflicting policies can cause economic instability. Interestingly, the analysis by Muscatelli, Tirelli, and Trecroci (2004) declared that the interaction depends on the nature of the shocks hitting the economy, for the cases of output shocks, fiscal and monetary policies tend to act in harmony, whereas they are used as substitutes following inflation shocks. They also urged that the fiscal–monetary interaction depends on the model used to fit the data. The strategy of employing different methodological frameworks in this study (DSGE and Econometrics) will further elaborate any dependence of fiscal–monetary interaction on empirical framework.

As in the Euro Zone, macroeconomic policies are formulated at union (monetary) as well as national (fiscal) levels. The policy formulation at different levels has created a situation where there might be chances of conflicting policies. A study on conflict of monetary and fiscal policies in currency union by Sanchez (2010) showed that in a currency union due to the free ride of fiscal policies on monetary authority a high volatility in Money markets occurs (interest rates). Therefore, it was suggested that small countries should maintain their monetary sovereignty. Although they did not provide empirical support to their theoretical inferences, yet recent Euro crises is a clear evidence on this issue. Moreover, their arguments were supported by a study analysing the strategic interaction between monetary and fiscal policies in a currency union carried out by Grimm and Ried (2007). They found that in a currency union where monetary policy is formulated union wide, fiscal policy is formulated strategically at country level (heterogeneously) for national objectives. The best outcome is, in the case, when monetary and fiscal policies are agreed on optimal output and inflation level, however, they declared it unrealistic. Therefore, the preferences may not coincide leading to worst effects. It was suggested that the monetary authority should be given a lead role. They urged to reduce heterogeneity of fiscal policies for long-term economic stability in EMU. A later study on the same issue of country size asymmetries by Machado and Ribeiro (2010) showed that in a non-cooperative scenario, small countries lead to active fiscal policy, while large countries adopt a moderate fiscal stance. Furthermore, non-cooperation leads to improved (reduced) outcome for small (large) economies. However, they also supported the policy cooperation as it leads to overall better outcome on union level.

Heterogeneity of agents (fiscal authorities) in EMU has also created a complex situation for macroeconomic policy responses to a shock; it would be interesting to briefly acknowledge a study by Aarle, Garretsen, and Huart (2003) as they analysed monetary and fiscal policies' interaction in the light of spill-over effects between Euro area and non-Euro area economies. It was shown that the exchange rates' adjustment acts as an important stabilizer in the case of external shock to the Euro zone. However, in the case of internal and asymmetric shocks, it is not the case. They associated this feature with the common monetary policy by ECB. Moreover, they also acknowledged that in the case of symmetric shock and symmetric economic structure, it is easier to implement appropriate monetary policy than in case with asymmetries. Similarly, the heterogeneity in EU and its implications for policy interaction were investigated by Asensio (2007) using a Keynesian framework. It showed that the heterogeneity has important implications for policy interaction in monetary union. Contrary to symmetric, monetary–fiscal instruments respond to almost every shock in a heterogeneous environment. The interaction could result in inefficiencies, for instance, unemployment and inflation. It was suggested that monetary policy should focus on common effects of shocks, while fiscal authorities should focus on idiosyncratic shocks. They associated it with a subsidiary principle of macroeconomic policy in the Euro zone.

Particularly, in a scenario when substantial aspect of research on interaction is only focused on Euro zone (Semmler & Zhang, 2003) where monetary policy is formulated by the European Central Bank (ECB) at union level but fiscal policies are formulated at country level, it may not be appropriate to generalize the policy recommendation to an economy with monetary sovereignty. Perhaps, the role of macroeconomic policies and their interrelation in the EU has its own idiosyncratic nature and may not be appropriate to be generalized for economy like the British. In this context, on the basis of comprehensive study, Viegi (1999) concluded that in a monetary union, the default risk can be used as a tool to gain bail out, particularly by large countries, although this privilege may not be available to non-union members. It was also cautioned that ignoring the long-term consequences of fiscal indiscipline could cause high debt and inflation issues; therefore, sound fiscal policies should be adopted. Moreover, in a monetary union, fiscal policy has spill-over effects and it was cautioned that it could lead to high inflationary stance by all fiscal members. Although the independence of central bank was appreciated, however, its possible conflict with fiscal policy was considered counterproductive. The independence of central bank leads to active use of fiscal policy by the government as price becomes a less important objective and associated with monetary authority. Obviously, this could not be the case in the UK where fiscal authorities would have some concern about inflation due to country-wide scope.

7.8. Macroeconomic policy interaction and crowding out

Although the crowding out aspect of fiscal policy in stock and bond markets could not be evident, a study by Stemp (2001) on investigating Australian foreign exchange markets concluded that fiscal policy can affect the exchange rate temporarily as an expansionary fiscal policy is crowded out by exchange rate appreciation, while contractionary policy is crowded out by exchange rate depreciation. There were no empirical methods used; critical analysis was based on arguments stemming from theories and current economic situation. The important point here is if we add exchange rate crowding out to consumption and investment crowding out (mentioned earlier), are there some crowding out effects of fiscal policy on bond and stock markets? If so, how does interaction with monetary policy influence fiscal policy and the financial sector relationship? In this regard, the study on foreign exchange markets and macroeconomic policies by Cook and Devereux (2006) supported flexible exchange rate as it can increase performance of fiscal policy and capital inflow and also emphasized on coordination between fiscal and monetary policies.

7.9. Favouring non-coordination

Apart from frequent evidences in favour of macroeconomic coordination cited in previous paragraphs, there are also some studies, for instance Adam and Billi (2011), which argued that the fiscal policy could adopt a non-cooperative stance. Therefore, a conservative monetary authority should completely focus on its mandate of price stability and determine its stance after fiscal policy. Nevertheless, on this aspect, analysing interaction between monetary and fiscal policies in the EMU, a comparatively comprehensive theoretical framework (without empirical validation) by Staudinger (2003) showed that the monetary authority (ECB) is always better off if it takes a leading role (Stackelberg leader); however, for fiscal policy, it depends on the weights given to the inflation and output, which was non-cooperative (Nash) in most of the scenarios considered. Similarly, analysing the roles of optimal fiscal and monetary policies in economic stabilization, Beetsma and Jensen (2005) claimed that if the price rigidities between countries in a monetary union become equal, the stabilization is only done by monetary policy without requiring effort from fiscal policy. On the other hand, we must remember that a non-coordination scenario was discouraged in the same framework (Game Theory), prominently by Leitemo (2004) and Chadha and Nolan (2007) as they cautioned that the Nash game between monetary and fiscal authorities could be harmful to economy; therefore, fiscal policy should support the monetary policy objective.

Some support to independent macroeconomic policy formulation was given by Leciejewicz (2010) while analysing the need for macroeconomic coordination vs. independence in the light of theoretical framework (Game Theory). It was shown that there is also a possibility of a different situation, where the independent decision between monetary and fiscal authorities may not lead to an adverse (Pareto non-optimal) scenario. However, it was also stated that the choice of instrument and policy mix depends on the effectiveness of that policy or instrument and background economic scenario. Most importantly, the idea of coordination could not be fully rejected in this study, as it was also acknowledged that for higher output growth, expansionary monetary policy should be coupled with tight fiscal stance.

Instead of monetary–fiscal coordination, a comparative analysis between monetary–fiscal and fiscal–fiscal policies' coordination in EMU was made by Carlberg (2004). It was argued that the cooperation between fiscal authorities (German and French) and monetary authorities leads to full employment. The monetary independence and cooperation between fiscal authorities also leads to full employment; therefore, it was urged that the cooperation is not compulsory as the required output could also achieved without cooperation. Although their assertions lacked empirical support, in a non-union country, for instance UK, there is only one fiscal authority; thus, we cannot go far on this dimension.

Analysing the implications of macroeconomic policy coordination in the long and short terms in EMU, Hagen and Mundschenk (2002) argued that in the long run, the price stability can be achieved without coordination as tight fiscal policy in future would offset the expansionary (inflationary) stance of the present fiscal policy. However, this argument raises a few doubts as what if an automatic stabilizer would not work in the long term? Future taxes could not balance the books and what if inflation could not be stabilized? Nevertheless, they implicitly answered these concerns by acknowledging the need for coordination in the short term as lack of it could lead to adverse economic conditions. Therefore, it needs to have consensus on aggregate output and price level in EMU between monetary and fiscal authorities. They also declared current level and arrangements of policy coordination insufficient.

An important implication of FTPL is that the "Inflation is also a Fiscal phenomena". The validity of FTPL and monetarist doctrine was carried out by McCallum and Nelson (2006). They showed that both interest rates' rules and money stock rules share the opinion that the inflation is also a function of fiscal policy. However, they suggested that detailed coordination between macroeconomic policies is not needed as monetary authority can achieve price stability at its own. Nevertheless, their unwarranted assertion raises a major concern that if fiscal policy also has a permanent impact on economy, how could monetary policy achieve its objectives on its own in case of a policy conflict?

A study in this context was performed by Buti, Roeger, and Veld (2001); their theoretical analysis and numerical simulation showed that the complementarity (coordination) and substitutability of macroeconomic policies and their preferences with respect to each other depend on shock hitting the economy. In the case of supply shocks, they move in opposite ways, while in demand shock, they move in same direction; although their comprehensive analysis favoured coordination to some extent, yet they associated coordination as dependent on shock hitting the economy which implies *that the coordination is vulnerable to the exogenous factors.*

Regarding the issue to coordinate or not to coordinate, Niemann and Hagen's (2008) argument is that the independent monetary authorities are reluctant to coordinate with fiscal authorities. To support their point of view, they gave the reference of European Central Bank's (ECB) first President Duisenberg (2003); there is clearly no scope for coordination between monetary and fiscal policies, If that is really the case, the practises by the monetary authorities are not in line with the researchers. Nevertheless, supportive arguments on non-coordination were given by Nyamonga, Sichei, and Mutai (2008) while analysing the behaviour of macroeconomic policies in Kenya. It was reported that during the time horizon of study, the monetary and fiscal policies have shown coordination in a few periods while some periods lacked coordination. They found evidence of monetary policy dominance and declared it as a cause of less harmful outcome during times of non-cooperation. On the other hand, a study on providing evidence on practises of macroeconomic policy coordination in the USA, Astudillo showed that most of the time policies were complementary to each other for stability. We would see this phenomenon in the context of UK economy in the next section.

They majority of studies on economic policy interaction have urged for coordination between policies. Followed by many others, a landmark study was by Dixit and Lambertini (2001, 2003) which gave the thought of "Symbiosis"; how to coincide for the financial sector's stability is still an un-answered question. Moreover, when we compare the empirical work on macroeconomic policy coordination, there are differences of opinion. von Thadden (2004), Schabert (2006) and Ferrero (2009) urged to avoid very strict monetary policy for inflation control and emphasized on fiscal discipline. Similarly, passive monetary and expansionary fiscal policy was suggested by Traum and Yang (2011) for increased output. Contrarily, Barnett (2005), Pappa and Vassilatos (2007) and very recently Davig, Leeper, and Walker (2011) urged for constrained fiscal policy but strict monetary policy for the same objectives. Focusing on real economy (inflation and output), these studies have conflicting conclusions. Obviously, in the light of these contradictory arguments, we cannot suggest a solution for the financial sector of a particular economy unless a comprehensive empirical analysis is performed.

7.10. Interaction and institutional arrangements

The significance of intuitional arrangements for an individual policy role has been acknowledged earlier; however, its implications in addition to macroeconomic events could affect the way macroeconomic policy interacts. In this context, analysing macroeconomic policy interaction in Indonesia, Mochtar (2004) found that the Asian Financial Crises (1997) lead central bank to run Quasi Fiscal Activity (QFA). They also briefly looked into the central bank independence and urged that the central bank has given independence in Indonesia, yet it demands fiscal discipline in controlling inflation. They cautioned that the fiscal indiscipline could put the inflation-targeting effort by monetary authority in vein. Moreover, it causes tight monetary policy which leads to further appreciation of exchange rates and results in further inflation. Therefore, they urged on fiscal policy cooperation in inflation control, despite monetary independence. However, briefly acknowledging the role of intuitional arrangements in macroeconomic policy interaction, Javed and Sahinoz (2005) argued that the fiscal authorities have conflicting incentives, targets and objectives. Therefore, they urged allocation of intuitional arrangement to monetary policy with regard to fiscal stance. Nevertheless, they also agreed on the idea of coordination for external and internal balances in economy.

There are conflicting opinions on independence of monetary authority; analysing the policy interaction in Russia, Merzlyakov (2011) argued that the independence of a central bank does not considerably influence policy impact. The macroeconomic policy interaction was most influential under fiscal policy as Stackelberg and cooperation and Cournot interaction (complete non-coordination) lead to adverse economic outcome. Contrarily, a similar study with an advantage of empirical support on the effects of setting an inflation target for monetary policy on performance of macroeconomic policies by Franta, Libich, and Stehlik (2011) showed that the fiscal indiscipline could affect monetary policy role; however, a legislative inflation target could help monetary policy control excessive fiscal spending. Moreover, the explicit inflation targeting could also lead to fiscal discipline.

Analysing the macroeconomic policy interaction under various exchange rates' regime, Claeys (2004) showed that the expansionary fiscal policies for output growth cause monetary policy to adopt a tighter stance, particularly in countries with a flexible exchange rate. However, in countries with fixed exchange rates, the results were not significant. It was also emphasized that the shifts in exchange rate policy regime are important. A similar and more recent study on macroeconomic policy exchange rates and implication of monetary independence was carried out by Park (2008). Interestingly, it was argued that often the exchange rate policy was not affected by monetary and fiscal policies; the central bank degree of independence does not affect price level. In specific to the UK economy, there have been prominent changes in exchange rate mechanism, for instance, abandoning the Exchange Rate Mechanism (ERM) in 1992 which may have important implications for policy coordination and interaction.

The importance of institutional design and arrangement in the light of various studies has also been acknowledged in literature review chapters; however, we would very briefly revisit a few evidences to refresh the memory of the reader and to establish its relevance with subject study. The addition of institutional arrangements aspects is motivated by the arguments by Srinivasan, Jain, and Ramachandran (2009), that the institutions must be designed so that the central bank's commitment to its objectives is not in doubt. In this context, the financial stability has not been a prime objective of any central bank, at least not explicitly, to the best of our knowledge; however, if intuitional design affects the outcome of macroeconomic policy, it raises the question about its implications for the financial sector.

One of the major institutional arrangement been made during the time of study was independence of the Bank of England. This may sound a simple case of giving autonomy to monetary authority to achieve its prime objective for price stability; perhaps, it was the explicit good intention. Nevertheless, it was rather a more complex and vital change in the functioning of the BoE. Specifically, subject decision resulted in a big shift in intuitional design and certain responsibilities related with financial stability, e.g. banking sector supervision and management of sovereign debt were transferred to Financial Serves Authority (FSA) and DMO. *The most significant are: a) the supervision of banking sector which was transferred to Financial Services Authority (FSA) and b) the responsibility of sovereign debt stabilization which was transferred to Debt Management Office (DMO).* These are the major shifts in responsibilities and authorities with an intention to increase the efficiency of policy formulation; however, these changes may have important implications for the financial sector. Perhaps the recent or post-financial crises development and revival of the BoE role in financial stability is something that requires plentiful attention. The Financial Services Act (2012) leads to major reform in the form of formulation of FPC. The prime objective of the Committee is to identify, monitor and take action to reduce systemic risk for the protection and resilience of the British financial sector. In addition to that the Prudential Regulation Authority (PRA) as a part of the BoE also started to function from April 2013 with the objection of banking sector supervision. In specific to effectiveness of macroeconomic policies and financial stability, these intuitional changes raise questions whether the withdrawal of earlier cited responsibilities of financial supervision from the BoE influenced macroeconomic policy role.

In this context, a study by Weymark (2007) declared that a fully independent central bank is only concerned with achievement of economic objectives, whereas fiscal authority may influence monetary framework. However, we need to validate these assertions and extend them to the financial sector. We can report some evidence on this aspect in a US case; Lobo (2000) concluded that the Federal Reserve policy of immediate disclosure has resulted in change of volatility of stock market from before to after the announcement of monetary policy decisions. Later investigation by Lobo, Darrat, and Ramchander (2006) also acknowledged that the Federal Reserve disclosure policy has influenced the impact of monetary policy on foreign exchange markets. However, we need to see it in the context of Optimal Policy Combination as well as both financial market (stock and bond). In specific to our case, Bank of England has been independent since 1997 which may have important implications for macroeconomic policy interaction and the financial sector. With regard to the macroeconomic policy interaction and real economy, we can associate the remarks by Dixit and Lambertini (2001) as they argued that in the case of disagreement, the outcome can be influenced by institution design.

Despite the fact that we could not evidence, many studies on policy coordination in the light of institutional design, yet there is a work done by Arby and Hanif (2010). It was showed that the monetary policy stance has shown a poor coordination with fiscal policy in Pakistan. The institutional arrangements, i.e. establishment of Monetary and Fiscal Policies Coordination Board, could not contribute towards coordination. This finding would be interesting in the UK context as MPC of the BoE responsible for formulation of monetary policy has representation of Fiscal authority (HM Treasury); our empirical findings in this study would give us further insight if this arrangement has been successful for policy coordination.

In addition to the independence of the BoE, a major change in the institutional framework of the BoE was an explicit target of price stability by keeping inflation to 2% of Consumer Price Index (CPI) or *Target 2.0*. On this aspect, Haldane and Read (2000) investigated the role of monetary policy under the influence of inflation targeting and its effects on bond market (yield curve). They found that introduction of inflation targeting in UK has significantly decreased the effects of monetary policy surprises on yield curve. They associated it with the increased transparency of monetary policy due to inflation targeting. Yet, we are seeing this shift in association with addition of interaction with fiscal policy stock market.

If we review the literature on the performance of policy framework, institutional design of monetary policy in the UK was praised by Bhundia and Donnell (2002), arguing that independence of central bank and institutional arrangements is based on the principles of credibility, flexibility and democratic legitimacy. Therefore, the independence of the BoE has not only increased the effectiveness of monetary policy, it has increased the fiscal coordination. Their arguments were logical, but there was no empirical evidence. In addition, this assertion also requires validity for the financial sector and most importantly its combination with fiscal policy.

More recently, analysing institutional changes, Osborn and Sensier (2009) found that there was a strong evidence of structural break coinciding with the introduction of inflation targeting. They declared the inflation targeting as more important change than the independence of BoE. Similarly, Lildholdt and Wetherilt (2004) concluded that the ability of market participants to predict monetary policy stance by BoE has been improved. Later, analysing economic and structural changes in the UK economy (output, inflation and Forex), under different monetary regimes, Baumeister, Liu, and Mumtaz (2010) found that there had been a shift in response of monetary policy from economic growth and exchange rates' fluctuation to inflation at present. They also acknowledged that economic fluctuation was less frequent after 1992 until recent past, though they did not associate it with any institutional aspect. The subject study urges to see their assertions in the light of comprehensive and alternative empirical frameworks and its implications for the financial sector.

7.11. Tinbergen principle not asserting a solution

An important aspect in policy interaction of combination is the Tinbergen Principle, according to which there should be equal numbers of instruments and targets. Therefore, one could argue that the idea of policy combination is based on Tinbergen thoughts. In this context, there are very interesting arguments by Hughes Hallett et al. (2011). They argued that "Let us note that **there will be no additional policy instrument to achieve the financial stability goal** (in the spirit of Tinbergen, 1952). Nevertheless, they also urged on the joint use of policies to achieve optimal results and warned that **it is never socially optimal for monetary policy to do the job on its own**." Furthermore, the ability of macroeconomic policies to stabilize the household and public debt depends on features of economy and preferences of monetary and fiscal policies about output and inflation. In some cases, both policies could be used while in some situations, one single policy is beneficial. It was also warned that the both policies could have a moral hazard of being not very active and passing the responsibility to other for which they used to term "Passing the Buck". Similarly, discoursing the generalization of the Tinbergen Principle, Agenor and Silva (2012, p. 6) argued that the "Tinbergen's principle is concerned with the existence and location of a solution to the system; it does not assert that any given set of policy responses will, in fact, lead to that solution. To assert this, it is necessary to investigate the stability properties of a dynamic system." In simple words, one policy combination does not fit all and Tinbergen does not suggest any policy combination either. Most importantly, it is not only the number of instruments, as some policy instruments might be more effective than others in particular scenarios (state dependency).

7.12. Interaction and the financial sector (stock and bond markets)

Studies on macroeconomic policy interaction acknowledged in the above lines have been only focused on real economy (inflation and output) and none of them brought the financial sector (stock and bond markets) into consideration, despite its accepted importance. The very first and probably only study which jointly considered fiscal and monetary policies in the financial sector analysis was carried out by Jansen et al. (2008). Though they did not suggest any optimal combination of policies, they reported that the relationship between monetary policy and the US stock market could be influenced by fiscal policy. They showed that the impact of monetary policy on the asset markets varies with the state of fiscal deficits or surpluses. Their empirical results were consistent with the notion of strong interdependence between monetary and fiscal policies. Perhaps, they also declared it as the first effort in this dimension, but with limited empirical framework (semi-parametric regression); policy interaction or combination was not considered thoroughly and the study was only focused on analysing the impact of monetary policy on the financial market under fiscal policy influence. Semi-parametric regression contains assumptions which could lead to inconsistency and misspecification. Equally focusing on both monetary and fiscal policies, this study offers DSGE and VAR models which are very comprehensive frameworks. Most importantly, this study aims to find optimal policy combination for financial stability (stock and bond markets) in the light of state dependency. Perhaps, the US stock markets have certain characteristic which make them different from the UK as identified by Yang et al. (2009), i.e. risk and behaviour/pattern of markets. In the next section, we would briefly review the financial sector (stock and bond markets) in the UK and evidence the performance of macroeconomic policies.

8. Conclusions

The macroeconomic policy is a vast subject and an important aspect of macroeconomics, perhaps due to its importance as well as its national and international implications it has been given significant attention to. Moreover, a substantial review of macroeconomic policy literature in the above lines indicates that the performance of the financial sector has crucial implications for real economy. The volatility in financial markets could hamper the economic growth and objective of macroeconomic policy-makers. It has also been acknowledged that the macroeconomic policies could influence the financial sector. Hence, due to the importance of financial stability for the real economy and effectiveness of macroeconomic policies for the financial sector, it creates scope of active policy responses to the financial sector's dynamics. Nevertheless, it is also evident that the solo efforts of a macroeconomic policy have not been very successful and often bring some adverse side effects.

Therefore, it is absolutely vital to consider both monetary and fiscal policies and analyse how their combination could positively influence the financial sector.

In addition, there are three more aspects we need to consider. Firstly, we are to consider the intuitional changes in macroeconomic policy framework. The existing studies have evidenced significant effects and implications of intuitional changes in the role of macroeconomic policies. We need to look at this factor in the context of macroeconomic policy interaction and its influence on financial markets. Secondly, there is evidence on the shift of monetary policy and financial market relationship after a major macroeconomic event. Therefore, we also need to consider the implications of such events on optimality of policy combination for financial stability. Thirdly, studies in the existing literature on the subject have either used Econometric or General Equilibrium framework and Frequentist or Bayesian approach. However, both frameworks and empirical approaches have their own advantages and limitations. Some recent studies have also urged the use of alternative approaches. Therefore, in specific to the subject, we are incorporating both empirical frameworks and approaches for the validation and robustness of our results.

9. Macroeconomic policies' framework and the financial sector in the UK

Macroeconomic policies in subject economy are formulated by separate institutions at country level; this is in contrast to the Euro zone; therefore, we can expect more national interest and perhaps country-specific context. In the UK, Her Majesty's Treasury (HMT) is responsible for the formulation and implementation of fiscal policy, whereas monetary policy is autonomously formulated by the BoE since its independence in May 1997. Moreover, the BoE has an explicit price stability objective, i.e. 2% rate of inflation (consumer price index), which is targeted by interest rate instrument. The decisions on monetary policy are made by the MPC on monthly bases. In case the inflation target is missed by 1% below or above the target rate, the Governor of the BoE has to write a letter to the Chancellor of the Exchequer to explain the causes. The MPC consists of nine members including five members from the BoE and four external members selected by the Chancellor of the Exchequer.

Before we go towards macroeconomic policy interaction, it is worth mentioning here that the performance of macroeconomic policy framework in subject economy is controversial as Haldane (1997), Bakhshi, Haldane, and Hatch (1997) and Osborn and Sensier (2009) appreciated its role, whereas Henry (2001) hugely criticized the performance of macroeconomic policies. In a later study, Lee (2009) also joined the criticism arguing that the fiscal policy rules[13] were violated and monetary policy effectiveness was undermined by financial market volatility and economic instability. Though arguments by the latter lack empirical evidence, this study would view them in the light of comprehensive empirical framework, the financial sector's performance and scope for policies interaction in this context.

Among prominent critics of monetary and fiscal policies' performance in the UK, Henry (2001) argued that the present framework of macroeconomic policies does not work well in the case of adverse shocks to the economy. Fiscal policy had been loosed which has caused the monetary policy to adopt a tight stance to control inflation. Policy framework has caused the appreciation in exchange rates which have resulted in worsening of current account balance. Furthermore, the stability of inflation was associated with international outlook and if the world inflation gets worse, the UK would be strongly affected. It was also suggested that there is need of a council of economic advisors which can analyse the fiscal stance and publish its appraisals. Though the conclusion was not supported by empirical evidences, arguments were quite logical. Analogously, later study by Angeriz and Arestis (2007) criticized tight monetary policy; they concluded that inflation targeting has been successful in the context of HM treasury target level and inflation had been "locked in". Yet, the inflation had also been low in a non-inflation targeting country like the USA. Furthermore, they also declared globalization as a cause of low inflation, instead of monetary policy success.

Macroeconomic policies also have political implications in this context; Lee (2009) criticizing the government argued that the UK economy had started moving towards recession before the financial crises. Moreover, the claim of monetary policy effectiveness was undermined by the financial market and economic volatility. Although the arguments made by Lee (2009) lacked empirical support, the behaviour of financial markets depicted in Figure 3 provides support to these arguments. The London Stock Exchange (LSE) showed frequent hideous episodes of sharp decline from the last quarter of 2008 till the first quarter 2009.

The Green line represents Quarterly, Blue line represents the daily, while Red line represents monthly averages of FTSE-100 index. It took market several quarters with very volatile behaviour to return close to the pre-crises level. As seen in Figure 5, the stock market started slow recovery at the end of the first quarter in 2009, almost the same time when the BoE carried out Quantitative Easing (QE) and Asset purchases.

Nevertheless, the bond market has also responded to the financial crises and macroeconomic policy responses as we can evidence in Figure 6.

There is negative yield on 10-year Gilts, a clear representation of expansionary monetary policy and Quantitative Easing (QE) which have suppressed the yield on gilts. It implies that although the government could borrow at negative real interest rates, saving household would get negative real returns.

Coming back towards the theoretical arguments, Lee (2009) declared that the British model of competitive policy failed as fiscal policy's Golden rule (borrow to invest public investment not consumption) and sustainable investment rule (Debt-to-GDP 40%) were violated. Importantly, the

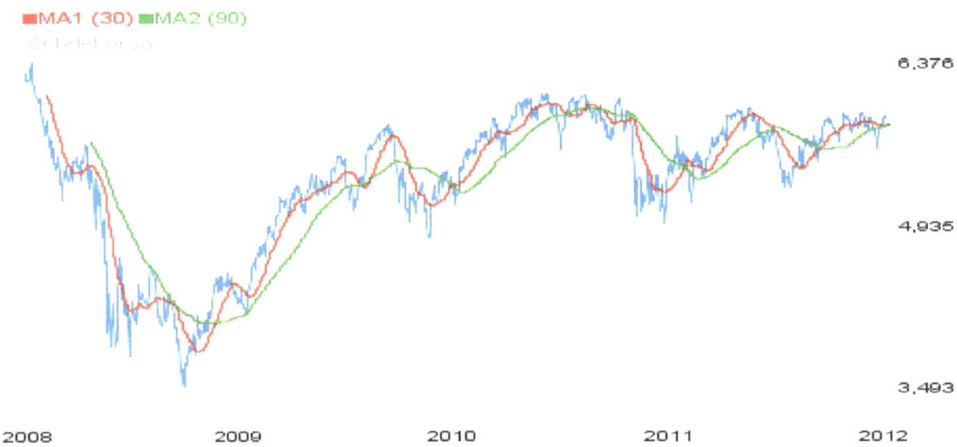

Figure 5. FTSE 100 (July 2007 to July 2012).

Note: 90 Days Moving Avg (green line), 30 Days Moving Avg (red line), and Daily Avg (blue line).
Source: London Stock Exchange.

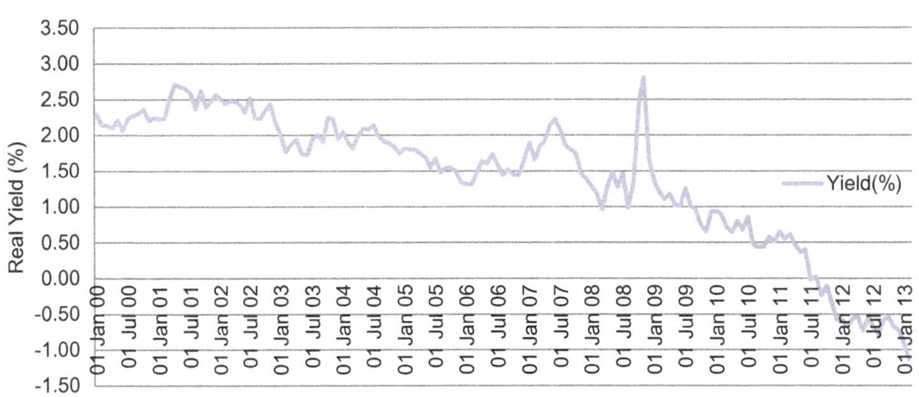

Figure 6. Real yield on 10-year Gilts, January 2000–February 2013.

Source: Bank of England (2012).

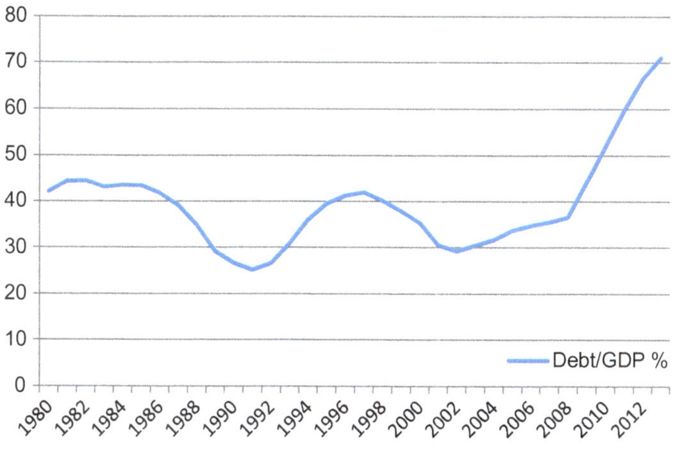

Figure 7. UK sovereign debt in comparison with income.

Source: Office of National Statistics (2012).

crucial aspect was risk-based financial regulation which caused the economy to be badly hurt during financial crises, although the blame had been put on the American subprime mortgage market for a year. Similarly, a study on stabilization of business cycle volatility as a key motive of economic policies in the UK, Atanasova and Gang (2008) declared that there was no significant evidence on declined business cycle volatility. Arguments by Lee (2009) lacked empirical support as no statistical method was used; however, the aforementioned outlook of the financial sector and below-cited fiscal situation prominent in Figure 7 support their arguments.

This study aims to provide empirical evidence to argument and make concluding remarks without any political context. In the next few sections, we will review some studies on the role of macroeconomic policies and their interaction.

10. Monetary policy role

The role of monetary policy has been very significant for the UK economy; in this context, a study by Beladi and Samanta (1988) is worth mentioning. They analysed the relation between money growth and output growth in the light of Rational Expectation Structural Neutrality (RESN) hypothesis, which emphasizes that the only unanticipated money growth affects economic activity. Interestingly, empirical findings did not support RESN hypothesis which has the implication that monetary policy effective in the UK, whether it is anticipated or unanticipated by market participants.

In practice, the response of stock and bond markets to monetary policy in the UK is acknowledged by the Bank of England (2011), stating that the bonds and equities are inversely related to monetary policy (interest rates) due to the high rates on which future income is discounted. In the macroeconomic policy literature, Bredin el al. (2005) showed that the contractionary monetary policy leads to a negative response in various sectors of the stock market. More recently, Gregoriou, Kontonikas, MacDonald, and Montagnoli (2009) also showed that stock market response to contractionary monetary policies is negative, which has become positive during the credit crisis. "They associated it with limitation of monetary policy, i.e. further rate cuts; this situation provides rationale to bring in fiscal policy which is the premise of this study."

In the light of the literature reviewed so far, it has been observed that there has not been substantial research performed on the interaction of economic policies, in particular to UK's economic and financial environments. Yet, there are a few studies which we could acknowledge. Interesting, in the context of financial sector, Kontonikas and Montagnoli (2006) urged that due to wealth effects and inefficiency of markets, responses of asset prices should be incorporated in monetary policy formulation. However, it is not part of practise so far. In addition, Allen and Yang (2004) found that apart from the dividend growth and monetary policy, the stock prices are also affected by un-explained innovation. There was no further investigation to analyse the unexplained innovation which might be due to several factors including fiscal policy.

11. Fiscal policy role

In specific to subject economy, the role of contractionary fiscal policy was investigated by Barrell and Riley (2004). Their simulation and empirical analysis showed that the economy seems imbalanced; however, a fiscal contraction (spending) without increase in taxes would affect exchange rate (depreciation) markets and money markets (lower interest rates). In contrast, if there had been fiscal expansion (spending) accompanied by the increases in taxes, the effectiveness of fiscal policy decreases. Their analysis prominently supported the limited role of fiscal policy; however, it was contrary to Keynesian philosophy of active fiscal responses when the economy is in recession and financial volatility. Earlier to them, a similar study by Alec Chrystal and Dowd (1989) performed in the light of various economic schools of thoughts showed that contrary to Keynesian ideology, the fiscal expansion had negative impacts on economy output. Their results support the Real Business Cycle theory. On the other hand, a quite interesting and recent study by Creel, Monperrus-Veroni, and Saraceno (2009) found that the New Classical Macroeconomic framework which opposes the Keynesian idea of active fiscal policy has illuminated the importance of fiscal policy. They argued that the fiscal policy may dominate the monetary policy without having any negative influence on economic stability. Moreover, the effectiveness of Fiscal policy (Keynesian Multiplier) has been increased over time in France and the UK. They also considered it disappointing that even the accepted importance of fiscal policy central bank dominance, rules and fiscal constraints has not changed. Their arguments received further support by an investigation made by Malley, Philippopoulos, and Woitek (2009), who showed that the dependence of counter cyclical fiscal policy on output and debt dynamics causes indeterminacy, whereas under counter cyclical fiscal policy, welfare gains were greater. Therefore, they recommended active counter cyclical fiscal policy in countries like the UK. Nevertheless, a study by Kirsanova, Stehn, and Vines (2005) concluded that best outcome is achieved when both fiscal and monetary policies perform together, which is also the theme of this study.

12. Macroeconomic policy interaction in the UK

An extensive review of literature on macroeconomic policies shows that the monetary–fiscal policy interaction, even their joint analysis, had not been popular, in particular to the UK economic environment; perhaps it has been more popular in the EMU. Pointing out this fact, Semmler and Zhang (2003) associated a whole aspect of existing macroeconomic policy interaction literature to EMU, declaring it crucial for Euro economy.

Among very rare studies from the UK which jointly considered the role of monetary and fiscal policies, an investigation by Kirsanova et al. (2005) which was limited to a theoretical framework (no empirical validation) argued that the best outcome is achieved when macroeconomic policies are cooperative and monetary policy perform actively for economic stabilization (inflation, output and debt). Results were consistent when fiscal policy performs actively, acknowledging monetary policy does not play Nash (non-cooperatively). In their theoretical framework, they only acknowledged behaviour of the output and inflation under macroeconomic policy interaction and did not perform any empirical analysis. Moreover, the financial sector could not gain any attention. Later study by Creel et al. (2009) showed that the fiscal policy may dominate monetary policy without having any negative influence on economic stability. Nevertheless, they only focused on the role of fiscal policy and little insight was given into the monetary policy behaviour; moreover, no optimal combination of policies was suggested either.

The implications for monetary–fiscal interaction for economic stabilization in a rather recent study were investigated by Blake and Kirsanova (2011). They showed that in case when there is conservative monetary authority, the strategic action by fiscal authority could lead to welfare losses; interestingly, they gave a notion that having two policy-makers could lead to conflict and stabilization bias. They argued that the strategic behaviour of fiscal authority may have costs which should also be considered. Moreover, the monetary policy should also support if there is high debt. In a non-cooperative scenario, the Nash leads to high volatility. The main conclusion of their comprehensive analysis was the coordination between policies. Yet, most importantly, recent study by Fragetta and Kirsanova (2010) showed that in the UK, macroeconomic policies act in non-cooperative manner. Although they did not mention the cause of non-cooperation and recommendation for cooperation, their findings are distressing as the poor financial and economic scenarios could be attributed to non-cooperation between macroeconomic policies.

13. Institutional changes in policy framework

An important aspect of this study is the state dependency of optimal policy combination. In this regard, there have been a few remarkable changes in the intuitional arrangements of macroeconomic policy framework in the last few decades. Significant among them are withdrawal from Exchange Rate Mechanism (1992), independence of the BoE and formulation of MPC (1997), inflation targeting (1992 and 2003) and Fiscal Responsibility Act (2010). Although, it would be quite interesting to see the implications of all the institutional changes for optimal policy combination, the most important and interesting change in the context of this study might be independence of the BoE in 1997. Apparently, it is just giving autonomy to monetary authority with the intention that it could focus on its prime object of price stability. Nevertheless, there were some vital responsibilities related to financial stability, which were transferred from the Bank of England to other institutions. "The most important are: (1) the supervision of the banking sector was transferred to Financial Services Authority (FSA) and (2) the responsibility to stabilize sovereign was debt transferred to Debt Management Office (DMO)." These are major shifts in responsibilities and authorities from the BoE to FSA and DMO. Perceptibly, the rationale of these arrangements would be to increase the efficiency of policy formulation; however, these changes may have important implications for UK's financial sector and economy as we have provided some evidence on other economics earlier.

Among the studies which analysed the impact of intuitional changes in macroeconomic policy framework in the UK, Haldane and Read (2000) investigated the role of monetary policy under the influence of inflation targeting and its effects on the bond market (yield curve). They found that introduction of inflation targeting in the UK has significantly decreased the effects of monetary policy surprises on yield curve. They associated it with the increased transparency of monetary policy due to inflation targeting. Yet, we are seeing this shift in association with the addition of interaction with fiscal policy. Institutional design of macroeconomic policy in the UK was praised by Bhundia and Donnell (2002) who argued that independence of central bank in the UK and institutional arrangements are based on the principles of credibility, flexibility and democratic legitimacy. Therefore, the independence of the BoE has not only increased the effectiveness of monetary policy, it has increased the fiscal coordination. Their arguments were logical but there was no empirical evidence.

Analysing institutional changes, Osborn and Sensier (2009) found that the there was strong evidence of a structural break coinciding with the introduction of inflation targeting. They declared the inflation targeting as a more important change than the independence of the BoE. Similarly, Lildholdt and Wetherilt (2004) concluded that the ability of market participants to predict monetary policy stance by the BoE has been improved. Later, analysing economic and structural changes in the UK economy (output, inflation and Forex) under different monetary regimes, Liu and Mumtaz (2010) found that there had been a shift in response of monetary policy from economic growth and exchange rates (1975s) to inflation at present. They also acknowledged that economic fluctuation was less frequent after 1992 until recent past, though they did not associate it with any institutional aspect. The subject study would see their assertions in the light of comprehensive and alternative empirical frameworks and its implications for the financial sector.

14. Macroeconomic events and shift in policy effectiveness

The second context of state dependency in which we analyse the impact of optimal policy combination is the major macroeconomic event and resulting shift in policy effects. In specific to subject economy and the financial sector, we have three major events in the last two decades which include the Collapse of Exchange Rate Mechanism (ERM), Dotcom bubble or Stock Exchange Crash of (2002) and earlier acknowledged Global Financial Crises and Lehman Brother's bankruptcy (2008) which severely hit global as well as the British stock market. It must be acknowledged here not many studies have considered the implications of these events on macroeconomic policy role, particularly in subject economy. Nevertheless, we have some evidence on this aspect; a study by Gregoriou et al. (2009) analysed the influence of stock exchange crash on monetary policy effectiveness. A structural break was found in between contractionary monetary policy and stock market relationship which changed from negative to positive in the post-financial crisis (2008) period. "They associated it with limitation of monetary policy, i.e. further rate cuts; this situation provides rationale to bring in the fiscal policy which is the premise of this study." They also declared their study as the first to consider the shift in monetary policy and stock relationship in the light of financial crises (2008). However, there are two major aspects we must consider: (1) as cited earlier, the monetary policy, particularly interest rate instrument in Britain, is in the Liquidity Trap since March 2009; (2) in the light of enormous arguments in favour of joint policy analysis, it is vital to consider fiscal policy as well. Therefore, in subject study, we are considering both policies and in context of major economic events, it would be helpful to understand which policy instrument is more useful and how to optimally combine them for financial stability.

15. Alternative empirical frameworks

Macroeconomic policy literature shows that either GE modelling or Econometrics techniques have been used for empirical analysis. Acknowledging this fact, Bhattarai (2011) urged that the DSGE and Econometrics should be considered complementary techniques rather than competitive. In Econometrics framework, structural parameters are estimated from time series data to make forecasts about the impact of economic policies; however, the Econometric models do not focus enough on the optimization behaviour of household and firm. This deficiency can be complimented by DSGE framework which generates time series on which forecasts of Econometrics analysis can be assessed. The idea of using both frameworks in this study is also supported by comprehensive analysis of Consolo et al. (2009) as they concluded that the combination of DSGE model and FAVAR (Econometric) dominates other frameworks. Nevertheless, we are suggesting alternative frameworks as well as alternative empirical approaches, i.e. Frequentist and Bayesians, in addition to a brief account in introductory section. On the ability of empirical methods to lead to a meaningful conclusion, Chari (2010, p. 1) made very concise and remarkable comments that "the models are purposeful simplifications that serve as guides to the real world; they are not the real world". Thus, in effort to reach to the best estimation and simulation of our optimal policy combination, subject study is considering both empirical framework and approaches. Though this element makes this study prominent from the previous research acknowledged in above lines, in particular to the UK, there is no evidence of this strategy in the subject area of research.

16. Conclusions

In specific to the, under analysis, UK, the macroeconomic policy interaction has not been very popular among researchers; perhaps, much of the space being given to the EMU. The financial sector of the UK also has great significance and contribution towards the economy and national income. Since financial crises (2008–2009), the financial markets, particularly bond and stock markets, have been very volatile; perhaps, the high volatility of the financial sector was the basic factor resulting in the formulation of the FPC by the Bank of England. Hence, on the academic and research side, it requires having deep insight into the role of macroeconomic policies and their interaction for the financial sector of the UK.

Moreover, there have been substantial intentional arrangements made into the macroeconomic policy framework in the last few years. The last two decades have also seen extraordinary major macroeconomic and financial events. It would also be interesting to analyse the implications of these institutional changes and events for optimal macroeconomic policy combination and their effectiveness for financial stability. Most of the studies on macroeconomic policy analysis have been focused on either Econometric or General Equilibrium framework or Bayesians or Frequentist approach; both approaches have their own advantages and limitations. This study has provided an exhaustive discussion in the context of existing paradigm and evidence on the subject and concomitantly suggested to consider an alternative empirical framework for the robustness and validity of empirical results.

It would be appropriate to acknowledge the limitations of this study as it would also point us towards the potential venues of future research. At first, we acknowledge here that the scope of subject study has been limited to stock and bond markets due to a limited time horizon. However, the future possible extensions could be made to include other aspects of the financial sector, for instance, foreign exchange markets, money markets and even derivative markets would be interesting additions. Secondly, we can also extend this study to a scenario where monetary policy is in the liquidity trap; however, considering the limited time horizon, we abstained from going further in this direction. Thirdly, on empirical and methodological grounds, the theoretical framework we have developed and the critical reasoning we have documented require an empirical validation. Fourth and last limitation of this study is related to the particular macroeconomic policy and financial sector environment of the UK on which we have been focusing on. Considering the fact that the British macroeconomic policy intuitions and financial sector are both the most established and ancient in the world, as cited in the introduction, the market capitalization as share of national income is the highest in the world. Hence, the conclusions and recommendations may not be equally applicable and should be taken with a grain of salt when applied to any other economy, particularly to developing economies. This aspect also provides the rationale for the future research.

Funding
The authors received no direct funding for this research.

Author details
Muhammad Ali Nasir[1]
E-mail: m.a.nasir@leedsbeckett.ac.uk
Junjie Wu[1]
E-mail: j.wu@leedsbeckett.ac.uk
Milton Yago[1]
E-mail: m.yago@leedsbeckett.ac.uk
ORCID ID: http://orcid.org/0000-0001-6709-8522
Alaa M. Soliman[1]
E-mail: a.soliman@leedsbeckett.ac.uk
[1] Faculty of Business & Law, Leeds Beckett University, Leeds, UK.

Notes

1. Bank stats (Monetary & Financial Statistics) are official symbols and abbreviations http://www.bankofengland.co.uk/statistics/ms/symbols.htm.
2. The part of the economy that is concerned with actual production of goods and services.
3. This refers to the period before the current financial and economic crises that started in 2008.
4. According to Foot (2003), there is no particular definition of financial stability; however, it could be defined in the context of financial assets price volatility (details in next sections).
5. In the current economic scenario, interest rates in many major economies cannot be cut any much further, e.g. in the UK, the current interest rate is 0.5, in the US 0 -0.25 and in the Euro zone 0.25%.
6. The Ricardian Equivalence refers to idea that any effort by the government to stimulate economy by debt-financed spending would be counter by the increased household savings to pay the higher taxes in future.
7. (a) Expansionary Fiscal– Expansionary Monetary, (b) Expansionary Fiscal–Contractionary Monetary, (c) Contractionary Fiscal–Contractionary Monetary and (d) Contractionary Fiscal–Expansionary Monetary.
8. An economic state where resources are allocated in the most efficient manner.
9. Banks and building societies were allowed to swap their high-quality mortgage-backed and other securities for UK Treasury Bills for up to three years.
10. Headed by Governor of the Bank of England, this committee would monitor the UK financial sector and its effects on the economy. http://www.bankofengland.co.uk/publications/news/2011/041.htm
11. Mishkin (2011) and Niemann and Pichler (2011) the optimal combination can be defined as "stance of Monetary & Fiscal policy which leads to simultaneous positive response from Stock & Bond markets".
12. In the light of the Fiscal theory of price level (FTPL), a non-Ricardian scenario exists where fiscal policy has deterministic effects on price stability (Moreira, Soares, Sachsida, & Loureiro, 2011).
13. Fiscal policy's golden rule (borrow to invest) and sustainable investment rule (Debt-to-GDP 40%) were violated.

References

Aarle, B. V., Garretsen, H., & Huart, F. (2003, September). *Transatlantic monetary and fiscal policy interaction* (Cesifo Working Paper No. 1042 Category 6: Monetary Policy and International Finance). Munich: CESifo GmbH (Munich Society for the Promotion of Economic Research)
Adam, K., & Billi, R. M. (2011). *Distortionary fiscal policy and monetary policy goals*. Mannheim: Department of Economics, Mannheim University.
Agenor, P. R., & Silva, L. A. P. D. (2012). Macroeconomic stability, financial stability, and monetary policy rules. *International Finance, 15*, 205–224.

Airaudo, M., Cardani, R., & Lansing, K. J. (2011). *Monetary policy and asset prices with belief-driven fluctuations and news shocks*. Philadelphia, PA: LeBow College of Business, Drexel University.

Airaudo, M., Nistico, S., & Zanna, L. F. (2008). Learning monetary policy and asset prices. *Journal of Money, Credit and Banking, 47*, 1273–1307.

Albulescu, C. T. (2011). *Macro-financial risks and central banks: What changes has the crisis triggered?* Romania: Poly-Technique University of Timisoara.

Alec Chrystal, K., & Dowd, K. (1989). Disaggregate supply: Evidence for the UK. *Applied Economics, 21*, 1397–1409. http://dx.doi.org/10.1080/758522332

Allen, D. E., & Yang, W. (2004). Do UK stock prices deviate from fundamentals? *Mathematics and Computers in Simulation, 64*, 373–383. http://dx.doi.org/10.1016/S0378-4754(03)00103-4

Altissimo, F., Georgiou, E. Sastre, M. Valderrama, M. T. Stocker, G. S. M. Weth, M. ... William, A. (2005, June). *Wealth and assets price effects on economic activity* (Occasional Paper Series No. 29). Frankfurt: European Central Bank.

Andrew, H. H., Libich, J., & Stehlik, P. (2011). Welfare improving coordination of fiscal and monetary policy. *AUCO Czech Economic Review, 5*, 7–26.

Angelini, P., Neri, S., & Panetta, F. (2010). *Grafting macro-prudential policies in a macroeconomic framework choice of optimal instruments and interaction with monetary policy*. Rome: Bank of Italy, Economic Outlook and Monetary Policy Department.

Angeriz, A., & Arestis, P. (2007). Monetary policy in the UK. *Cambridge Journal of Economics, 31*, 863–884. http://dx.doi.org/10.1093/cje/bem014

Arby, M. F., & Hanif, M. N. (2010). Monetary and fiscal policies coordination: Pakistan's experience. *SBP Research Bulletin, 6*, 3–13.

Ardagna, S. (2009). Financial markets' behavior around episodes of large changes in the fiscal stance. *European Economic Review, 53*, 37–55. http://dx.doi.org/10.1016/j.euroecorev.2008.07.003

Arnold, I. J. M., & Vrugt, E. B. (2010). Treasury bond volatility and uncertainty about monetary policy. *The Financial Review, 45*, 707–728. http://dx.doi.org/10.1111/(ISSN)1540-6288

Asensio, A. (2007). *Monetary and budgetary-fiscal interactions in a Keynesian heterogeneous monetary union*. CEPN, University Paris.

Atanasova, C. V., & Gang, J. (2008). The decline in the volatility of the business cycles in the UK. *Manchester School, 76*, 14–36. http://dx.doi.org/10.1111/manc.2008.76.issue-s1

Auerbach, A. J., & Gorodnichenko, Y. (2012). Measuring the output responses to fiscal policy. *American Economic Journal: Economic Policy, 4*, 1–27.

Bakhshi, H., Haldane, A. G., & Hatch, N. (1997). *Some costs and benefits of price stability in the United Kingdom, Bank of England*. Retrieved February 23, 2016, from http://www.bankofengland.co.uk/archive/Documents/historicpubs/workingpapers/1998/wp78.pdf ISSN 1368-5562.

Bank of England. (1997). *Monetary policy framework*. Author. Retrieved 30 June, 2011, from http://www.bankofengland.co.uk/monetarypolicy/framework.htm

Bank of England. (2011). *The transmission mechanism of monetary policy*. The Monetary Policy Committee Bank of England. Retrieved 3 December, 2011, from www.bankofengland.co.uk

Barnett, R. C. (2005). Coordinating macroeconomic policy in a simple AK growth model. *Journal of Macroeconomics, 27*, 621–647. http://dx.doi.org/10.1016/j.jmacro.2004.04.002

Barrell, R., & Riley, R. (2004). The impact of fiscal and monetary policy imbalances on the UK economy. *National Institute Economic Review, 189*, 61–63. http://dx.doi.org/10.1177/002795010418900106

Baum, A., Poplawski-Ribeiro, M., & Weber, A. (2012). *Fiscal multipliers and the state of the economy*. International Monetary Fund, WP/12/286. Washington, DC.

Baumeister, C., Liu, P., & Mumtaz, H. (2010). *Changes in the transmission of monetary policy: Evidence from a time-varying factor-augmented VAR* (Working Paper No. 401). Bank of England.

Beetsma, R. M. W. J., & Jensen, H. (2005). Monetary and fiscal policy interactions in a micro-founded model of a monetary union. *Journal of International Economics, 67*, 320–352.

Beladi, & Samanta (1988). Unanticipated monetary policy and real output—Some evidence from UK economy. *Applied Economics, 20*, 721–729.

Bénassy, J. P. (2003). Fiscal policy and optimal monetary rules in a non-Ricardian economy. *Review of Economic Dynamics, 6*, 498–512. http://dx.doi.org/10.1016/S1094-2025(03)00017-6

Benigno, G., Chen, H., Otrok, C., Rebucci, A., & Young, E. R. (2011). Financial crises and macro-prudential policies. *Journal of International Economics, 89*, 453–470.

Benigno, G., Chen, H., Otrok, C., Rebucci, A., & Young, E. R. (2012). *Optimal policy for macro-financial stability, Research Division Federal Reserve Bank of St. Louis* (Working Paper 2012-041A).

Bernanke, B. S., & Gertler, M. (2001). Should Central Banks respond to movements in asset prices? *The American Economic Review, 91*, 253–257.

Bhattarai, K. (2011). Econometric and stochastic general equilibrium models for evaluation of economic policies. *International Journal of Trade and Global Markets, 4*, 212–241.

Bhundia, A. O., & Donnell, G. (2002). UK policy coordination: The importance of institutional design. *Fiscal Studies, 23*, 135–164.

Blake, A. P., & Kirsanova, T. (2011). Inflation conservatism and monetary-fiscal policy interactions. *International Journal of Central Banking, 7*, 41–83.

Blanchard, O., Dell'Ariccia, G., & Mauro, P. (2010). *Rethinking macroeconomic policy* (IMF staff position note, SPN/10/03). Washington, DC.

Borio, C. (2011). *Rediscovering the macroeconomic roots of financial stability policy: Journey, challenges and a way forward* (BIS Working Papers No. 354). Retrieved February 23, 2016, from http://www.bis.org/publ/work354.htm

Bredin, D., Hyde, S., & Reilly, G. O. (2005). *UK stock returns & the impact of domestic monetary policy shocks*. Dublin: Department of Banking & Finance, Graduate School of Business, University College Dublin.

Broome, S., & Morley, B. (2004). Stock prices as a leading indicator of the East Asian financial crisis. *Journal of Asian Economics, 15*, 189–197. http://dx.doi.org/10.1016/j.asieco.2003.12.008

Buti, M., Roeger, W., & Veld, J. I. (2001). *Monetary and fiscal policy interaction under a stability pact* (EUI Working Paper ECO No. 2001/8). European University Institue, San Domenico di Fiesole FI.

Campbell, J. Y. (1995). Some lessons from the yield curve. *Journal of Economic Perspectives, 9*, 129–152. http://dx.doi.org/10.1257/jep.9.3.129

Caporale, G. M., & Soliman, A. M. (2013). Stock prices and monetary policy: An impulse response analysis. *International Journal of Economics and Financial Issues, 3*, 701–709.

Carlberg, M. (2004). *Monetary and fiscal policy interactions in the euro area*. Hamburg: Department of Economics, Federal University.

Carroll, C. D. (2004). *Housing wealth and consumption expenditure*. Baltimore: Department of Economics, Johns Hopkins University.

Carroll, C. D., Otsuka, M., & Slacalek, J. (2011). How large are housing and financial wealth effects? A new approach. *Journal of Money, Credit, and Banking, 43*, 55–79.

Case, K. E., Quigley, J. M., & Shiller, R. J. (2012). *Wealth effects revisited 1975–2012* (Cowles foundation discussion paper No. 1884). New Haven, CT: Yale University.

Chadha, J. S., & Nolan, C. (2007). Optimal simple rules for the conduct of monetary and fiscal policy. *Journal of Macroeconomics, 29*, 665–689. http://dx.doi.org/10.1016/j.jmacro.2005.01.005

Chari, V. V. (2010). *Testimony before the Committee on Science and Technology, Subcommittee on Investigations and Oversight, U.S. House of Representatives*. Minneapolis: University of Minnesota and Federal Reserve Bank of Minneapolis.

Chen, M. H. (2012). State dependence in the influence of monetary policy regime shifts on hospitality index returns. *International Journal of Hospitality Management, 31*, 1203–1212. http://dx.doi.org/10.1016/j.ijhm.2012.02.008

Claeys, P. (2004). *Monetary and budgetary policy interaction: An SVAR analysis of stabilization policies in Monetary Union* (EUI Working Paper ECO No. 2004/22). European University Institute, san domenico di fiesole.

Collard, F., Dellas, H., Diba, B., & Loisel, O. (2012). *Optimal monetary and prudential policies*. Bern: Department of Economics, University of Bern.

Consolo, A., Favero, C. A., & Paccagnini, A. (2009). On the statistical identification of DSGE models. *Journal of Econometrics, 150*, 99–115. http://dx.doi.org/10.1016/j.jeconom.2009.02.012

Cook, D., & Devereux, M. B. (2006). Capital inflows, fiscal discretion, and exchange rate policy. *European Economic Review, 50*, 1975–1992. http://dx.doi.org/10.1016/j.euroecorev.2005.08.003

Creel, J., Monperrus-Veroni, P. M., & Saraceno, F. (2009). Fiscal policy is back in France and the United Kingdom!. *Journal of Post Keynesian Economics, 31*, 645–667. http://dx.doi.org/10.2753/PKE0160-3477310407

Cúrdia, V., & Woodford, M. (2011). The central-bank balance sheet as an instrument of monetarypolicy. *Journal of Monetary Economics, 58*, 54–79. http://dx.doi.org/10.1016/j.jmoneco.2010.09.011

Davig, T., & Leeper, E. M. (2011). Monetary-fiscal policy interactions and fiscal stimulus. *European Economic Review, 55*, 211–227. http://dx.doi.org/10.1016/j.euroecorev.2010.04.004

Davig, T., Leeper, E. M., & Walker, T. B. (2011). Inflation and the fiscal limit. *European Economic Review, 55*, 31–47.

David Gulley, O., & Sultan, J. (2003). The link between monetary policy and stock and bond markets: Evidence from the federal funds futures contract. *Applied Financial Economics, 13*, 199–209. http://dx.doi.org/10.1080/09603100110115165

Dhami, S. Al-Nowaihi, A . (2009).*Strategic monetary and fiscal policy interaction in a liquidity trap*. Leicester: Department of Economics, University of Leicester.

Di Bartolomeo, G., & Giuli, F. (2011). Fiscal and monetary interaction under monetary policy uncertainty. *European Journal of Political Economy, 27*, 369–375. http://dx.doi.org/10.1016/j.ejpoleco.2010.11.001

Dixit, A., & Lambertini, L. (2001). Monetary-fiscal policy interactions and commitment versus discretion in a monetary union. *European Economic Review, 45*, 977–987. http://dx.doi.org/10.1016/S0014-2921(01)00134-9

Dixit, A., & Lambertini, L. (2003). Symbiosis of monetary and fiscal policies in a monetary union. *Journal of International Economics, 60*, 235–247. http://dx.doi.org/10.1016/S0022-1996(02)00048-X

Doughty, A. (1991). The relationship between fiscal policy and monetary policy. *Reserve Bank Bulletin, 54*, 228–234.

Duisenberg, W. (2003, June 3). Introduction. In W. F. Duisenberg (Ed.), *Monetary and fiscal policy in the euro area*. International Monetary Conference, Berlin. Retrieved from http://www.ecb.int/press/key/date/2003/html/sp030603.en.html

Dungey, M., & Fry, R. (2009). The identification of fiscal and monetary policy in a structural VAR. *Economic Modelling, 26*, 1147–1160. http://dx.doi.org/10.1016/j.econmod.2009.05.001

Eichengreen, B. (2005). Europe, the euro and the ECB: Monetary success, fiscal failure. *Journal of Policy Modeling, 27*, 427–439. http://dx.doi.org/10.1016/j.jpolmod.2005.04.008

Federal Reserve. (2011). *Federal Open Market Committee*. Board of Governors of Federal Reserve System. Retrieved June 30, 2011, from http://www.federalreserve.gov/monetarypolicy/fomc.htm

Ferré, M. (2008). Fiscal policy coordination in the EMU. *Journal of Policy Modeling, 30*, 221–235. http://dx.doi.org/10.1016/j.jpolmod.2007.04.007

Ferrero, A. (2009). Fiscal and monetary rules for a currency union. *Journal of International Economics, 77*, 1–10. http://dx.doi.org/10.1016/j.jinteco.2008.09.004

Financial Services Act. (2012). *Financial Services Act*. Retrieved February 23, 2015, from http://www.legislation.gov.uk/ukpga/2012/21/contents/enacted

Foot, M. (2003). *What is financial stability and how do we get it?* ACI (UK) The Roy Bridge Memorial Lecture. Retrieved March 7, 2012, from http://www.fsa.gov.uk/library/communication/speeches/2003/sp122.shtml

Forlati, C. (2006). *On optimal monetary and fiscal policy interaction in open economies*. Pompeu Fabra University.

Fragetta, M., & Kirsanova, T. (2010). Strategic monetary and fiscal policy interactions: An empirical investigation. *European Economic Review, 54*, 855–879. http://dx.doi.org/10.1016/j.euroecorev.2010.02.003

Franta, M., Libich, J., & Stehlik, P. (2011). The big picture of monetary-fiscal interactions. *Economic Papers, 30*, 6–14.

Funke, M., Paetz, M., & Pytlarczyk, E. (2010). Stock market wealth effects in an estimated DSGE model for Hong Kong. *Economic Modelling, and*. doi: http://dx.doi.org/10.1016/j.econmod.2010.08.016

Giorgio, D. G., & Nistico, S. (2007). Monetary policy and stock prices in an open economy. *Journal of Money, Credit and Banking, 39*, 1947–1985. http://dx.doi.org/10.1111/jmcb.2007.39.issue-8

Giorgio, D. G., & Nistico, S. (2008). *Fiscal deficits, current account dynamics and monetary policy* (Working Paper Series 8). Rome: Department of the Treasury, Ministry of the Economy and of Finance Italy.

Gomis-Porqueras, P., & Peralta-Alva, A. (2010). Optimal monetary and fiscal policies in a search theoretic model of monetary exchange. *European Economic Review, 54*, 331–344. http://dx.doi.org/10.1016/j.euroecorev.2009.08.007

Goodhart, C. A. E. (2004, June). *Some new directions for financial stability?* The 74th Annual General Meeting of the BIS, Zurich.

Gregoriou, A., Kontonikas, A., MacDonald, R., & Montagnoli, A. (2009). Monetary policy shocks and stock returns: Evidence from the British market. *Financial Markets and Portfolio Management, 23*, 401–410.

Grimm, O., & Ried, S. (2007). *Macroeconomic policy in a heterogeneous monetary union* (SFB 649 Discussion Paper 2007-028). Berlin: Humboldt University of Berlin.

Hagen, J. V., & Mundschenk, S. (2002). Fiscal and monetary policy coordination in EMU. *International Journal of Finance & Economics, 8*, 279–295.

Haldane, A., & Read, V. (2000). *Monetary policy surprises and the yield curve*. Bank of England. ISSN: 1368-5562.

Haldane, A. G. (1997). *Some issues in inflation targeting*. Bank of England. ISSN: 1368-5562.

Hanif, M, N., & Arby, M. F. (2009, September). *Monetary and fiscal policy coordination* (MPRA Paper No. 10307). Munich: Munich Personal RePEc Archive.

Henry, B. (2001). Fiscal policy in the UK. *Economic Outlook, 25*, 12–16. http://dx.doi.org/10.1111/ecol.2001.25.issue-3

Hallett, A. H. (2008). *Coordination without explicit cooperation: Monetary-fiscal interactions in an era of demographic change* (European Economy - Economic Papers 305). Directorate General Economic and Financial Affairs (DG ECFIN), European Commission.

Hughes Hallett, A., & Libich, J. (2007). Fiscal-monetary interactions: The effect of fiscal restraint and public monitoring on central bank credibility. *Open Economies Review, 18*, 559–576. http://dx.doi.org/10.1007/s11079-007-9017-9

Hughes Hallett, A. W., Libich, J., & Stehlík, P. (2011). Macroprudential policies and financial stability. *Economic Record, 87*, 318–334. http://dx.doi.org/10.1111/j.1475-4932.2010.00692.x

Isaac, A. G. (2009). *Monetary and fiscal interactions: Short-run and long-run implications, journal compilation*. Oxford: Blackwell.

Jansen, D. W., Li, Q., Wang, Z., & Yang, J. (2008). Fiscal policy and asset markets: A semiparametric analysis. *Journal of Econometrics, 147*, 141–150. http://dx.doi.org/10.1016/j.jeconom.2008.09.007

Javed, Z. H., & Sahinoz, A. (2005). Interaction of monetary and fiscal policy in case of Turkey, *Journal of Applied Sciences, 5*, 220–226.

Khorasgani, H. S. (2010). *Financial instability and optimal monetary policy rule* (FIW Working Paper No. 42). Vienna: Austrian Institute of Economic Research.

Kirsanova, T., Leith, C., & Lewis, S. W. (2010). Monetary and fiscal policy interaction: The current consensus assignments in the light of recent developments. *The Economic Journal, 119*, 482–596.

Kirsanova, T., Stehn, S. J., & Vines, D. (2005). The interactions between fiscal policy and monetary policy. *Oxford Review of Economic Policy, 21*, 532–564. http://dx.doi.org/10.1093/oxrep/gri031

Kontonikas, A., MacDonald, R., & Saggu, A. (2012). Stock market reaction to fed funds rate surprises: State dependence and the financial crisis. *Journal of Banking and Financial Crisis, 37*, 4025–4037.

Kontonikas, A., & Montagnoli, A. (2006). Optimal monetary policy and asset price misalignments. *Scottish Journal of Political Economy, 53*, 636–654. http://dx.doi.org/10.1111/sjpe.2006.53.issue-5

Landolfo, L. (2004). *Monetary and fiscal policy issues in the euro area*. York: Department of Economics and Related Studies, University of York.

Leciejewicz, I. W. (2010). Decision interactions of the monetary and fiscal authorities in the choice of policy mix. *Journal of Organisational Transformation and Social Change, 7*, 189–210.

Lee, S. (2009). The rock of stability? The political economy of the Brown government. *Policy Studies, 30*, 17–32.

Leeper, E. (1993). The policy tango; towards a holistic view of monetary and fiscal effects. *Economic Review, Federal Reserve Bank of Atlanta, 78*, 1–27.

Leitemo, K. (2004). A game between the fiscal and the monetary authorities under inflation targeting. *European Journal of Political Economy, 20*, 709–724. http://dx.doi.org/10.1016/j.ejpoleco.2003.08.004

Leith, C., & Wren-Lewis, S. (2006). Compatibility between monetary and fiscal policy under EMU. *European Economic Review, 50*, 1529–1556. http://dx.doi.org/10.1016/j.euroecorev.2005.04.003

Libich, J., Nguyen, D. T., & Stehlík, P. (2011). *Monetary exit strategy and fiscal spillovers* (CAMA Working Papers 2011-04). Centre for Applied Macroeconomic Analysis, Crawford School of Public Policy, The Australian National University.

Lildholdt, P., & Wetherilt, A. V. (2004). *Anticipation of monetary policy in UK financial markets*. London: Bank of England.

Lippi, F., & Trachter, N. (2012). *State dependent monetary policy*. Sassari: University of Sassari, EIEF.

Lobo, B. J. (2000). Asymmetric effects of interest rate changes on stock prices. *The Financial Review, 35*, 125–144. http://dx.doi.org/10.1111/fire.2000.35.issue-3

Lobo, B. J., Darrat, A. F., & Ramchander, S. (2006). The asymmetric impact of monetary policy on currency markets, *The Financial Review, 41*, 289–303. http://dx.doi.org/10.1111/fire.2006.41.issue-2

Lombardo, G., & Sutherland, A. (2004). Monetary and fiscal interactions in open economies. *Journal of Macroeconomics, 26*, 319–347. http://dx.doi.org/10.1016/j.jmacro.2003.11.016

Lu, X., & In, F. (2006). Monetary policy, open market operations and New Zealand interest-rate and exchange-rate markets. *Journal of the Asia Pacific Economy, 11*, 462–481. http://dx.doi.org/10.1080/13547860600924021

Machado, C., & Ribeiro, A. P. (2010). *Monetary and fiscal policy interactions in a monetary union with country-size asymmetry* (CEF.UP Working Paper 2010-03). Porto: Centre for Economics and Finance at University of Porto.

Malikane, C., & Semmler, W. (2008). Asset prices, output and monetary policy in a small open economy. *Metroeconomica, 59*, 666–686.

Malley, J., Philippopoulos, A., & Woitek, U. (2009). To react or not? Technology shocks, fiscal policy and welfare in the EU-3. *European Economic Review, 53*, 689–714. http://dx.doi.org/10.1016/j.euroecorev.2009.01.005

Merzlyakov, S. (2011). *Strategic interaction between fiscal and monetary policies in an export-oriented economy, laboratory for macroeconomic analysis*. Moscow: State University - Higher School of Economics.

Midthjell, N. L. (2011). Fiscal policy and financial crises, what are the actual effects of fiscal policy? *Norges Bank, Economics Bulletin, 82*, 24–38.

Minsky, H. P. (1974). The modeling of financial instability: An introduction. *Modeling and Simulation, Proceedings of the Fifth Annual Pittsburgh Conference*. Pittsburgh: University of Pittsburgh.

Mishkin, F. S. (2011). *Monetary policy strategy: Lessons from the crisis* (Working Paper 16755). Cambridge, MA: National Bureau of Economic Research.

Mochtar, F. (2004). Fiscal and monetary policy interaction: Evidences and implication for inflation targeting in Indonesia. *Bulletin of Monetary Economics and Banking, 7*, 359–386.

Moosa, I. A. (1998). An investigation into the cyclical behaviour of output, money, stock prices and interest rates. *Applied Economics Letters, 5*, 235–238.

Moreira, T. B. S., Soares, F. A. R., Sachsida, A., & Loureiro, P. R. A. (2011). The interaction of monetary and fiscal policy: The Brazilian case. *Modern Economy, 02*, 114–123. http://dx.doi.org/10.4236/me.2011.22016

Muscatelli, V. A., Tirelli, P., & Trecroci, C. (2004). Fiscal and monetary policy interactions: Empirical evidence and optimal policy using a structural new-Keynesian model. *Journal of Macroeconomics, 26*, 257–280. http://dx.doi.org/10.1016/j.jmacro.2003.11.014

Nakov, A., & Thomas, C. (2011). *Optimal monetary policy with state-dependent pricing* (Working paper No 1130). Frankfurt: Bank of Spain.

Nasir, M., Ahmad, A., Ali, A., & Rehman, F. (2010). Fiscal and monetary policy coordination: Evidence from Pakistan. *International Research Journal of Finance and Economics, 35*, 202–213.

Neri, S. (2003). *Structural VARs and DSGE models: Applications to macroeconomics* (Dissertation). Barcelona: University Pompeu Fabra.

Niemann, S., & Hagen, J. V. (2008). Coordination of monetary and fiscal policies: A fresh look at the issue. *Swedish Economic Policy Review, 15*, 89–124.

Niemann, S., & Pichler, P. (2011). Optimal fiscal and monetary policies in the face of rare disasters. *European Economic Review, 55*, 75–92.

Nordhaus, W. D. (1994). Policy games: Coordination and independence in monetary and fiscal policies. *Brookings Paper on Economic Activity, 2*, 139–216.

Nyamonga, M. E., Sichei, M. M., & Mutai, N. K. (2008). *The monetary and fiscal policy interaction in Kenya*. Nairobi: Central Bank of Kenya, Research Department.

Osborn, D.R, & Sensier, M .2009.UK inflation: Persistence, seasonality and monetary policy. *Scottish Journal of Political Economy, 56*(1), 24–44.

Pappa, E., & Vassilatos, V. (2007). The unbearable tightness of being in a monetary union: Fiscal restrictions and regional

stability. *European Economic Review, 51*, 1492–1513. http://dx.doi.org/10.1016/j.euroecorev.2006.10.006
Park, S. G. (2008). *Monetary, fiscal, and the exchange rate policy interactions with Central Bank Debt*. Bloomington: Department of Economics, University of Indiana.
Pierdzioch, C. (2004). Capital mobility and the effectiveness of fiscal policy in open economies. *Journal of Macroeconomics, 26*, 465–479. http://dx.doi.org/10.1016/j.jmacro.2003.04.001
Robert, C. P. (2013). *On the Jeffreys-Lindley's paradox* (Universit´e Paris-Dauphine, CEREMADE). Paris: University of Warwick, Department of Statistics, and CREST.
Rukelj, D. (2009). Modelling fiscal and monetary policy interactions in Croatia using structural vector error correction model. *Privredna kretanja i ekonomska politika, 121*, 24–58.
Sanchez, M. (2010). The interplay of monetary and fiscal policies in a multinational currency union. *International Journal of Monetary Economics and Finance, 3*, 33–49.
Sargent, T. J., & Wallace, N. (1981). *Some unpleasant monetarist arithmetic*. Minneapolis: Federal Reserve Bank of Minneapolis, Research Department.
Schabert, A. (2006). Central bank instruments, fiscal policy regimes, and the requirements for equilibrium determinacy. *Review of Economic Dynamics, 9*, 742–762. http://dx.doi.org/10.1016/j.red.2006.08.001
Semiromi, B., & Reza, M. (2010). Literatures about asset price bubbles and monetary policies. *International Conference on Applied Economics, ICOAE, 2010*, 695–703.
Semmler, W., & Zhang, W. (2003). *Monetary and fiscal policy interactions: Some empirical evidence in the euro-area*. Bielefeld: Centre for Empirical Macroeconomics, Bielefeld University.
Shively, P. A. (2004). The size and dynamic effect of aggregate-demand and aggregate-supply disturbances in expansionary and contractionary regimes. *Journal of Macroeconomics, 26*, 83–99. http://dx.doi.org/10.1016/j.jmacro.2002.01.002
Sims, C. A. (2011). Stepping on a rake: The role of fiscal policy in the inflation of the 1970s. *European Economic Review, 55*, 48–56. http://dx.doi.org/10.1016/j.euroecorev.2010.11.010
Srinivasan, N., Jain, S., & Ramachandran, M. (2009). Monetary policy and the behaviour of inflation in India: Is there a need for institutional reform? *Journal of Asian Economics, 20*, 13–24. http://dx.doi.org/10.1016/j.asieco.2008.07.003
Staudinger, S. (2003). *Monetary and fiscal policy interaction in the EMU*. Wien: Vienna University of Technology.
Stemp, P. J. (2001). Policy forum: Macroeconomic policies and exchange rates, fiscal policy, monetary policy and exchange rate. *The Australian Economic Review, 34*, 442–448.
Sullivan, A., & Sheffrin, S. M. (2003). *Economics: Principles in action*. Upper Saddle River, NJ: Pearson Prentice Hall.
Svensson, L. E. O. (2012). The relation between monetary policy and financial policy. *International Journal of Central Banking, 8*, 293–295.
Tager, M., & Van Lear, W. (2001). Fiscal and monetary policy rules revisited. *The Social Science Journal, 38*, 69–83. http://dx.doi.org/10.1016/S0362-3319(00)00117-8
Talvan, L. M. M., & Lupu, A. (2010). Fiscal and monetary policy measures to ensure price stability. *The Romanian Economic Journal, 13*, 155–170.
Traum, N., & Yang, S. C. S. (2011). Monetary and fiscal policy interactions in the post-war U.S.. *European Economic Review, 55*, 140–164. http://dx.doi.org/10.1016/j.euroecorev.2010.11.009
Tsouma, E. (2009). Stock returns and economic activity in mature and emerging markets. *The Quarterly Review of Economics and Finance, 49*, 668–685. http://dx.doi.org/10.1016/j.qref.2008.02.002
Viegi, N. (1999). *Fiscal interdependence, fiscal and monetary policy interaction and the optimal design of EMU*. Glasgow: Department of Economics, University of Strathclyde
von Thadden, L. V. (2004). Active monetary policy, passive fiscal policy and the value of public debt: Some further monetarist arithmetic. *Journal of Macroeconomics, 26*, 223–251. http://dx.doi.org/10.1016/j.jmacro.2003.11.013
Weymark, D. N. (2007). Inflation, government transfers, and optimal central bank independence. *European Economic Review, 51*, 297–315. http://dx.doi.org/10.1016/j.euroecorev.2006.01.005
Williams, N. (2012). Monetary policy under financial uncertainty, *Journal of Monetary Economics, 59*, 449–465.
Wong, W. K., Khan, H. K., & Du, J. (2006). Do money and interest rates matter for stock prices? An econometric study of Singapore and USA. *The Singapore Economic Review, 51*, 31–51. http://dx.doi.org/10.1142/S0217590806002214
Yang, J., Zhou, Y., & Wang, Z. (2009). The stock-bond correlation and macroeconomic conditions: One and a half centuries of evidence. *Journal of Banking & Finance, 33*, 670–680.
Zubairy, S. (2009). *On fiscal multipliers: Estimates from a medium scale DSGE model*. Ottawa: (Bank of Canada Working Paper 2010-30).

Factors influencing Sudanese microfinance intention to adopt mobile banking

Anwar Ammar[1] and Elsadig Musa Ahmed[2*]

*Corresponding author: Elsadig Musa Ahmed, Faculty of Business, Multimedia University, Melaka 75450, Malaysia

E-mail: elsadig1965@gmail.com

Reviewing editor: David McMillan, University of Stirling, UK

Abstract: Access to financial service has become a key phenomenon for economic development and poverty alleviation .Microfinance is one way of fighting poverty in Sudan, where most citizens are in need of it. However, despite the initial results showing a positive impact of microfinance on the livelihood of low-income people in Sudan, around 8 million of the Sudanese poor people are excluded from microfinance services. One potential remedy for the limited outreach of microfinance in Sudan may lie within enhancing the capacity of microfinance services providers (MFPs) in the utilization of modern technology. Recent innovation in providing financial services in a convenient and efficient way is the use of mobile banking (m-banking) technology in microfinance. M-banking promises to increase the efficiency and outreach of microfinance services in developing countries. This paper tries to examine the factors that influence the adoption of m-banking by microfinance sector in Sudan. In this respect, hypotheses were developed guided by Unified Theory of Acceptance and Use of Technology (UTAUT) and Technology-organization-Environment (TOE) models. Primary data were collected from MFPs and microfinance customers in Sudan using questionnaires and interviews. The study contributes to knowledge in terms of methods used by extending aforementioned theories through adding new variables to both models by putting both models in

ABOUT THE AUTHORS

Anwar Ammar is a PhD student at Faculty of Management, Multimedia University, Malaysia. His research interests are in mobile banking technology Adoption, Implementation and Effectiveness. He has 13 years of practical experience in ICT at International Airports Projects in Saudi Arabia and 5 years in electronic banking technology as a manager of banking technology department at the Central Bank of Sudan.

Elsadig Musa Ahmed is a professor of Economics and Technology Management and Senate member of Multimedia University, Malaysia. He has published more than 100 journals' publications, produced a number of PhD and other postgraduate students, completed 5 external research projects and has excellent international contributions in his research areas.

PUBLIC INTEREST STATEMENT

The Sudanese experience showed that microfinance—the major tool to combat poverty—has a positive impact on income-generating activities, poverty reduction, women's empowerment, and better access to education and health services. However, late statistics show that microfinance covers only 8% of the total potential clients leaving 8 million unserved people behind. With baby steps, microfinance industry in Sudan will never get anywhere. Nonetheless, the enormous growth of mobile banking (M-banking) has created a new opportunity to expand financial services to this unserved population. Sudan's mobile phone network covers 77% of the population, including the poor. The main objective of this study is to identify the major factors determining the adoption of M-banking in the Sudanese microfinance sector. The findings from this research study can be used by microfinance providers to improve m-banking facilities and to identify those factors that can contribute to either the failure or success of the m-banking services and this could be further used for decision-making.

one study to fill the gaps in past studies; via examination of the demand (customers) and supply (institutions) through modifying them to include new variables related to m-banking in microfinance.

Subjects: Arts & Humanities; Social Sciences; Technology

Keywords: M-banking; microfinance; Sudan; ICT; UTAUT; TOE

1. Introduction

According to the National Baseline Household Survey (2009), the poverty rate in Sudan is 46.5% nationwide and varies considerably between rural and urban areas (57.6 vs. 26.5%, respectively) (Sudan 2015 African Economic Outlook, 2015). Unemployment is also high in Sudan, according to The African Development Bank (2014) the unemployment rate stood at 10.8% in 2012, with male unemployment at 13% compared to 20% for females. Sudan is one of the countries which adopted microfinance as a tool to address issues of poverty and unemployment.

The Sudanese experience showed that microfinance has a positive impact on income-generating activities, poverty reduction, women's empowerment, and better access to education and health services. However, late statistics showed that the total number of clients is 970,000, i.e. 8% coverage of the total potential clients estimated at 7.2 million (Ibrahim, 2014).This might be due to several reasons such as lack of basic public infrastructures, high operation cost, MFPs [1] deliberately ignoring the rural areas' clients because of the high risk; microfinance programs offer only a limited number of products and limited management capacity of MFPs.

It is clear that the present delivery channels are not quite meeting the challenges of microfinance in Sudan, especially when it comes to serving communities in remote locations characterized by low population density. In recent years, Mobile technology was successfully used in many countries of similar situation to Sudan (e.g. MPESA in Kenya and WIZIT in South Africa) for delivering financial services to the poor. While microfinance in Sudan is still in fledgling stage (8% coverage), mobile phone estimated penetration rate in 2015 is 77% (BuddeComm, 2015). Based on this, many studies suggest m-banking as a solution to microfinance problems (Impact Evaluation Assessment MFI Sector in Sudan 2007–2012, 2013; Mapping, capacity assessment & capacity development of microfinance providers in Sudan, 2012; Situational Analysis of the Microfinance Sector in Sudan, 2006).

M-banking has its own challenges which according to this research include the need for strong institutions and technology infrastructure (HORUS CBOS, 2011; Khattab, Balola, & Eldabi, 2012; Mapping, capacity assessment & capacity development of microfinance providers in Sudan, 2012) an innovative business model that can reach microfinance customers with a broader range of financial products at lower costs (HORUS CBOS, 2011; Impact Evaluation Assessment MFI Sector in Sudan 2007–2012, 2013); understanding the factors that influence Sudanese microfinance customer's intentions to use m-banking services (Karma, Ibrahim, and Ali (2014); Tingari & Abdelrahman, 2012), partnerships, and collaboration between different stakeholders (HORUS CBOS, 2011; Khattab et al.,2012); and lack of a clear regulatory framework (HORUS CBOS, 2011; Khattab et al., 2012).

In Sudan, there are certain gaps on supply side of microfinance services that is evident from outreach statistics. The gap in the financial services market is creating a unique niche for m-banking, thus enabling a growing number of people to access to financial services for the first time. In Sudan, little research was conducted to understand m-banking and the environment needed to develop an effective m-banking for serving Sudan's microfinance sector. Thus, this paper aims to examine the factors that should be considered to develop a successful m-banking that is suitable for Sudan's microfinance sector.

2. Significance of the study

Theoretically, the study contributes to the available literature by filling the gap of past studies that did not examine both supply and demand in one study, and empirically examines the demand (customers) and supply (microfinance providers) of microfinance activities by using Unified Theory of Acceptance and Use of Technology (UTAUT) and Technology-organization-Environment (TOE) models.

The findings of this study are expected to contribute to the adoption literature in the area of m-banking in Sudan and developing nations. More specifically, to bridge the gap that exists for Sudan by serving as a starting point for further research. The findings provided by this research can be used by microfinance providers to improve m-banking facilities and to identify those factors that can contribute to either the failure or success of the m-banking services and this could be further used for decision-making. To academia, the research would serve as a source of academic reference for further studies.

3. Literature review

Microfinance around the globe has shown promise of providing financial services to the poor people. It is considered as an effective tool to alleviate poverty (Armendariz & Morduch, 2010). Moreover, microfinance has developed as the provision of financial services to micro entrepreneurs and small businesses that lack access to banking and related services due to the high transaction costs (Maneiah, 2012) and it is generally used in order to provide help to micro and small-scaled entrepreneurs and companies which generally have difficulties in reaching financial and banking services due to cost and financial resource limitations (Turner, 2011). Hartarska, Shen, and Mersland (2013) describe microfinance as the financial service supplied for poor people and micro-scaled companies. MFPs are now offering many financial services such as deposits, insurance, remittances, automatic teller machines (ATMs) services, housing and money transfer (Ahmed, 2012).

The Sudanese experience showed that microfinance has a positive impact on income-generating activities, women's empowerment, improvement in education, access to financial services, poverty alleviation, and better health services. Badri's (2013) study's main findings revealed that participation of women in micro-credit program helps in promoting women's empowerment, in particular the economic and sociocultural dimensions of empowerment. Impact Evaluation Assessment MFI Sector in Sudan 2007–2012 (2013) study shows that microfinance clients respondents reported an improvement in nutrition for their families (46.7% of clients), followed by better access to education (36.3%), better access to health services (33.8%), and purchase of property (30%). When compared to non-clients, less impact is reported by non-clients in all areas. El Habeeb, Maruod, and Elteama (2014) study the role of Rural Development Project (NKRDP) as a microfinance institution in women development in North Kordofan. The results showed that the project helped in providing education services, health services, water services, fuel services, and handcrafts, respectively. Siddig (2013) stated that microfinance providers in Sudan have shown impressive contribution in delivering financial services to the poor and their enterprises. Microfinance institutions enable poor low-income households to develop their microenterprises, which enhance their income earning capacity, and improve their living standard. Sayed and Belal (2013) study results show that there is a positive effect of microfinance on poverty reduction by 16%.

Furthermore, offering financial services to poor people under the traditional microfinance setting is sometimes costly, unproductive, unprofitable, and unappealing for MFPs; the main problem with poor people's access to finance is that they are too costly to serve (Mas, 2011). Sudan microfinance market maintains a high operating expense ratio at 56% (Situational Analysis of the Microfinance Sector in Sudan, 2006). Equally, for MFPs, the cost of reaching people is high. The lack of physical infrastructure increases the transaction costs for micro and small enterprises. Distance of microfinance institutions is a variable that is always associated with high transaction costs (Hassan & Bauer, 2013). Further, Hinson (2011) highlighted geographical distance as a main factor preventing poor people from accessing traditional banking services. Ivatury and Pickens (2006) study stresses that banks will aggressively target the poor as a market only if they find ways to serve these customers profitably.

It should be noted that microfinance is an important and influential tool to combat poverty in Sudan .The Sudanese microfinance project made moderate satisfactory progress toward achieving the proposed objectives. Microfinance in Sudan has proven to be an impressive tool for applying business practices to solutions of poverty. It is important to continue building on this success to develop innovative solutions that can reach all microfinance customers. Yousif, Elizabeth, Jacinta, and Olga (2013) claim that even now MFIs face two important barriers in achieving scale: operational inefficiencies and high operational costs, both of which contribute to keeping interest rate high. She noted that with the appearance and development of mobile payments, it comes to the promises for many MFIs to address these barriers and offer m-banking.

3.1. Mobile banking

To reach large clients and offer better services, MFPs should bring the banking services to the doorstep of poor people (Nestor & Edelstein, 2011). The mobile revolution has transformed the lives of many people in developing countries, providing not just communications, but also basic financial access in the forms of phone-based money transfer and storage (Demombynes & Thegeya, 2012).

It should be recalled that M-banking can carry financial services close to the poor peoples' lives (Alexandre, 2011); it can reduce the problem of lack of proximity and high cost to reach distant clients with bricks and mortars branches (Breul, 2012). Besides, M-banking uses mobile phones to perform various functions like mini statement, checking of account history, SMS alerts, access to card statement, balance check, mobile recharge, etc. (Vinayagamoorthy & Sankar, 2012). Researchers use various terms to refer to mobile banking, including M-banking (Liu, Min, & Ji, 2009), branchless banking (Ivatury & Mas, 2008), m-payments, m-transfers, m-finance (Donner & Tellez, 2008). M-banking, also known as mobile money, is used as a broad term to define the usage of a mobile phone to access financial services (Pierre-Laurent, 2011). It allows customers to use their mobile phone as another channel for their banking services, such as deposits, withdrawals, account transfer, bill payment, and balance inquiry.

Additionally, the implementations of m-banking have many advantages for microfinance institutions. M-banking helps microfinance institutions to serve existing customers better as well as to reach new customers. Due to mobile banking, rural banks in the Philippines reduced interest rate monthly from "2.5 to 2%" and "fees from 3 to 2.5%", mobile banking also reduces at least 2.20 cents travel costs for clients (Kumer, Mckay, & Rotman, 2010). Meanwhile, the Pakistan experience highlights an important point about the link between M-banking and microfinance. (Michel & Sarah, 2013) According to the PHB Development1, there are 154 microfinance institutions using m-banking channel around the world (Voorrips, Breul, & Coupienne, 2012) Nestor and Edelstein (2011) argued that m-banking can amplify trust and transparency for MFIs by sending short message services (SMS) to customers after repayment or disbursement of loan. Conzett, Pulido, Lacalle, and Javier's (2010) study with microfinance institutions in Tanzania shows that m- banking increases outreach in rural areas. Moshy and Mukwaya's (2011) survey results in Uganda and Tanzania show that mobile financial services reach rural areas and greater number of clients who were previously excluded from financial services. M-banking is considered more convenient for clients in terms of flexibility, especially in saving small amount, in obtaining loan and repayment (Goss, Mas, Radcliffe, & Stark, 2011) due to its reliability and convenience (Ivatury & Mas, 2008).

Moreover, realizing the importance of m-banking technology for Sudanese microfinance sector, in October 2010, the Central Bank of Sudan (CBOS) contracted two consultants from HORUS Development Finance to investigate a pro-poor branchless banking initiative in Sudan. Yassir's (PACT, Yassir & Hassan, 2012) study reveals that in Sudan, the traditional and informal mobile phone transfer is dominating the market by 62% varying from one region to another, but it seems that where the banking services are not accessible probably, this percent increased as appears in West 80% and

East 81% . Meanwhile, Aversano, Evers, Latif, and Vaca-Viana's (2013) study reveals that mobile phone coverage in Sudan is extremely high, with 80% of retailers owning one phone, and 18% owning two. Most importantly, the results highlight the direct positive impact of mobiles on business efficiency in Sudan. According to ZAIN PWC (report 2014), in Sudan, m-banking for the unbanked has the potential to include a huge part of the population in banking services. Ismail's (Ismail & Osman, 2012) study results show that 84% of the retail banking industry clients uses at least one of the e-banking services, among all e-banking channels in Sudan m-banking is used by 12.6% of the clients.

3.2. Factors influencing mobile banking adoption

An individual's acceptance and adoption of innovation differs from organization innovation adoption in terms of the factors that influence such adoption (Moon & Norris, 2005; Titah & Barki, 2006 cited in Al-Zoubi, Sam, & Eam, 2011).

In this regard, various factors may influence customers' adoption to new technology. There is a need, therefore, to understand users' acceptance and adoption of m-banking and to identify the factors affecting their intentions to use mobile banking. Masinge (2010) conducted a study on the factors influencing the adoption of m-banking services at the bottom of the pyramid (BOP) in South Africa. The results of the study revealed that perceived usefulness (PU), perceived ease of use (PEOU), perceived cost, and customer's trust had a significant effect on the adoption of M-banking at the BOP, while perceived risk (PR) was found to have no significant effect. Tingari and Abdelrahman (2012) use extended TAM to explore the evolution of banking technology in Sudan. The study found that demographic factors such as age, income, education, and bank treatment period have no effect on customers' intention to use bank technology. Using TAM, Crabbe, Standing, Standing, and Karjaluoto's (2009) study showed that social and cultural factors in the form of perceived credibility, facilitating conditions, and demographic factors play an important role in influencing adoption and sustained usage of m-banking in Ghana . Carlsson, Carlsson, Hyvönen, Puhakainen, and Walden (2006) studied the factors affecting intention to use mobile devices/services. The study reveals that performance expectancy and effort expectancy are affecting behavioral intention, but social influence is not influencing behavior intention to use mobile devices/services. Also, Yu (2012) employs the (UTAUT) to investigate what impacts people to adopt m-banking in Taiwan. His study concluded that the individual intention to adopt m-banking was influenced by; social influence, performance expectancy, perceived financial cost, and perceived credibility. Furthermore, Karjaluoto, Mattila, and Pento (2002) evinced that prior experience with computers and technology and attitudes toward computers influence both attitudes toward online banking and actual behaviors. McKay and Pickens (2010) argue that in order for the poor segments of the population to adapt the service, it is important for the service provider to develop products that meet their needs in terms of product characteristics as well as price. Moreover, a study by Laforet and Li (2005) on factors influencing the adoption of online banking among Chinese banking clients shows that two-thirds of their surveyed sample did not adopt online banking because they were either not aware of the service or were not clear about its benefits. Besides, Benjamin (2013) investigates the facilitators and obstacles to entrepreneurial mobile banking in Nigeria, the study found lack of basic needs for banking services arising from low income and unemployment was the main reason for financial exclusion. It should be recalled that banking needs refer to the variety of banking products and services required by an individual (Tan & Teo, 2000). Ketkar, Shankar and Banwet (2012) identify lack of basic need for banking/payment services as barriers to m-banking adoption. Luarn and Lin (2005) deem perceived self-efficacy as a necessary capability in using m-banking.

On the supply side, within the organization context, Muriuki's (2009) study aims to establish factors affecting the adoption of E- banking by microfinance institutions in Kenya. This study's results indicate that MFIs with a strong support and commitment to e-banking from top management are more likely to adopt it. MFIs that have requested ICT and business resource (Infrastructure, Infostructure, and skills) for e-banking adoption stands a better chance at adopting e-banking. Further, Khattab et al.'s (2012) study's aims are to investigate the factors that are essential to the development of branchless banking in Sudan using mobile technology. Their study results revealed that there are essential factors for the success of branchless banking in Sudan, e.g. the identification of the industry key players and their roles, the enabling regulatory environment, the infrastructure readiness, and Sudanese cultural values. Moreover, Benjamin's (2013) study's findings revealed that conservative and vague regulations; security issues; underdeveloped infrastructures; lack of interoperability; business model issues; and lack of basic need for banking/financial services were identified to be the obstacles to entrepreneurial m-banking. Further, Khatri's (Khatri & Kurnia, 2011) study's results show that lack of collaboration between the banks and telecommunications providers, consumer's lack of experience with technology, and poor network reception could be a reason as to why implementation of mobile-based services has been slow in Australia. A study conducted by Chong, Ooi, Lin, and Tan (2010) in Vietnam found out that a government support in connection with consumer intention to use online banking is highly essential. Toufaily and Daghfous (2009), using TOE framework, conducted study on success and critical factors in adoption of E-banking by Lebanese banks. The results of their study show that the organizational variables (bank size, functional divisions, technical staff, technical infrastructure, perceived risks, decision makers` international experience and mastery of innovation) are variables which exert significant impact on the adoption of E-banking. Ismail and Osman's (2012) study on e-banking usage in Sudan shows that available infrastructure in Sudan is not sufficient to fulfill the requirements of e-banking technology in all parts of the country. Besides, the government has a major role to play in promoting the basic infrastructure required to increase the diffusion of e-banking. Moreover, there is need to enact legislation to protect e-transactions. Financial resources are an important factor in facilitating innovation adoption for any organization and they are often correlated with the firm size (Iacovou, Benbasat, & Dexter, 1995; Kuan & Chau, 2001). Al Nahian Riyadh, Akter, and Islam's (2009) study aims to investigate the factors that affect SMEs' adoption of e-banking in Bangladesh. The study identified seven variables affecting e-banking adoption by SMEs. They are: organizational capabilities, perceived benefits, perceived credibility, perceived regulatory support, ICT industries readiness, lack of financial institutions readiness, and institutional influence. Moreover, Ramdani, Kawalek, and Lorenzo (2009) combined TPB, TRA, TAM, DOI, UTAUT, and TOE to study adoption of Enterprise Systems, including ERP, CRM, SCM, and E-procurement by SMEs in (UK). Their results indicate that firms with a greater perceived relative advantage, a greater ability to experiment with ES before adoption, a greater top management support, a greater organizational readiness, and a larger size are predicted to become adopters of ES. Further, Yousif et al. (2013) reviewed MFI experiences with mobile financial services. The study suggested that: the right market environment is essential (Mobile network operators dominate the MFS market, current markets are primarily urban and semi-urban, a vibrant mobile payments market—such as money transfers—is a necessary condition for the success of mobile financial services). There is a need to advance organizational structure, training, and communication strategies. Ensuring that MFIs successfully implement MFS requires a carefully thought-out change leadership strategy. There are challenges with IT/M IS integration. IT/MIS integration is one of the greatest challenges faced by MFIs today. Innovation in products and services is limited. The regulatory environment influences everything. A CGAP research about microfinance and mobile (Michel & Sarah, 2013) noted that MFIs that have been successful in using m-banking for their operations are located in mature m-banking markets where customers are already aware that the mobile phone can be used for payments. Ongwenyi (2012) study was carried out to examine the influence of mobile phone banking technology on traditional banking transactions with reference to Kenya's banking institutions. The study's findings indicated that mobile phone banking can be said to have transformed the way banking activities are undertaken. This has been through introduction of new products and services that as per the study findings include cash transfers, payment of bills, deposits and account statement inquiries. Ketkar et al. (2012) show that, Critical mass of users for growth, as barriers to m-banking implementation. Zhu and Kraemer (2005) developed theoretically and evaluated empirically an integrative research model incorporating TOE factors, for assessing e-business use and value at the firm level, based on which a series of hypotheses are developed. The study found that technology competence, firm size, financial commitment, competitive pressure, and regulatory support are important antecedents of e-business use.

3.3. Technology adoption theories

There are various models that help to study the adoption behavior of mobile banking services. These models include various attributes that judge the intention of the mobile banking user and his/her attitude toward it. These models are: Theory of Reasoned Action (TRA) Fishbein and Ajzen (1975); Technology Acceptance Model (TAM) Davis (1989); Theory of Planned Behaviour (TPB) Taylor and Todd (1995); Innovation Diffusion Theory (IDT) Rogers (1995); Unified Theory of Acceptance and Use of Technology Model (UTUAT) Venkatesh, Morris, Davis, and Davis (2003) and Technology-organization-Environment framework (TOE) (Tornatzky & Fleischer, 1990).

In this respect, the factors that affect the technology adoption decision of m-banking services by individuals were studied using either the Technology Acceptance Model (TAM) such as Masinge (2010), Tingari and Abdelrahman (2012), Luarn and Lin (2005), Crabbe et al. (2009), Sripalawat, Thongmak, and Ngramyarn (2011), Al Nahian Riyadh et al. (2009), Tobbin and Kuwornu (2011), Ramdani et al. (2009) or the Unified Theory of Acceptance and Use of Technology (UTAUT) model such as Park, Yang, and Lehto (2007), Yu (2012), Carlsson et al. (2006), Ramdani et al. (2009).

It should be mentioned that TAM is a popular technology model and is a widely applied model for the acceptance and usage of ICT. According to Bagozzi (2007), TAM fails to take the group, cultural, or social aspects of technology acceptance into account. TAM has limited use in explaining users' attitudes and behavioral intentions to adopt mobile services (Venkatesh & Davis, 2000). The UTAUT model successfully integrates key constructs from existing ICT adoption models and is able to explain 70% of the variance in intention to use a system, as compared to 40% by TAM (Aldhaban, 2012; Yun, Han, & Lee, 2011). The UTAUT model explains the determinants of behavioral intention and use behavior of technology systems. The direct determinants include performance expectancy, effort expectancy, social influence, and facilitating conditions. The key moderators include gender, age, experience, and voluntariness of use. According to Park et al. (2007) UTAUT has been considered the most prominent and unified model in the stream of information technology adoption research with high robustness of the instruments regarding the key constructs.

Meanwhile, the Technology-organization-Environment (TOE) framework identifies three aspects of an enterprise's context that influence the process by which it adopts and implements a technological innovation: technological context, organizational context, and environmental context. Although TOE was not used widely in the m-banking context, it has been employed in e-business (Zhu & Kraemer, 2005), e-banking (Al Nahian Riyadh et al., 2009; Ayana, 2014; Kurnia, Peng, & Liu, 2010; Toufaily & Daghfous (2009)), e-government (Sara, 2012) Enterprise Systems (Ramdani et al., 2009). These applications have similar contexts and share common features with m-banking.

3.4. Theoretical framework

To build the research framework, we need to first identify the factors that affect M-banking intention to use and adoption by Sudan microfinance sector. Based on the literature review, there are five factors, microfinance customer factors, microfinance service providers' factors, mobile banking model, stakeholder's collaboration, and the enabling environment.

In this regard, UTAUT framework is selected to investigate factors influencing intention to use M-banking by microfinance customers for two reasons: firstly, it is the most widely utilized IS/IT adoption-based theory after TAM (Tobbin & Kuwornu, 2011). Secondly, it is a unified theory mapped onto the constructs of eight individual theories of adoption and diffusion (i.e. TRA, TAM, TPB, C-TAM-TPB, MM, SCT, MPCU, and DOI/IDT) and found to outperform all of them with a variance of as much as 70%. This study also aims to further extend UTAUT model with the inclusion of six additional factors, namely Previous Experience, Banking Needs, Perceived Self-efficacy, Awareness, Perceived credibility, and Perceived financial cost factors.

Meanwhile, the TOE has been used extensively by IS researchers to explain ICT adoption in enterprises and provides a useful analytical framework for the development and discussion of specific factors that influence the adoption decision. It has a solid theoretical basis, consistent empirical support, and the potential for application across various IS innovations domains (Oliveira & Martins, 2011). Based on this, TOE is employed to investigate the factors that influence microfinance providers (MFPs) adoption of M-banking technology. TOE framework (Tornatzky & Fleischer, 1990) was extended by adding factors related to the adoption of M-banking within the organization and environment contexts such as *Business Model, Market and Products*, and *Partners Collaboration* (Figures 1 and 2).

The proposed framework of this study combines UTAUT, TOE and Banking Needs, Perceived Self-efficacy, Awareness, Perceived Credibility, Prior Experience, and Perceived financial cost factors to investigate factors influencing intention to use M-banking by microfinance customers and microfinance services providers in Sudan. As depicted in Figure 3.

3.5. Hypotheses development

To explain the key drivers and barriers to M-banking adoption in Sudan microfinance sector, this study is guided by UTAUT model, and the technology-organization-environment (TOE) framework proposed by Tornatzky and Fleischer (1990). Based on these models, five types of factors are described below.

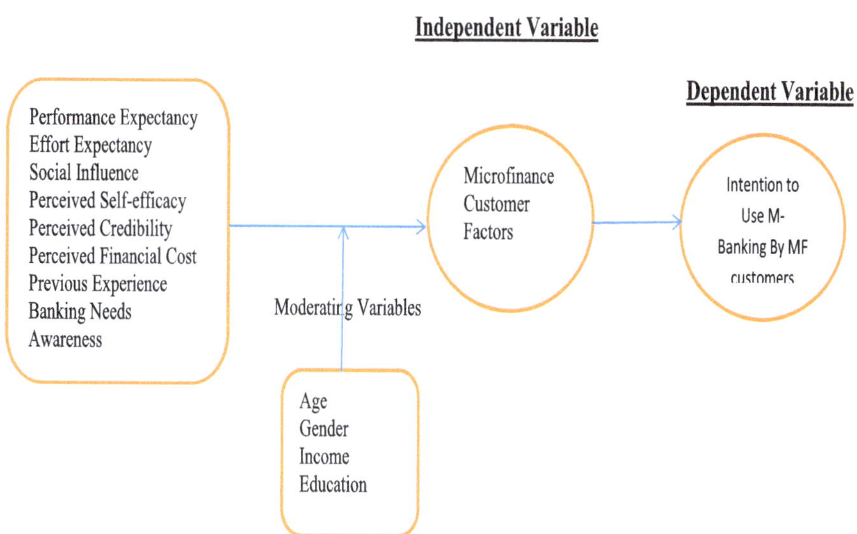

Figure 1. Microfinance customer factors based on UTAUT framework.

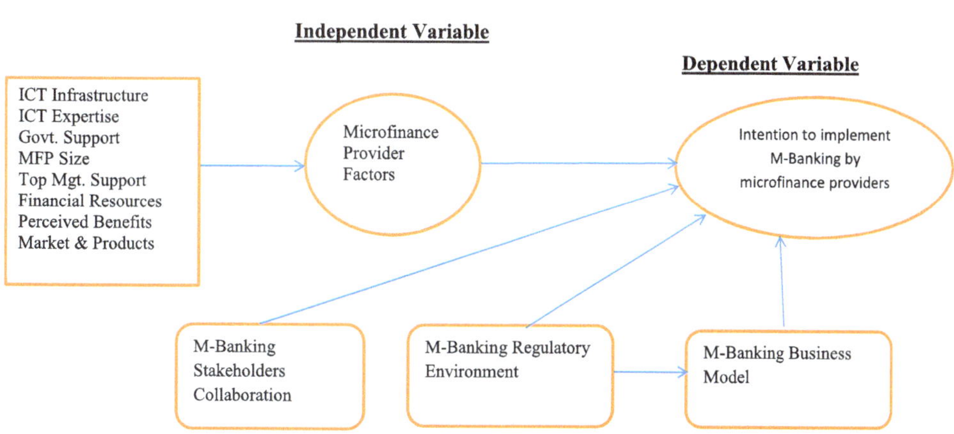

Figure 2. Microfinance service providers factors based on TOE framework.

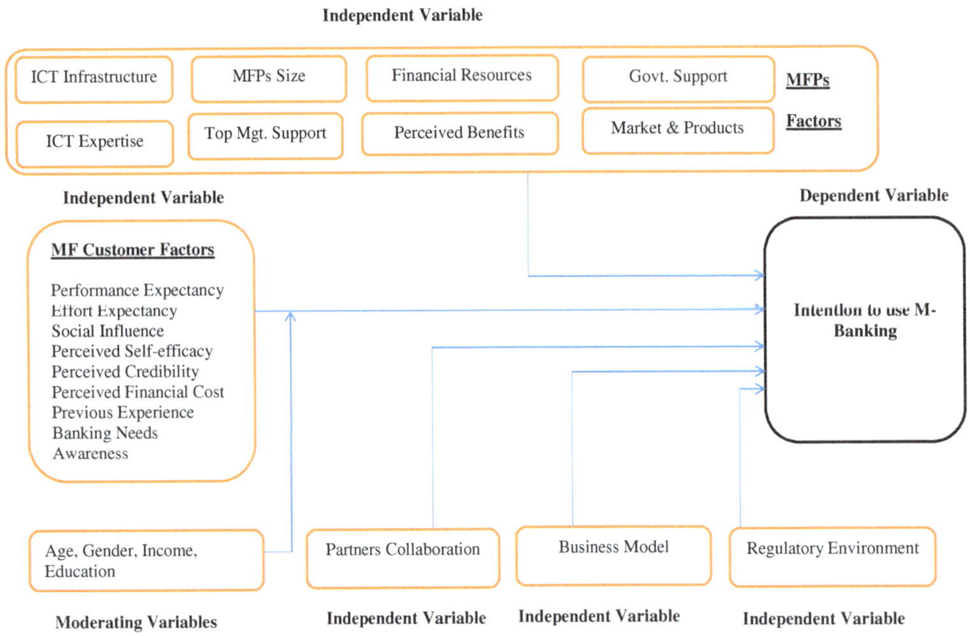

Figure 3. The combined study framework.

3.6. Microfinance customer factors

H1: Performance Expectancy: Performance Expectancy (PE) is the degree to which an individual believes that using the system will help him/her attain gains in job . Performance expectance significantly affects individual intention to use M-banking.

H2: Effort Expectancy: is the degree of ease associated with the use of system. Effort expectation significantly affects individual intention to use M-banking.

H3: Social Influence: is the degree to which an individual perceives that important others believe he/she should use the new system. Social influence significantly affects individual intention to use M-banking.

H4: Perceived Self-Efficacy: is defined as the "judgement of one's ability to use M-banking." Perceived self-efficacy significantly affects individual behavior of using M-banking.

H5: Perceived Credibility: is defined as the "one's judgment on the privacy and security issues of M-banking." Perceived credibility significantly affects individual intention to use M-banking.

H6: Perceived Financial Cost: Are the monetary expenses incurred when adopting an innovation. Perceived financial cost significantly affects individual intention to use M-banking.

H7: Previous Experience: Previous experience of M-banking will have a significant influence on adoption of M-banking adoption.

H8: Banking Needs: is defined as "the variety of banking products and services required by an individual.' The greater the extent to which m-banking meets the individual's needs for banking products and services, the more likely that M-banking will be adopted".

H9: Awareness: Awareness about M-banking has a positive effect on intention to adopt and use M-banking.

Demographic Variables: demographics characteristics, such as gender, age, business sector, and income affect M-banking user acceptance.

H10: Age will moderate the relationships among the proposed model constructs.

H11: Gender will moderate the relationships among the proposed model constructs.

H12: Education level will moderate the relationships among the proposed model constructs.

H13: Income will moderate the relationships among the proposed model constructs.

3.7. Microfinance service providers (MFPs) factors

H14: ICT Infrastructure: Increased ICT infrastructure will increase the likelihood of successful M-banking adoption.

H15: ICT Expertise: Higher level of ICT Expertise is positively related to M-banking adoption.

H16: MFP Size: The greater the MFPs size (number of employees), the more likely M-banking technology will be adopted by MFPs.

H17: Top Management Support: Top management support will positively influence M-banking adoption.

H18: Financial Resources: MFPs with greater financial commitment are more likely to achieve a greater extent of M-banking adoption.

H19: Perceived benefits: The greater the perceived benefits of M-banking, the more likely M-banking technology will be adopted by MFPs.

H20. Governmental Support: Government support affects the adoption of M-banking by MFPs.

H21: Market and Products: M-banking services adoption in a country is affected by its market conditions and Produces provided.

H22: Business Model: Business model have effect on the adoption of M-banking. Regulatory framework has effect on the business model.

H23: Regulatory: Enabling Regulatory Environment affect the adoption of M-banking by MFPs.

H24: Stakeholders' collaboration: The greater the degree of partner collaboration, the more likely the MFP will adopt and use M-banking services.

4. Methodology and estimation procedure

The study used the survey research methodology. The population of the study was the microfinance customers in Khartoum, Kasala and North Kordofan states, and microfinance services providers MFPs in Sudan. Personal administered questionnaires were employed to collect the data from the customers and MFPs. Several items were used to measure all variables and for each item, a corresponding Likert Scale with anchors ranging from 1 as "Strongly Disagree" and 5 as "Strongly Agree" was used. For each item listed, the respondents were requested to mark any of the five options given. The collected data were analyzed using SPSS Version 16. Altogether, a total of 550 questionnaires were distributed and 413 were returned. However, only 393 were found usable for data analysis.

4.1. Data collection instruments

4.1.1. Primary data

Two types of questionnaires were developed to collect primary data from microfinance customers and microfinance services providers (MFPs). To ensure content validity, four (4) knowledgeable individuals, including MF and MB experts and faculty members participated in a pre-testing with an initial draft of the questionnaires. The comments and suggestions received from these individuals helped to improve the quality of the final questionnaire. This study also used a semi-structured interview for collecting relevant qualitative data.

The interviewees include microfinance sector senior staff and consulting firms.

4.1.2. Secondary information

Secondary sources of data collection were obtained for additional information. The study relied on both unpublished and published data such as articles from journals and the internet which is related to the topic.

4.2. Data analysis

Data was analyzed using descriptive statistics such as frequencies and percentages. The analysis of data was done with the help of the statistical software of Statistical Package for Social Sciences (SPSS version 21).

4.3. Reliability

To analyze the data, internal reliability of the data was first tested using SPSS. The Cronbach's alpha for the microfinance customer variables is shown in Table 1, and for MFPs variables in Table 2. Cronbach's alpha for all microfinance customer variables and MFPs variables are greater than 0.7, and therefore, the reliability of data is acceptable.

5. Results and discussion

The main purpose of this section is to present the analysis and discussion of the findings of the study. The analysis is done in line with the objectives.

Table 1. Cronbach's alpha for the microfinance costumers' variables

No.	MF customer variables	Items	Alpha
1	Performance expectance	4	0.860
2	Effort expectance	4	0.860
3	Social influence	4	0.865
4	Perceived credibility	4	0.869
5	Perceived financial cost	4	0.865
6	Perceived self-efficacy	4	0.863
7	Banking needs	3	0.865
8	Awareness	3	0.860
9	Gender		0.870
10	Age		0.871
11	Education		0.874
12	Income		0.869
13	Mobile phone experience		0.868

Table 2. Cronbach's alpha for the microfinance service provider's variables

No.	MFPs and external variables	Items	Alpha
1	ICT infrastructure	3	.944
2	ICT expertise	3	.941
3	Government support	3	.941
4	Top management support	3	.938
5	Financial resources	4	.941
6	Perceived benefits	10	.940
7	Market and services	8	.939
8	Business model	6	.940
9	Business partners collaboration	6	.942
10	Regulatory environment	4	.941
11	MFP size (number of employees)		.649

5.1. Microfinance customer

Females represent the majority of respondents with 57%. The breakdown of age groups is dominated by the group of 28–37 years which consists of 35%, this is followed by those respondents aged 38–47, which had 33%. The majority (36%) of respondents earn income ranged 1,001–2,000 Sudanese pounds, followed by (34%) an earning income less than 1000 Sudanese pounds. University graduates compose the majority of respondents (35%), followed by intermediate (19%) and Secondary (16%). Table 3 below displays major demographic data of respondent.

Majority of respondents (99%) own a mobile phone, evidencing a very high cell phone penetration rate in microfinance communities. As for the purpose of using mobile phones, 69% reported using it for personal and business reasons, followed by those who used it for personal (26%). The most preferable way to communicate using mobile phones were reported to be call and talk to people (48%), followed by those who use mobile to transfer money 31%, the least important way of communication was sending only texts 10%. In terms of years of using the mobile phone, majority (61%) had good experience in using the mobile phone since their usage is more than 6 years, followed by those who used it between 3 and 5 years (19%). In response to frequency of usage, majority (85%) use mobile on daily basis. Table 4 displays customer characteristics related to mobile phone.

Majority of respondents belong to trade sector (40%), the respondents were asked to indicate which financial services were needed, majority of respondent (60%) want Send / Receive Money services, followed by loan request 58%, paying utilities bills 56%, balance enquiry 52%, payment for services and products 51%, 49% request bank statement, 48% Saving, 42% buy airtime, and the least services needed is insurance 34%.

The data also showed that among the respondents, 56% of them owning bank accounts, 55% get microfinance services from banks, followed by 34% from MFIs. Only 48% of respondents were aware of mobile banking services; however, a huge proportion (84%) believe that m-banking is important

Table 3. Demographic statistics

Variable	Description	Frequency	Percent (%)
Gender	Male	170	43.3
	Female	223	56.7
Age	18–27	65	16.5
	28–37	138	35.2
	38–47	125	31.8
	48–60	65	16.5
Education level	Illiterate	36	9.3
	Primary	39	9.9
	Intermediate	76	19.4
	Secondary	64	16.1
	Diploma	41	10.4
	University	137	34.9
Income level	Rather not say	52	13.2
	<1,000	132	33.6
	1,001–2,000	142	36.2
	2,001–3000	48	12.2
	3,001–4,000	13	3.3
	>4,000	6	1.5

Source: Field data 2015.

Table 4. Mobile phone ownership and usage

Mobile phone	Frequency	Percentage (%)
Ownership		
Yes	388	99
No	5	01
Mobile usage purposes		
Personal	95	26
Business	17	05
Both	250	69
Mobile services		
Calls	177	48
SMS	37	10
Money transfer	116	31
Other	42	11
Mobile experience		
One year	25	06
One-to-two years	53	14
Three-to-five years	73	19
Six to eight years	235	61
Frequency of usage		
Daily	327	85
2–5 times a week	19	05
Once a week	7	02
When required	32	08

Source: Field Data 2015.

for Sudanese community, 1% of respondent use m-banking, as per customer view only 1% of the MFPs provide m-banking services.

As shown in Figure 4, the major factors affecting adoption of m-banking from customer perspective are performance expectancy (perceived usefulness) 77%, effort expectancy (perceived ease of use) 72%, and perceived credibility (security and privacy) 71%.

As for moderating effects of gender, age, education, and income, gender significantly moderated the effects of performance expectancy and Social Influence, Perceived Credibility perceived financial cost, Perceived Self-Efficacy, and awareness to behavioral intention. Age significantly moderated the effects of Social Influence, Perceived Credibility, Perceived Self-Efficacy, and Banking Needs. Education significantly moderated the effects of Performance Expectance, Effort Expectance, Social Influence, Perceived Credibility, Perceived Financial Cost, Perceived Self-Efficacy, and Banking Needs. Income significantly moderated the effects of Performance Expectance, Effort Expectance, Social Influence, Perceived Credibility, Perceived Financial Cost, Perceived Self-Efficacy, and Banking Needs.

5.2. Microfinance service providers (MFPS)

Majority (90%) of the responding MFPs serve in urban areas, 60% of them are banks, 20% are MFIs, 10% are companies, and 7% are NGOs. The majority of the respondents (52%) have more than 15 years in operation, 24% have six to ten years in operation, and 21% have one to five years in operation. Most of the responding MFPs (52%) have less than 5,000 active clients, 26% have more than 30,000 active clients, and 16% have between 5,001 and 10,000 active clients. The study revealed that 41% of responding MFPs have between 50 and 200 employees, and 41% have more than 200 employees.

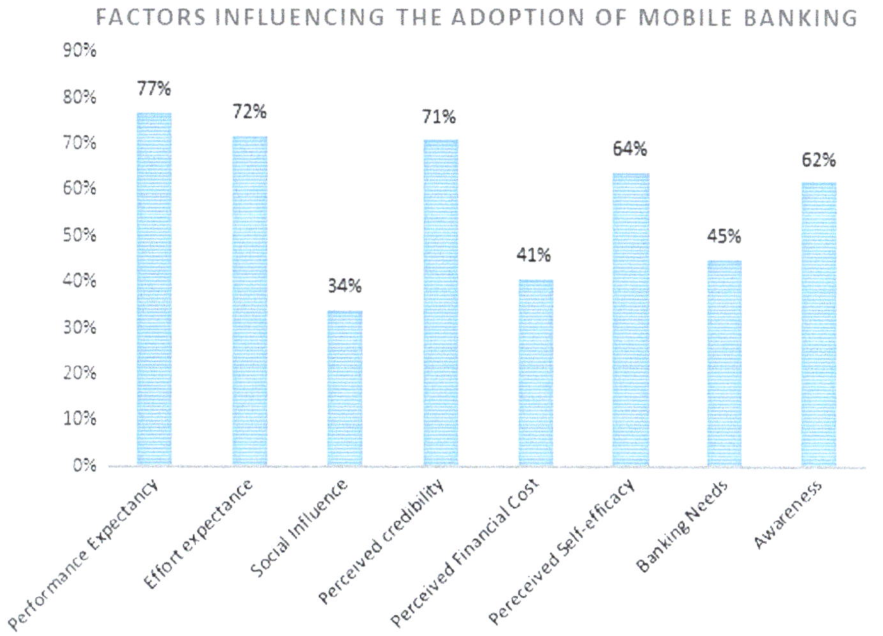

Figure 4. Factors influencing the adoption of m-banking based on microfinance customer perspectives.
Source: Field Data 2015.

All MFPs use computerized systems in operation, majority (61%) have 100 computers, and 26% have more than 300 computers. The majority of responding MFPs (70%) have more than 5 years' experience with computers, 20% have between 3 and 5 years' experience with computers, and the rest (10%) have less than 3 years' experience with computer systems. There are 63% of the MFPs have MIS, 53% have LTS, 53% provide ATM services, and 27% provide m-banking services. Results show that majority of MFPs (87%) have a WEB page, 48% of them use it for marketing, and 31% for status, 80% for information, and 7% use the WEB page for sales purposes.

The factors affecting adoption of m-banking by MFPs are depicted in Figure 5. Majority of respondents 77% articulated benefits of m-banking to their organization as a major factor of adoption, 71% of the respondents testify that their organizations have adequate ICT infrastructure to

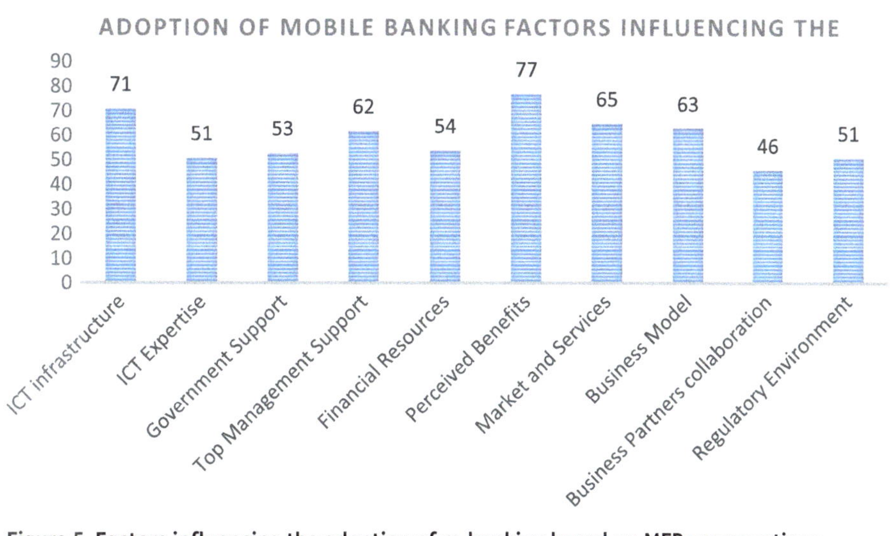

Figure 5. Factors influencing the adoption of m-banking based on MFPs perspectives.

accommodate m-banking applications, 65% articulated that their organization understands customers` requirements and in which market to announce its products and services. Based on Likert, MFPs that have more than 200 employees (measurement of MFP size) give high scores to ICT infrastructure readiness, ICT skills, top management support, Financial Resources, Perceived Benefits, Market and Services, Business Model, and Business Partners Collaboration.

5.3. Interview interpretation

Qualitative semi-structured face-to-face interviews were conducted with microfinance senior staff in Khartoum and Kassal states. The main objectives of the interviews were to understand the major problems facing microfinance sector outreach in Sudan and the role of mobile banking to resolve these problems. The results reveal that there is a huge market for microfinance market in Sudan, but operating cost is a major problem especially in rural areas due to local population density and poor road infrastructure. Hence, the need for m- banking services is obvious. Implementing mobile banking would require reliable ICT infrastructure mainly in rural and semi-urban areas. Most of the microfinance providers rely on traditional core banking systems, which is not suitable for the inclusion of the poor and micro-financing activities. There is no significant mobile banking initiative which can be launched in Sudan without ensuring that microfinance services providers are equipped with a stable and scalable MIS such as loan tracking system LIS, managed by competent ICT staff. There are huge differences in the degree of satisfaction and perception of clients according to the differences in geographical locations, gender types, and age intervals. Hence, the nature of products, their level of sophistications of processes and technology used should be adapted to the targeted clients, supplying such services will require adapting their organization, products, and processes. Innovation in products and services in Sudanese microfinance are limited, for example, savings and remittance services are a real need for clients of microfinance, but remain underdeveloped. Respondents claimed that government support is one of the important factors that influence adoption of mobile banking in Sudan. Issues related to customers illiteracy and awareness were also raised as factors influencing the acceptance of mobile banking services. Collaboration of different mobile banking stakeholders was also mentioned by banks' senior staff as one of the most important factors. There are two banks and one MFI realizing the benefits of mobile banking and they have begun a practical action to proceed.

6. Empirical findings discussion

The findings of the study showed that most of the microfinance customers are female, age range 28–47, educated, have moderate income, majority need financial services such as loan, saving, money transfer. Besides, majority have bank accounts, own a mobile phone, and have more than six years of mobile experience. Moreover, majority did not hear about mobile baking services but they think it is important for the Sudanese community.

The research showed that a lot of people in microfinance sector had no knowledge at all about mobile banking services, as evidenced by 48% citing lack of knowledge of the services. Results also showed that there were more people with cell phones (99%) than with bank accounts (56%). Majority of respondents (99%) don't use the m-banking service, these findings are in line with Chitungo and Munongo's (2013) findings that stated that mobile banking is a new phenomenon in developing countries and has not been well adopted by customers.

From this research finding, perceived performance expectancy (perceived usefulness), perceived effort expectancy (ease of use), perceived credibility (security and privacy), perceived self-efficacy, and awareness are seen as determinants of mobile banking adoption by microfinance customers in Sudan. As such, the study's findings were supported by the studies undertaken by Masinge (2010); Yu (2012), and Carlsson et al. (2006) that reveal that performance expectancy is a major factor in intention to use m-banking. Meanwhile, Tingari and Abdelrahman (2012); and NG Karma et al. (2014) supported perceived ease-of-use as a determinant impacting people to use m-banking. Perceived Credibility was supported by Yu (2012); and Luarn and Lin (2005) studies. Luarn and Lin (2005) deem perceived self-efficacy as a necessary capability in using m-banking. Moreover, Laforet and Li's

(2005) study reveals lack of awareness and understanding of benefits is the main factor affecting mobile banking adoption. Contrary to the author" expectation Social influence, perceived financial cost, and banking needs were found to have no influence on the microfinance customers " intention to use m-banking". According to Carlsson et al. (2006), social influence does not seem to be a major factor influencing behavior intention to use mobile devices/services. Studies from Koening-Lewis, Palmer, and Moll (2010), Petrova and Yu (2010) suggest that there is no significant relationship between cost and behavioral intention to use technology.

Within the MFPs factors, all factors mentioned in the study—except collaboration between stakeholders—ICT infrastructure, ICT expertise, MFP size, Top management Support, organization financial resources, perceived benefits, government support, market and products, business model, and enabling regulatory environment were found to have influence on m-banking implementation by MFPs. Many empirical studies support these findings such as studies undertaken by Ayana (2014) in Ethiopia, Muriuki's (2009) study in Kenia, and Khattab et al. (2012) in Sudan revealed that infrastructure readiness is an essential factor for the success of m-banking. Ayana (2014) and Muriuki (2009) studies consider ICT expertise as a major factor in E- banking implementation. Toufaily and Daghfous (2009) and Zhu and Kraemer's (2005) studies support the importance of firm size. Top management support findings are in line with Muriuki (2009) and Zhu and Kraemer's (2005) studies. Zhu and Kraemer (2005), and Kuan and Chau's (2001) studies support organization financial resources as an influencing factor in the adoption of E-channels. Importance of perceived benefits in technology adoption has been supported by Xu, Zhu, and Gibbs (2010). Government support findings are in line with Chong et al. (2010) study in Vietnam. Market and Products findings are in line with Yousif et al. (2013) and Khattab et al. (2012) studies. According to Benjamin (2013), and Khattab et al. (2012) studies, business model is a major factor in m-banking adoption. Enabling Regulatory Environment factor was supported by Yousif et al. (2013), Khattab et al. (2012); Ismail and Osman (2012), Ayana (2014) and Zhu and Kraemer's (2005) studies.

7. Conclusion and policy implications

A significant contribution of this study is that this study extends UTAUT model with the inclusion of six additional variables, namely Previous Experience, Banking Needs, Perceived Self-efficacy, Awareness, Perceived credibility, and Perceived financial cost factors to study MF customers intention to use m-banking. The second significant contribution is that TOE framework developed by (Tornatzky & Fleischer, 1990) was also extended by adding variables related to the adoption of m-banking within the organization and environment contexts in Sudan such as Business Model, Market and Products, and Partners Collaboration. The two extended framework were combined to identify the factors influencing adoption of m-banking in the Sudanese microfinance sector. The study fills the gaps in both demand and supply of this area of important study, as most of the studies studied them individually.

We notice with optimism that most respondents of microfinance customers and MFPs had strong intentions to use m-banking. Performance expectancy and effort expectancy were the primary determinants of behavior intention in our study. This is also related to the education, age, gender, income, mobile phone ownership and customer's experience with mobile phone. Most of the MFPs (especially banks) have long experience with technology. ICT Infrastructure and ICT experts in the country are ready for m-banking. The study's results also show that participants are familiar with mobile phone technology. The use of mobile phone in Sudan microfinance sector is high. High usage of mobile phone motivates MFPs to implement mobile banking; in this case, people are familiar with the main tools of mobile banking and can use it efficiently. Moreover, the results also indicate that intention to use M-banking services is predicted by most of the factors that we used in the research models. The existing E-banking regulations can pave the road for m-banking regulations.

There are several limitations evidenced in this study. These limitations should be considered for future research and improvement. Firstly, the results of this study are collected within a few microfinance communities (three states) in Sudan and the results may not be generalized and inapplicable to other nationalities. Secondly, most of MFPs contributed in the questionnaire are banks with good organization setup (technical, managerial, and financial). Also, most of the face-to-face interviews were carried out with senior knowledgeable MFPs staff, most of whom were exposed to microfinance experience both inside and outside the country.

Since the adoption and usage of mobile technology highly varies across countries with different adoption levels and perceptions, researchers may want to further research on multi-nationalities through expanding geographical areas to gain better generalizations in future studies.

Based on the study's findings, following are the recommendations to be considered by the concerned groups in this area:

(1) There is a need to address security issues associated with M-banking technology so as to ensure success of m-banking technology implementation. More specifically, the issues that need to be addressed in the time being is to ensure security and privacy of existing e-channels such as ATM, EPOS and resolve all network problems.
(2) Building customer awareness and informing the public on benefits and use of m-banking products and services is required. There should be rigorous marketing campaigns by mobile banking service providers; banks and MNOs alike, especially targeting the urban and rural communities.
(3) Proper regulatory environment, respecting user guidelines, trusts, rights and protections, proper integration and partnership between mobile network operators and MFPs, adequate staff training and introducing client literacy for proper use, developing reliable and adequate ICT infrastructure and better product and service design are necessary to implement m-banking.
(4) Success of m-banking implementation is highly dependent on the dedication and specialization of capacities of the MFPs. Microfinance customers need safer, more reliable, affordable, and convenient ways to manage the little money they have. A deep and realistic understanding of financial needs, constraints, and opportunities of the microfinance customers are needed to address in its proper designing.

Acknowledgments
We would like to thank Islamic Research and Training Institute (IRTI) of Islamic Development Bank (IDB) based on Jeddah, KSA for funding this research through the research grant provided. Special thanks to Professor Dr Abdul Ghafar Ismail and Professor Dr Abdulrahman Elzahi.

Funding
This work was supported by Islamic Research and Training Institute, Islamic Development Bank, Jeddah, KSA.

Author details
Anwar Ammar[1]
E-mail: anwar_ammar@yahoo.com
Elsadig Musa Ahmed[2]
E-mail: elsadig1965@gmail.com
[1] Faculty of Management, Multimedia University, Cyberjaya, Malaysia.
[2] Faculty of Business, Multimedia University, Melaka 75450, Malaysia.

Note
1. Throughout this paper, an organization providing microfinance to the poor is referred to as MFP (Microfinance Provider) rather than MFI (Microfinance Institute). There are many microfinance-providing organizations which are not MFIs, namely NGOs, CBOS, commercial banks, etc. Microfinance is one of the programs/sectors they undertake.

References
Ahmed, F. (2012). *Identifying the result of mobile banking implementation for microfinance institutions* (Unpublished Master Thesis). Solvay Brussels Institute of Business and Management, University Libre de Bruxelles.
Al Nahian Riyadh Md., Akter, S., & Islam, N. (2009). The adoption of e-banking in developing countries: A theoretical model for SMEs. *International Review of Business Research Papers, 5*, 212–230
Aldhaban, F. (2012). Exploring the adoption of smartphone technology. Literature review. In *Proceeding of the Technology anagement for Emerging Technologies* (pp. 2758–2770). Washington, DC: IEEE Computer Society.
Alexandre, C. (2011, November 14–17). *What can branchless banking do to advance the field, and what can it not do? From mobile banking to point of service*. Paper presented at the 2011 Global Microcredit Summit. Valladolid.
Al-Zoubi, M., Sam, T. L., & Eam, L. H. (2011). E-Government adoption among businesses in Jordan. *Academic Research Institute ISSN, 1*, 2223–9553.
Armendariz, B., & Morduch, J. (2010). *The economics of microfinance* (2nd ed.). Massachusetts: MIT Press.
Aversano, A., Evers, S., Latif, A., & Vaca-Viana, M. (2013, October 10). *Mobile telephony in developing countries: A global perspective* (I Quaderni Di THINK! N°4 I Quaderni di THINK. THINK! Report). Retrieved from www.thinkinnovation.org

Ayana, G. B. (2014). Factors affecting adoption of electronic banking system in Ethiopian banking industry. *Journal of Management Information System and E-commerce, 1.*

Badri, A. Y. (2013). The role of micro-credit system for empowering poor women. *Developing Country Studies,* 3(5). ISSN 2224-607X (Paper) ISSN 2225-0565 (Online). Retrieved from www.iiste.org

Bagozzi, R. (2007). The legacy of the technology acceptance model and a proposal for a paradigm shift. *Journal of the Association for Information Systems, 8,* 244–254.

Benjamin, O. A. (2013). *Mobile banking and entrepreneurship in developing countries: A case study of Nigeria* (Master Thesis). Department of Industrial Economics Master in Entrepreneurship, Blekinge Institute of Technology, Karlskrona.

Breul, P. (2012). *Analyzing the result of mobile banking implementation for microfinance institutions in emerging countries.* Slide presentation at PHB Development. PHB Development.

Carlsson, C., Carlsson, J., Hyvönen, K., Puhakainen, J., & Walden, P. (2006, January 4–7). Adoption of mobile devices/services - Searching for answers with the UTAUT. *Proceedings of the 39th Annual Hawaii International Conference on System Sciences, 2006. HICSS '06, 6,* 132a–132a. doi:10.1109/HICSS.2006.38

Chitungo, S. K., & Munongo, S. (2013). Extending the technology acceptance model to mobile banking adoption in rural Zimbabwe. *Journal of Business Administration and Education, 3,* 51–79.

Chong, A. Y., Ooi, K., Lin, B., & Tan, B. (2010). Online banking adoption: An empirical analysis. *International Journal of Bank Marketing, 28,* 267–287.

Conzett, C., Pulido, P. R., Lacalle, M., & Javier, A. G. (2010). *Impact of mobile money services on MFI's operational costs in Tanzania.* IMTFI Institute for Money, Technology & Financial Inclusion.

Crabbe, M., Standing, C., Standing, S., & Karjaluoto, H. (2009). An adoption model for mobile banking in Ghana. *International Journal of Mobile Communications, 7,* 515–543. http://dx.doi.org/10.1504/IJMC.2009.024391

Davis, F. (1989). Perceived usefulness, perceived ease of use, and user acceptance of information technology. *MIS Quarterly, 13,* 319–340. http://dx.doi.org/10.2307/249008

Demombynes. G., & Thegeya, A. (2012, March). *Kenya's mobile revolution and the promise of mobile savings* (World Bank Policy Research Working Paper, No. 5988).

Donner, J., & Tellez, C. A. (2008). Mobile banking and economic development: Linking adoption, impact, and use. *Asian Journal of Communication, 18,* 318–332. http://dx.doi.org/10.1080/01292980802344190

El Habeeb, H. E., Maruod, M. E., & Elteama, M. S. (2014). The role of North Kordofan rural development project (NKRDP) in women development in Bara locality, North Kordofan State, Sudan. *International Journal of Education and Research, 2*(10).

Fishbein, M., & Ajzen, I. (1975). *Belief, attitude, intention and behavior: An introduction of theory and research.* Reading, MA: Addison-Wesley.

Xu, S., Zhu, K., & Gibbs, J. (2004). Global technology, local adoption: A cross-country investigation of Internet adoption by companies in the United States and China. *Electronic Markets, 14,* 13–24.

Goss, S., Mas, I., Radcliffe, D., & Stark, E. (2011, April). *The next challenge: Challenging savings through mobile money schemes* (World Economic Forum Report).

Hartarska, V., Shen, X., & Mersland, R. (2013). Scale economies and input price elasticities in microfinance institutions. *Journal of Banking & Finance, 37,* 118–131.

Hassan, A. I., & Bauer, S. (2013). Access to micro credit and its impact on farm profit among rural farmers in dryland of Sudan. *Global Advanced Research Journal of Agricultural Science, 2,* 088–102, ISSN: 2315-5094.

Hinson, R. E. (2011). Banking the poor: The roles of mobiles. *Journal of Financial Services Marketing, 15,* 320–333.

HORUS CBOS. (2011, January). *Study for the establishment of pro-poor branchless banking in Sudan* (Final Report).

Iacovou, C. L., Benbasat, I., & Dexter, A. S. (1995). Electronic data interchange and small organizations: Adoption and impact of technology. *MIS Quarterly, 19,* 465–485. http://dx.doi.org/10.2307/249629

Ibrahim, B. El. D. A. (2014, October 22–25). Microfinance Sectors in two African countries -Sudan & Ethiopia. In *AEMFI 8th biennial conference.* Hawassa.

Impact Evaluation Assessment MFI Sector in Sudan 2007–2012 (2013, May). *Sudanese Microfinance Development Facility (SMDF) Draft Report May 2013 PACT.*

Ismail, M. A., & Osman, M. A. Y. (2012). Factors influencing the adoption of e-banking in Sudan: Perceptions of retail banking clients. *Journal of Internet Banking and Commerce, 17*(3), 1–16. Retrieved from http://www.arraydev.com/commerce/JIBC/2012- 12/mohamedismailv02.pdf

Ivatury, G., & Mas, I. (2008). *The early experience with branchless banking* (CGAP Focus Note No. 46). Retrieved from http://ssrn.com/abstract=1655257

Ivatury, G., & Pickens, M. (2006). *Mobile phone banking and low-income customers.* Washington, DC: CGAP.

Karjaluoto, H., Mattila, M., & Pento, T. (2002). Electronic banking in Finland: Consumer beliefs and reactions to a new delivery channel. *Journal of Financial Services Marketing, 6,* 346–361.

Karma N. G., Ibrahim S. B., Ali, A. H. (2014). Key factors affecting mobile banking adoption among banks' customers in Sudan. *International Journal of Liberal Arts and Social Science, 2*(6).

Ketkar, S. P., Shankar, R., & Banwet, D. K. (2012). Structural modeling of m-banking influencers. *Journal of Electronic Commerce Research, 13,* 70–87.

Khatri, A., & Kurnia, S. (2011). Mobile banking adoption in australian rural areas. *PACIS 2011 Proceedings Paper 95.* Retrieved from http://aisel.aisnet.org/pacis2011/95

Khattab, I., Balola, Y., & Eldabi T. (2012, June 7–8). Factors influencing branchless banking for microfinance in Sudan: Theoretical perspectives and future directions. In *European, Mediterranean & Middle Eastern Conference on Information Systems 2012 (EMCIS2012).* Munich.

Koening-Lewis, N., Palmer, A., & Moll, A. (2010). Predicting young consumers' take up of mobile banking services. *International Journal of Banking Marketing, 28,* 410–432.

Kuan, K. K. Y., & Chau, P. Y. K. (2001). A perception-based model for EDI adoption in small businesses using a technology-organization environment framework. *Information and Management, 38,* 507–521. http://dx.doi.org/10.1016/S0378-7206(01)00073-8

Kumer, K., Mckay, C., & Rotman, S. (2010, July). *Microfinance and mobile banking: The story so far* (Focus note-62). Washington, DC: CGAP.

Kurnia, S., Peng, F., & Liu, Y. R. (2010). Understanding the adoption of electronic banking in China. In *Proceedings of the 43rd Hawaii International Conference on System Sciences* (pp. 1–10). IEEE.

Laforet, S., & Li, X. (2005). Consumers' attitudes towards online and mobile banking in China. *International Journal of Bank Marketing, 23,* 362–380.

Liu, Z., Min, Q., & Ji, S. (2009). An empirical study on mobile banking adoption: The role of trust. In *2009 Second International Symposium on Electronic Commerce and Security* (pp. 7–13). IEEE. doi:10.1109/ISECS.2009.150

Luarn, P., & Lin, H. H. (2005). Toward an understanding of the behavioral intention to use mobile banking. *Computers in*

Human Behavior, 21, 873–891. http://dx.doi.org/10.1016/j.chb.2004.03.003
Maneiah, K. (2012). Micro finance – An effective tool for women empowerment. *Asian Academic Research Journal of Social Sciences & Humanities, 1*, 139–145.
Mapping, capacity assessment & capacity development of microfinance providers in Sudan. (2012, June). PACT (Project Report to CBOS).
Mas, I. (2011). Why are banks so scarce in developing countries? A regulatory and infrastructure perspective. *Critical Review, 23*, 135–145.
Masinge, K. (2010). Factors influencing the adoption of mobile banking services at the bottom of the pyramid in South Africa (A Research Report submitted to the Gordon Institute of Business Science). University of Pretoria.
McKay, C., & Pickens, M. (2010). *Branchless banking 2010: Who's served? At what price? What's next?* (Focus Note 66). Washington, DC: CGAP. Retrieved from http://www.cgap.org/sites/default/ files/CGAP-Focus-Note-Branchless-Banking-2010-Who-Is-Served-At-What-Price-What-Is-NextSep-2010.pdf
Michel H., & Sarah, R. (2013, August). Microfinance and mobile banking: Blurring the lines? (CGAP Focus Note No. 88).
Moon, M. J., & Norris, D. (2005). Does managerial orientation matter? The adoption of reinventing government and e-government at the municipal level. *Information Systems Journal, 15*, 43–60. http://dx.doi.org/10.1111/isj.2005.15.issue-1
Moshy, B., & Mukwaya, P. L. (2011). *An assessment of adoption and use of mobile money services in East Africa-Case Studies from Uganda and Tanzania.* Slide presentation at IMTFI Annual Conference Schedule 2011.
Muriuki, E. (2009). *Factors affecting adoption of e-banking by microfinance institutions in Kenya* (Unpublished MBA project). Moi, Moi University.
National Baseline Household Survey. (2009). *Sudan Central Bureau of Statistics.*
Nestor, C., & Edelstein, D. (2011, November 14–17). *How technology is working for clients and MFIs especially for those living and working in the hardest to reach areas.* 2011 Global Microcredit Summit Commissioned Workshop Paper. Valladolid: Ndiwalana, A., Morawczynski.
Oliveira, T. and Martins, M. F. (2011). Literature review of information technology adoption models at firm level. *Electronic Journal Information Systems Evaluation, 14*, 110–121.
Ongwenyi, O. (2012). Influence of mobile phone banking on traditional banking transactions; A case of banking institutions in Nairobi central business district (A Project Report submitted in partial fulfillment of the requirements of the Degree of Master of Arts (M.A), Planning and Project, Management School of Continuing and Distance Education) University of Nairobi.
Park, J., Yang, S., & Lehto, X. (2007). Adoption of mobile technologies for Chinese consumers. *Journal of Electronic Commerce Research, 8*, 196–206.
Petrova, K., & Yu, S. (2010). SMS Banking. *International Journal of E-Services and Mobile Applications, 2*, 19–43. http://dx.doi.org/10.4018/IJESMA
Pierre-Laurent, C. (2011). *Protecting mobile money against financial crimes global policy challenges and solutions.* Washington, DC: World Bank Publications.
Ramdani, B., Kawalek, P., & Lorenzo, O. (2009). Knowledge management and enterprise systems adoption by SMEs: Predicting SMEs adoption of enterprise systems. *Journal of Enterprise Information Management, 22*, 10–24.
Rogers, E. (1995). *Diffusion of innovations* (4th ed.). New York, NY: Free Press.
Sara, A. (2012). *An e-government adoption framework for developing countries: A case study from Sudan* (Ph.D. Dissertation). Cranfield University.
Sayed, F. E., & Belal, I. (2013, September 17–19). *The impact of microfinance on rural poor households' income & vulnerability to poverty: Case study of North Kordofan State.* Stuttgart-Hohenheim: Tropentag.
Siddig, K. (2013). Role of women small enterprises in poverty alleviation in urban Sudan (1998–2012) (A thesis submitted for the degree of Doctor of Philosophy in Economic). Sudan: AlzaeemAlazhari University.
Situational Analysis of the Microfinance Sector in Sudan. (2006, March). *Unicons* (Project report to CBOS).
Sripalawat, J., Thongmak, M., & Ngramyarn, A. (2011). M-banking in metropolitan Bangkok and a comparison with other countries. *The Journal of Computer Information Systems, 51*,67–76.
Sudan 2015 African Economic Outlook. (2015). AfDB, OECD, UNDP. Retrieved from www.africaneconomicoutlook.org
Tan, M., & Teo, T. (2000). Factors influencing the adoption of Internet banking. *Journal of the Association for Information Systems, 1*(5), 1–42.
Taylor, S., & Todd, P. A. (1995). Understanding information technology usage: A test of competing models. *Information Systems Research, 6*, 144–176. http://dx.doi.org/10.1287/isre.6.2.144
The African Development Bank. (2014). *A partner of choice for the Eastern Africa we want* (EARC Report).
Tingari, W. M., & Abdelrahman A. B. (2012). Study acceptance of banking technology in Sudan: An analytical study. In *ICCIT 2012.*
Titah, R., & Barki, H. (2006). E-Government Adoption and Acceptance. *International Journal of Electronic Government Research, 2*, 23–57 http://dx.doi.org/10.4018/IJEGR.
Tobbin, P., & Kuwornu, J. K. (2011). Adoption of mobile money transfer technology: structural equation modeling approach. *European Journal of Business and Management, 3*, 59–77.
Tornatzky, L., & Fleischer, M. (1990). *The process of technology innovation.* Lexington, MA: Lexington Books.
Toufaily, E., & Daghfous, N. (2009). The adoption of E-banking by Lebanese banks: Success and critical factors. *International Journal of Eservices and Mobile Applications (IJESMA), 1*, 67–93.
Turner, M. (2011). Effectiveness of micro finance loans in Pakistan. *American Journal of Law and Public Policy, 1*(4).
Venkatesh, V., & Davis, F. D. (2000). A theoretical extension of the technology acceptance model: Four longitudinal field studies. *Management Science, 46*, 186–204. http://dx.doi.org/10.1287/mnsc.46.2.186.11926
Venkatesh, V., Morris, M. G., Davis, F. D., & Davis, G. B. (2003). User acceptance of information technology: Towards a unified view. *MIS Quarterly, 27*, 425–478.
Vinayagamoorthy, A., & Sankar, C. (2012). Mobile banking –An overview. *Advances In Management, 5*, 24–29.
Voorrips, G., Breul, P., & Coupienne, F. (2012, May). *Mobile financial services:-The microfinance perspective* (PHB briefing note No. 2). PHB Development. Retrieved from http://www.microfinancegateway.org/library/mobile-financial-services-microfinance-perspective .
Yassir, A., & Hassan, J. (2012). The market demand research of Agriculture Bank of Sudan. *PACT 2012.*
Yousif, F., Elizabeth, B., Jacinta, M., & Olga, M. (2013). *Best practice in mobile microfinance.* Grameen Foundation and Institute for Money, Technology & Financial Inclusion.
Yu, C. (2012). Factors affecting individuals to adopt mobile banking: Empirical evidence from the UTAUT model. *Journal of Electronic Commerce Research, 13*(2).
Yun, H., Han, D., & Lee, C. C. (2011). Extending UTAUT to predict the use of location based. In *Proceedings of the 32nd International Conference of Information Systems* (pp. 1–9).
Zhu, K., & Kraemer, K. L. (2005). Post-adoption variations in usage and value of e-business by organizations: Cross-country evidence from the retail industry. *Information Systems Research, 16*, 61–84. http://dx.doi.org/10.1287/isre.1050.0045

9

Measuring systemic risk of Greek banks: New approach by using the epidemic model "SEIR"

Abdelkader Derbali[1*] and Slaheddine Hallara[2]

*Corresponding author: Abdelkader Derbali, Department of Finance, Higher Institute of Management of Sousse, University of Sousse, 22 Street Zarkaa Al Yamama, Sousse Erriadh 4023, Tunisia
E-mail: derbaliabdelkader@outlook.fr

Reviewing editor: David McMillan, University of Stirling, UK

Abstract: In the last decade of the financial crisis of 2007, the international financial system appeared to be on the brink of a major systemic crisis which leads to a failure of a systemically important European bank. This type of scenario highlights the need for identifying and measuring of the contribution of banks to systemic risk in the financial system. Then, the aim of this paper is to propose, for the first time, a new approach to measure systemic risk in the financial institutions. This approach is based on the epidemic model methodology. Then, we use the SEIR model with four compartments: Susceptible, Exposed, Infected, and Removed. We apply this model for a sample of 18 Greek banks listed in the Athens Exchange over the period from 2 January 2006 to 31 December 2012. Based on the empirical results, we find the existence of 12 times of default transmission during the study period and the transmission of default coincides with the number of Greek banks that have declared failure and then leaving the Athens Exchange. Also, we remark that the continuation of aid and recovery plans granted by international and national regulatory authorities did enough to save Greek banks.

Subjects: Banking; Corporate Finance; Risk Management

Keywords: systemic risk; epidemic model; SEIR; Greek banks; transmission

JEL classifications: D53; E02; E44; G21; G32; C52

ABOUT THE AUTHORS

Abdelkader Derbali is an assistant professor in Finance at the Higher Institute of Management of Sousse in University of Sousse, Tunisia. He is one of the editorial board members in the *African Journal of Accounting, Auditing and Finance*. His research interests include Risk Management and Capital markets and institutions. He has published articles, among others, in *Research in International Business and Finance, The Journal of Energy Markets, African Journal of Accounting, Auditing and Finance, International Journal of Critical Accounting*, and *International Journal of Trade and Global Market*.

Slaheddina Hallara is a professor of Finance at Higher Institute of Management of Tunis in University of Tunis, Tunisia. His research interests are pricing, credit risk, and financial markets. He obtained his PhD in Finance from Rennes University, Tunisia. His research has been published in journals such as *Research in International Business and Finance, International Journal of Monetary Economics and Finance*.

PUBLIC INTEREST STATEMENT

This paper analyzes the propagation of the default in the Greek financial system. This propagation justifies the presence of the systemic risk in Greece. So, this study is important because, after the outbreak of the financial crisis of 2007, the task of processing bank failures and its negative impact requires approaches to assess systemic risk and to determinate the role of Greek regulators. Thus, we find the existence of 12 transmissions of default during the period of study (02/01/2006–31/12/2012). Then, the role of the central bank is inadequate and even absent for the period of study. There is a deficiency in own regulations. Also, we find that the default probability, the recovery rate, the default correlation, the exposure at default, the frequency of default in the case of loss, the market capitalization, and the regulatory authorities are the main factors of the systemic risk in the financial system of Greece.

1. Introduction

The magnitude of the recent financial crisis has led to a redesign of the mechanisms' supervision of the financial sector. In particular, following the Larosière report (2009), the European Parliament voted to create a new instance of supervision: The European Systemic Risk Board (ESRB for European Systemic Risk Board). Part of the European policy response to the financial crisis, therefore, to have a dedicated instance for the systemic risk in addition to the usual trio of Financial Supervisory Authorities: the financial market authority (ESMA for European Securities and Market Authority), the bank authority (EBA to European Banking Authority), and the Insurance authority (EIOPA for European Insurance and Occupational Pensions Authority). According to Regulation EU (European Union) 1092/2010, the European Systemic Risk Board should have the task to monitor and to assess the systemic risk in normal times to mitigate the system's exposure to the risk of failure of systemic components and improve the resilience of the financial system to shocks. This mandate specifies both objectives and how to fill them. A key point is that the way—monitor and assess systemic risk—requires measurement tools.

The arrangement of systemic risk measurement tools is a new challenge in finance. New for this type of risk, and thus a part of the difficulty is in the subject of measurement. In financial literature, Acharya, Pedersen, Philippon, and Richardson (2009) examine the identification and the understanding of the systemic risk, Martínez-Jaramillo, Pérez, Embriz, and Dey (2010) and Amelia and Philip (2013) study the systemic risk and the phenomenon of financial contagion, Sanjiv and Raman (2004) and Silvan and Paolo (2007) learn an importance on the modeling of the systemic risk of a credit portfolios, and Mejra, Alenka, and Sebastijan (2011) investigate the macro-economic factors of systemic risk.

The financial crisis of 2007 proves to be the start of systemic events in most banking systems. The determination of these events is maintained using several models and approaches which find the existence of excessive propagation of banking failures. Greece is one among many countries which their banking system is strongly affected by the financial crisis of 2007. This gives rise to several questions which revolve around the following: the transmission date, the number of transmission, the transmission rate, the value or the size of bank assets in default and can pass this defect to other banks.

Even with the intervention of regulators, the state of uncertainty about the nature and causes of systemic risk is reflected in the potentially conflicting views on the relationship between financial network structure and the extent of financial contagion. Consequently, the presence of a more interconnected architecture improves the probability of systemic collapse events in the entire financial system and subsequently spread risk throughout the economy. This gives rise to the spread of financial contagion that promotes the increase in the scale and number of negative shocks to financial institutions, which in turn improves system instability. This view is also shared by Blume, David, Jon, Robert, and Eva (2011), Blume, Easley, Kleinberg, Kleinberg, and Tardos (2013) who considered the interbank contagion like an epidemic. This consideration has drawn our attention to develop a measure of systemic risk approach based on epidemic models.

This paper contributes to the systemic risk indicator building literature in several ways. First, we employ market data which reflect the real financial situation of Greek institution. Then, this paper expands the applicability of the measures proposed to assess the default transmission by the SEIR model. Also, we contribute to the determination of the systemic risk factors, as the default probability, the recovery rate, the default correlation, the exposure at default, the frequency of default in the case of loss, the market capitalization, and the regulatory authorities. Additionally, the proposed measure of the systemic risk explains the default transmission between Greek banks. Furthermore, we find that the presence of recovery plans decided by the international and the national regulatory authorities did enough to save Greek banks.

In this paper, we suggest a new approach to measure the systemic risk of the Greek banks. We will make use of an epidemic model to measure systemic risk. The epidemic models are used to model the spread of a disease in a population. These mathematical models of infectious diseases, initially purely theoretical tools, began to be practiced with the problem of infectious diseases in the 1980. The course of an epidemic in a population highly dependent on many parameters, mathematical models, have gradually established themselves as decision support tools for public policy. Our goal is to measure the systemic risk of Greek banks by adopting a biofinancial approach based on the use of an epidemic model "'SEIR."

We employ a sample composed of 18 Greek banks listed in the Athens Exchange from 2 January 2006 to 31 December 2012. The empirical results show the existence of 12 transmission fault of times during the study period. We remark that the failure of the transmission coincides with the failure of some Greek banks. The results presented in this paper are based on a set of assumptions that allow the validity of an epidemic model used to assess the systemic risk in the case of Greece. In addition, we show that the Greek financial system has a low exposure to the systemic events. Finally, we find that the aid programs and recovery plans implied by the international regulatory authorities did enough to save Greek banking system.

The rest of this paper is organized as follows: in Section 2, we develop a related literature concerning the measurement of systemic risk. Section 3 introduces the econometric approach and details the properties of the epidemic model used in this paper. Section 4 describes data. We explain the factors of systemic risk in section 5. Section 6 presents the main empirical results and analysis. Section 7 highlights the major conclusions of the different part of the present paper.

2. Literature review

Adrian and Brunnermeier (2008) used the approach of the Conditional VaR (CoVaR) to examine the effect of failure of a bank to other banks or to an entire banking system. To validate their approach, Adrian and Brunnermeier (2008) used stock prices and balance sheet data for a sample of 1224 institutions from 4 financial sectors and for a period of 25 years (1986–2010).

Based on Adrian and Brunnermeier (2008, 2009), Chan-Lau (2010) introduced an approach denoted CoRisk to study the risk of interdependence between the various financial institutions. Chan-Lau (2010) measured the default risk of transmission from one bank to other banks or to the entire financial system. The data employed to assess systemic risk are the implied default probabilities of CDS for 26 banks during the period from 2 May 2003 to 27 February 2009.

Segoviano and Goodhart (2009) propose a model for measuring systemic risk, the joint probability of default (JPod). This model was used to analyze conditional probabilities between institutions and the Banking Stability Index (BSI). The joint probability of default is the probability that the entire system fails at the same time. In addition, the index of banking stability is based on the measurement of conditional default probabilities. Their study is based on sample of 17 banks on Latin America, Eastern Europe, and Asia during the period from 1 January 2007 to 30 October 2008. Segoviano and Goodhart (2009) built their analysis on the distress or default dependency matrix between banks to determine the joint probability of default (JPod) and the index of banking stability (BIS).

Huang, Hao, and Zhu (2009, 2010) studied the phenomenon of systemic risk from 2001 to 2008. They propose a new measure of systemic risk denoted Distress Insurance Premium. Huang et al. (2009, 2010) gave two main indicators of systemic risk, the individual probability of default of each bank and the asset correlation. Besides, they found five indicators of systemic risk which are as follows: the values of CDS, the implied probability of default of CDS, the expected default frequency (EDF), the correlation of asset yields, and recovery rates. Their results show that all these indicators have a direct effect on systemic risk in Asian banks employed in their study.

Brownlees and Engle (2012) proposed an approach to determine the systemic risk. This approach is denoted SRISK measures which is used to identify the contribution of a financial institution to systemic risk on the whole financial system. Brownlees and Engle (2012) used a sample into four groups of US firms that have a market capitalization more than 5 billion dollars at the end of June 2007. The four groups are: repositories (29 institutions), brokers (32 institutions), companies insurance (10 institutions), and non-depository institutions (23 institutions). The period of study is from 3 June 2000 to 30 June 2010. Their results demonstrate that the companies with the highest SRISK have a strong contribution to the under-capitalization of the financial market crisis. These companies are considered to be the most systemically risky.

Acharya, Engle, and Richardson (2012), Acharya, Pedersen, Philippon, and Richardson (2010), and Acharya et al. (2009) proposed a model for measuring the systemic risk. This approach is named the Systemic Expected Shortfall (SES) or the expected systemic failure. Acharya et al. (2009, 2010, 2012) used a sample of 102 American financial institutions into 4 groups during a period of one year (June 2006–June 2007). They utilize the Expected Shortfall to estimate the systemic risk. Acharya et al. (2009, 2010, 2012) demonstrated the importance of the level of indebtedness of firms in their contributions to systemic risk.

Gray and Jobst (2010, 2011) developed a model called the systemic Contingent Claims Analysis (CCA). They used a sample of 36 largest institutions in the USA divided into 4 groups: investment banks, commercial banks, insurance companies, and specialized financial institutions. The period of study began on 1 January 2007 and ended on 31 January 2010. Their results show that the magnitude of systemic risk depends on the size of companies and on their interconnections in a multivariate system.

Derbali, Hallara, and Sy (2015) employed a conditional approach to estimate the systemic risk which allows decomposing the risk of the aggregate financial system of Greece. They employed the SRISK index to assess the systemic risk contribution of each Greek bank.

3. The modeling approach

3.1. The initial forma of model "SEIR"

In this paper, we adopt the epidemic model "SEIR" for the measurement of the systemic risk. The SEIR model consists of four compartments (Figure 1). This model is presented in the form of differential equations which measures the transfers between the four compartments (S, E, I, and R) (Al-Sheikh, 2012; Zhou & Cui, 2011):

This is the fraction of initially defaulted banks. E is the value of banks exposed to default (Exposed). This is the fraction of the banks that are infected but not yet capable of transmitting the default to the infected banks. I is the value of the banks not exposed to default (Infected). This is the portion of the banks may become in default if they are in contact with the portfolios that initially are defaulted. R is the value of banks resistant or withdrawn (Removed). This is the portion of the credit portfolios immunized against default. These are honest portfolios that do not change regardless of the situation they may find themselves. γ is the mean recovery rate (RR). β is the mean default correlation (DC). μ is the mean probability of default (PD). α is the mean exposure at default (EAD). θ is the

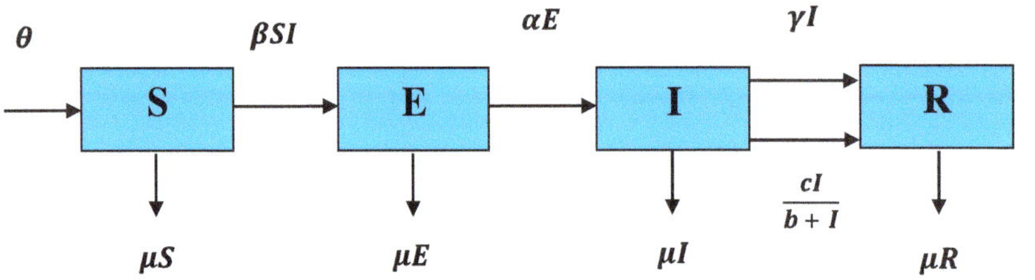

Figure 1. The SEIR model.

Notes: P is the total value of banks ($P = S + E + I + R$), S is the value of susceptible banks (susceptible).

growth rate of the total value of market capitalization of all banks (GRMC). b is the frequency of default in case of Loss ($b = 1 -$ Recovery Rate) (FDL). c is the maximum recovery rate at time (MAXRR). The total value of population (all banks) is measured as follow:

$$P = S + E + I + R \Rightarrow P(t) = S(t) + E(t) + I(t) + R(t) \tag{1}$$

So, we can see that $f(I, P)$ is the force of default transmission ($f(I, P) \geq 0$). In addition, the function f is increasing according to I and decreasing according to P and it can be written:

$$f(IP) \geq 0 \tag{2}$$

where $f(I, P) = \frac{\beta I}{P}$ if the population is not constant and $f(I, P) = \beta I$if the population is constant.

$$\text{The proportion ob banks in default} = \frac{I}{P} \tag{3}$$

The fundamental assumptions of standard SEIR model are:

Assumption 1: The total value of banks is assumed closed. Therefore, the effects related to changes in the total value of the banks are ignored and the P size is constant over time t, where: $S(t)$, $E(t)$, $I(t)$, *and* $R(t)$ are the fractions of four compartments at time t. $P(t) = S(t) + E(t) + I(t) + R(t)$.

Assumption 2: At $t = 0$, all banks are expected to be susceptible to default with the exception of the first banks that is in default.

Assumption 3: The model is assumed to be homogeneous. The total of banks is assumed to be homogeneous in terms of different types of financial institutions. Thus, the contact between the various portfolios (banks) is expressed by the mean of default correlations between the various portfolios. These contacts are homogeneous. Therefore, a portfolio is likely infected after a single random contact with infectious portfolio.

Moreover, the assumption of homogeneity implies that a bank (Infectious) transmits the failure to other portfolios which an independent and equiprobable manner with the same rate of infection.

Thus, the transmission process of the failure of a portfolio to other portfolios with a standard SEIR model is defined by the following non-linear system of differential equations (Al-Sheikh, 2012; Chowell et al., 2008; Zhou & Cui, 2011):

$$\begin{cases} \frac{dS(t)}{dt} = \theta - f(I, P)S(t) - \mu S(t) \\ \frac{dE(t)}{dt} = f(I, P)S(t) - \alpha E(t) - \mu E(t) \\ \frac{dI(t)}{dt} = \alpha E(t) - \gamma I(t) - \mu I(t) - \frac{cI(t)}{b+I(t)} \\ \frac{dR(t)}{dt} = \gamma I(t) - \mu R + \frac{cI(t)}{b+I(t)} \end{cases} \tag{4}$$

Then,

$$\begin{cases} \frac{dS(t)}{dt} = \theta - \beta I(t)S(t) - \mu S(t) \\ \frac{dE(t)}{dt} = \beta I(t)S(t) - (\alpha + \mu)E(t) \\ \frac{dI(t)}{dt} = \alpha E(t) - (\gamma + \mu)I(t) - \frac{cI(t)}{b+I(t)} \\ \frac{dR(t)}{dt} = \gamma I(t) - \mu R(t) + \frac{cI(t)}{b+I(t)} \end{cases} \tag{5}$$

where, $h(I) = \frac{cI(t)}{b+I(t)}$ is the recovery of infection implied by the regulatory authorities (mainly the Central Bank or other international authorities in the case of a portfolio of banks). The estimate of a basic SEIR model is to estimate its various parameters in the case of a deterministic model or in the case of a stochastic model.

In this respect, the estimation method used is not unique but depends on the nature of the data used and observations on the contagion process.

Whatever the nature of deterministic or stochastic SEIR model, the standard version is the simplest version, since it assumes homogeneity of the structure of banks at two levels:

- The first level concerns the transmission of default, that is to say, each bank is lacking transmits this defect to another bank may become in default with the same transmission rate.
- The second level concerns the level of correlation between banks, that is to say, the transmission of default is due to defects equal to the correlations between default portfolios and portfolios may be in fault.

In this paper, we will try to model the different parameters following its stochastic nature. This model ensures the homogeneity of all portfolios of banks. The resolution of the system (S) used to calculate the rate of default transmission which will be adopted as a measure of systemic risk. The rate of default transmission between portfolios takes values that will be compared to 1 (Ducrot, 2010; Touzeau, 2010). Following this rate R_0, the calculation results can be interpreted as follows:

- If $R_0 \leq 1$, then the DFE (disease-free equilibrium) is Locally Asymptotically Stable (LAS). The default will disappear and there is no transmission of the defect to other portfolios. In this case, we can observe a very low default correlation level or even non-existent between the portfolios.
- If $R_0 > 1, R_0$, then the DFE is unstable and there is a transmission of default. So, we're talking at this point a fairly significant level of default correlation between portfolios.

In this alignment, the mathematical resolution of the system (S) is shown in the following. Moreover, we set X the vector of portfolios (E), (I), and (S). That is to say, $X = (E, I, S)$.

The theorem on the resolution of this type of system, assuming that the DFE is unstable, is presented as follows:Theorem 1The disease-free equilibrium justifies the absence of infection. So, $E^* = I^* = R^* = 0$ and $S^* = P$. In our study, we speak of the absence of default is to say, a flawless state of equilibrium (DFE: Default Equilibrium Free).

In this case, we have $E^* = I^* = R^* = 0$ and $S^* = P$. Thus, $(S, E, I, R) = (S^*, 0, 0, 0) \leftrightarrow (S^*, 0, 0, 0) = \left(\frac{\theta}{\mu}, 0, 0, 0\right)$. $\mathcal{F}(X)$ and $\mathcal{V}(X)$ are functions of X.

In this context, the transmission rate R_0, which measures the systemic risk equals to FV^{-1}. The DFE assume that R_0 is equal to the dominant eigenvalue of which FV^{-1} is the maximum value of FV^{-1}.

The dynamics of changes in the various compartments of the total portfolio of banks will be represented by the following equation:

$$\frac{dx_i}{dt} = \mathcal{F}(x) - \mathcal{V}(x) \tag{6}$$

where, x_i refers to all portfolios which form the total of banks ($i = 1, \ldots, n$) and $\mathcal{F}(x)$ refers to the rate of appearance of new banks in a default state, that is to say what comes from other compartments of the total portfolio of banks in the defaulting bank compartment following a transmission failure and $\mathcal{V}(x)$ denotes the set of banks that go into default category of banks following the other causes that are beyond the compartment I.

In the case of a default-free state was $X_s = \{x|x_1 = \ldots = x_m = 0\}$ with $m \leq n$.Theorem 2The first three equations of the system (S) are independent of the compartment R. In this case, it is sufficient to use the new system (6) which is in the form of a system of differential equations.

$$\begin{cases} \frac{dS(t)}{dt} = \theta - \beta I(t)S(t) - \mu S(t) \\ \frac{dE(t)}{dt} = \beta I(t)S(t) - (\alpha + \mu)E(t) \\ \frac{dI(t)}{dt} = \alpha E(t) - (\gamma + \mu)I(t) - \frac{cI(t)}{b+I(t)} \end{cases} \quad (7)$$

In the absence of the default, we have $E^* = I^* = 0$ and $S^* = P$. In other words, $(S, E, I) = (S^*, 0, 0) \leftrightarrow (S^*, 0, 0) = \left(\frac{\theta}{\mu}, 0, 0\right)$.

We notes $X = (E, I, S)^T$ and $\frac{dX}{dt} = \mathcal{F}(X) - \mathcal{V}(X)$.

So we have,

$$\mathcal{F}(X) = \begin{pmatrix} \beta SI \\ 0 \\ 0 \end{pmatrix} \quad (8)$$

and,

$$\mathcal{V}(X) = \begin{pmatrix} (\alpha + \mu)E \\ -\alpha E + (\gamma + \mu)I + \frac{cI}{b+I} \\ -\theta + \beta IS + \mu S \end{pmatrix} \quad (9)$$

The Jacobean matrix $\mathcal{F}(X)$ and $\mathcal{V}(X)$ in the case of default transmission are shown, respectively, as follows:

$$D\mathcal{F}(X) = \begin{pmatrix} F & 0 \\ 0 & 0 \end{pmatrix} \quad (10)$$

$$D\mathcal{V}(X) = \begin{pmatrix} V & 0 \\ J_1 & J_2 \end{pmatrix} \quad (11)$$

Thereafter, we can write,

$$F = \begin{pmatrix} \frac{\partial \mathcal{F}}{\partial E} & \frac{\partial \mathcal{F}}{\partial I} \\ \frac{\partial \mathcal{F}}{\partial E} & \frac{\partial \mathcal{F}}{\partial I} \end{pmatrix} = \begin{pmatrix} 0 & \beta S \\ 0 & 0 \end{pmatrix} = \begin{pmatrix} 0 & \frac{\beta\theta}{\mu} \\ 0 & 0 \end{pmatrix} \quad (12)$$

and,

$$V = \begin{pmatrix} \frac{\partial \mathcal{V}}{\partial E} & \frac{\partial \mathcal{V}}{\partial I} \\ \frac{\partial \mathcal{V}}{\partial E} & \frac{\partial \mathcal{V}}{\partial I} \end{pmatrix} = \begin{pmatrix} (\alpha + \mu) & 0 \\ -\alpha & \left(\gamma + \mu + \frac{c}{b}\right) \end{pmatrix} \quad (13)$$

So, we can calculate the matrix V^{-1}:

$$V^{-1} = \left(\begin{pmatrix} \frac{\partial \mathcal{V}}{\partial E} & \frac{\partial \mathcal{V}}{\partial I} \\ \frac{\partial \mathcal{V}}{\partial E} & \frac{\partial \mathcal{V}}{\partial I} \end{pmatrix}\right)^{-1} = \begin{pmatrix} (\alpha + \mu) & 0 \\ -\alpha & \left(\gamma + \mu + \frac{c}{b}\right) \end{pmatrix}^{-1} \quad (14)$$

First of all, we calculate the determinant of the matrix V:

$$\det(V) = \left((\alpha + \mu) * \left(\gamma + \mu + \frac{c}{b}\right)\right) - (0 * (-\alpha)) = (\alpha + \mu) * \left(\gamma + \mu + \frac{c}{b}\right) = (\alpha + \mu)(\gamma + \mu) \quad (15)$$

Then,

$$V^{-1} = \frac{1}{\det(V)} V^{ct} \tag{16}$$

with,

$$V^{ct} = \begin{pmatrix} (\gamma + \mu + \frac{c}{b}) & 0 \\ \alpha & (\alpha + \mu) \end{pmatrix} \tag{17}$$

and

$$\begin{aligned} V^{-1} &= \frac{1}{\det(V)} V^{ct} = \frac{1}{\det(V)} \begin{pmatrix} (\gamma + \mu + \frac{c}{b}) & 0 \\ \alpha & (\alpha + \mu) \end{pmatrix} \\ &= \frac{1}{(\alpha + \mu)\left(\gamma + \mu + \frac{c}{b}\right)} \begin{pmatrix} (\gamma + \mu + \frac{c}{b}) & 0 \\ \alpha & (\alpha + \mu) \end{pmatrix} \end{aligned} \tag{18}$$

$$V^{-1} = \begin{pmatrix} \frac{(\gamma+\mu+\frac{c}{b})}{(\alpha+\mu)\left(\gamma+\mu+\frac{c}{b}\right)} & \frac{0}{(\alpha+\mu)\left(\gamma+\mu+\frac{c}{b}\right)} \\ \frac{\alpha}{(\alpha+\mu)\left(\gamma+\mu+\frac{c}{b}\right)} & \frac{(\alpha+\mu)}{(\alpha+\mu)\left(\gamma+\mu+\frac{c}{b}\right)} \end{pmatrix} = \begin{pmatrix} \frac{1}{(\alpha+\mu)} & 0 \\ \frac{\alpha}{(\alpha+\mu)\left(\gamma+\mu+\frac{c}{b}\right)} & \frac{1}{\left(\gamma+\mu+\frac{c}{b}\right)} \end{pmatrix} \tag{19}$$

Finally, we can calculate the value of FV^{-1} which is written as follows:

$$\begin{aligned} FV^{-1} &= \begin{pmatrix} 0 & \frac{\beta\theta}{\mu} \\ 0 & 0 \end{pmatrix} \begin{pmatrix} \frac{1}{(\alpha+\mu)} & 0 \\ \frac{\alpha}{(\alpha+\mu)\left(\gamma+\mu+\frac{c}{b}\right)} & \frac{1}{\left(\gamma+\mu+\frac{c}{b}\right)} \end{pmatrix} = \begin{pmatrix} \frac{\frac{\beta\theta}{\mu}\alpha}{(\alpha+\mu)\left(\gamma+\mu+\frac{c}{b}\right)} & \frac{\frac{\beta\theta}{\mu}}{\left(\gamma+\mu+\frac{c}{b}\right)} \\ 0 & 0 \end{pmatrix} \\ &= \begin{pmatrix} \frac{\beta\theta\alpha}{\mu(\alpha+\mu)\left(\gamma+\mu+\frac{c}{b}\right)} & \frac{\beta\theta}{\mu\left(\gamma+\mu+\frac{c}{b}\right)} \\ 0 & 0 \end{pmatrix} \end{aligned} \tag{20}$$

Then,

$$FV^{-1} = \frac{1}{\mu(\alpha + \mu)\left(\gamma + \mu + \frac{c}{b}\right)} \begin{pmatrix} \beta\theta\alpha & \beta\theta \\ 0 & 0 \end{pmatrix} \tag{21}$$

$$R_0 = FV^{-1} = \frac{\beta\theta\alpha}{\mu(\alpha + \mu)\left(\gamma + \mu + \frac{c}{b}\right)} = \frac{1}{\mu}\left(\frac{\alpha}{(\alpha + \mu)}\right)\left(\frac{\beta\theta}{\left(\gamma + \mu + \frac{c}{b}\right)}\right) \tag{22}$$

The rate of default transmission rate is calculated based on the basis property, such as:

$$(S(0), E(0), I(0), R(0)) \in \left\{ (S, E, I, R) \in [0, P]^4 : S + E + I + R = P \right\} \tag{23}$$

After obtaining the value of R_0, so we can therefore interpret the result of this rate by comparing it to 1. The interpretation of the result is done by the following analysis (Porter, 2012):

- If $R_0 \leq 1$, then the DFE (disease-free equilibrium) is Locally Asymptotically Stable (LAS). The default will disappear and there is no transmission of the default to other portfolios. One speaks in this case, a very low default correlation level or even non-existent between credit portfolios. Therefore, we can assume that $R_0 = SR \leq 1 \Rightarrow \lim_{t \to +\infty}(S(t), E(t), I(t), R(t)) = DFE = (P, 0, 0, 0)$

- Where $R_0 > 1$, then the DFE is unstable and there is a transmission failure. So we're talking at this point a fairly significant level of default correlation between credit portfolios. The calculation of R_0 is to prove the stability of the DFE. So systemic risk or failure of the transmission rate justifies the following equations:

$$R_0 = SR > 1, I(0) > 0 \text{et} E(0) > \Rightarrow \lim_{t\to+\infty}(S(t), E(t), I(t), R(t)) = (S^*, E^*, I^*, R^*)$$

THEOREM 3 *For a value of transmission rate (systemic risk) greater than 1, the system of differential equations (6) admits one positive solution* $X^* = (S^*, E^*, I^*)$:

$$\begin{aligned} S^* &= \frac{\theta}{\beta I^* + \mu} = \frac{\theta}{\mu R_0} \\ E^* &= \frac{I^*(\gamma+\mu)}{\alpha} = \frac{\mu(\gamma+\mu)}{\alpha\beta}(R_0 - 1) \\ I^* &= \frac{\mu}{\beta}(R_0 - 1) \end{aligned} \tag{24}$$

Thus, to determine the equilibrium values of the various compartments S^*, E^*, R^*, and I^*, we will try to solve the system (24).

$$\begin{cases} \theta - \beta I^* S^* - \mu S^* = 0\,(i) \\ \beta I^* S^* - (\alpha + \mu)E^* = 0\,(ii) \\ \alpha E^* - (\gamma + \mu)I^* + \frac{cI^*}{b+I^*} = 0\,(iii) \end{cases} \tag{25}$$

According to this system, one can deduce the following equations:

$$S^* = \frac{\theta}{\beta I^* + \mu} \tag{26}$$

$$E^* = \frac{\beta I^* S^*}{(\alpha + \mu)} = \frac{(\beta I^*)(\frac{\theta}{\beta I^* + \mu})}{(\alpha + \mu)} = \frac{\beta I^* \theta}{(\alpha + \mu)(\beta I^* + \mu)} = \frac{\beta I^* \theta}{\mu^2 + \alpha\mu + (\beta\alpha + \beta\mu)I^*} \tag{27}$$

In this case, we use the value of E^* and integrating in the equation (iii). Therefore:

$$E^* - (\gamma+\mu)I^* + \frac{cI^*}{b+I^*} = \frac{\alpha\beta I^*\theta}{\mu^2+\alpha\mu+(\beta\alpha+\beta\mu)I^*} - (\gamma+\mu)I^* + \frac{cI^*}{b+I^*} = \frac{[(\alpha\beta I^*\theta)*(b+I^*)] - \left[\left(\mu^2+\alpha\mu+(\beta\alpha+\beta\mu)I^*\right)*(\gamma+\mu)I^**(b+I^*)\right] + \left[cI^**\left[\mu^2+\alpha\mu+(\beta\alpha+\beta\mu)I^*\right]\right]}{\left[\mu^2+\alpha\mu+(\beta\alpha+\beta\mu)I^*\right]*\left[b+I^*\right]} =$$

$$\frac{\alpha b\beta\theta I^* + \alpha\beta\theta I^{*2} - \left(\left[\left(\mu^2+\alpha\mu\right)(\gamma+\mu)*b\right]I^* + \left[(\beta\alpha+\beta\mu)(\gamma+\mu)*bI^{*2}\right] + \left[\left(\mu^2+\alpha\mu\right)(\gamma+\mu)\right]I^{*2} + [(\beta\alpha+\beta\mu)(\gamma+\mu)]I^{*3}\right) + c\left(\mu^2+\alpha\mu\right)I^* + c(\beta\alpha+\beta\mu)I^{*2}}{\left[\mu^2+\alpha\mu+(\beta\alpha+\beta\mu)I^*\right]*\left[b+I^*\right]} =$$

$$\frac{\alpha b\beta\theta I^* + \alpha\beta\theta I^{*2} - \left[\left(\mu^2+\alpha\mu\right)(\gamma+\mu)*b\right]I^* - \left[(\beta\alpha+\beta\mu)(\gamma+\mu)*bI^{*2}\right] - \left[\left(\mu^2+\alpha\mu\right)(\gamma+\mu)\right]I^{*2} - [(\beta\alpha+\beta\mu)(\gamma+\mu)]I^{*3} + c\left(\mu^2+\alpha\mu\right)I^* + c(\beta\alpha+\beta\mu)I^{*2}}{\left[\mu^2+\alpha\mu+(\beta\alpha+\beta\mu)I^*\right]*\left[b+I^*\right]} =$$

$$\frac{I^*\left[\alpha b\beta\theta + \alpha\beta\theta I^* - \left[\left(\mu^2+\alpha\mu\right)(\gamma+\mu)*b\right] - [(\beta\alpha+\beta\mu)(\gamma+\mu)*b]I^* - \left[\left(\mu^2+\alpha\mu\right)(\gamma+\mu)\right]I^* - [(\beta\alpha+\beta\mu)(\gamma+\mu)]I^{*2} + c\left(\mu^2+\alpha\mu\right) + c(\beta\alpha+\beta\mu)I^*\right]}{\left[\mu^2+\alpha\mu+(\beta\alpha+\beta\mu)I^*\right]*\left[b+I^*\right]} = 0 \quad (28)$$

To solve this equation, we must have two possible cases:

1st case: $I^* = 0$

For this case, the solution obtained I^* is rejected.

2nd case:

$$\begin{aligned}[\alpha b\beta\theta + \alpha\beta\theta I^* &- [(\mu^2 + \alpha\mu)(\gamma+\mu)^* b] - [(\beta\alpha + \beta\mu)(\gamma+\mu)^* b]I^* - [(\mu^2+\alpha\mu)(\gamma+\mu)]I^* \\ &- [(\beta\alpha+\beta\mu)(\gamma+\mu)]I^{*2} + c(\mu^2+\alpha\mu) + c(\beta\alpha+\beta\mu)I^*] - [(\beta\alpha+\beta\mu)(\gamma+\mu)]I^{*2} \\ &+ [\alpha\beta\theta - [(\mu^2+\alpha\mu)(\gamma+\mu)]]I^* = 0 \end{aligned} \tag{29}$$

Thus,

$$\alpha b\beta\theta - \left(\mu b(\alpha+\mu)(\gamma+\mu)\right) + \mu c(\alpha+\mu) - [\beta(\alpha+\mu)(\gamma+\mu)]I^{*2} + \left[\alpha\beta\theta - \beta b(\alpha+\mu)(\gamma+\mu) - \mu b(\alpha+\mu)(\gamma+\mu) + c\beta(\alpha+\mu)\right]I^* = 0 \tag{30}$$

This equation is in the form of a second-degree equation $ax^2 + bx + c = 0$. To solve this equation, we must calculate the value of Δ which is equal to $\left[b^2 - 4ac\right]$. So, Δ can have three possible values:

- If $\Delta < 0$: then this equation has no solution.
- If $\Delta = 0$ then this equation has two equal solutions, $x_1 = x_2 = \frac{-b}{2a}$
- If $\Delta > 0$ then this equation has two solutions x_1 and x_2. With the value of $x_1 = \frac{-b-\sqrt{\Delta}}{2a}$ and the value of $x_2 = \frac{-b+\sqrt{\Delta}}{2a}$.

So we will try to solve the equation:

$$\alpha b\beta\theta - \left(\mu b(\alpha+\mu)(\gamma+\mu)\right) + \mu c(\alpha+\mu) - [\beta(\alpha+\mu)(\gamma+\mu)]I^{*2} + \left[\alpha\beta\theta - b(\beta+\mu)(\alpha+\mu)(\gamma+\mu) + c\beta(\alpha+\mu)\right]I^* = 0 \tag{31}$$

Thus, it has

$$\begin{cases} a = -\beta(\alpha+\mu)(\gamma+\mu) \\ b = \alpha\beta\theta - (\alpha+\mu)\left(b(\beta+\mu)(\gamma+\mu) - c\beta\right) \\ c = \alpha b\beta\theta - (\alpha+\mu)\left(\mu b(\gamma+\mu) - \mu c\right) \\ x = I^* \end{cases} \tag{32}$$

So now,

$$\Delta = b^2 - 4ac = \left[\alpha\beta\theta - (\alpha+\mu)\left(b(\beta+\mu)(\gamma+\mu) - c\beta\right)\right]^2 - 4*(-\beta(\alpha+\mu)(\gamma+\mu))*(\alpha b\beta\theta - (\alpha+\mu)\left(\mu b(\gamma+\mu) - \mu c\right)) \tag{33}$$

Subsequently, there may be three possible cases:

- If $\Delta < 0$, then Equation (32) has no solution.
- If $\Delta = 0$, then Equation (32) has two equal solutions $I_1^* = I_2^* = \frac{-b}{2a}$. I_1^* and I_2^* must be positive. Thus, to obtain a positive sign of I_1^* and I_2^* we should a and b have different signs. If a and b have the same sign, therefore the solutions obtained will be rejected.
- If $\Delta > 0$, then Equation (32) has two solutions x_1 and x_2. With the value of $I_1^* = \frac{-b-\sqrt{\Delta}}{2a}$ and the value of $I_2^* = \frac{-b+\sqrt{\Delta}}{2a}$. Similarly, we should taken the positive value of I_1^* or I_2^*. So, four cases are observed:

- If $a < 0$ and $b > 0$, then, $I_1^* > 0$ and $I_2^* = 0$. In this case, it takes the value of $I_1^* = I^*$ and we can be calculated the values of S^*, E^* and R^*.
- If $a < 0$ and $b < 0$, so, $I_1^* < 0$ and $I_2^* = 0$. In this case, we must reject the two solutions I_1^* and I_2^*.
- If $a > 0$ and $b > 0$, then, $I_1^* < 0$ and $I_2^* = 0$. In this case, we must reject the two solutions I_1^* and I_2^*.
- If $a > 0$ and $b < 0$, then $I_1^* > 0$ and $I_2^* = 0$. In this case, we can takes the value of $I_1^* = I^*$ which used to obtain the value of S^*, E^*, and R^*.

Thus, for both possibilities ($a < 0$ and $b > 0$) and ($a > 0$ and $b < 0$), the value of $I_1^* = I^*$ can be written as follows:

$$I_1^* = I^* = \frac{-b - \sqrt{\Delta}}{2a} \tag{34}$$

Furthermore, the resolution of the system at equilibrium will be as follows:

$$\begin{cases} S^* = \frac{\theta}{\beta I^* + \mu} = \frac{\theta}{\beta\left(\frac{-b-\sqrt{\Delta}}{2a}\right) + \mu} \\ E^* = \frac{I^*(\gamma+\mu)}{\alpha} = \frac{\left(\frac{-b-\sqrt{\Delta}}{2a}\right)(\gamma+\mu)}{\alpha} \\ I^* = \frac{-b-\sqrt{\Delta}}{2a} \\ R^* = \frac{\gamma I^*}{\mu} = \frac{\gamma\left(\frac{-b-\sqrt{\Delta}}{2a}\right)}{\mu} \end{cases} \tag{35}$$

3.2. The final form of model "SEIR"

In this part, we present in Figure 2 the final form of the SEIR model which used to quantify the systemic risk between financial institutions (portfolio of banks).

This model will be transformed into a system (36) which presented in the form of stochastic differential equations:

$$\begin{cases} \frac{dS(t)}{dt} = GRMC - DC * I(t)S(t) - PD * S(t) \\ \frac{dE(t)}{dt} = DC * I(t)S(t) - (EAD + PD)E(t) \\ \frac{dI(t)}{dt} = EAD * E(t) - (RR + PD)I(t) - \frac{MAXRR * I(t)}{FDL + I(t)} \\ \frac{dR(t)}{dt} = RR * I(t) - PD * R(t) + \frac{MAXRR * I(t)}{FDL + I(t)} \end{cases} \tag{36}$$

We note that the term $h(t) = \frac{MAXRR * I(t)}{FDL + I(t)}$ represent the role of regulatory authorities to save banks with default risk. Primarily, the regulatory authorities come from the central bank that organizes, directs, and supervises the banking system. The central bank is to guarantee the healthy situation of the banking system.

The resolution of this system has allowed us to measure systemic risk (SR) of a portfolio of banks. That is to say, we will determine a measure of systemic risk to verify the existence of a transmission of default of a portfolio to other portfolios. Thus, systemic risk will be measured by the following formula:

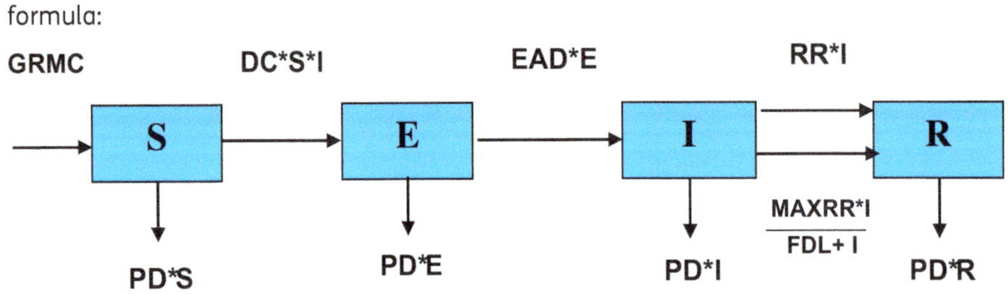

Figure 2. The final form of systemic risk.

$$R_0 = FV^{-1} = \frac{\beta\theta\alpha}{\mu(\alpha+\mu)\left(\gamma+\mu+\frac{c}{b}\right)} = \frac{1}{\mu}\left(\frac{\alpha}{(\alpha+\mu)}\right)\left(\frac{\beta\theta}{\left(\gamma+\mu+\frac{c}{b}\right)}\right) \tag{37}$$

Then,

$$SR = \frac{DC * EAD * GRMC}{PD(EAD+PD)\left(RR+PD+\frac{MAXRR}{FDL}\right)} = \frac{1}{PD}\left(\frac{EAD}{(EAD+PD)}\right)\left(\frac{DC * GRMC}{\left(RR+PD+\frac{MAXRR}{FDL}\right)}\right) \tag{38}$$

We can also determine the fractions of the four categories of the banks. These fractions are calculated based on the value of systemic risk:

$$\begin{cases} S^* = \frac{GRMC}{DC\left(\frac{-b-\sqrt{\Delta}}{2a}\right)+PD} \\ E^* = \frac{\left(\frac{-b-\sqrt{\Delta}}{2a}\right)(RR+PD)}{EAD} \\ I^* = \frac{-b-\sqrt{\Delta}}{2a} \\ R^* = \frac{RR\left(\frac{-b-\sqrt{\Delta}}{2a}\right)}{PD} \end{cases} \tag{39}$$

4. Data

The data used in this paper composed of 18 Greek banks listed in the Athens Exchange from 02 January 2006 to 31 December 2012. Then, daily prices are transformed to daily logarithmic returns

Table 1. List of Greek banks

Name of bank	The period of study
ALPHA BANK	02/01/2006-31/12/2012
ASPIS BANK	02/01/2006-30/06/2010
ATE	02/01/2006-31/12/2012
ATTICA BANK	02/01/2006-31/12/2012
BANK OF CYPRUS	02/01/2006-31/12/2012
BANK OF GREECE	02/01/2006-31/12/2012
ΕΓΝΑΤΙΑ BANK (KO)	02/01/2006-20/09/2007
ΕΓΝΑΤΙΑ BANK (ΠΟ)	02/01/2006-20/08/2007
EMPORIKI BANK	02/01/2006-29/04/2011
EUROBANK EFG	02/01/2006-31/12/2012
GENIKI BANK	02/01/2006-31/12/2012
MARFIN EGNATIA BANK	02/01/2008-31/03/2011
MARFIN FINANCIAL GROUP	02/01/2006-30/03/2007
MARFIN POPULAR BANK	02/01/2008-11/04/2012
NATIONAL BANK	02/01/2006-31/12/2012
PIRAEUS BANK	02/01/2006-31/12/2012
PROTON BANK	02/01/2006-30/12/2011
TT HELLENIC POSTBANK	02/01/2008-31/12/2012

which used to calculate the fundamental factors of systemic risk. Table 1 reports the list of all Greek banks used in this paper. In this table, we present the name of the bank. So, we remark that the period of existing in the Athens Exchange of each banks is not identical to other banks during the period of study. This is justified by the default situation of these banks which accomplished by their leave for the Athens Exchange before the final date of study (31/12/2012).

5. The determinants of systemic risk

In this section, we present the potential indicators of systemic risk. These indicators are the parameters used for modeling systemic risk through the development of a biofinancial approach. Determining the different systemic risk parameters is based on the assumptions of epidemic models. The parameters to be determined are mainly the probability of default, default correlation, recovery rate, the frequency of default in case of loss, the growth rate of the value of the market capitalization, and exposure to default now.

In this paper, we used a SEIR epidemic model type that is based on assumptions is mainly justified by the assumption regarding the characteristics of the portfolios of banks that will be used in our sample. The development of the SEIR model assumes that the study population is homogeneous.

In addition, we used a sample of 18 banks that are homogeneous (Zhou & Cui, 2011). Here, the basic assumption is verified that the population is characterizing by the homogeneity (Liu, Ruan, & Zhang, 2015).

For the transmission of the default, it is assumed that a default in the bank passes the default immediately when he went into failure.

The exchange between portfolios initially defaulted and portfolios may become in default is in proportion to the statistical average of default correlations (CD). The exchange between portfolios initially defaulted and portfolios exposed to the default are in proportion to the statistical average exposures default time (EAD). The relationship between portfolios initially defaulted and portfolios immunized to default are in proportion to the statistical average recovery rate (RR). The other parameters used are: the frequency of default for loss (FDL), the maximum average of recovery rate (MAXRR), and the growth rate of the value of market capitalization of portfolio of banks (GRMC).

5.1. The probability of default and the recovery rate

The probability of default was estimated using the analysis developed by Merton (1974). The basic assumption of the model is that the value of the assets of a company V follows a stochastic process and that failure is realized if V crosses the default barrier. The latter may be regarded as the recovery value for failure. It measures the amount $TR * D$. With TR means the recovery rate at date t and D debt per share of the company that varies in time.

The firm is said to be in default if at time t the value of its assets is less than its nominal value, i.e. though $V_t < F_t$. The recovery rate is then written as follows:

$$TR = \frac{F_t}{V_t} \tag{40}$$

And loss given default (P_t) is:

$$P_t = 1 - TR = \frac{F_t - V_t}{F_t} \tag{41}$$

The value of assets is assumed to follow a geometric Brownian process given by the following equation:

$$dV_t = \mu V_t dt + \sigma V_t dW_t \quad (42)$$

In other words,

$$\frac{dV_t}{V_t} = \mu dt + \sigma dW_t \quad (43)$$

which, is μ the drift of the value of the assets of the firm, σ is the asset volatility and W_t is a standard Brownian process. It is assumed that $\mu = 0$.

According to the development of the KMV model, the fault distance is defined as follows (Crosbie & Bohn, 2003):

$$DD = \frac{V_A - X}{\sigma_A V_A} \quad (44)$$

From the fault distance, one can deduce the value of the probability of default as follows (Schäfer & Koivusalo, 2013):

$$P_{KMV} = Prob\{V_A(T) < X\} = N\left(-\frac{ln\left(\frac{V_A}{X}\right) + \left(\mu - \frac{1}{2}\sigma_A^2\right)T}{\sigma_A\sqrt{T}}\right) = N(-DD) \quad (45)$$

In the biofinancial approach to the measurement of systemic risk, we referred to the estimate of the average probability of default of individual banks used in our paper at each time *t*. According to the results found in the first chapter, we can deduce the average default probability of the different banks in our sample. Figure 3 shows the dispersion of the average probability of default during the study period in the case of banks in Greece. According to this figure, we found that the probability of default is characterized by an increasing rate.

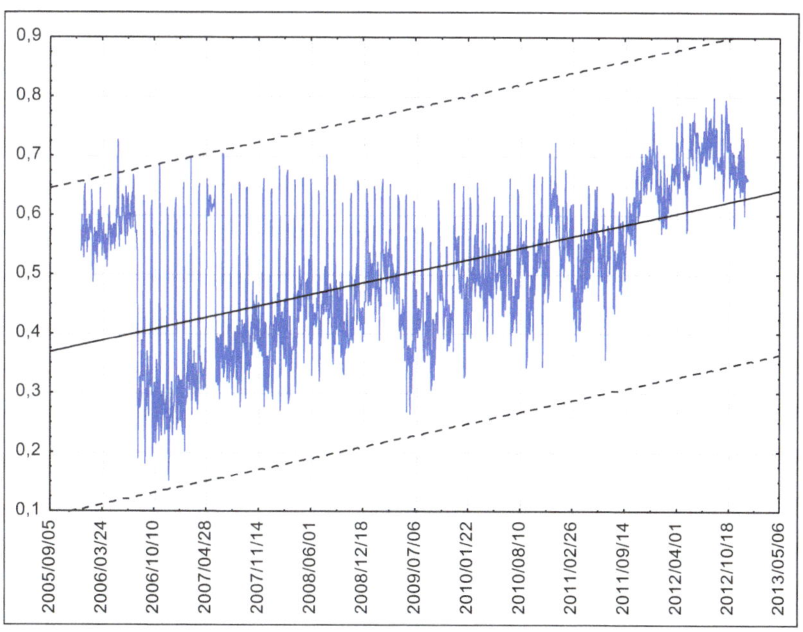

Figure 3. The average default probability of Greek banks.

Note: This figure report the average probability of default of 18 banks used in this paper for the study period from January 02, 2006 to December 31, 2012.

The level of the Greek bank default is increasing during the study period, mainly following the declaration of bankruptcy of Greece in 2009. The accumulation level of sovereign debt in the euro area has an impact on the economy Economic Greece and especially its banking system.

The effect of the subprime crisis was transmitted from the USA to the euro zone. The impact of this crisis manifests itself in the bankruptcy of several banks, the excess of the level of unemployment, the imbalance in the balance of payments of these countries, and the increase in external debt.

Greece is one of the most affected countries by the financial crisis even in the presence of stimulus plans against the risk of loss. The failure of banks to Greece was passed from one bank to other banks. This was the objective of our paper, in which we try to model the systemic risk of a loan portfolio. This model aims to verify the existence of a communication failure in the banking system of Greece.

The default accumulation is justified by the low recovery rate charged by banks. What justifies the lack of effective management in banks and also the absence of control and supervision by the central bank and banks too.

Figure 4 shows the ineffectiveness of the recovery rate of the banks in Greece. According to this figure, we noticed that after the third quarter of 2011 the average recovery rate was fairly high levels to cover bank losses. Increasing the level of the recovery rate is verified by the stimulus packages and aid granted by the Member States of the European Union. Greece has benefited from aid granted by the EU to support its economy in general and it's banking system in particular.

In Figure 5, we presented the distribution of the maximum recovery rate (MAXRR). This parameter is directly related to the function $h(t)$ in the SEIR model that measures the intervention of regulatory authorities in the fight against bank failure propagation in Greece during the study period. The intervention of the national and international regulatory authorities did not ensure the soundness of the banking system of Greece.

Descriptive statistics of average recovery rate and maximum recovery rate for all banks used in our study and for each date t are presented in Table 2.

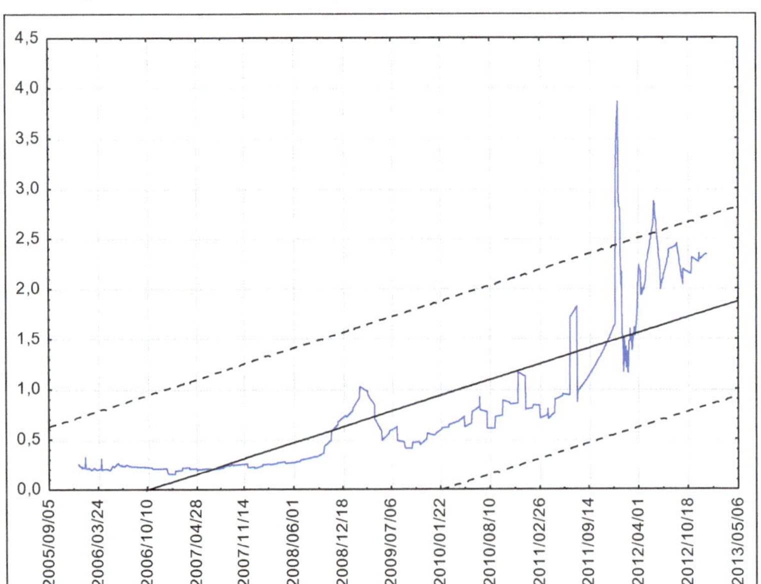

Figure 4. The average recovery rate of banks in Greece.

Note: This figure summarizes the average recovery rate of 18 banks used in our research for the study period from January 02, 2006 to December 31, 2012.

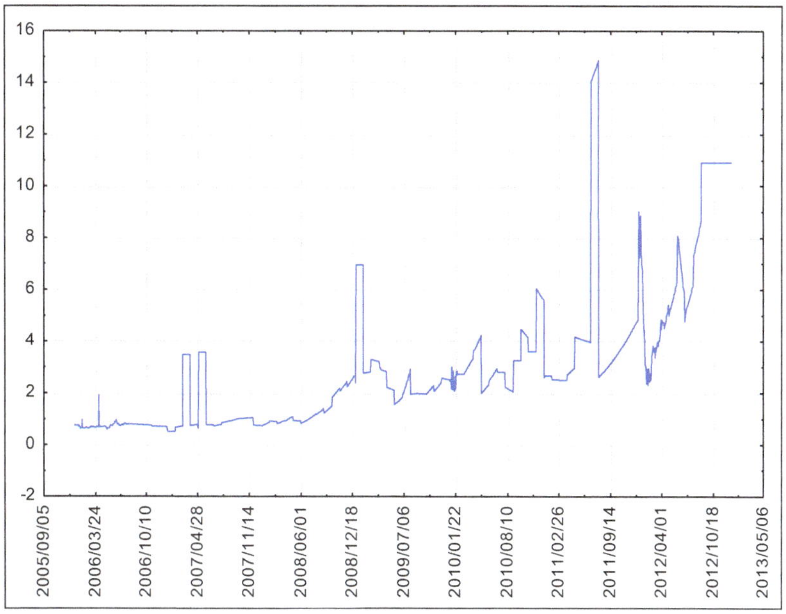

Figure 5. The maximum recovery rate (MAXRR) bank of Greece.

Note: This figure report the maximum recovery rate of 18 banks used in our research for the study period from January 02, 2006 to December 31, 2012.

Table 2. Descriptive statistics

	Obs.	Mean	Min	Max	Variance	Std. dev	Skewness	Kurtosis
RR	1,748	0.775939	0.149549	3.85324	0.467068	0.683424	1.449630	1.353938
MAXRR	1,748	2.973614	0.498459	14.85419	7.698507	2.774618	2.016648	4.223239

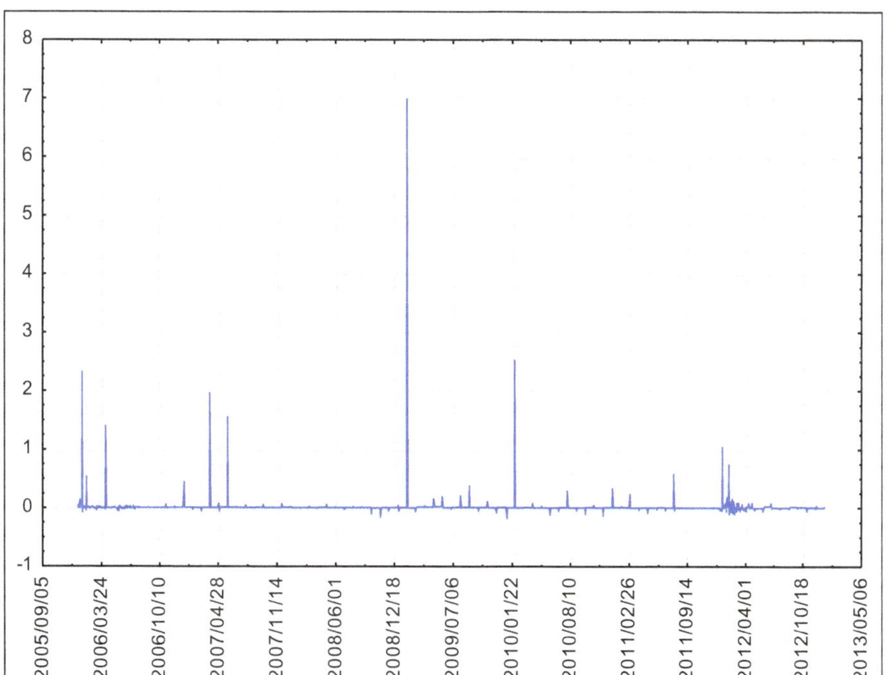

Figure 6. The growth rate of the market capitalization (GRMC) of Greek banks.

Similarly, in Figure 6, we represented the growth rate of the value of the loan portfolio. In epidemic models, the growth rate measures the rate of increase in the size of the study population. In our work, we used the KMV model to measure the probability of default of banks in Greece. KMV model is based on the use of historical price action of the studied companies. In this case, we determined the growth rate of the total market capitalization of 18 banks that make up the sample of our study. Table 3 summarizes the descriptive statistics of the growth rate of the value of studying portfolio.

5.2. Exposure to default time and default frequency for loss

The other parameters used for the measurement of systemic risk of a credit portfolio are the exposure to the default time (EAD) and the default frequency for loss (FDP) (Bellotti & Crook, 2012; Leow & Mues, 2012). The FDP is often considered to be constant but it is sometimes regarded as a random variable. As for EAD, it is often defined as the amount of capital to be paid at the time of default by borrowers, but in some cases, it may include lost interest (Basel Committee on Banking Supervision, 2006).

Exposure to the default time (EAD) is calculated as follows:

$$EAD = \frac{PA}{PD * FDP} \tag{46}$$

where, PD is the probability of default, FDL is the frequency of default in case of loss and EL is the expected loss ($PA = 1 - \frac{V_t}{F_t}$) (Giovanni, Levchenko, & Mejean, 2012; Schäfer & Koivusalo, 2013).

In Figure 7, we present the volatility of the average exposure at default of Greek banks.

Table 3. Descriptive statistics

	Obs.	Mean	Min	Max	Variance	Std. dev	Skewness	Kurtosis
GRMC	1,748	0.010817	−0.188745	6.979145	0.041150	0.202855	26.22219	828.3062

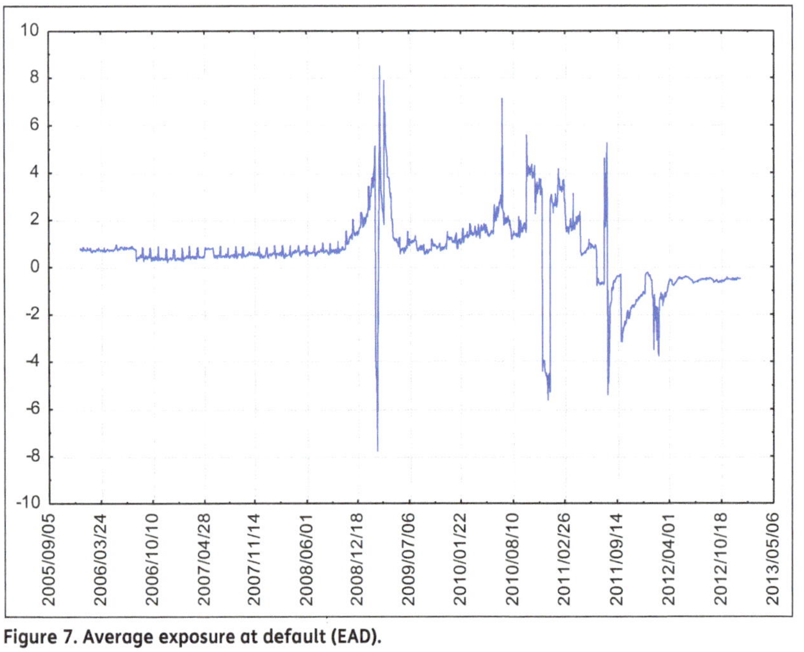

Figure 7. Average exposure at default (EAD).

Note: This figure report the average exposure at default of 18 banks used in this paper for the study period from 02 January 2006 until 31 December 2012.

The default frequency for loss is the amount of money that is lost by a financial institution or a bank when a borrower defaults on a loan. Hartmann-Wendels, Miller, and Töws (2014) suggest that there are several methods to calculate the loss given default, but the most frequently used method is the comparison between the actual total loss and total potential exposure at default. Most banks have experienced difficulties in calculating the value of the FDL for a loan. Faced with this difficulty, the banks examine their overall portfolios by determining the FDL based on cumulative losses and exposure.

Thus, the FDL is calculated as follows:

$$FDP = \frac{Perted^{'}unportefeuille}{EAD} \tag{47}$$

According Schäfer and Koivusalo (2013), the loss of a portfolio is calculated as follows:

$$Perted^{'}unportefeuille = PD * PA \tag{48}$$

In this case, the default frequency in the event of loss is measured by the following relationship:

$$FDP = \frac{PD * PA}{EAD} \tag{49}$$

Figure 8 summarizes the evolution of the default frequency in the event of average loss of banks in Greece during the study period going from 2 January 2006 to 31 December 2012.

Table 4 summarizes the descriptive statistics of the two parameters; EAD and FDL. These statistics relate to exposure to average default time and default frequency in the event of average loss.

5.3. The default correlation

The default correlation of the measurement problem is well-developed in the financial literature. Thus, different approaches have been proposed for the modeling of the default correlation. Wang, Shan, and Geng (2015) proposed a scoring model of the transition probabilities of default, which are driven by economic factors. This model is explained by a dynamic process.

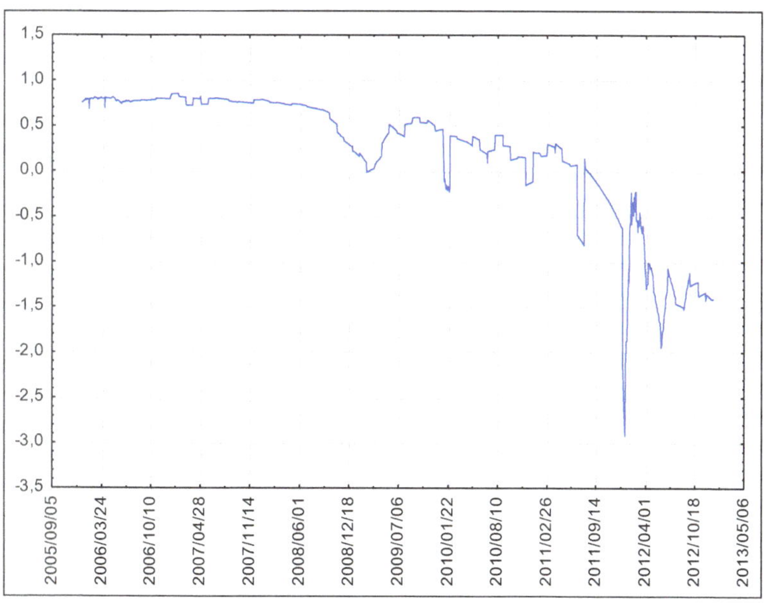

Figure 8. The average frequency of default in the case of loss (FDL).
Note: This figure report is the average frequency of default for the case of loss of 18 banks used in this paper for the study period from 02 January 2006 until 31 December 2012.

Table 4. Descriptive statistics								
	Obs.	**Mean**	**Min**	**Max**	**Variance**	**Std. dev**	**Skewness**	**Kurtosis**
FDL	1,748	0.204368	-2.92824	0.850451	0.499190	0.706534	−1.45359	1.333923
EAD	1,748	0.620046	-7.79659	8.498492	2.126643	1.458301	−0.24817	4.605794

In this paper, we use a model based on KMV model to estimate default correlation between the Greek banks. KMV model calculated the default correlation between two borrowers. The default correlation between two banks *A* and *B* is written as follows:

$$\rho_{AB}^{D} = \frac{(JDF_t)_{AB} - (PD_t)_A * (PD_t)_B}{\sqrt{[(PD_t)_A(1 - (PD_t)_A)] * [(PD_t)_B * (1 - (PD_t)_B)]}} \tag{50}$$

where, ρ_{AB}^{D} is the default correlation between the two banks *A* and *B*, $(PD_t)_A$ is the probability of default of bank *A* at time *t*, $(PD_t)_B$ is the probability of default of bank *B* at time *t*, and $(JDF_t)_{AB}$ is the joint default probability between the two banks *A* and *B* at time *t*. In this case, the joint default probability between the two banks *A* and *B* at time *t* will be expressed as follows:

$$(JDF_t)_{AB} = (PD_t)_{AB} = \Phi_2(\Phi^{-1}((PD_t)_A), \Phi^{-1}((PD_t)_B), \rho_{AB}) \tag{51}$$

where, $\Phi_2(.)$ is the function of bivariate normal cumulative distribution, $\Phi^{-1}(.)$ is the inverse function of univariate cumulative normal distribution, and ρ_{AB} is the correlation between the asset returns of the two banks *A* and *B*.

$$\rho_{AB} = \frac{\sigma_{AB}}{\sigma_A \sigma_B} = \frac{cov(R_A, R_B)}{\sigma_{R_A} \sigma_{R_B}} \tag{52}$$

$$cov(R_A, R_B) = \sigma_{AB} = \sum_{i=1}^{2} P_i (R_{Ai} - E(R_A))(R_{Bi} - E(R_B)) \tag{53}$$

where, $cov(R_A, R_B)$: is the covariance between asset returns of banks *A* and *B*, σ_A is the standard deviation of the asset returns of bank *A*, σ_B is the standard deviation of the asset returns of bank *B*, R_{Ai} is the asset returns of portfolio *A*, R_{Bi} is the asset returns of portfolio *B*, $E(R_A)$ is the expected asset returns of bank *A*, and $E(R_B)$ is the expected asset returns of bank *B*.

We calculated the average default correlation value for the different years (2006–2012) for a daily frequency. Table 5 summarizes the various statistics on the distribution of the average default correlation (DC).

Figure 9 reports the evolution of the average default correlation. We can observe that the default correlation is highly and positive during the period of study.

However, the number of default correlations varies with the number of existing banks in the Athens Exchange. Table 6 summarizes the number of default correlations based on the number of banks and date, as the number of banks listed in the Athens Exchange is not the same for each time *t*.

Table 5. Descriptive statistics								
	Obs.	**Mean**	**Min**	**Max**	**Variance**	**Std. dev**	**Skewness**	**Kurtosis**
DC	1,748	0.276925	−0.115776	0.864569	0.047681	0.218359	0.490966	−0.365925

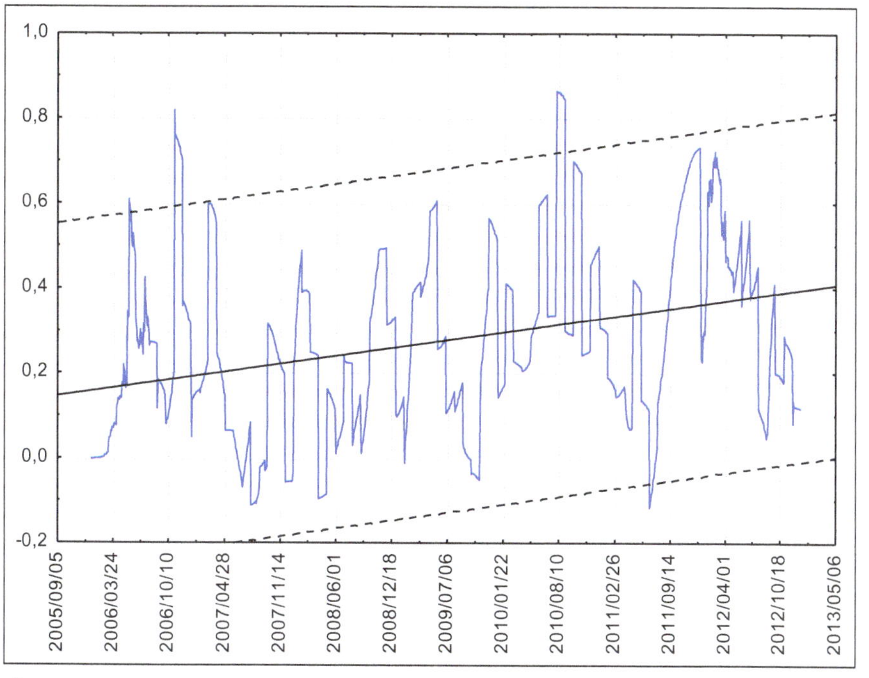

Figure 9. The evolution of default correlation (DC).

Note: This figure summarizes the mean of default correlation between 18 Greek banks used in this paper for the study period from 02 January 2006 to 31 December 2012.

Table 6. The number of default correlations

Period	Number of days	Number of existing banks in the Athens exchange	Number of default correlation
02/01/2006 to 30/03/2007	312	15	32,448
02/04/2007 to 20/08/2007	97	14	8,730
21/08/2007 to 20/09/2007	23	13	1,771
21/09/2007 to 31/12/2007	70	12	4,550
02/01/2008 to 30/06/2010	616	15	64,064
01/07/2010 to 31/03/2011	191	14	17,190
01/04/2011 to 29/04/2011	19	13	1,463
02/05/2011 to 30/12/2011	171	12	11,115
02/01/2012 to 11/04/2012	70	11	3,780
12/04/2012 to 31/12/2012	179	10	7,876

6. Empirical results

According to the empirical results, we found that there are 12 dates of transmission of default in the case of banks in Greece:

- One transmission in 2006.
- Two transmissions in 2007.
- Five transmissions in 2009.
- Two transmissions in 2010.
- One transmission in 2011.
- One transmission in 2012.

Figure 10 reports the volatility of systemic risk during the period from 2 January 2006 to 31 December 2012.

Generally, the main transmission dates are deducted immediately after the declaration of failure of Greece in 2009 except for three dates in 2006 and 2007. The different results of the estimation of systemic risk are shown in Table 7.

Table 8 reports the descriptive statistics of systemic risk and of the different compartments of SEIR model. From this table, we note that systemic risk has a higher level of volatility. For the four compartments of systemic risk, we remark that the Susceptible portfolios are likely to become more volatile than Exposed, Infected, and Removed portfolios.

Figure 11 reports the volatility of four compartments of systemic risk measured by epidemic model 'SEIR' during the period from 2 January 2006 to 31 December 2012.

In epidemic models, the default correlation is very important in the assessment of systemic risk and in solving the system of differential equations. In addition, the default correlation justifies the level of dependence between different Greek banks that constitute the study population used in this paper. During the period of study, the number of default correlation number varies according to the number of existing banks on the Athens Exchange and depending on the time of transmission of default. Table 9 summarizes the volatility of default correlation on default transmission periods.

From Table 9, we tried to determine the number of declared default after each transmission of default. In Table 10, we presented the different dates transmission of default dates accomplished by the number of bank which had declared failure and left the Athens Stock Exchange.

Based on the results presented in Table 10, we decomposed the study period into five subperiods based on the failure dates, the number of banks that had declared failure and left the Athens Exchange. Table 11 summarizes all the subperiods and their dates and the number of transmission combine them.

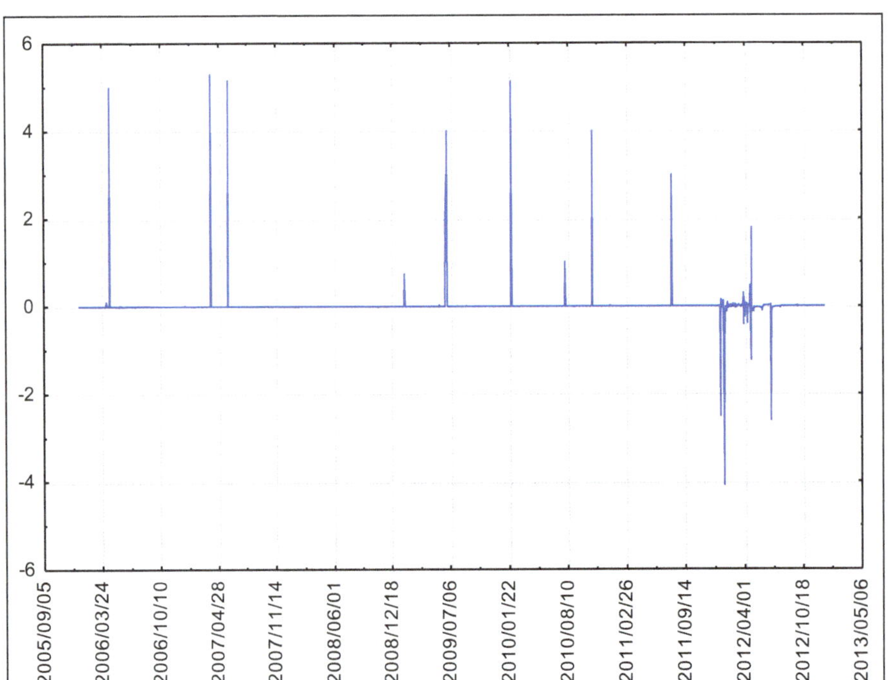

Figure 10. Systemic risk (SR).

Table 7. The different dates of default transmission

The default transmission date (SR > 1)	SR value	The value of S^*	The value of E^*	The value of I^*	The value of R^*
19/04/2006	5.0006153	0.44488648	0.41960956	0.13531776	0.0001862
30/03/2007	5.2970103	0.99984395	6,9385E-05	6,5959E-05	2,0703E-05
31/05/2007	5.1573438	0.99901469	0.00043651	0.00041721	0.00013159
19/06/2009	2.0006752	0.41217565	0.31751271	0.27023112	8,0517E-05
22/06/2009	3.0007966	0.4397149	0.31579495	0.24442201	6,81481E-05
23/06/2009	1.0007579	0.43504867	0.3140503	0.25082958	7,14472E-05
24/06/2009	4.0006830	0.42201318	0.31228201	0.26562574	7,90646E-05
25/06/2009	2.0006179	0.40917982	0.31049095	0.28024218	8,70542E-05
29/01/2010	5.1349557	0.989464612	0.00296003	0.00384998	0.00372538
30/07/2010	1.0159414	0.34178886	0.28082659	0.36526491	0.012119647
29/07/2011	3.0010208	0.50264181	0.1214959	0.37242186	0.003440431
24/04/2012	1.7918449	0.49982389	0.12799133	0.37195427	0.000230502

Table 8. Descriptive statistics

	Obs.	Mean	Min	Max	Variance	Std. dev	Skewness	Kurtosis
SR	1,748	0.017843	−0.000003	−4.08346	5.297010	0.340306	9.2759	162.085
S	1,748	0.997080	1.000000	0.34179	1.000000	0.040644	−13.9783	194.938
E	1,748	0.001444	0.000000	0.00000	0.419610	0.021070	15.4041	244.403
I	1,748	0.001465	0.000000	0.00000	0.372422	0.020992	14.9805	230.959
R	1,748	0.000012	0.000000	0.00000	0.012120	0.000314	34.4760	1282.523

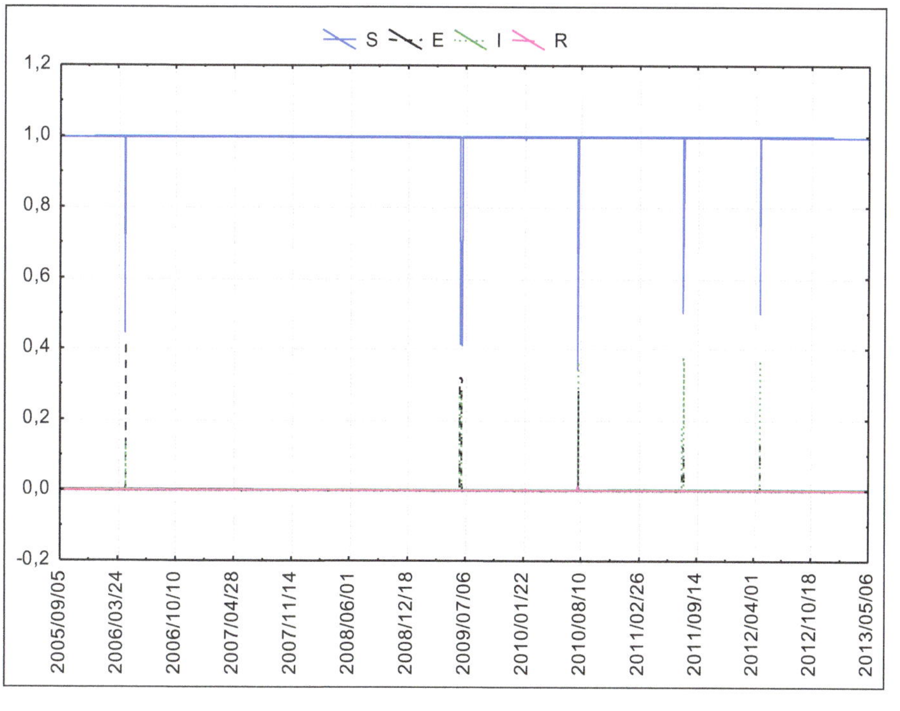

Figure 11. The volatility of the four compartments of SEIR model (*S*, *E*, *I*, and *R*).

Table 9. The volatility of default correlation

Date of transmission of default	Study period	Number of days	Number of existing banks in the Athens Exchange	Number of default correlation
19/04/2006	02/01/2006 to 19/04/2006	74	15	7,696
30/03/2007	20/04/2006 to 30/03/2007	238	15	24,752
31/05/2007	02/04/2007 to 31/05/2007	41	14	3,690
19/06/2009	01/06/2007 to 20/08/2007	56	14	5,040
	21/08/2007 to 20/09/2007	23	13	1,771
	21/09/2007 to 31/12/2007	70	12	4,550
	02/01/2008 to 19/06/2009	358	15	37,232
22/06/2009	19/06/2009 to 22/06/2009	1	15	104
23/06/2009	22/06/2009 to 23/06/2009	1	15	104
24/06/2009	23/06/2009 to 24/06/2009	1	15	104
25/06/2009	24/06/2009 to 25/06/2009	1	15	104
29/01/2010	26/06/2009 to 29/01/2010	151	15	15,704
30/07/2010	01/02/2010 to 30/06/2010	103	15	10,712
	01/07/2010 to 30/07/2010	22	14	1,980
29/07/2011	02/08/2010 to 31/03/2011	169	14	15,210
	01/04/2011 to 29/04/2011	19	13	1,463
	02/05/2011 to 29/07/2011	64	12	4,160
24/04/2012	01/08/2011 to 30/12/2011	107	12	6,955
	02/01/2012 to 11/04/2012	70	11	3,780
	12/04/2012 to 31/12/2012	179	10	7,876

According to Table 10, we found that there are seven banks that have left the Athens Exchange after their failure and after the high depreciation of their values in the stock market of Greece.

The transmission of default is based on the application of a SEIR epidemic model. The advantage of these models is the determination of the date of transmission of default and the number of default for a population consisting of a set of banks in this paper.

The SEIR model is composed of four compartments that we have determined based on the assumptions of epidemic models. The evolutions of the different compartments (S, E, I, and R) are shown in Figures 12–16. This representation is based on the distribution of the different subperiods that we have chosen.

This paper is based on the development of biofinancial approach for measuring systemic risk of a portfolio of banks. This approach is based on the selected sample (18 Greek banks), the assumptions of our empirical evidence, and the econometric techniques used to test this approach. In addition, we used an epidemic model (SEIR) from which we tested the transmission of default in banks in Greece during the study period (02/01/2006–31/12/2012).

Note that, even in the presence of an intervention by the central bank and other regulatory authorities, we noticed that there are banks that have declared failure. We can say that the role of the central bank of Greece is not enough to save bank on default and to prevent the propagation of the default from one bank to another, or to the entire banking system.

Table 10. The presentation of different transmission fault dates

The date of transmission of default (SR > 1)	The date of default of a bank and its exit from the Athens Exchange	Banks that had declared failure
19/04/2006		
30/03/2007	30/03/2007	MARFIN FINANCIAL GROUP
31/05/2007	20/08/2007	ΕΓΝΑΤΙΑ BANK (ΚΟ)
	20/09/2007	ΕΓΝΑΤΙΑ BANK (ΠΟ)
19/06/2009		
22/06/2009		
23/06/2009		
24/06/2009		
25/06/2009		
29/01/2010	30/06/2010	ASPIS BANK
30/07/2010	31/03/2011	MARFIN EGNATIA BANK
	29/04/2011	EMPORIKI BANK
29/07/2011	11/04/2012	MARFIN POPULAR BANK
24/04/2012		

Table 11. The representation of the different subperiods

Period	Date	Number of transmissions of default	Number of banks leaving the Athens exchange
1	02/01/2006 to 30/05/2007	2	1
2	31/05/2007 to 18/06/2009	1	2
3	19/09/2009 to 29/07/2010	6	1
4	30/07/2010 to 28/07/2011	2	2
5	29/07/2011 to 31/12/2012	1	1

The variable measuring the role of Greece regulatory authorities is less than 1 until the end of the first half of 2008. During this period, we noticed that there were only three banks that have left the Athens Exchange. The role of regulators is insufficient because the variable $h(t)$ exceeded 1 (Liu, Yu, & Zhu, 2015). Following the period of 2008, we note that there are four banks that had declared failure and left the Athens Exchange. This is justified by the high level of the variable $h(t)$ since it reaches a very important value equal to 11. In addition, during the second period, just after the first half of 2008 until 31 December 2012, the Greece declared its failure and several help have granted by the member countries of the European Union. Even these plans have not stopped the propagation of the failure of banks in Greece. The intervention of the International Monetary Fund, the European Central Bank, the Government of Greece and the Greek central bank is insufficient to save Greece and to prevent systemic risk in the Greek banking system. Figure 17 reports the volatility of $h(t)$.

Then, since the financial crisis of 2007, successive plans succeed aid to Greece with a lot of absurd demands to save them and also save his creditors. We note that at the end of 2014 Greece have a total of debts that are equal to 300 billion dollars. Figure 18 summarizes the main creditors of Greece.

The results found in this paper are consistent with the assumptions of the model used and thereafter, we validated the use of this model. The SEIR model used allowed us to determine the different

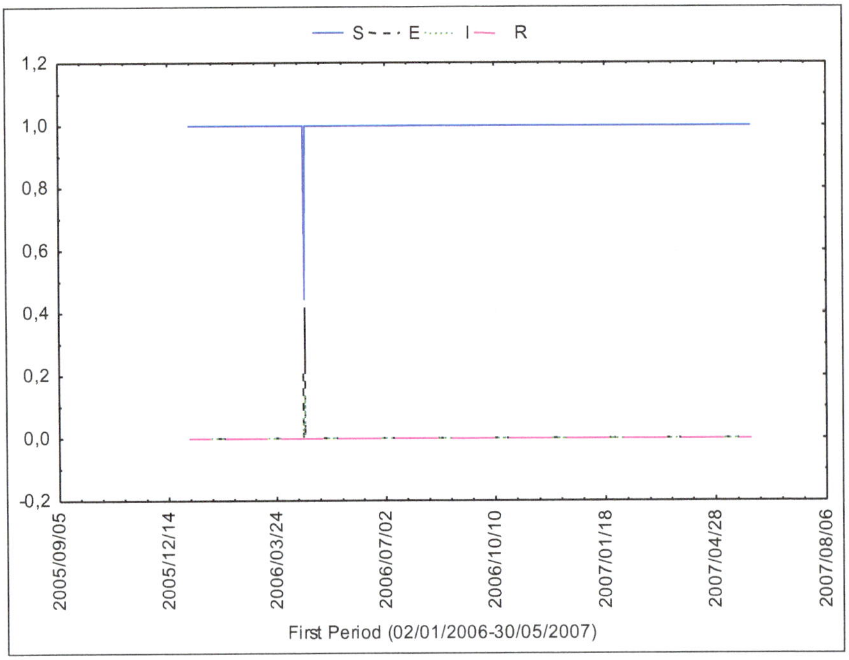

Figure 12. The presentation of the first period.

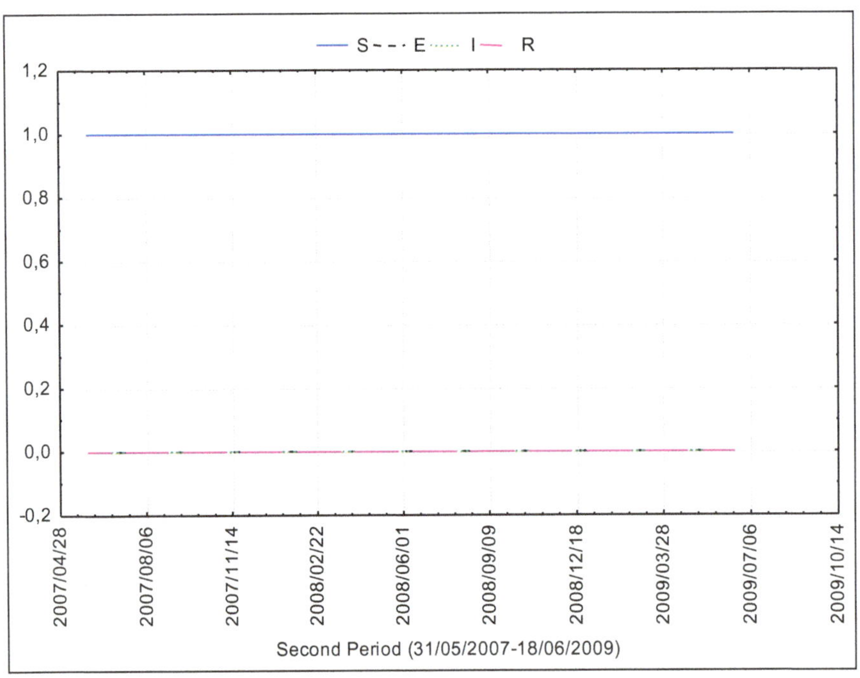

Figure 13. The presentation of the second period.

dates of transmission of default between banks in Greece. In addition, following this transmission there are seven banks that have declared their failure and left the Athens Exchange.

7. Conclusion

Measurement of risk is considered to be one of the most interesting issues in the recent literature in finance, especially after the outbreak of the financial crisis of 2007. This concept is developed recently by several authors, while the measures discussed systemic risk are different from one author

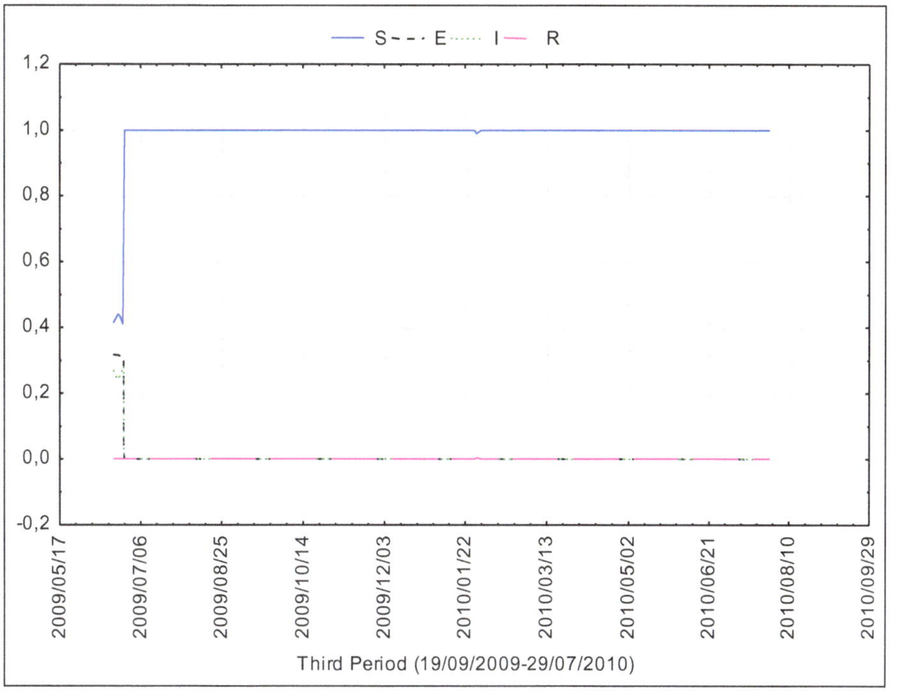

Figure 14. The presentation of the third period.

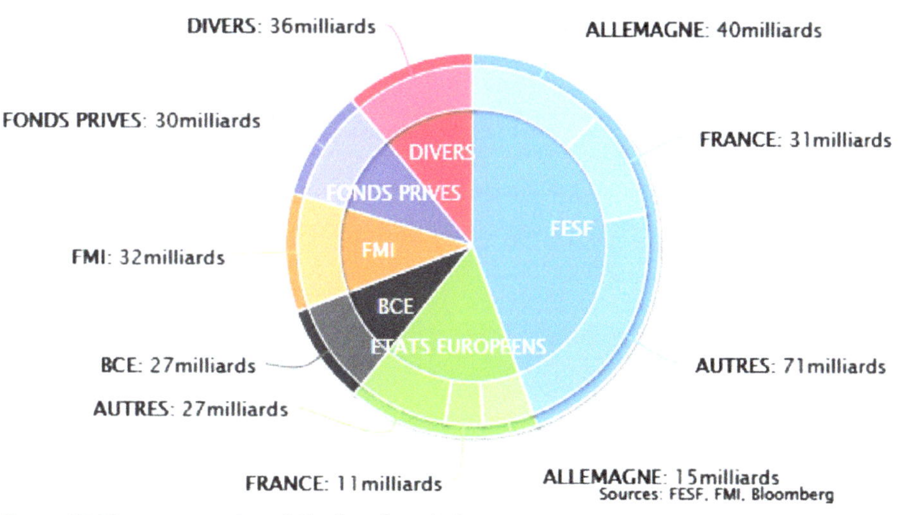

Figure 15. The presentation of the fourth period.

to another. In this paper, we present a biofinancial approach adopted for the modeling of systemic risk. We estimated the potential indicators of systemic risk as measured by the SEIR epidemic model. This model has four categories of portfolios. In addition, this model can measure the rate of transmission of default from portfolio to other portfolios. However, the transmission is conditioned by the value of systemic risk found in every moment. This value is compared to a threshold equal to 1. If the value of the systemic risk is less or equal to 1, there is no default transmission and if it is greater than 1, therefore there is a transmission of default.

We use a sample of 18 Greek banks listed in the Athens Exchange from 02 January 2006 to 31 December 2012. By observing the empirical results found in this paper, we found the existence of 12 transmissions of default during the period of study (02/01/2006-31/12/2012). The transmission of default coincides with the default of Greek banks that have declared failure then leaving the Athens

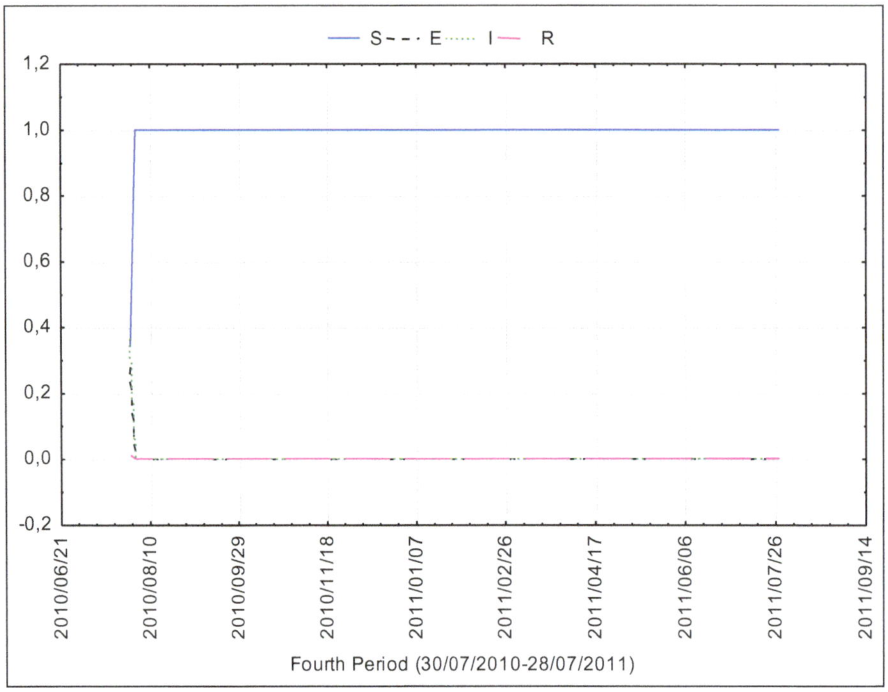

Figure 16. The presentation of the fifth period.

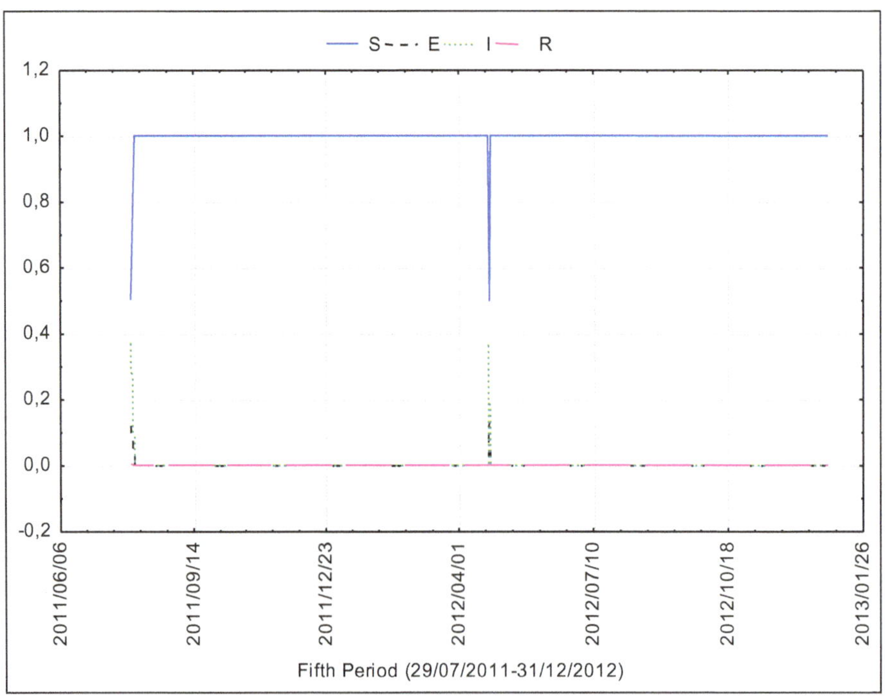

Figure 17. The evolution of the function *h*(*t*).

Exchange. The results presented in this paper are based on a set of assumptions that allow the validity of "SEIR" model of systemic risk. We have shown that the Greek banking system is in recession. The continuation of aid plans employed by regulatory authorities did enough to help Greece.

We find that the main factors of the systemic risk are the default probability, the recovery rate, the default correlation, the exposure at default, the frequency of default in the case of loss, the market capitalization, and the regulatory authorities.

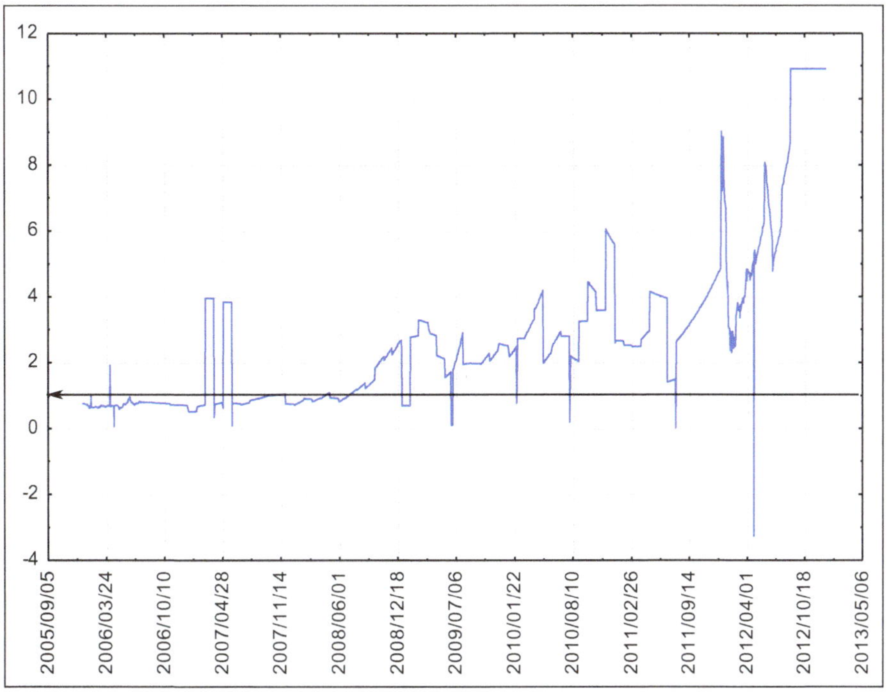

Figure 18. The Greek debt.

The role of the central bank is inadequate and even absent for the period of study. There is a deficiency in own regulations. We note that seven years are sufficient for 40% of the sample (7 banks) that declared their failure and left the stock market in Greece. Thus, two major observations are necessary: strong regulation is not always synonymous with financial stability and improving the transparency of information should be at the heart of any regulatory reform to prevent systemic risks that may arise from the traditional banking industry. The regulatory authorities are required to restore the new micro-prudential and macro-prudential reforms to control and to manage the systemic risk.

Acknowledgments
The authors would like to thank the editor and anonymous reviewers for their supportive comments and suggestions.

Funding
The authors received no direct funding for this research.

Author details
Abdelkader Derbali[1]
E-mail: derbaliabdelkader@outlook.fr
Slaheddine Hallara[2]
E-mail: ihet@gnet.tn
[1] Department of Finance, Higher Institute of Management of Sousse, University of Sousse, 22 Street Zarkaa Al Yamama, Sousse Erriadh 4023, Tunisia.
[2] Department of Finance, Higher Institute of Management of Tunis, University of Tunis, Tunis, Tunisia.

References

Acharya, V. V., Engle, R., & Richardson, M. (2012). Capital shortfall: A new approach to ranking and regulating systemic risks. *American Economic Review, 102*, 59–64. http://dx.doi.org/10.1257/aer.102.3.59

Acharya, V. V., Pedersen, L. H., Philippon, T., & Richardson, M. P. (2009). Regulating systemic risk. *Financial Markets, Institutions & Instruments, 18*, 174–175.

Acharya, V. V., Pedersen, L. H., Philippon, T., & Richardson, M. P. (2010). *Measuring systemic risk*. Federal Reserve Bank of Cleveland, Working Paper, No. 10-02.

Adrian, T., & Brunnermeier, M. K. (2008). *CoVaR* (Staff Reports 348). Federal Reserve Bank of New York.

Adrian, T., & Brunnermeie, M. K. (2009). *CoVaR* (Working Paper Staff Reports No. 348). Princeton University and Federal Reserve Bank of New York.

Al-Sheikh, S. A. (2012). Modeling and analysis of an SEIR epidemic model with a limited resource for treatment. *Global Journal of Science Frontier Research Mathematics and Decision Sciences, 12*, 56–66.

Amelia, P., & Philip, A. S. (2013). Bank size and systemic risk. *European Financial Management, 19*, 429–451.

Basel Committee on Banking Supervision. (2006). *Basel II: International convergence of capital measurement and capital standard*. Bank for International Settlements Press & Communications CH-4002 Basel.

Bellotti, T., & Crook, J. (2012). Loss given default models incorporating macroeconomic variables for credit cards.

International Journal of Forecasting, 28, 171–182. http://dx.doi.org/10.1016/j.ijforecast.2010.08.005
Blume, L., David, E., Jon, K., Robert, K., & Eva, T. (2011). Which networks are least susceptible to cascading failures? In *52nd IEEE Annual Symposium on Foundations of Computer Science (FOCS)* (pp. 393–402). doi:10.1109/FOCS.2011.38
Blume, L., Easley, D., Kleinberg, J., Kleinberg, R., & Tardos, É. (2013). Network formation in the presence of contagious risk. *ACM Transactions on Economics and Computation, 1*(2), 1–20. http://dx.doi.org/10.1145/2465769
Brownlees, C. T., & Engle, R. F. (2012). *Volatility, correlation and tails for systemic risk measurement* (Working Paper). New York University. Retrieved from http://scrc.stern.nyu.edu/scrc/?p=2241
Chan-Lau, J. (2010). Regulatory capital charges for too-connected-to-tail institutions: A practical proposal. *Financial Markets, Institutions, and Instruments, 19*, 355–380.
Chowell, G., Torre, C. A., Munayco-Escate, C., Suárez-Ognio, L., López-Cruz, R., Hyman, J. M., & Castillo-Chavez, C. (2008). Spatial and temporal dynamics of dengue fever in Peru: 1994–2006. *Epidemiology and Infection, 136*, 1667–1677. http://dx.doi.org/10.1017/S0950268808000290
Crosbie, P. J., & Bohn, J. R. (2003). *Modeling default risk* (White Paper). Moody's KMV.
Derbali, A., Hallara, S., & Sy, A. (2015). Systemic risk of the Greek financial institutions: Application of the SRISK model. *African Journal of Accounting, Auditing and Finance, 4*, 7–28. http://dx.doi.org/10.1504/AJAAF.2015.071751
Ducrot, A. (2010). *Autour de quelques modèles épidémiques* (INRIA Bordeaux Sud-Ouest ANUBIS & IMB UMR CNRS 5251).
Giovanni, J. D., Levchenko, A., & Mejean, I. (2012). *The role of firms in aggregate fluctuations*. Retrieved from VoxEU.org
Gray, D. F., & Jobst, A. A. (2010). New directions in financial sector and sovereign risk management. *Journal of Investment Management, 8*, 23–38.
Gray, D. F., & Jobst, A. A. (2011). Modelling systemic financial sector and sovereign risk. *Sveriges Riksbank Economic Review, 2*, 68–106.
Hartmann-Wendels, T., Miller, P., & Töws, E. (2014). Loss given default for leasing: Parametric and nonparametric estimates. *Journal of Banking & Finance, 40*, 364–375.
Huang, X., Hao, Z., & Zhu, H. (2009). A framework for assessing the systemic risk of major financial institutions. *Journal of Banking & Finance, 33*, 2036–2049.
Huang, X., Hao, Z., & Zhu, H. (2010). Assessing the systemic risk of a heterogeneous portfolio of banks during the recent financial crisis. *Journal of Financial Stability, 8*, 193–205.
Larosière, J. (2009). *Report of the high-level group on financial supervision in the eu* (Report de Larosière).
Leow, M., & Mues, C. (2012). Predicting loss given default (LGD) for residential mortgage loans: A two-stage model and empirical evidence for UK bank data. *International Journal of Forecasting, 28*, 183–195. http://dx.doi.org/10.1016/j.ijforecast.2011.01.010
Liu, S., Ruan, S., & Zhang, X. (2015). On avian influenza epidemic models with time delay. *Theory in Biosciences, 134*, 75–82.
Liu, H. L., Yu, J. Y., & Zhu, G. T. (2015). Stability results for an age-structured SIS epidemic model with vector population. *Journal of Applied Mathematics*, 1–12. doi:10.1155/2015/838312
Martínez-Jaramillo, S., Pérez, O. P., Embriz, F. A., & Dey, F. L. G. (2010). Systemic risk, financial contagion and financial fragility. *Journal of Economic Dynamics and Control, 34*, 2358–2374. http://dx.doi.org/10.1016/j.jedc.2010.06.004
Mejra, F., Alenka, K., & Sebastijan, R. (2011). The macroeconomic sources of systemic risk in the banking sectors of five new EU member states. *Journal of Banking & Finance, 35*, 310–322.
Merton, R. C. (1974). On the pricing of corporate debt: The risk structure of interest rates'. *Journal of Finance, 29*, 449–470.
Porter, A. T. (2012). *A path-specific approach to SEIR modeling* (Dissertation). University of Lowa. Retrieved from http://ir.uiowa.edu/etd/2963
Sanjiv, R. D., & Raman, U. (2004). Systemic risk and international portfolio choice. *Journal of Finance, American Finance Association, 59*, 2809–2834.
Schäfer, R., & Koivusalo, A. F. R. (2013). Dependence of defaults and recoveries in structural credit risk models. *Economic Modelling, 30*, 1–9. http://dx.doi.org/10.1016/j.econmod.2012.08.033
Segoviano, M. A., & Goodhart, C. A. E. (2009). *Banking stability measures* (IMF Working Paper, No. 09/04).
Silvan, E., & Paolo, V. (2007). Credit portfolios: What defines risk horizons and risk measurement? *Journal of Banking & Finance, 31*, 3663–3679.
Touzeau, S. (2010). Modèles épidémiologiques (R_0). *UR341 Mathématiques et Informatique Appliquées*, Jouy-en-Josas.
Wang, Y., Shan, X., & Geng, J. (2015). Estimating the systemic risk of China's banking industries based on Merton model. *Applied Mathematics & Information Sciences, 9*, 957–964.
Zhou, X., & Cui, J. (2011). Analysis of stability and bifurcation for an SEIR epidemic model with saturated recovery rate. *Communications in Nonlinear Science and Numerical Simulation, 16*, 4438–4450. http://dx.doi.org/10.1016/j.cnsns.2011.03.026

10

Day-of-the-week effect on the Tunisian stock market return and volatility

Abdelkader Derbali[1]* and Slaheddine Hallara[2]

*Corresponding author: Abdelkader Derbali, Department of Finance, Higher Institute of Management of Sousse, University of Sousse, 22 Street Zarkaa Al Yamama, Erriadh City, Sousse, 4023, Tunisia

E-mail: derbaliabdelkader@outlook.fr

Reviewing editor: David McMillan, University of Stirling, UK

Abstract: In this paper, we examine empirically the day-of-the-week effect on the Tunisian stock exchange index (TUNINDEX) return and volatility. We use three multivariate general autoregressive conditional heteroscedasticity models (GARCH (1,1), EGARCH (1,1), and TGARCH (1,1)) to examine the presence of daily anomalies in the TUNINDEX returns and volatilities during the period from 31 December 1997 to 07 April 2014. The empirical results of GARCH (1,1), EGARCH (1,1), and TGARCH (1,1) model indicate the existence of a significance and positive effect for Thursdays and for the return at ($t-1$) on the return and volatility of TUNINDEX in a threshold of 1%. Additionally, we find the presence of a significance and negative effect for Tuesday on the TUNINDEX return and volatility. Also, we can show the persistence of volatility in the case of Tunisian stock market index.

Subjects: Corporate Finance; Mathematical Economics; Risk Management; Social Sciences

Keywords: day of the week; volatility; returns; GARCH; T-GARCH; E-GARCH; TUNINDEX

JEL classifications: C22; G10; G12

1. Introduction

The hypothesis of efficiency of markets (HEM) postulates that the stock exchanges must effectively reflect all information available on their fundamental value. The assumption of efficiency of the

ABOUT THE AUTHORS

Abdelkader Derbali is an assistant professor in Finance at the Higher Institute of Management of Sousse in University of Sousse, Tunisia. He is one of the editorial board members in the *African Journal of Accounting, Auditing and Finance*. His research interests include Risk Management and Capital Markets and Institutions. He has published articles, among others, in *Research in International Business and Finance, The Journal of Energy Markets, African Journal of Accounting, Auditing and Finance, International Journal of Critical Accounting*, and *International Journal of Trade and Global Market*.

Slaheddina Hallara is a professor of Finance at Higher Institute of Management of Tunis in University of Tunis, Tunisia. His research interests are pricing, credit risk, and financial markets. He obtained a PhD in Finance from Rennes University, Tunisia. His research has been published in journals such as *Research in International Business and Finance*, and *International Journal of Monetary Economics and Finance*.

PUBLIC INTEREST STATEMENT

The movements of the stock market prices are among some phenomena that have been studied through several academic disciplines and have cumulative research evidence. This study investigates the presence of the day-of-the-week anomalies in the case of the Tunisian stock exchange index (TUNINDEX) using three GARCH models. The day-of-the-week effect is a phenomenon that constitutes a form of anomalies of the efficient capital markets theory. This paper examines day-of-the-week effect on the available data of daily returns on the weighted index in the Tunisian stock exchange index during the period from 31 December 1997 to 07 April 2014. The empirical findings of this paper show the persistence of volatility in the case of Tunisian stock market index.

market was contradicted by anomalies such as the calendar of the anomalies, the fundamental anomalies, and the technical anomalies. The calendar of the anomalies refers to the tendency of the titles to behave differently over a particular day of the week, or month of the year. Among these anomalies, the effect of the day of the week was seen like one of the most important models and it was noted in several actions on several financial markets (Balaban, 1995; French, 1980; Jaffe & Westerfield, 1985; Lian & Chen, 2004).

The effect of the day of the week indicates that the returns are abnormally high over certain days of the week than other days. More precisely, the results resulting from several empirical studies showed that the average return of Friday is abnormally raised, and the average return of Monday is abnormally low. Moreover, the rational investor must take account of the risk or the volatility of the returns while making decisions of investment.

However, the investors could buy actions with abnormal daily returns and sell actions with high abnormal daily returns. This phenomenon was developed in several former work such as Aggarwal & Rivoli (1989), French (1980), and Gibbons and Hess (1981). However, all studies above concentrates only on the equations of the average returns of the stock exchange markets and uses the methods of ordinary least squares (OLS) like method of estimate to regress the outputs on five daily dummy variables.

In this paper, we investigate empirically the effect of the day of the week on the stock returns and volatility of the Tunisian stock exchange market. We use daily returns of the Tunisian stock exchange index (TUNINDEX) over the period from 31 December 1997 to 07 April 2014. For the econometric methodology, we employ a general autoregressive conditional heteroscedasticity models based in the GARCH (1,1), EGARCH (1,1), and TGARCH (1,1).

The empirical findings of estimated GARCH models indicate the existence of the impact of the day of the week on the stock returns and volatility of the TUNINDEX. Then, the results of GARCH (1,1), EGARCH (1,1), and TGARCH (1,1) models show the existence of a highly and positive effect for Wednesday, Thursdays, Friday, and the past return at date $(t - 1)$ on the stock returns and volatilities. However, Tuesday have a negative effect. The estimation results of EGARCH (1,1) and TGARCH (1,1) models indicate the highly impact of the returns observed at date $(t - 1)$ and a significance and positive impact of Thursdays on the TUNINDEX returns.

The rest of this paper is organized as follows: Section 2 provides a review of the related literature. In Section 3, we present the econometric methodology based on the GARCH models. We expose the data used in our paper in Section 4. Section 5 shows and analyzes the empirical results of the estimation of the conditional heteroscedasticity models. Section 5 concluding remarks.

2. Literature review

Many empirical works on the effect of the day of the week in the outputs of the actions was undertaken so much on the developed and emergent markets as French (1980) and Gibbons and Hess (1981). All these studies have obtained different conclusions on the effect of the day from the week on the stock returns and volatility.

Athanassakos and Robinson (1994) and Dubois and Louvet (1996) examine the effect of the day of week for the emerging developed markets. Their empirical results show that Monday has a negative effect on the stock exchange returns for the United States, the European markets, and in Hong Kong, Tuesday has a negative effect on the stock returns for Australia, Japan, and South Korea.

The studies made by Kato (1990) show that Tuesday has a weak effect but Wednesday has a highly effect on the stock returns for Japan.

The study developed by Poshakwale and Murinde (2001) show that Monday has a negative and significant effect while Friday has a positive effect on the stock returns in the stock exchange markets of Hungary and Poland.

Brooks and Persand (2001) evaluate the elements of proof of the day of the week for five countries of the South Asia: Malaysia, South Korea, Philippines, Taiwan, and Thailand. They found one day of the week which has a significant effect among three of the five studied stock markets. However, they concluded moreover that the risk of market alone can be insufficient to capture the anomalies of calendar.

Hui (2005), by using the nonparametric test, examines the effect of the day of the week for four markets of the Asia-Pacific and two developed markets. The empirical results show that Hong Kong, Taiwan, and Singapore show higher average returns on Fridays and of the weak influence of Monday in the average returns, but for the United States, Japan, and South Korea we can show the existence of a mixed model. As a whole, it is only in Singapore that one day ago of the week which has an important effect.

In their studies of the Chinese stock market, Cai, Yuming, and Yuehua (2006) found the presence of the day-of-the-week effect with negative returns on Mondays and Tuesday.

Some of the studies in Africa include Agathee (2008), Aly, Mehdian, and Perry (2004), Chukwuogor-Ndu (2006) and Tachiwou (2010). For example, Aly et al. (2004) examine the day-of-the-week effect on the stock returns in Egypt. On average, its study indicated that Monday has a positive and significant effect on the stock returns. Tachiwou (2010) develops an analysis on the effect of the day of the week on regional stock market in West Africa over the period 1998–2007. Their empirical results show that the returns are the lowest on Tuesday and Wednesday and they are higher on Friday.

AL-Mutairi (2010) finds an evidence of the presence of the day-of-the-week effect in the stock exchange of Kuwait. Their empirical results show that the outputs of Saturday have a positive and higher impact than other days of the week except Wednesday, which suggests that the Kuwaiti stock exchange market is ineffective.

Hussain, Hamid, Akash, and Khan (2011) analyze the effect of the day of the week on Karachi stock exchange. They revealed significant effects for Tuesday.

Ulussever, Yumusak, and Kar (2011) study the stock exchange of Saudi and they provided evidence of the presence of the day-of-the-week effect on the daily stock returns.

The study of Gonzalez-Perez and Guerrero (2013) utilizes data belonging to S&P 500 during the period from 2004 to 2011. Their empirical findings are supportive of US market efficiency with the absence of DoW effect in the daily S&P 500 returns. Therefore, they conclude that designing a trading strategy without taking any risk will not lead to attaining abnormal returns as there is no deterministic seasonal pattern. Confirmative findings that are opposite to the DoW effect are also documented by Carlucci, Junior, and Lima (2013) for the main stock exchange indices of Canada and US over the period from 2002 to 2012. Furthermore, another research conducted by Puja (2010) shows insignificant results for S&P 500 during the period from 01 January 1990 to 30 November 2004.

Berument and Dogan (2012) investigate the stock market returns and volatility nexus using US daily returns over the period from 26 May 1952 to 29 September 2006. The empirical findings report did not confirm the proposition that the return–volatility relationship is present and the same for each day of the week.

More recently, Abdalla (2012) studies the anomalies of calendar in the stock exchange market of Khartoum. The empirical results did not reveal the presence of an effect of the day of the week on the stock returns and volatility.

Gharaibeh and Al Azmi (2015) investigate empirically the day-of-the-week effect on the available data of daily returns on the weighted index in the Kuwait stock exchange (KSE) during the period from January 2002 to September 2011. Their empirical findings show that the KSE exhibits positive returns on the first and the last day of the week with significant negative returns on the second day of the trading week.

3. Methodology

In this section, we define the econometric methodology used in this paper which based in a three general autoregressive conditional heteroscedasticity models, such as GARCH, EGARCH, and TGARCH.

3.1. Generalized Autoregressive Conditional Heteroscedasticity (GARCH) model

The standard GARCH (p, q) model was introduced by Bollerslev (1986) which suggests that the conditional variance of returns is not only dependent on the squared residuals of the mean equation but also on its own past values. The standard GARCH model captures the volatility clustering of financial time series. Then, by using an appropriate GARCH model, while controlling for time-varying property of volatility, one can estimate the changes in the information flows, i.e. the impact of recent and old news on volatility. Specifically, log likelihood ratio tests on the GARCH model for $p, q \in \{1, 2, ..., 5\}$ are employed in order to find the most parsimonious GARCH representation of the conditional variance of returns. A GARCH (p, q) process is represented as follows:

$$R_t = a_1 R_{t-1} + \sum_{t=1}^{5} \lambda_i D_{it} + \varepsilon_t \quad (1)$$

$$h_t = \omega_1 + \sum_{i=1}^{p} \alpha_i \varepsilon_{t-1}^2 + \sum_{j=1}^{q} \delta_1 h_{t-j} + \sum_{t=1}^{4} \lambda_i D_{it} \quad (2)$$

where Equations (1) and (2) denote the conditional mean equation and the conditional variance equation, respectively. R_t is the spot returns of the TUNINDEX indexes at time t. R_{t-1} is a proxy for the mean of R_t conditional on past information. h_t is the conditional variance of the period t. Only four out of five days in the week are included in the conditional variance equation to avoid the dummy variable trap in the regression model. Thus, D_{it}'s (i = 1, 2, ..., 4) are dummy variables for Monday, Tuesday, Thursday, and Friday, respectively, and Wednesday is excluded. The GARCH (1,1) is weakly stationary if ($\alpha_i + \delta_1 < 1$), α_i and δ_1 are nonnegative, α_i (ARCH parameter) represents the news about volatility from the previous period and δ_i (GARCH parameter) represents a persistence coefficient. If the sum of ARCH and GARCH coefficients ($\alpha + \delta$) is very close to one, the volatility shocks are very persistent. It is an indication of a covariance stationary model with a high degree of persistence and long memory in the conditional variance.

The basic GARCH is symmetric and does not capture the asymmetry effect that is inherent in most stock markets return data also known as the "leverage effect". In the context of financial time series analysis, the asymmetry effect refers to the characteristic of times series on asset prices that "bad news" tends to increase volatility more than "good news" (Black, 1976 and Nelson, 1991). The exponential GARCH (EGARCH) model and the threshold GARCH (TGARCH) model proposed by Glosten, Jagannathan, and Runkle (1993) and Nelson (1991), respectively, are specifically designed to capture the asymmetry shock to the conditional variance.

3.2. Exponential Generalized Autoregressive Conditional Heteroscedasticity (EGARCH) model

Nelson (1991) proposes the exponential GARCH model which allows the conditional volatility to have asymmetric relation with past data. Statistically, this effect occurs when an unexpected drop in stock price due to bad news increases volatility more than an unexpected increase in price due to good news of similar magnitude. This model expresses the conditional variance of a given variable as a nonlinear function of its own past values of standardized innovations that can react asymmetrically to good and bad news (Drimbetas, Sariannidis, & Porfiris, 2007). Specifically, log likelihood ratio tests on an EGARCH model for $p, q \in \{1, 2, ..., 5\}$ are employed in order to find the most parsimonious EGARCH representation of the conditional variance of returns. The EGARCH (1,1) model can be specified as follows:

$$R_t = a_1 R_{t-1} + \sum_{t=1}^{5} \lambda_i D_{it} + \varepsilon_t \tag{3}$$

$$\ln\left(\sigma_t^2\right) = \omega_1 + \delta_1 \ln\left(\sigma_{t-1}^2\right) + \alpha_1 \left|\frac{\varepsilon_{t-1}}{\sigma_{t-1}}\right| + \gamma_1 \frac{\varepsilon_{t-1}}{\sigma_{t-1}} + \sum_{t=1}^{4} \lambda_i D_{it} \tag{4}$$

where σ_{t-1}^2 denotes the estimation of the variance of the previous time period that stands for the linkage between current and past volatility. In other words, it measures the degree of volatility persistence of conditional variance in the previous period. $\left|\frac{\varepsilon_{t-1}}{\sigma_{t-1}}\right|$ represents information concerning the volatility of the previous time period. It signifies the magnitude impact (size effect) coming from the unexpected shocks. $\frac{\varepsilon_{t-1}}{\sigma_{t-1}}$ indicates information concerning the leverage ($\gamma_1 > 0$) and the asymmetry ($\gamma_1 \neq 0$) effects. δ_1, α_1, and γ_1 are the constant parameters to be estimated. The parameters, λ_i's are employed to capture the daily effects. ε_t represents the innovations distributed as a generalised error distribution (GED), a special case of which is the normal distribution (Nelson, 1991).

3.3. Exponential Generalized Autoregressive Conditional Heteroscedasticity (EGARCH) model

The threshold GARCH model (TGARCH) was introduced by Glosten et al. (1993) that captures asymmetric in terms of negative and positive shocks and adds multiplicative dummy variable to check whether there is statistically significant different when shocks are negative. In TGARCH model, it has been observed that positive and negative shocks of equal magnitude have a different impact on stock market volatility, which may be attributed to a "leverage effect" (Black, 1976). In the same sense, negative shocks are followed by higher volatility than positive shocks of the same magnitude (Engle & Ng, 1993). The conditional variance for the simple TGARCH model is defined by

$$R_t = a_1 R_{t-1} + \sum_{t=1}^{5} \lambda_i D_{it} + \varepsilon_t \tag{5}$$

$$\sigma_t^2 = \omega_1 + \delta_1 \sigma_{t-1}^2 + \alpha_1 u_{t-1}^2 + \gamma_1 u_{t-1}^2 d_{t-1} + \sum_{t=1}^{4} \lambda_i D_{it} \tag{6}$$

where d_t takes the value of 1 if u_{t-1} is negative, and 0 otherwise. So "good news" and "bad news" have a different impact. If $\gamma_1 > 0$ the leverage effect exists and news impact is asymmetric if $\gamma_1 \neq 0$. Notably, the additional parameters, λ_i's are employed to capture the daily effects.

4. Data

In this study, we use daily closing prices of the principal index in the stock exchange of Tunisia (TUNINDEX). The data-set was considered during the period from 31 December 1997 to 07 April 2014, which including a total of 4,043 observations. The data-set was collected from the website of the stock exchange of Tunisia. In our paper, the stock exchange returns are defined by ln of the return between two dates (t) and ($t - 1$). The return R_t is calculated as follows:

$$R_t = \ln\left(\frac{P_t}{P_{t-1}}\right) = \ln(P_t) - \ln(P_{t-1}) \tag{7}$$

where P_t and P_{t-1} are the daily closing prices of index TUNINDEX at the date (t) and date ($t - 1$), respectively. Let us note that t indicates the time (day).

Table 1 summarizes the descriptive statistics for the TUNINDEX daily returns for each day of the week. According to this table, we can remark that on average the highly return is for Wednesday (0.201088), followed by Thursday (0.200346) and Friday (0.200099). The lowest average of TUNINDEX returns is for Monday (0.198615) followed by Tuesday (0.199852) during the period of study.

The highly value of standard deviation is for Wednesday (0.400863), followed by Thursday (0.400309), Friday (0.400124), Monday (0.399938), and Tuesday (0.399007).

According to the two statistics of skewness (asymmetry) and kurtosis (leptokurtic), we can remark that all variables used in this paper are characterized by non-normal distribution. The skewness coefficients reflect that the variable is skewed to the right and it is far from being symmetric for all variables. Also, the Kurtosis coefficient indicates that the leptokurtic for all variables used in this study show the existence of a high peak or a fat-tailed in their volatilities.

Then, the positive sign of estimate coefficients of Jarque-Bera statistics show that we reject the null hypothesis of normal distribution of the variables used in our study. Also, the high value of Jarque-Bera coefficients reflects that the series is not normally distributed at the level of 1%.

Figure 1 reports the distribution of the TUNINDEX returns. So, we can observe that the Tunisian stock market index is very volatile which explain the persistence of volatilities.

Figure 2 presents the evolution of the residual series of the TUNINDEX returns during the period of study from 31 December 1997 to 07 April 2014. This figure indicates the presence of highly volatility, implying the existence of time-varying volatilities in the case of the TUNINDEX returns.

The Augmented Dickey-Fuller (ADF) test and the Philips-Perron (PP) test are used to examine the stationary of the time series of the data used in this study. Then, the results of these two tests are presented in Table 2. From this table, we can reject the null assumption of nonstationary of the

Table 1. Descriptive statistics

	D1 Monday	D2 Tuesday	D3 Wednesday	D4 Thursday	D5 Friday
Mean	0.199852	0.198615	0.201088	0.200346	0.200099
Maximum	1.000000	1.000000	1.000000	1.000000	1.000000
Minimum	0.000000	0.000000	0.000000	0.000000	0.000000
Std. Dev.	0.399938	0.399007	0.400863	0.400309	0.400124
Skewness	1.501160	1.510864	1.491524	1.497297	1.499227
Kurtosis	3.253481	3.282709	3.224643	3.241899	3.247682
Jarque-Bera	1,529.295*	1,551.629*	1,507.539*	1,520.524*	1,524.898*
Probability	0.000000	0.000000	0.000000	0.000000	0.000000
Observations	4,043	4,043	4,043	4,043	4,043

Notes: This table presents the main statistical features for the TUNINDEX returns. The data period is from 31 December 1997 through 07 April 2014.

*Indicate a significance level at 1%.

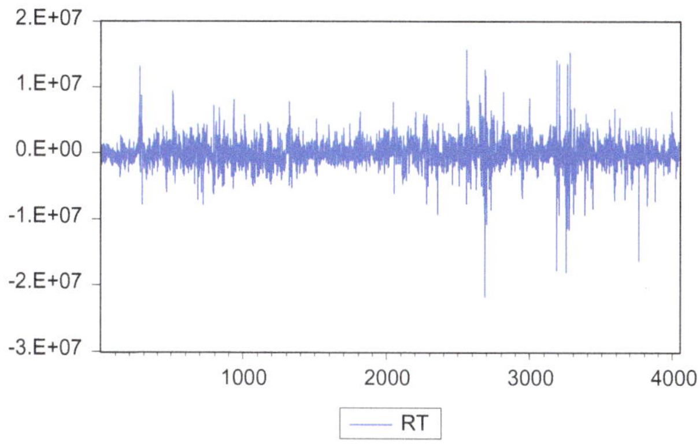

Figure 1. TUNINDEX returns over the period from 31 December 1997 to 07 April 2014.

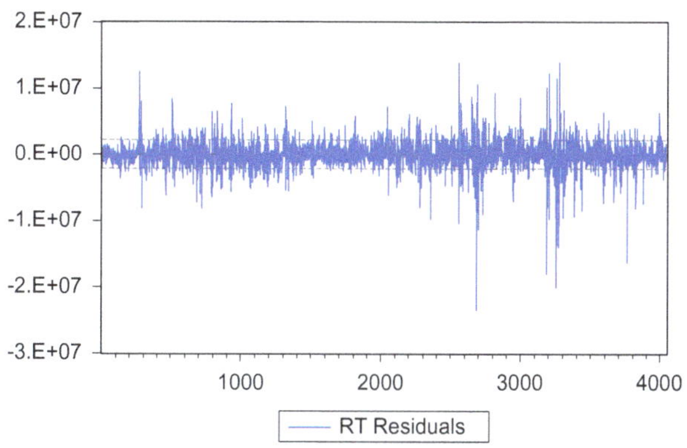

Figure 2. Residuals series of TUNINDEX Return during the period from 31 December 1997 to 07 April 2014.

TUNINDEX returns. Then, we can conclude that the TUNINDEX returns are stationary during the period of study from 31 December 1997 to 07 April 2014.

5. Empirical results

The estimation results of three general autoregressive conditional heteroscedasticity models in the case of TUNINDEX returns are presented in Table 3.

Based on the estimation results of GARCH (1,1) model, we can show that, in the mean equation, we observe the existence of a significance and positive effect for Thursdays and the returns at date (t − 1) with a significance level of 1%. Also, we can remark that Wednesday have a positive impact on the TUNINDEX returns. This impact is significant with a significance level of 5%. Then, Tuesday present a negative impact on the TUNINDEX returns during the period of study from 31 December 1997 to 07 April 2014. However, the results of the variance equation indicate a highly significance level of all GARCH (1,1) parameters specification in the level of 1%. For the daily effect, we can

Table 2. Unit root test results

Augmented Dickey–Fuller test			
Variable	**Intercept**	**With trend and intercept**	**Without trend and intercept**
TUNINDEX	−26.27386*	−26.27168*	−26.05671*
Phillips–Perron test			
Variable	Intercept	With trend and intercept	Without trend and intercept
TUNINDEX	−48.30104*	−48.29572*	−48.24050*

Notes: This table presents the unit root test for the TUNINDEX returns. The data period is from 31 December 1997 through 07 April 2014.

*Indicate a significance level at 1%.

Table 3. Results of estimated GARCH models for TUNINDEX returns

Mean equation			
	GARCH (1,1)	**EGARCH (1,1)**	**TGARCH (1,1)**
R_{t-1}	0.265470	0.260781	0.268641
	(15.86556)*	(15.79673)*	(15.91967)*
$Monday_t$	69,688.57	45,686.04	58,881.39
	(1.397639)	(0.967173)	(1.147096)
$Tuesday_t$	−151,204.8	−171,702.2	−167,487.8
	(−2.969272)*	(−3.817989)*	(−3.210058)*
$Wednesday_t$	122,045.7	81,629.03	107,051.5
	(2.347673)**	(1.678873)***	(2.057791)**
$Thursday_t$	158,493.7	115,680.6	146,589.2
	(3.033942)*	(2.364359)**	(2.794679)*
$Friday_t$	142,960.7	131,136.5	125,421.5
	(2.867363)*	(2.687249)*	(2.405137)*
Variance equation			
ω_1	3.84E + 11	2.894581	3.68E + 11
	(16.42245)*	(15.14099)*	(16.41509)*
α_1	0.283312	0.465095	0.259363
	(24.06536)*	(35.41839)*	(17.04848)*
δ_1	0.653288	0.009105	0.039778
	(64.49909)*	(2.955389)*	(4.091736)*
γ_1		0.888044	0.662790
		(132.7530)*	(64.37662)*
$Monday_t$	34,775.11	70,886.76	116,439.8
	(0.649272)	(1.556719)	(2.358142)*
$Tuesday_t$	−222,719.8	−158,043.0	−147,690.3
	(−4.112683)*	(−3.420643)*	(−2.817204)*
$Wednesday_t$	294,984.30	273,942.41	228,394.5
	(0.663743)	(3.99304)*	(4.839843)*
$Thursday_t$	70,542.08	110,151.9	150,838.0
	(1.296325)	(2.354543)**	(2.903925)*
$Friday_t$	94,424.81	152,695.5	171,105.2
	(1.759013)***	(3.289716)*	(3.366130)*
ARCH-LM test	4.986955	6.008870	4.710778
	(0.225594)	(0.314276)	(0.230032)

Notes: This table summarizes the estimated coefficients from GARCH (1,1), EGARCH (1,1), and TGARCH (1,1) models. To test empirically this model, we used daily returns of the Tunisian stock market index (TUNINDEX) over the period from 31 December 1997 to 07 April 2014. Statistical significance at the 1, 5, and 10% threshold is denoted by *, **, and ***.

observe a negative impact of Tuesday in a significance level of 1% and a positive impact of Friday in a significance level of 10%.

Additionally, in the mean equation, we can observe that the estimation results from EGARCH (1,1) and TGARCH (1,1) models are in conformity with the estimation results of GARCH (1,1) model for the highly impact of the return observed at date ($t - 1$). But, these results are not in conformity with the estimation of GARCH (1,1) model for Thursdays.

From the estimation results of EGARCH (1,1) model, we can find the existence of a significance and positive effect for the TUNINDEX returns at date ($t-1$) with a significance level of 1%. We can observe that Tuesday present a negative impact on the TUNINDEX returns in a significance level of 1% during the period of study from 31 December 1997 to 07 April 2014. Then, we can show that Wednesday have a positive impact on the TUNINDEX returns. This impact is significant with a significance level of 10%. We can show the existence of a significance and positive effect for Thursdays with a significance level of 1%. Friday affect positively the TUNINDEX returns at the significance level of 1%. In the results of the variance equation, we can find a highly significance level of all EGARCH (1,1) parameters specification in the level of 1%. For the daily effect, we can observe a negative impact of Tuesday in a significance level of 1% and a positive impact of Thursday and Friday in a significance level of 5 and 1%, respectively.

By using the estimation results of TGARCH (1,1) model, we can observe the existence of a significance and positive effect for the TUNINDEX returns at date ($t-1$) with a significance level of 1%. We can remark that Tuesday present a negative impact on the TUNINDEX returns in a significance level of 1% during the period of study from 31 December 1997 to 07 April 2014. Also, we can show that Wednesday have a positive impact on the TUNINDEX returns in a significance level of 5%. We can find the existence of a significance and positive effect for Thursdays and Friday with a significance level of 1%.

From the results of the variance equation, we can show a highly significance level of all TGARCH (1,1) parameters specification in the level of 1%. For the daily effect, we can remark a negative impact of Tuesday in a significance level of 1% and a positive impact of Thursday and Friday in a significance level of 1%.

Finally, the results of ARCH-LM test indicate the absence of an important ARCH effect in the residual series which imply the importance of the conditional variance equations in GARCH models.

6. Conclusion

In this paper, we investigate empirically the day-of-the-week effect on the Tunisian stock exchange returns and volatility. We use a conditional heteroscedasticity specification based on GARCH (1,1), EGARCH (1,1), and TGARCH (1,1) models to examine the presence of the daily anomalies during the period of study from 31 December 1997 to 07 April 2014.

The empirical findings of three GARCH models indicate the presence of the day-of-the-week effect on the Tunisian stock exchange returns and volatility. Then, the estimated results of the GARCH (1,1) model indicate a highly and positive effect for Wednesday, Thursday, Friday, and the past return at date ($t-1$). However, Tuesday have a negative effect on the TUNINDEX returns and volatility.

The estimation results of EGARCH (1,1) and TGARCH (1,1) models show a highly impact of the returns observed at date ($t-1$). Also, in the case of these two models Thursday have a significance and positive effect on the TUNINDEX returns. We can find that Tuesday have a negative and significant impact with a significance level of 1% on mean and variance equation in the case of EGARCH (1,1) and TGARCH (1,1) models. In consequence of the existence of the effect of the day of the week on the TUNINDEX returns and volatilities, we can suggest that the Tunisian stock market is weak-form inefficient.

Additionally, further research can be directed toward investigating the existence of day-of-the-week anomalies on firm basis rather than focusing on stock market indices.

Funding
The authors received no direct funding for this research.

Author details
Abdelkader Derbali[1]
E-mail: derbaliabdelkader@outlook.fr
Slaheddine Hallara[2]
E-mail: ihet@gnet.tn
[1] Department of Finance, Higher Institute of Management of Sousse, University of Sousse, 22 Street Zarkaa Al Yamama, Erriadh City, Sousse 4023, Tunisia.
[2] Department of Finance, Higher Institute of Management of Tunis, University of Tunis, Tunis, Tunisia.

References

Abdalla, S. (2012). Day-of-the-week effect on returns and conditional volatility: Empirical evidence from Sudanese stock market. *Middle Eastern Finance and Economics, 16*, 167–180.

Agathee, U. S. (2008). Day of the week effect: Evidence from the stock exchange of Mauritius (SEM). *International Research Journal of Finance and Economics, 17*, 7–14.

Aggarwal, R., & Rivoli, P. (1989). Seasonal and day of the week effects in four emerging stock markets. *Financial Review, 24*, 541–550.

AL-Mutairi, A. (2010). An Investigation of the day-of-the-week effect in the Kuwait stock exchange. *Research Journal of International Studies, 16*, 191–197.

Aly, H., Mehdian, S., & Perry, M. (2004). An analysis of the day-of-the-week effects in the Egyptian stock market. *International Journal of Business, 9*, 301–308.

Athanassakos, G., & Robinson, M. J. (1994). The day-of-the-week anomaly: The Toronto Stock exchange experience. *Journal of Business Finance and Accounting, 21*, 833–856. http://dx.doi.org/10.1111/jbfa.1994.21.issue-6

Balaban, E. (1995). Day of the week effects: New evidence from an emerging stock market. *Applied Economics Letters, 2*, 139–143. http://dx.doi.org/10.1080/135048595357465

Berument, M., & Dogan, N. (2012). Stock market return and volatility: Day-of-the-week effect. *Journal of Economics and Finance, 36*, 282–302. http://dx.doi.org/10.1007/s12197-009-9118-y

Black, F. (1976). The pricing of commodity contracts. *Journal of Financial Economics, 3*, 167–179. http://dx.doi.org/10.1016/0304-405X(76)90024-6

Bollerslev, T. (1986). Generalized autoregressive conditional heteroskedasticity. *Journal of Econometrics, 31*, 307–327. http://dx.doi.org/10.1016/0304-4076(86)90063-1

Brooks, C., & Persand, G. (2001). Seasonality in southeast Asian stock markets: Some new evidence on the day-of-the-week effects. *Applied Economics Letters, 8*, 155–158.

Cai, J., Yuming, L., & Yuehua, Q. (2006). The day-of-the-week effect. *The Chinese Economy, 39*, 71–88.

Carlucci, F. V., Junior, T. P., & Lima, F. G. (2013). A study on the day of the week effect in the four major capitals markets of the Americas. *Journal of International Finance & Economics, 13*, 11–20.

Chukwuogor-Ndu, C. (2006). Stock market returns analysis, day-of-the-week effect, volatility of returns: Evidence from European financial markets 1997–2004. *International Research Journal of Finance and Economics, 1*, 112–124.

Drimbetas, E., Sariannidis, N., & Porfiris, N. (2007). The effect of derivatives trading on volatility of the underlying asset: Evidence from the Greek stock market. *Applied Financial Economics, 17*, 139–148. http://dx.doi.org/10.1080/09603100500461702

Dubois, M., & Louvet, P. (1996). The day-of-the-week effect: The international evidence. *Journal of Banking and Finance, 20*, 1463–1484. http://dx.doi.org/10.1016/0378-4266(95)00054-2

Engle, R. F., & Ng, V. K. (1993). Measuring and testing the impact of news on volatility. *The Journal of Finance, 48*, 1749–1778. http://dx.doi.org/10.1111/j.1540-6261.1993.tb05127.x

French, K. R. (1980). Stock returns and the weekend effect. *Journal of Financial Economics, 8*, 55–69. http://dx.doi.org/10.1016/0304-405X(80)90021-5

Gharaibeh, A. M. O., & Al Azmi, A. A. T. S. (2015). Test of the day of the week effect: The case of Kuwait stock exchange. *Asian Economic and Financial Review, 5*, 757–765.

Gibbons, M., & Hess, P. (1981). Day of the week effects and asset returns. *The Journal of Business, 54*, 579–596. http://dx.doi.org/10.1086/jb.1981.54.issue-4

Glosten, L. R., Jagannathan, R., & Runkle, D. (1993). On the relation between the expected value and the volatility of the nominal excess return on stocks. *The Journal of Finance, 48*, 1779–1801. http://dx.doi.org/10.1111/j.1540-6261.1993.tb05128.x

Gonzalez-Perez, M. T. & Guerrero, D. E. (2013). Day-of-the-week effect on the VIX. A parsimonious representation. *The North American Journal of Economics and Finance, 25*, 243–260. http://dx.doi.org/10.1016/j.najef.2012.06.003

Hui, T. K. (2005). Day-of-the-week effects in US and Asia-Pacific stock markets during the Asian financial crisis: A non-parametric approach. *The International Journal of Management Science, 33*, 277–282.

Hussain, F., Hamid, K., Akash, R. S. I., & Khan, M. I. (2011). Day of the week effect and stock returns: Evidence from Karachi stock exchange-Pakistan. *Far East Journal of Psychology and Business, 3*, 25–31.

Jaffe, J., & Westerfield, R. (1985). The week-end effect in common stock returns: The international evidence. *The Journal of Finance, 40*, 433–454. http://dx.doi.org/10.1111/j.1540-6261.1985.tb04966.x

Kato, K. (1990). Weekly patterns in Japanese stock returns. *Management Science, 36*, 1031–1043. http://dx.doi.org/10.1287/mnsc.36.9.1031

Lian, K. K., & Chen, W. K. (2004). Seasonal anomalies of stocks in ASEAN equity markets. *Sunway College Journal, 1*, 1–11.

Nelson, D. B. (1991). Conditional Heteroskedasticity in asset returns: A new approach. *Econometrica, 59*, 347–370. http://dx.doi.org/10.2307/2938260

Poshakwale, S., & Murinde, V. (2001). Modelling the volatility in East European emerging stock markets: Evidence on Hungary and Poland. *Applied Financial Economics, 11*, 445–456. http://dx.doi.org/10.1080/096031001300314009

Puja, P. (2010). Days-of-the-week-effect and stock return volatility: Theory and empirical evidence. *Advances in Management, 3*, 14–21.

Tachiwou, A. M. (2010). Day-of-the-week-effects in west African regional stock market. *International Journal of Economics and Finance, 2*, 167–173.

Ulussever, T., Yumusak, I. G., & Kar, M. (2011). The day-of-the-week effect in the Saudi stock exchange: A non-linear garch analysis. *Journal of Economic and Social Studies, 1*, 9–23. http://dx.doi.org/10.14706/JECOSS11

11

CEO age and gender: Subsequent market performance

Marcelo Eduardo[1]* and Brooks Poole[1]
*Corresponding author: Marcelo Eduardo, Mississippi College School of Business, Clinton, MS, USA
E-mail: eduardo@mc.edu
Reviewing editor: David McMillan, University of Stirling, UK

Abstract: The issue of CEO age and gender vs. concurrent performance is extensively examined, but the association with subsequent performance has limited treatment in the financial literature, and with conflicting findings. In the current study, we examine the association between CEO age and gender, and subsequent company market performance using a more recent set of observations and the standard four-factor model to estimate future cumulative abnormal shareholder returns. We find that subsequent abnormal shareholder returns are marginally significantly higher for female CEOs than for their male counterparts, but no material pattern is observed between CEO age and subsequent abnormal shareholder return performance.

Subjects: Corporate finance; Economics, Finance, Business & Industry; Finance; Social Sciences

Keywords: finance; CEO compensation; gender; market efficiency

1. Introduction

The role of CEO age and gender in explaining concurrent or past shareholder returns has been extensively explored in recent financial literature with mixed findings. The examination of the association between CEO age and gender, and *subsequent* abnormal shareholder return performance, however, indicates limited investigation. The research question of this study is as follows: are CEO age and gender correlated with a company's subsequent abnormal shareholder return performance?

ABOUT THE AUTHOR

Marcelo Eduardo is the "Sam Anderson Professor of Finance" at the Mississippi College School of Business. His research interests have centered on the areas of Financial Institutions, Financial Education, and Corporate Finance. In terms of institutions, the author has published articles in the area of Banking and regulation with particular emphasis on CRA regulations and their impact. Eduardo's research in financial education includes award-winning cases dealing with cost of capital and ratio analysis scenarios. More recently, Eduardo has researched the topic of behavioral finance as it impacts capital structure corporate decisions, as well as the impact that CFO rankings have on company performance. This CEO gender and age study fits into this area of research.

PUBLIC INTEREST STATEMENT

An interesting aspect of CEO performance discussions is the impact that CEO age and gender has, if any, on the performance of the company as measured by its stock market returns. Previous studies that search for a relationship between these characteristics and current or past company performance have produced mixed results showing in some cases that female CEO's outperform their male counterparts, while other studies have found no such relationship or even a negative impact by female CEO's. This study attempts to provide a different perspective into this question by examining the impact of gender and age on subsequent performance. By looking at the company's excess stock returns over a market benchmark for the year *following* the year of CEO compensation, the study reveals that such subsequent returns are slightly higher for female CEO's. The study also finds that CEO age has no impact on company's subsequent performance.

The current paper contributes to the literature by investigating the relationship between CEO age and gender and subsequent cumulative abnormal shareholder return. The study's sample draws current data from Fortune 500 companies. A standard four-factor market model is employed to capture the impact of market parameters in measuring subsequent cumulative abnormal shareholder return. While no significant association between CEO age and subsequent market performance is observed, the association between CEO gender and subsequent market performance is observed to be marginally significant with female CEOs outperforming their male counterparts. Including females in the management structure benefits an organization, but CEO age does not affect the organization's future abnormal performance.

2. Literature review

2.1. CEO gender and company performance

Studies on the importance of CEO-specific characteristics and performance are generally mixed. With regard to gender, some studies find companies benefit more from females occupying high-level management positions. Companies led by female CEOs or chairs are associated with higher ROAs (Peni, 2014). Female executives are viewed to be better suited to comprehending customer needs (Brennan & McCafferty, 1997), although no relationship is observed between gender and company performance (Dezsö & Ross, 2008). A positive relationship is found between the percentage of women on top management teams and organizational performance (Krishnan & Park, 2005). In a study of Danish firms, a positive relationship is observed between the percentage of females in top management and firm performance (Smith, Smith, & Verner, 2006). Using the Fama-French valuation framework, a positive relationship is observed between the proportion of female officers and abnormal returns for firms operating in complex environments (Francoeur, Labelle, & Sinclair-Desgagné, 2008). Small service businesses led by female CEOs outperform their male counterparts, primarily due to their stronger market orientation (Davis, Babakus, Englis, & Pett, 2010). When the CEO of a US company is female, company risk is less than when the CEO is male (Khan & Vieito, 2013). In a study of Singaporean companies, investors react positively to the addition of women on the board of directors (Kang, Ding, & Charoenwong, 2010). The presence of female directors on Norwegian companies increases board efficiency through reduced conflicts (Nielsen & Huse, 2010a). A study of Fortune 1,000 companies reveals a positive relationship between the percentage of the board represented by either females or ethnic minorities and firm value (Carter, Simkins, & Simpson, 2003). In a study of female director appointments in Spain, the market is observed to react positively in the short-run (Campbell & Minguez Vera, 2010). Companies led by female CEOs or chairs produce higher ROAs, and age is positively related to performance (Peni, 2014; Krishnan & Park, 2005; Smith et al., 2006). Female executives are better suited to comprehending customer needs (Brennan & McCafferty, 1997).

Conversely, other studies find the presence of females in upper management to be associated with negative consequences in terms of performance. Among Chinese-listed corporations, CEO gender and firm performance have a limited association (Lam, McGuinness, & Vieito, 2013). The average effect of the presence of women on the boards of American companies is negative, driven by the lack of takeover defenses in those companies (Adams & Ferreira, 2009). In a study of FTSE 100 companies, while there is no observed relationship between women's presence on boards and accounting performance, a negative relationship is observed with subjective stock valuation performance measures (Haslam, Ryan, Kulich, Trojanowski, & Atkins, 2010). The perception of women as unequal board members in Norwegian companies reduces their potential to contribute to board policy formulation (Nielsen & Huse, 2010b).

Finally, some studies find upper management gender is found to be unassociated with company performance. CEO gender is found to have a negative, but insignificant relationship with corporate social responsibility (Huang, 2012). While the percentage of board members that are female is positively related to company financial performance in Spain, the relationship is not statistically significant (Campbell & Mínguez-Vera, 2008). No relationship is observed between female CEOs and company performance (Dezsö & Ross, 2008). The evidence on the ability of women directors to influence shareholder value is mixed (Simpson, Carter, & D'Souza, 2010).

2.2. CEO age and company performance

Studies examining the role of executive age in relation to company performance are limited and also produce mixed findings. One study observes executive age to be inversely related to firm performance (Bertrand & Mullainathan, 2003; Davidson, Xie, Xu, & Ning, 2007). Also, older executives are found to be prone to be more conservative as they approach retirement focusing on projects that produce earlier results (Gibbons & Murphy, 1992), while younger CEOs are more prone to focus on short-term performance to establish reputation (Hirshleifer, 1993). However, executive experience is postulated to have a positive influence on performance (Baysinger & Hoskisson, 1990). Finally, executive age may have an impact on company performance that may be positive or negative (Bertrand & Schoar, 2003). The findings between CEO age and performance are mixed, while experience and quality of upper management are positively associated with performance (Peni, 2014).

3. Sample

Sample inclusion requires that the company be listed in the Fortune 500 for each year within the 2007–2012 time period, and also be publicly traded for the five years immediately preceding each observation year for purposes of model parameter estimation. Inclusion restrictions reduce the initial potential sample of 3,000 company-years to 1,306 company-years.

4. Methodology

An ANACOVA (analysis of variance with a covariate) is applied to test the association between the independent variables (age and gender) and performance (subsequent cumulative abnormal market returns).

4.1. Dependent variable

The cumulative abnormal monthly returns on the stock for the year *following* the year of CEO compensation serves as the dependent variable in the current study. Monthly returns estimated for the 60-month time period ending in the year of published CEO-specific data are used to establish model parameters. Standardized cumulative abnormal returns for the 12 months immediately following the CEO-specific data publication year serve as the measure of excess returns.[1] Monthly expected returns are generated using the four-factor model prescribed by Fama and French (1996) and Carhart (1997), as follows:[2]

$$E(r_i, t) - R_{f,t} = \beta_i[E(R_{M,t}) - R_{f,t}] + s_i E(SMB_t) + h_i E(HML_t) + m_i E(MF_t) - \varepsilon_{f,t} \quad (1)$$

where $E(r_i, t)$ is the expected monthly return on company *i* for month *t*, β_i, s_i, h_i, and m_i are the coefficients of the return model for company *i* for the 60-month estimation period ending just prior to the start of the 12-month period of observation, $R_{f,t}$ is the Treasury Bill rate for month *t*, $R_{M,t}$ is the return on the market portfolio *M* for month *t*, SMB_t is the difference between the return on a portfolio of small stocks and the return on a portfolio of big stocks for month *t*, HML_t is the difference between the return on a portfolio of high book-to-market stocks and the return on a portfolio of low book-to-market stocks for month *t*, MF_t is the momentum factor found by the average return on two high prior return portfolios minus the average return on two low prior return portfolios for month *t*, and $\varepsilon_{f,t}$ is the error term.

Scaled abnormal returns are then calculated for each company for each estimation period month as:

$$AR_{it} = (R_{it} - \bar{R}_{it})/s_i \quad (2)$$

where AR_{it} is the scaled abnormal (residual) return for company *i* for month *t*, $\bar{R}_{it}$ is the predicted return for company *i* for month *t*, R_{it} is the observed return for company *i* for month *t*, and s_i is the sample standard deviation of monthly residual returns for company *i* over the estimation period.

Cumulative scaled abnormal returns are then defined for the subsequent 12-month observation period, where $t = 0$ is the last month of the 60-month model formulation period, as:

$$CAR_t = \sum_{t=1}^{12} AR_t \tag{3}$$

4.2. Independent variables

CEO age and gender are the independent variables in the analysis, perhaps serving as proxies for experience and the gender pay disparity, respectively. CEO age for each year from 2006 to 2012 inclusive is obtained from Fortune Magazine.[3] CEO gender for the same time periods is obtained from SEC registration statements via SEC website (EDGAR).[4]

5. Results and analysis

Sample characteristics are presented in Table 1. Results indicate a subsequent cumulative abnormal scaled return for the sample that is not statistically different from zero. Average CEO age is roughly 57 years, and the presence of female CEOs in the sample is quite low, with only 43 of the 1,306 CEO years represented by female CEOs.

Observation of the ANCOVA model with both AGE (covariate) and GENDER (factor) reveals that gender is marginally significant while age is insignificant, but the ANCOVA model is statistically insignificant (see PANEL A in Table 2). A scatterplot for CAR and CEO gender is included (see Graph C). The lack of relationship between subsequent market performance and CEO age is also presented in the form of a scatterplot (see Graph A). There appears to be no visual relationship between CAR and CEO age. The insignificance of CEO age is in contrast with other studies that submit mixed results. Other research efforts observe CEO age to be positively associated with shareholder benefit (e.g. Baysinger & Hoskisson, 1990), or negatively associated with shareholder welfare (e.g. Bertrand & Mullainathan, 2003; and Davidson et al., 2007), or a pattern that may be positive or negative (Bertrand & Schoar, 2003; and Peni, 2014). However, few studies incorporate the standard four-factor model (Carhart, 1997; Fama & French, 1996) to control for systematic effects in measuring abnormal returns, and other studies are based on an earlier time period of observation.

Additionally, we controlled for size (log of sales). The results in Table 3 (PANEL A) suggest that including size into the model does not change the results and still renders GENDER as significant while AGE remains insignificant. The model is rerun without GENDER in (PANEL B).

The model is regenerated without the covariate (see PANEL B1), with the results demonstrating marginal significance for both the model and gender. Observation of the categorical mean CAR values reveals that female CEOs outperform their male CEO counterparts (see PANEL B2). This finding is visually reinforced with the bar chart displayed in Graph B. This findings is consistent with those of other studies that observed a positive benefit from the presence of females in the management structure (e.g. Francoeur et al., 2008; Kang et al., 2010; Khan & Vieito, 2013; Krishnan & Park, 2005; Peni, 2014; Smith et al., 2006). The results are also contradictory to those of other studies who either

Table 1. Sample characteristics

N = 1,306	Mean/(standard deviation)
Variable	
CAR[a]	−0.363/(5.860)
CEO age (Years)	56.870/(5.458)
CEO gender (1-female 2-male)	1.970/(0.179)
(Male CEO years = 1,263)	
(Female CEO years = 43)	

[a]CAR is the subsequent cumulative scaled annual abnormal return as defined in Equation (3).

Table 2. CEO Age and gender vs. subsequent market performance

Source	Sum of squares	df	Mean square	*F*	Sig.
PANEL A					
Corrected model	113.854	2	56.927	1.660	0.191
Intercept	7.514	1	0.219	0.219	0.640
Age	16.693	1	0.487	0.487	0.486
Gender	104.573	1	104.573	3.049	0.081
Error	44,692.075	1,303	34.299		
Total	44,977.822	1,306			
Corrected total	44,805.929	1,305			
PANEL B1					
Corrected model	97.161	1	97.161	2.834	0.093
Intercept	20.511	1	20.511	0.598	0.439
Gender	97.161	1	97.161	2.834	0.093
Error	44,708.768	1,304	34.286		
Total	44,977.822	1,306			
Corrected total	44,805.929	1,305			
PANEL B2					
Gender	Mean		Standard deviation	*N*	
Female	1.115		6.120	43	
Male	−0.413		5.846	1263	
Total	−0.363		5.860	1306	

Notes: In both models, the dependent variable (CAR) is the subsequent cumulative scaled abnormal returns as defined in Equation (3). In the first ANCOVA model (PANEL A), both gender (factor) and age (covariate) serve as independent variables. In the second model (PANEL B1), only gender is included as an independent factor. Mean values of the second model are displayed in PANEL B2.

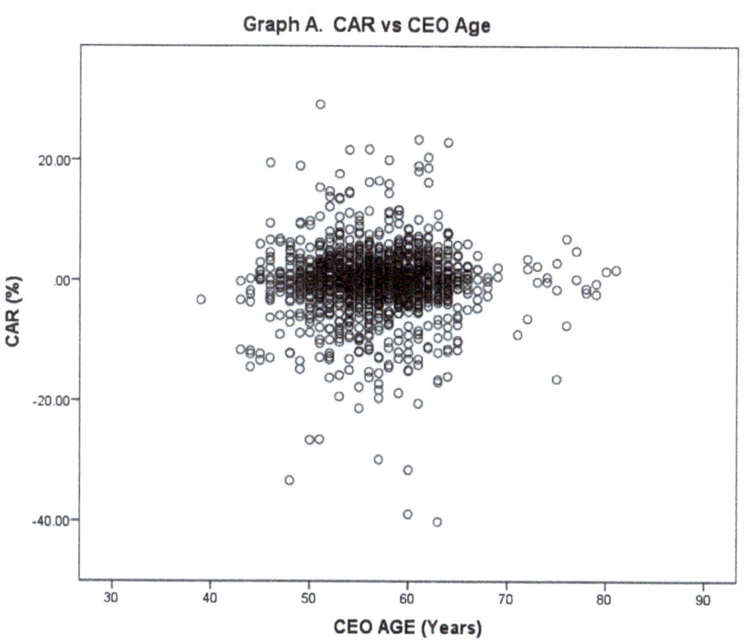

Graph A. CAR vs. CEO age.

Table 3. CEO age and gender vs. subsequent market performance controlling for size				
Model	**Coefficients**	**S. error**	**t**	**Sig.**
PANEL A				
Constant	4.895	4.638	1.056	.291
Age	.022	.030	.795	.427
Gender	–.490	.914	–1.776	.076
SIZE	–.023	.404	–.827	.409
PANEL B				
Constant	5.694	4.527	1.258	.209
Gender	–.470	.908	–1.701	.089
Size	–.020	.401	–.734	.463

Notes: In the model (PANEL A), the dependent variable (CAR) is the subsequent cumulative scaled abnormal returns as defined in Equation (3). Gender, age, and now size serve as independent variables. In the second model (PANEL B), only gender and size are included as the independent variables.

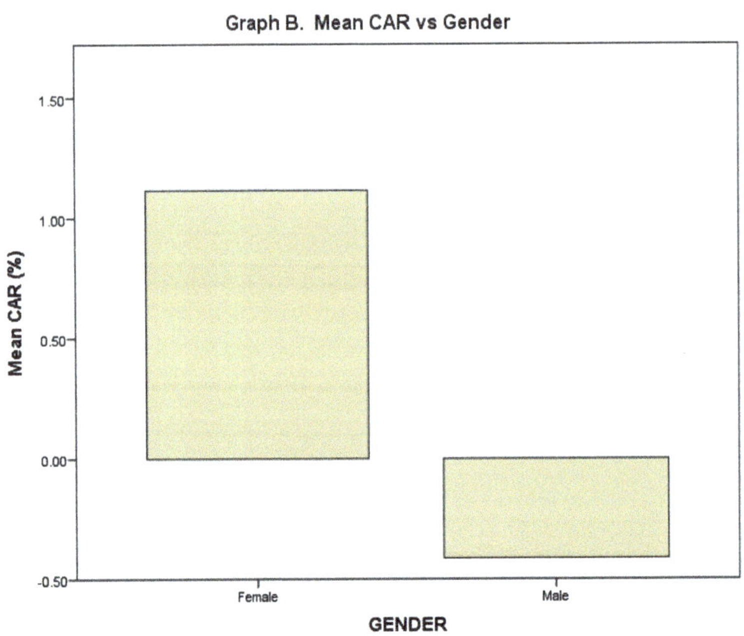

Graph B. Mean CAR vs. gender.

observed a negative impact of females in management (e.g. Adams & Ferreira, 2009; Haslam et al., 2010; Lam et al., 2013; Nielsen & Huse, 2010b), or no significant association in terms of performance (e.g. Campbell & Mínguez-Vera, 2008; Dezsö & Ross, 2008; Huang, 2012; and Simpson et al., 2010).

6. Conclusions

The current study examines the relationship between CEO age and gender and subsequent market performance. The subsequent market performance is measured as the cumulative abnormal shareholder returns in the following year based on the standard four-factor market model (Carhart, 1997; Fama & French, 1996). While no significant association between CEO age and subsequent market performance is observed, the association between CEO gender and subsequent market performance is observed to be marginally significant with female CEOs outperforming their male counterparts. The study's findings support the beneficial aspects of including females in the management structure, but no shareholder benefit is observed to be associated with CEO age.

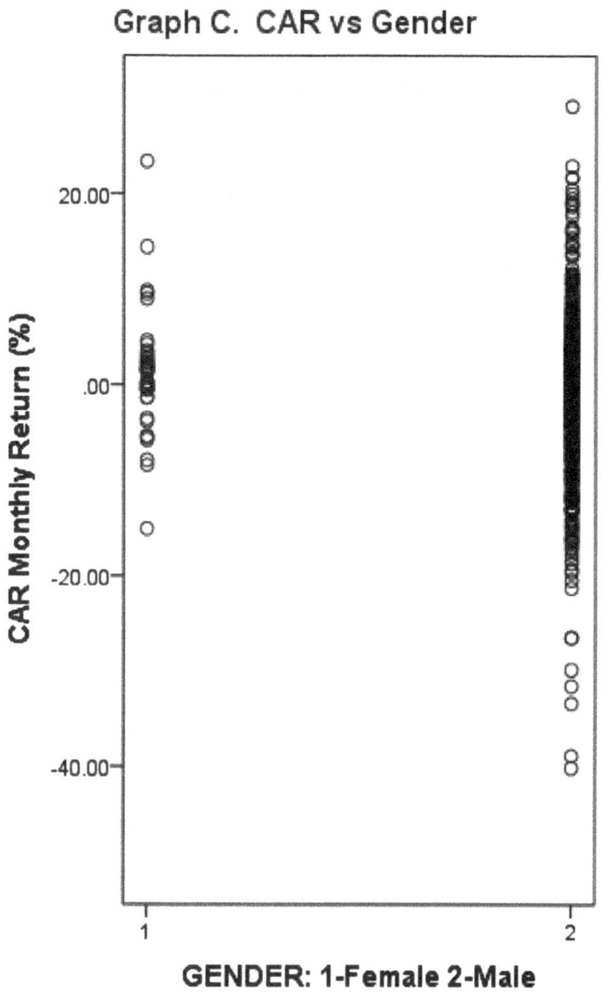

Graph C. CAR vs. gender.

The study does not address additional issues such as years of CEO experience within the same industry, or the benefit of females on the company boards. Those and other issues are left for further study.

Funding

The authors received no direct funding for this research.

Author details

Marcelo Eduardo[1]

E-mail: eduardo@mc.edu

Brooks Poole[1]

E-mail: vpoole@mc.edu

[1] Mississippi College School of Business, Clinton, MS, USA.

Notes

1. For example, for CEO-specific data published for 2012, the expected returns model parameter estimates are based on the 60 months comprising the 2008–2012 time period, with cumulative abnormal return performance based on the 12 months comprising the 2013 year. A likewise procedure is used for each of the other five observation years of the study.
2. Returns are obtained from monthly closing prices, adjusted for splits and dividends, via the. *Wall Street Journal* online website at: http://quotes.wsj.com. The four-factor model develops parameter estimates based on the three systematic factors introduced by Fama and French (1996) and Carhart's (1997) momentum factor. These data are publicly available from the Kenneth French Data Library at: http://mba.tuck.dartmouth.edu/pages/faculty/ken.french/data_library.html.
3. Publication of these data by *Fortune* ceased with the 2012 year.
4. http://edgar.gov.

References

Adams, R., & Ferreira, D. (2009). Women in the boardroom and their impact on governance and performance. *Journal of*

Financial Economics, 94, 291–309. http://dx.doi.org/10.1016/j.jfineco.2008.10.007

Baysinger, B., & Hoskisson, R. (1990). The composition of boards of directors and strategic control: The effects on corporate strategy. *Academy of Management Review, 15*, 72–87.

Bertrand, M., & Mullainathan, S. (2003). Enjoying the quiet life? Corporate governance and managerial preferences. *Journal of Political Economy, 111*, 1043–1075. http://dx.doi.org/10.1086/376950

Bertrand, M., & Schoar, A. (2003). Managing with style: The effect of managers on firm policies. *The Quarterly Journal of Economics, 118*, 1169–1208. http://dx.doi.org/10.1162/003355303322552775

Brennan, N., & McCafferty, J. (1997). Corporate governance practices in Irish companies. *Irish Journal of Management, 17*, 116–135.

Campbell, K., & Minguez Vera, A. (2010). Female board appointments and firm valuation: Short and long-term effects. *Journal of Management and Governance, 14*, 37–59. http://dx.doi.org/10.1007/s10997-009-9092-y

Campbell, K., & Mínguez-Vera, A. (2008). Gender diversity in the boardroom and firm financial performance. *Journal of Business Ethics, 83*, 435–451. http://dx.doi.org/10.1007/s10551-007-9630-y

Carhart, M. (1997). On persistence in mutual fund performance. *The Journal of Finance, 52*, 57–82. http://dx.doi.org/10.1111/j.1540-6261.1997.tb03808.x

Carter, D., Simkins, B., & Simpson, W. (2003). Corporate governance, board diversity, and firm value. *The Financial Review, 38*, 33–53. http://dx.doi.org/10.1111/fire.2003.38.issue-1

Davidson, W., III, Xie, B., Xu, W., & Ning, Y. (2007). The influence of executive age, career horizon and incentives on pre-turnover earnings management. *Journal of Management and Governance, 11*, 45–60. http://dx.doi.org/10.1007/s10997-007-9015-8

Davis, P., Babakus, E., Englis, P., & Pett, T. (2010). The influence of CEO gender on market orientation and performance in service small and medium-sized service businesses. *Journal of Small Business Management, 48*, 475–496. http://dx.doi.org/10.1111/jsbm.2010.48.issue-4

Dezsö, C., & Ross, D. (2008). Girl power: Female participation in top management and firm quality (Working Paper). University of Maryland.

Fama, E., & French, K. (1996). Multifactor explanations of asset pricing anomalies. *The Journal of Finance, 51*, 55–84. http://dx.doi.org/10.1111/j.1540-6261.1996.tb05202.x

Francoeur, C., Labelle, R., & Sinclair-Desgagné, B. (2008). Gender diversity in corporate governance and top management. *Journal of Business Ethics, 81*, 83–95. http://dx.doi.org/10.1007/s10551-007-9482-5

Gibbons, R., & Murphy, K. (1992). Does executive compensation affect investment? *Journal of Applied Corporate Finance, 5*, 99–109. http://dx.doi.org/10.1111/jacf.1992.5.issue-2

Haslam, A., Ryan, M., Kulich, C., Trojanowski, G., & Atkins, C. (2010). Investing with prejudice: The relationship between women's presence on company boards and objective and subjective measure of company performance. *British Journal of Management, 21*, 484–497.

Hirshleifer, D. (1993). Managerial reputation and corporate investment decisions. *Financial Management, 22*, 145–160. http://dx.doi.org/10.2307/3665866

Huang, S. (2012). The impact of CEO characteristics on corporate sustainable development. *Corporate Social Responsibility and Environmental Management, 20*, 234–244.

Kang, E., Ding, D., & Charoenwong, C. (2010). Investor reaction to women directors. *Journal of Business Research, 63*, 888–894. http://dx.doi.org/10.1016/j.jbusres.2009.06.008

Khan, W., & Vieito, J. (2013). Ceo gender and firm performance. *Journal of Economics and Business, 67*, 55–66. http://dx.doi.org/10.1016/j.jeconbus.2013.01.003

Krishnan, H., & Park, D. (2005). A few good women—On top management teams. *Journal of Business Research, 58*, 1712–1720. http://dx.doi.org/10.1016/j.jbusres.2004.09.003

Lam, K., McGuinness, P., & Vieito, J. P. (2013). CEO gender, executive compensation and firm performance in Chinese-listed enterprises. *Pacific-Basin Finance Journal, 21*, 1136–1159. http://dx.doi.org/10.1016/j.pacfin.2012.08.006

Nielsen, S., & Huse, M. (2010a). The contribution of women on boards of directors: Going beyond the surface. *Corporate Governance: An International Review, 18*, 136–148. http://dx.doi.org/10.1111/corg.2010.18.issue-2

Nielsen, S., & Huse, M. (2010b). Women directors' contribution to board decision-making and strategic involvement: The role of equality perception. *European Management Review, 7*, 16–29. http://dx.doi.org/10.1057/emr.2009.27

Peni, E. (2014). CEO and Chairperson characteristics and firm performance. *Journal of Management and Governance, 18*, 185–205. http://dx.doi.org/10.1007/s10997-012-9224-7

Simpson, G., Carter, D., & D'Souza, F. (2010). What do we know about women on boards? *Journal of Applied Finance, 20*, 27–39.

Smith, N., Smith, V., & Verner, M. (2006). Do women in top management affect firm performance? A panel study of 2,500 Danish firms. *International Journal of Productivity and Performance Management, 55*, 569–593. http://dx.doi.org/10.1108/17410400610702160

12

Nonprofit financial assessment and research service learning: Evaluating the performance of an animal welfare nonprofit organization

Karen A. Maguire[1]*

*Corresponding author: Karen A. Maguire, Department of Accounting, Coastal Carolina University, PO Box 261954, Conway, SC 29528, USA

E-mail: KMaguire@coastal.edu

Reviewing editor: Collins Gyakari Ntim, University of Huddersfield, UK

Abstract: The objective of this project is to evaluate the current financial and compliance status of an animal welfare nonprofit organization (NPO) by: analysis of trends over time using information reported on tax filings (Form 990); vertical and horizontal analyses of financial statements; analysis of trends over time using information from financial statements; reconciliation of financial statements to Form 990; ratio analysis of Form 990 Information; and comparison of reported information to local analogs and national standards. This project is conducted in collaboration with The Chapin Foundation. This research serves as a research service learning project with the participation of Master of Accountancy graduate students at Coastal Carolina University. Once the results are presented, recommendations are given for improving operational efficiency and achieving best practices. These recommendations are presented in the form of both short-term items to be addressed immediately—defined in this study as within 60 days—and long-term items to be undertaken in the future. Resources for applicable standards and requirements are also provided.

Subjects: Accounting; Accounting Education; Government & Non-Profit Accounting

Keywords: accounting; auditing; governance; nonprofit organizations; animal welfare organizations; research service learning

ABOUT THE AUTHOR

Karen A. Maguire, PhD, MSF, CFE, CFS, CPA, is a professor of Accounting and the William J. Baxley Jr. Endowed Professor at Coastal Carolina University. This multi-phase, graduate research service learning process—conducted in Dr. Maguire's Master of Accountancy classes—is intended to assist nonprofit organizations (NPOs) achieve compliance with best practices for financial accountability, fundraising, and board governance. Essentially, by strengthening the financial knowledge and practices of NPOs: donors will have more confidence; NPOs will have the ability to obtain the funding needed to reach their goals; achieving efficiency in "back-room operations" will increase effectiveness in "front-room operations;" NPOs can build capacity; and NPOs can continue providing charitable services to our communities. This research provides a mutual benefit to both Coastal Carolina University and the NPO community.

PUBLIC INTEREST STATEMENT

The recommendations presented are intended to enable the NPO to:

- Obtain affordable audits and reviews
- Develop and utilize cost-effective techniques
- Improve the internal control process
- Adhere to the grant compliance requirements
- Promote leadership and governance
- Enhance community engagement

Research with the participation of Master of Accountancy graduate students at Coastal Carolina University provides the opportunity to assist the NPOs in several areas. Through the research, assistance can be provided to help NPOs achieve best practices for corporate governance, accounting, and auditing, and reduce the costs of attaining these goals.

1. Introduction

Mahatma Gandhi once said that "The greatness of a nation and its moral progress can be judged by the way its animals are treated." With this in mind, it is imperative that those organizations concerned with the well-being of animals have the abilities and resources necessary to fulfill their function in society. Toward this end, the objective of this project is to evaluate the current financial and compliance status of an animal welfare nonprofit organization (NPO) by:

- Analysis of trends over time using information reported on tax filings (Form 990)
- Vertical and Horizontal analyses of financial statements
- Analysis of trends over time using information from financial statements
- Reconciliation of financial statements to Form 990
- Ratio analysis of Form 990 Information
- Comparison of reported information to local analogs and national standards

Once the evaluation is complete, recommendations are made that are intended to enable the NPO to:

- Obtain affordable audits and reviews
- Develop and utilize cost-effective techniques
- Improve the internal control process
- Adhere to the grant compliance requirements
- Promote leadership and governance
- Enhance community engagement

2. Facilities walkthrough

An important first step in assessing the current status of an animal welfare NPO is an initial facilities walkthrough. By physically inspecting the facility, it is possible to get a sense of the day-to-day operations of the facility that may not be apparent through inspection of financial data alone. For this project, an official scheduled visit was conducted by the entire Advanced Auditing class. In addition, two visits were conducted in secret with no advanced notice given.

The scheduled site visit was conducted on 24 September 2015 after the close of normal business hours. The Advanced Auditing class was guided around the facility by the Director of Operations as well as two members of the Board of Directors. During this visit, the condition of the facility was observed, as was the condition of the animals housed within the facility. In general, it was agreed that during the walkthrough, the facilities and animals appeared clean and relatively happy.

The additional, informal visits were undertaken by Candelyn Bond and Dr. Karen Maguire some days before the official visit occurred. The conditions observed during these visits were reported to be at odds with the conditions observed during the official walkthrough. Of greatest concern was the observance of dirty animal housing with dogs being observed standing in their own feces. Additionally, it was noted that many of the staff appeared to only undertake any duties while being directly observed by the Director of Operations. Of further concern was that in several instances, it appeared that employees indicated that an animal was in the process of being adopted simply to avoid the work required to adopt the animal to the inquiring person.

The information gathered during both the formal and informal visits has proven invaluable for the project, providing a basis that was used to identify areas of concern. The areas of concern are addressed in the individual sections that follow, along with recommendations for addressing these concerns.

3. Mission statement

In addition to physical and financial analyses, it is important to determine what the organization itself views as the most important functions it undertakes. One of the best ways to ascertain this information is to obtain and review any mission statement produced by the organization.

A mission statement is an important item for any organization. The statement should reflect the core values of the organization and reflect what the organization strives to be. A mission statement is more important to employees of an organization than customers, as it presents the ideals toward which employees should be working. This is an important fact to keep in mind when creating a mission statement for your organization. The stated mission of the Grand Strand Humane Society as taken from their website is:

> The Grand Strand Humane Society (GSHS) takes in animals brought in by the City of Myrtle Beach Animal Control. We are committed to the care and humane treatment of all homeless and abandoned animals in the Myrtle Beach Metropolitan Area. When we made the decision to step out of the cookie-cutter style of shelters and stop euthanizing healthy, adoptable animals for space, it was the right decision and we felt the only option for the GSHS. The decision did increase our financial struggle, but we will continue finding every healthy, adoptable animal a forever family as long as it is financially feasible. We are further committed to providing excellent guest service to people visiting our facilities in the hope that all our animals can find caring and loving homes. We also work at educating our community about responsible pet ownership and finally, to investigate and attempt to prevent cruelty to all animals. We strive to provide all communities within our area with cost-effective adoption rates as well as spay/neutering and preventative healthcare services. (Grand Strand Humane Society, 2015).

In addition, the Grand Strand Humane Society has included the following mission statement on the Form 990 tax forms filed with the IRS:

> To care for and place animals and to provide for adoption, spay/neuter operations, preventive care, rabies and other vaccinations, and boarding of animals. (Foundation Center, 2015).

4. Five freedoms of animal welfare

Related to the mission statement of an animal welfare NPO are the Five Freedoms of Animal Welfare. While they may not be explicitly stated in the mission statement, these freedoms are key issues to keep in mind when drafting a mission statement.

Animal welfare, according to the World Organization for Animal Health (OIE), refers to the ability of an animal to cope with its current living conditions. An animal is in a good state of welfare if it is comfortable, safe, healthy, and well nourished. Such an animal is free from distress, pain, and fear, and can express innate behavior. Consequently, good animal welfare requires humane handling of animals, provision of shelter, proper nutrition, and prevention of diseases (OIE, 2015).

There are five recognized factors that influence an animal's welfare. These factors are referred to as the Five Freedoms (Bousfield & Brown, 2010). The concept of Five Freedoms originated in the United Kingdom in 1965 after the government commissioned an investigation into the welfare of animals kept in intensive farming conditions (Bousfield & Brown, 2010). These Five Freedoms are defined as:

(1) Freedom From Hunger and Thirst

- By ready access to fresh water and diet to maintain health and vigor

(2) Freedom From Discomfort

- By providing an appropriate environment including shelter and a comfortable resting area

(3) Freedom From Pain, Injury, or Disease

- By prevention or rapid diagnosis and treatment

(4) Freedom to Express Normal Behavior

- By providing sufficient space, proper facilities, and company of the animal's own kind

(5) Freedom From Fear and Distress

- By ensuring conditions and treatment which avoid mental suffering (Bousfield & Brown, 2010)

5. Compliance and responsibility

While the Five Freedoms provide a framework assessing the welfare of animals cared for by an animal welfare NPO, they do not carry the full force and weight of legal regulations. There are a number of areas where an animal welfare NPO is legally required to comply with published standards. We have grouped compliance for animal welfare NPOs into five categories based on the entity governing the compliance standards. Detailed appendices were provided to the GSHS. The areas of compliance determined by this project are as follows:

- Accounting Standards
  - Financial Accounting Standards Board (FASB)
- Business Regulations
  - Internal Revenue Service (IRS)
- Fundraising and Solicitation
  - Secretary of State
- OSHA Compliance
  - Occupational Safety and Health Act (OSHA)
- DHEC Compliance
  - Drug Enforcement Administration (DEA)

With respect to FASB standards, all nonprofit organizations have to report information about their financial performance, liquidity, and cash flow. Special procedures have been established for the handling of contributions, where FASB Statement No. 116 regulates Contributions Received and Contributions Made. FASB Statements No. 124 and 135 are specifically related to nonprofit organizations (Financial Accounting Standards Board, 2015).

FASB Statement No. 117 requires that all nonprofit entities provide:

- Statement of financial position
- Statement of activity
- Statement for functional expenses
- Statement of cash flows

Full disclosure of the donor-imposed restrictions on net assets should be made in these financial statements (Financial Accounting Standards Board, 2015).

Following IRS guidelines, nonprofit organizations may apply to the IRS in order to be exempt from federal income taxes. The IRS requires reporting on organization's exempt status, finances, governance, compliance with federal tax filings (including the IRS Form 990), and other activities. IRS also regulates charitable contributions and unrelated business expense (IRS, 2015b).

Charitable fundraising in South Carolina is administered by the Division of Public Charities of the office of the South Carolina Secretary of State. All charities that intend to solicit contributions or have someone solicit contributions for them must register with the Division of Public Charities before solicitations are made and thereafter on an annual basis. For annual financial reports, a charity can submit its IRS Form 990, 990-EZ, or 990-PF to the Division of Public Charities in lieu of filing a report on the Division of Public Charities' annual report form. Failure to timely submit registration statements and reports can result in administrative fines of up to $2,000 per violation (South Carolina Secretary of State, 2015).

Under OSHA, employers are responsible for providing a safe and healthful workplace. Employers must comply with all applicable OSHA standards. Employers must also comply with the General Duty Clause of OSHA, which requires employers to keep their workplace free of serious recognized hazards. Under OSHA, organizations must comply with:

- Record-keeping
- Reporting
- Inspection Rules
- Hazard Prevention and Infection Control
- Physical Safety
- Chemical Safety
- Biological Safety
- Other Hazards (Occupational Safety & Health Administration, 2015)

According to the US Drug Enforcement Administration, all nonprofit organizations have to maintain minimum standards with respect to:

- Controlled Substances Registration
- Inventory
- Storage
- Administration (Drug Enforcement Administration, 2015)

The South Carolina Department of Health and Environmental Control's (DHEC's) Bureau of Drug Control enforces the S.C. Controlled Substances Act, which closely parallels the federal Controlled Substances Act of 1970. The S.C. Controlled Substances Act:

- Requires that every person or entity who engages in controlled substances activity in South Carolina:
  - Obtain an annual registration from DHEC
  - Register with the US Drug Enforcement Administration (DEA) prior to engaging in such activity. (Section 44-53-290)
- Empowers DHEC to decrease the diversion of controlled substances from legal sources to illegal ones by maintaining a closed system of distribution

- Authorizes DHEC to use South Carolina-licensed pharmacists who are also commissioned as state law enforcement officers (Section 44-53-480). These pharmacists have received certification training at the S.C. Criminal Justice Academy (South Carolina Department of Health & Environmental Control, 2015).

6. Overall operations

The overall operations of the Grand Strand Humane Society—and other animal welfare NPOs conducting an assessment—can first be analyzed by observing the trends over time of data reported on tax Form 990 and financial statements. This analysis will begin with graphical representations of the data contained on filed and publicly available Tax Form 990s. The information from the GSHS has been plotted against publicly available Form 990 data from other local animal welfare organizations (Foundation Center, 2015).

The GSHS is a larger operation than the animal welfare NPOs closest geographically. In 2011, the GSHS took in roughly twice the total revenue of the Humane Society of North Myrtle Beach (HSNMB), and roughly six times the total revenues of Coastal Animal Rescue (CAR) and Waccamaw Animal Rescue Mission (WARM). By 2013, reported revenues on the Form 990 for the GSHS are almost three times that of the HSNMB. CAR and HSNMB experienced an upward trend in revenues from 2012 to 2013 along with the GSHS. WARM, already the smallest NPO of the group with respect to total revenue, experienced a drop in revenue (Figure 1).

Similar to revenue, GSHS's total expenses have increased from year to year. The same is true for CAR. HSNMB decreased its total expenditures in 2013, even though its total revenues increased for the year. WARM's decrease in total revenues from 2012 to 2013 is evident in the corresponding decrease in total expenses over the same period (Figure 2).

Taken all together, the information on the preceding charts indicates that from an overall perspective the financial status of the GSHS in on an upward trend. Revenues have increased for every year analyzed at a rate that outpaces the increase in expenses and contributes to an upward trend in net income. Of concern, however, is the fact that the GSHS has operated at a net loss for all years analyzed (Figure 3).

Of the animal welfare NPOs, only HSNMB reported positive net income, and this was only for one of the three years studied, in 2013. CAR moved toward the breakeven point from 2012 to 2013. WARM's net loss increased over the same period.

The GSHS kindly provided and approved the use of the financial statements used by management and the board of directors for internal reporting services. This allowed us to segregate data by

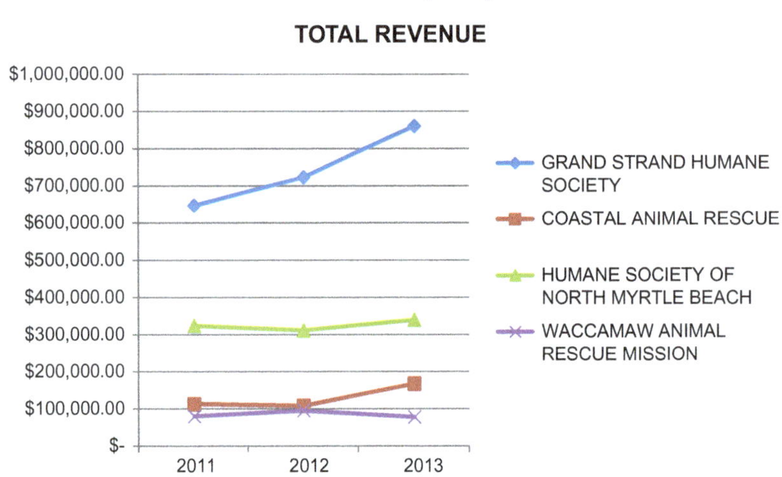

Figure 1. Total revenue, local animal welfare organizations.

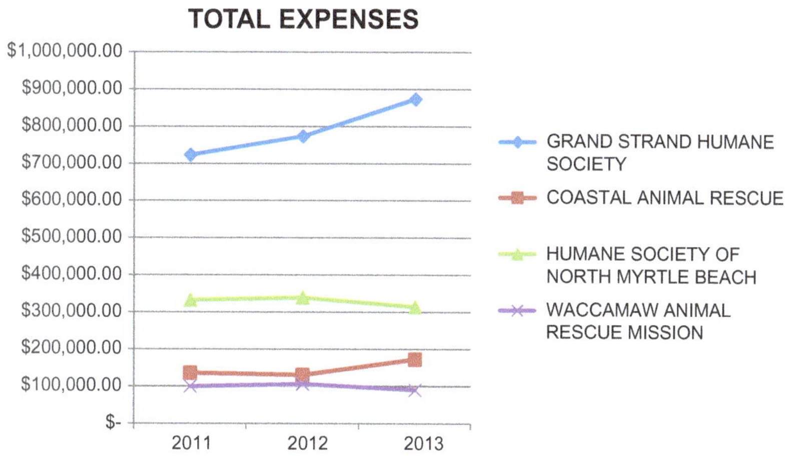

Figure 2. Total expenses, local animal welfare organizations.

function, and to analyze fiscal year data from 2012 to 2015. The Form 990s for fiscal years 2014 and 2015 for any of the aforementioned animal welfare NPOs are not yet publicly available. Therefore, in analyzing the financial statement data, the overall results for the GSHS were plotted against the results for the separate operational units within the GSHS—Shelter, Clinic, and Fundraising/Administration. These individual operations are included in the charts below, and will also be analyzed in more detail in subsequent sections (Figure 4).

Similar to the data provided on the tax Form 990, financial statement analysis reveals that income for the GSHS is on an upward trend that appears to be accelerating. Of concern is the fact that while income from the shelter and clinic operations has increased, the income from fundraising exhibits a downward trend. In an NPO, the majority of funds are expected to be generated by fundraising activities; therefore, this trend indicates an area that must be addressed. The National Center for Charitable Statistics provides benchmarks created by multiple philanthropic organizations. These organizations estimate that between 20 and 40% of expenses are typically spent on fundraising (National Center for Charitable Statistics, 2015).

As with revenue, Cost of Goods Sold has increased every year for the time period under review. Total Cost of Goods Sold mirrors the trend in Shelter Cost of Goods Sold (Figure 5). Of particular note in this graph are the completely different behaviors of the three operating units. While shelter is consistently increasing, clinic is decreasing, and fundraising has remained steady as it declines to almost no fundraising expenses at all.

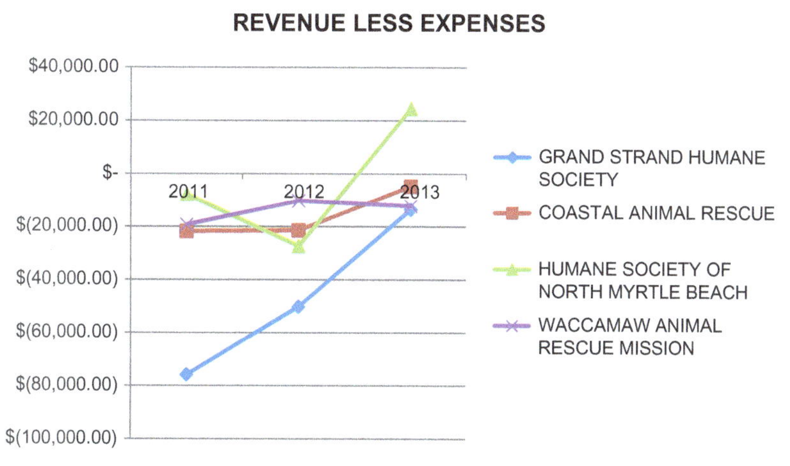

Figure 3. Revenue less expenses, local animal welfare organizations.

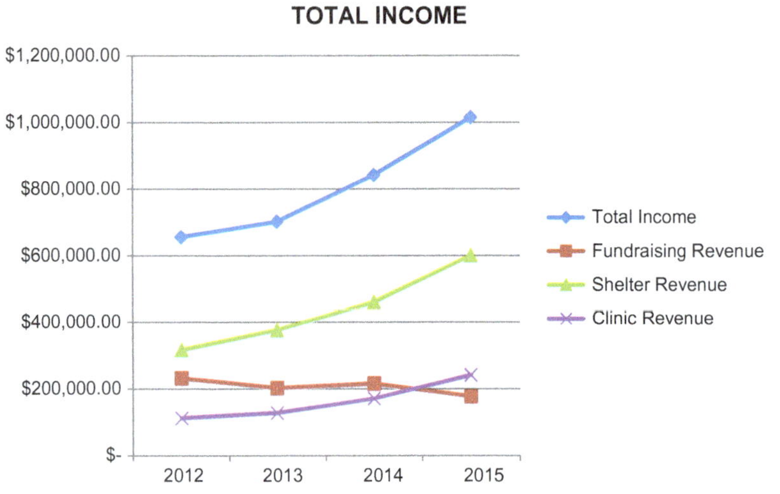

Figure 4. GSHS total income and by operational unit.

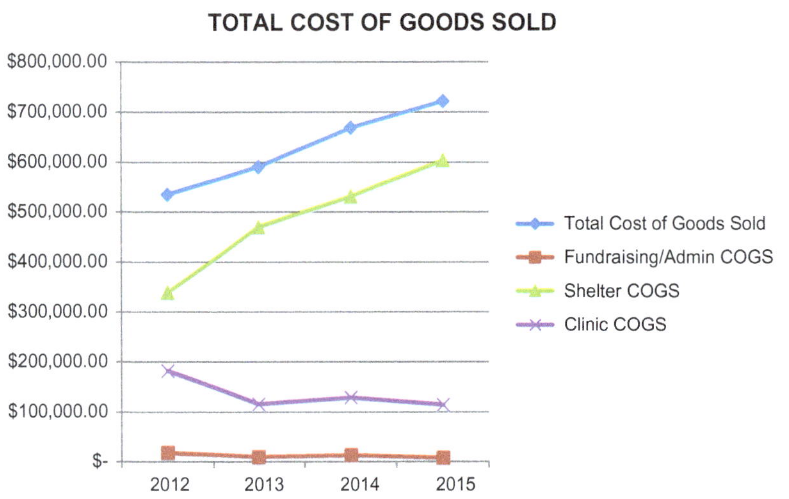

Figure 5. GSHS total CGS and by operational unit.

When the gross profit, revenue less cost of goods sold, is plotted, the results are dramatic (Figure 6). Where once fundraising was solely responsible for the GSHS generating a positive gross profit, results from recent years indicate that the shelter and clinic have become the driving force. If trends continue, shelter and clinic gross profit will eclipse the gross profit generated by fundraising activities in the near future.

When compared to other analyses, the amount of total expenses seems completely disconnected (Figure 7). While revenues, cost of goods sold, and gross profit have undergone large changes during the time period in question, expenses have remained abnormally flat with almost no change from year to year. When the other analyses are taken into account, this flat behavior represents an area of concern that should be examined. Further charts and tables representing the analysis were provided to the GSHS. In addition, Appendices for every section of this paper were provided to GSHS. These deliver a more detailed view that can be used by the board of directors and management during their decision-making processes.

In addition to the trend over time analysis represented above, ratio analysis was undertaken using the information contained on filed tax Form 990s. Two sets of ratios were computed. The first set compared the Form 990 ratio results of the GSHS to other animal welfare NPOs within the state, specifically the Charleston Animal Society and the Greenville Humane Society. The second set of

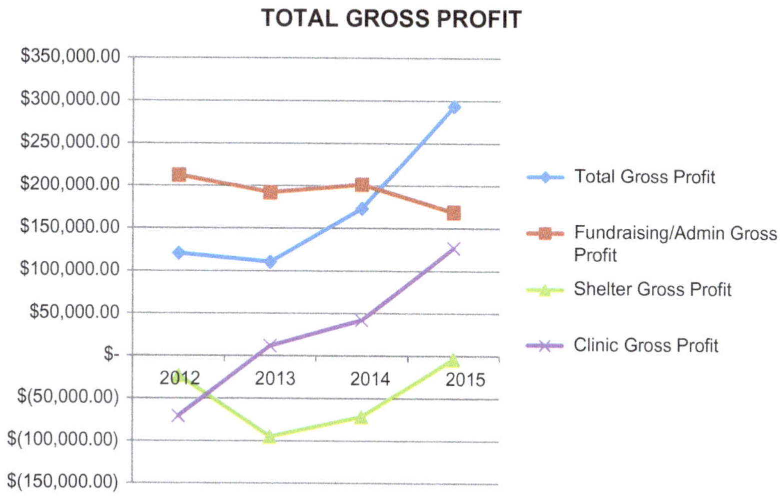

Figure 6. GSHS total gross profit and by operational unit.

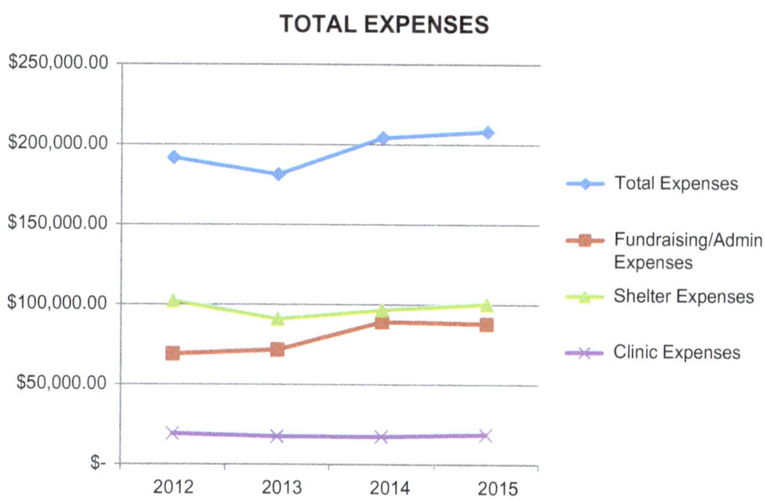

Figure 7. GSHS total expenses and by operational unit.

Table 1. Form 990 ratio analysis, state animal welfare organizations

2013 Form 990 data	Grand Strand Humane Society	Charleston Animal Society	Greenville Humane Society
Current ratio	2.31	11.43	3.91
Fundraising efficiency ratio	0.18	0.10	0.64
Program efficiency ratio	0.89	0.85	0.96
Working capital	$31,057	$1,279,737	$465,074

ratios compared the financial statement results of the GSHS to the Humane Society of the United States (HSUS, 2015). Form 990 analysis for 2013 (Table 1) includes the following:

The current ratio measures an NPO's ability to meet short-term financial obligations (Guidestar, 2004). For the GSHS, the NPO has $2.31 in current assets for every dollar of current liabilities. A current ratio of 1.00 is the breakeven point, and a higher number is better. The GSHS has a lower current ratio than the Charleston Animal Society and the Greenville Humane Society. However, their ratio does indicate that in 2013 the GSHS can meet its financial obligations. This result is contrary to GSHS's current ratio for 2011 and 2012, which was 0.9 and 0.8, respectively. Working capital measures in dollars the excess of current assets over current liabilities (Guidestar, 2004). The GSHS had $31,057 to devote toward building capacity. This number is on a smaller scale than the other animal welfare NPOs presented.

7. Shelter operations

When analyzing the overall financial health of an organization, it is helpful to look at its financial data over a period of time. This displays the organization's strengths and weaknesses. This same analysis can be applied to the financial data of the individual components of the overall organization. This section builds on the analysis of the overall status of the organization completed in the previous section. The following charts present an analysis of the Shelter Operations of the Grand Strand Humane Society (Figure 8).

When looking at the revenue generated by the shelter, it is clearly on an upward trend.

The upward trend noticed in shelter revenue is also apparent when reviewing the cost of goods sold for the shelter (Figure 9). In both instances, these items are moving at approximately the same rate as the overall humane society measures of revenue and cost of goods sold.

The GSHS shows a dramatic increase in net income over the past few years (Figure 10). The shelter's net income has improved in the sense that every year its net loss decreases. While the GSHS has been increasing with regard to net income, the shelter has been somewhat erratic. The year 2013 provides a unique result. The total GSHS net income remained at almost the same level as the year before. For the shelter, the net income in 2013 saw a sharp decline from the previous year. The shelter then struggled to make a positive contribution to overall net income as it recovered. The main culprit contributing to the negative net income from the shelter is the rapidly increasing Cost of Goods Sold Other Than Personnel as indicated in the chart below (Figure 11).

The Cost of Goods Sold Personnel account is unclear with respect to both definition and allocation. When calculating cost of goods sold, the IRS delineates organizations that make, buy, or sell goods, organizations that sell or charge for supplies used in a service business, and purchases less cost of items withdrawn for personal use (IRS, 2015a). It appears that this account includes elements of all three types.

Otherwise, there appears to be two main drivers for these increased shelter costs:

- Shelter supplies
- Shelter preventative medications.

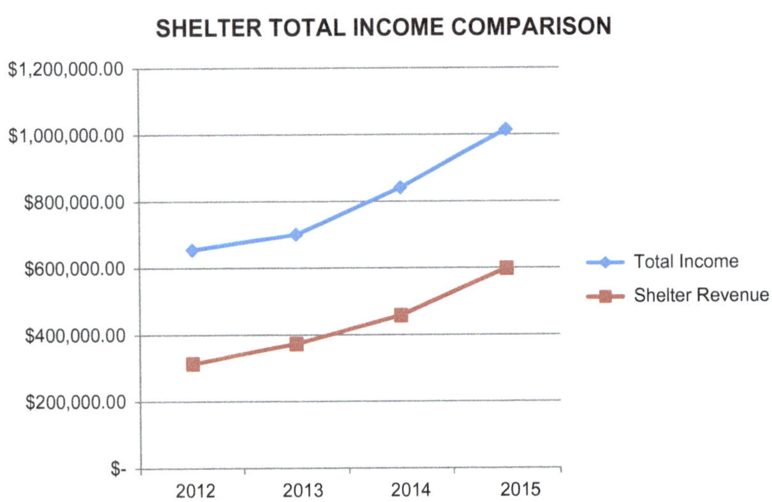

Figure 8. GSHS comparison of total and shelter unit income.

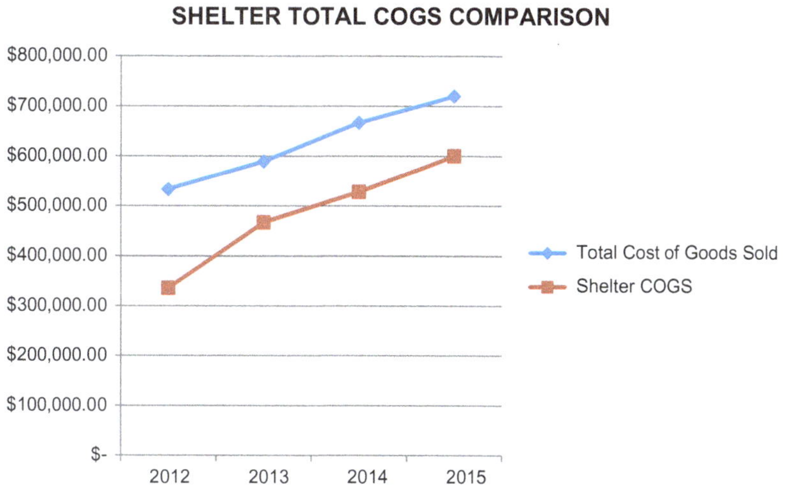

Figure 9. GSHS comparison of total and shelter unit CGS.

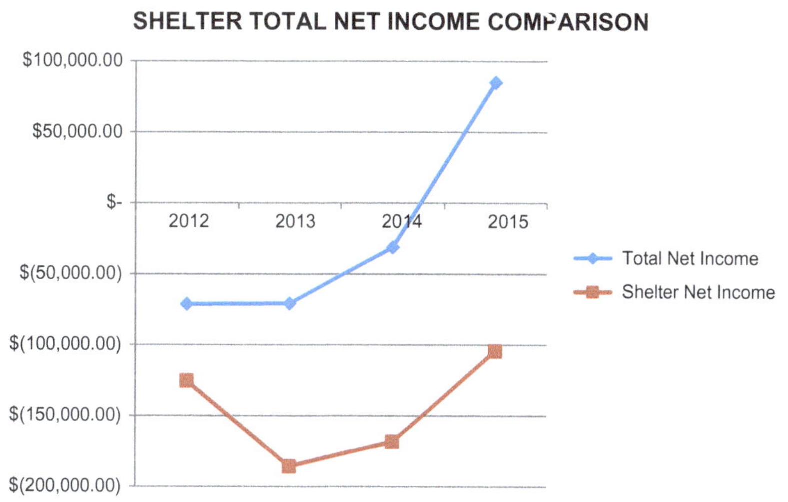

Figure 10. GSHS comparison of total and shelter unit net income.

From 2012 to 2015, the costs recorded in the general ledger account labeled Shelter Supplies increased by 262%. During the same time period, the costs recorded in the general ledger account labeled Shelter Preventative Medications increased by just over 300%. During this time period, the variance between budgeted amounts and actual amounts was also quite large. This indicates either operational inefficiencies or unrealistic budgeting parameters. These two accounts make up over 98% of the costs that are recorded under Cost of Goods Sold Other Than Personnel.

There are also several items that are currently not tracked by the GSHS that would create greater accuracy in financial reporting and lead to better decision-making. First, it is important to know the maximum and current capacity with regard to effectively serving animals. This will allow for effective budgeting and allow the organization to determine an accurate cost of treating an individual animal (ASPCA, 2015a).

Additionally, one of the most comprehensive figures that can be used to evaluate the performance of an animal welfare NPO is live release rate (ASPCA, 2015b). To effectively implement this measure, the organization will have to identify animals under one of four segments: Healthy, Treatable, Unhealthy, and Untreatable. This will allow accurate record-keeping and can be used by the organization to identify areas to improve. Simply put, the live release rate is the percentage of

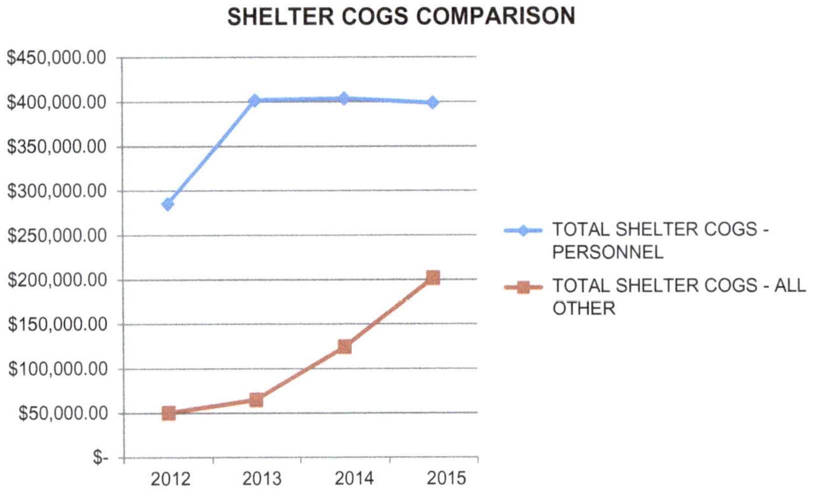

Figure 11. GSHS shelter unit CGS.

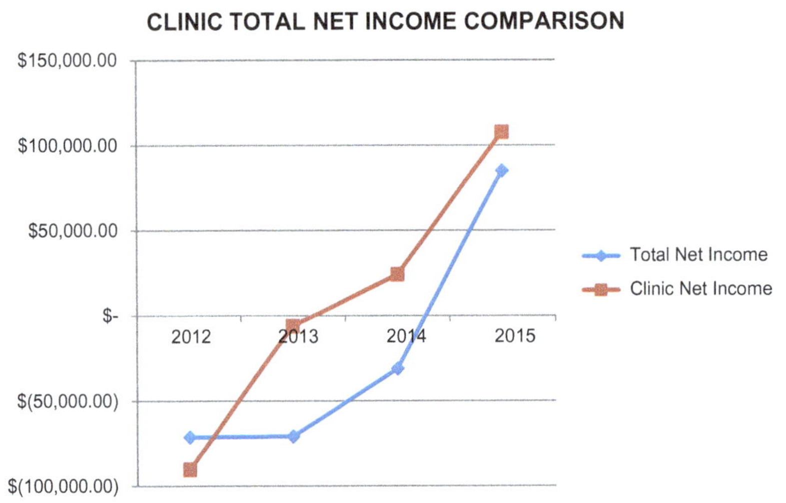

Figure 12. GSHS comparison of total and clinic unit net income.

animals that left the facility with a live outcome. To measure this effectively, the organization needs to record the following things in detail:

- Animal intakes
- Live outcomes
- Euthanasia outcomes
- Owner requested euthanasia
    - Whether the animal was treatable/untreatable
- All outcomes (Asilomar Accords, 2004)

A template for calculating the live release rate can be found at: http://www.asilomaraccords.org/statistics_and_formulas/annual_animal_statistics_table_template_2-07.pdf.

In the short term—defined in this study as within 60 days—the recommendation for shelter operations is to begin using the features of the Pet Point application already purchased by and available to the GSHS. The GSHS needs to begin using Pet Point immediately for animals currently residing in the shelter. Performance measurements available via Pet Point include:

- Intake/Outcome Tracking
- Receipt
- Behavior
- Inventory/Order Management
- Enhance Animal Profile
- Lost/Found Tracking
- Pet Request (Pet Point, 2015).

Not only does Pet Point provide tracking for the items needed to calculate the live release rate, it also provides inventory tracking which would help identify the causes of the rapid increase in supply usage and help with the development of a more effective budgeting procedure. Additionally, Pet Point also provides monthly reports of total national intakes of cats and dogs, total national cats and dogs that left animal welfare organizations, and average adoption fees for cats and dogs under and over one year of age (Pet Point, 2015).

8. Clinic operations

Building upon the analysis done in the overall operations and shelter operations sections, this section analyzes the financial data related to the clinic operations of the GSHS. During the 2013 fiscal year, the clinic transitioned from operating at a net loss to operating with a substantial net income. Net Income for both the GSHS overall and the clinic are presented in the following chart (Figure 12):

The above chart plots the GSHS's total revenue with that of the clinic (Figure 13). When the net income measures and revenue measures in the two previous charts are examined in tandem, results indicate that while clinic revenue is increasing at a slower rate than total revenue, clinic net income has in fact outpaced the net income of GSHS as a whole.

Whereas total cost of goods sold has increased, the clinic cost of goods sold from 2012 to 2015 shows a significant decrease (Figure 14). This is particularly evident from 2012 to 2013. Recall that the shelter cost of goods sold in the previous section showed an increase in shelter supplies of 262% and an increase in shelter preventative supplies of over 300% over the 2012 to 2015 period. At a minimum, these results suggest that record-keeping and allocation of the budgeted and actual cost of goods sold are inconsistent.

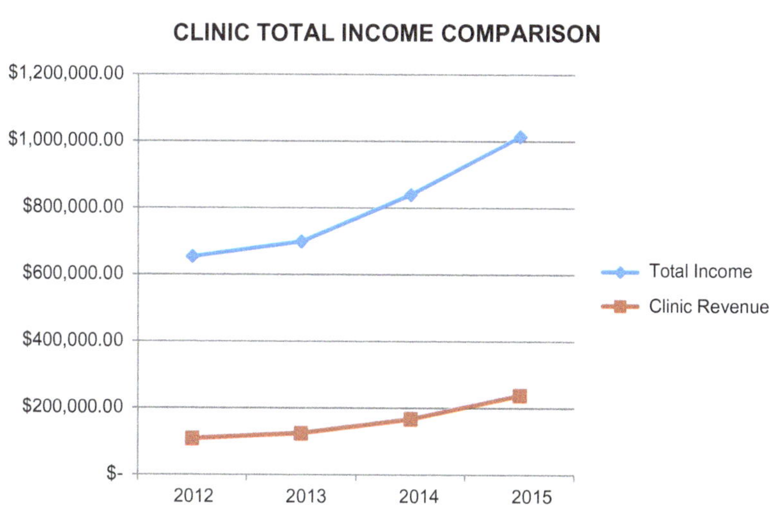

Figure 13. GSHS comparison of total and clinic unit income.

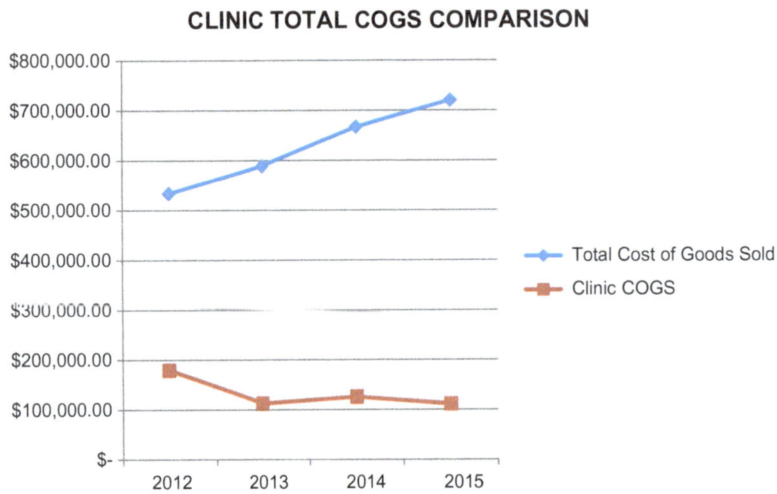

Figure 14. GSHS comparison of total and clinic unit CGS.

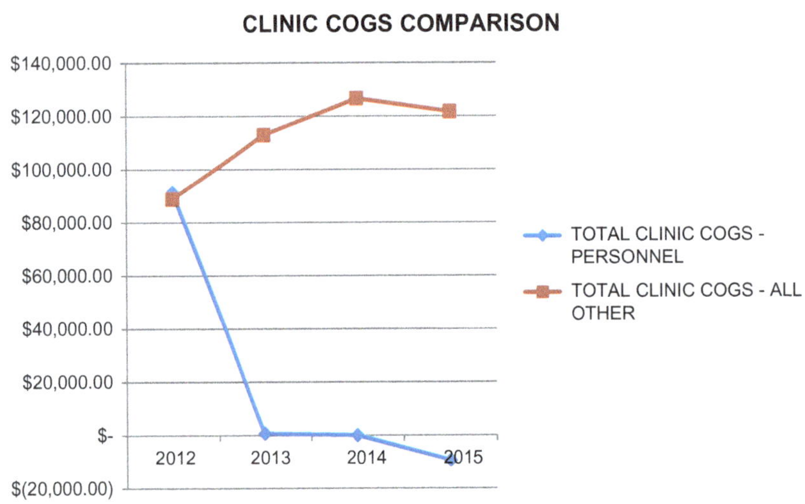

Figure 15. GSHS clinic unit CGS.

Looking further into the decrease in clinic cost of goods sold, it can be observed on the chart above that the decrease can be almost wholly attributed to the rapid decrease in clinic personnel costs that occurred following the 2012 fiscal year (Figure 15).

This decrease in cost of goods sold can be attributed to the fact that for all four years, the Services to Shelter—Clinic account is allocated over to the Shelter COGS from the Veterinarian Services—Shelter account. Each year, but 2014, the dollar amounts in both accounts balance, offsetting each other. In 2014, the amount of $141,091.90 in the Service to Shelter—Clinic account does not match the amount of $141,288.00 in the Veterinarian Services—Shelter. This improper allocation causes a huge decrease in the overall total of the Clinic COGS—Personnel account. This is evident in the 2015 Total Clinic COGS—Personnel account with a balance of negative $9,299.93. Additional charts and tables reflecting this data were provided to GSHS. Ratios relating directly to clinic operations were also performed and these results were provided to GSHS.

In addition to the issues related to financial information, a number of issues related to day-to-day operations were noted. These issues relate to the areas of:

- Sufficient Record-Keeping
- Proper Cost Allocation

- Timely Inventory Tracking
  - Storage, Handling, and Preparation of Vaccinations
- Compliance With Established Standards
  - OSHA
  - DHEC
  - DEA
  - IRS

The recommended actions to be taken related to each of these areas are detailed in the Long-Term Recommendations section later in this paper. In the short term, the recommendation is that the GSHS immediately begin using the Pet Point application for animals currently being treated in the clinic. Performance measures available via Pet Point include:

- Medical
- Receipt
- Inventory and Order Management
- Enhanced Animal Profile
- Flexible Reports

In addition, Pet Point will allow the clinic to immediately begin tracking inventory and can provide tailored reports on the results of operations (Pet Point, 2015).

9. Fundraising operations

In addition to the shelter and clinic functions, the GSHS engages in fundraising activities. Fundraising is an essential part of nonprofit operations. Many NPOs rely mainly upon donations from individuals and corporations in order to sustain operations. As with the other segments of GSHS operations, this section begins with an analysis of the financial data related to fundraising activities. In this section, the analysis begins with a comparison of GSHS Form 990 reported tax data to that of other local animal welfare organizations. Of note, in this section is that fundraising and administration are considered a single cost center for the GSHS.

The chart above appears to represent that the GSHS is outperforming other local animal welfare organizations in terms of fundraising revenue (Figure 16). The next test will be this revenue as a percentage of total revenue.

When looked at as a percentage of total revenue, it becomes apparent that the fundraising revenues of the GSHS not only lag behind most other local organizations, they have also been contributing a smaller percentage of total revenue every year (Figure 17).

In addition to fundraising revenue (Figure 18), fundraising expenses are tracked in the Form 990. The GSHS exhibits some peculiar behavior in regard to fundraising expenses. While the fundraising revenue slightly increased in dollar value from year to year, the associated fundraising expenses have fluctuated wildly from a high of above $16,000 to a low of less than $8,000.

The fluctuation of fundraising expenses is again evident when the fundraising expenses are expressed as a percentage of total expenses (Figure 19).

Before transitioning from Form 990 data to analyzing financial statement data, it is important to point out that the amounts attributed to fundraising/administration on the financial statements do not directly correlate to the fundraising amounts reports on the GSHS Form 990. This project was unable to determine the basis for the conversion that resulted in the Form 990 numbers.

An example of the lack of reconciliation between the Form 990 and financial statement numbers is indicated above in Total Income. While the reported Form 990 income has been increasing, the amount of income attributed to fundraising/administration on the financial statements has been on a downward trend (Figure 20).

The source of the downward trend referenced above becomes apparent when the individual sources of fundraising revenue are examined. Donations, which is the largest component of fund-raising revenue, had been holding steady but suffered a decrease in excess of 20% during the 2015 fiscal year (Figure 21). Additional charts and tables reflecting this data were provided to GSHS.

As seen above, GSHS fundraising revenue does not comprise a high percentage of total income. Clear delineation of these revenues and expenses is vital for accurate financial reporting (IRS, 2015c). In order to begin increasing the level of donations, donor trust must be re-established and the GSHS must become more compliant in terms of its fundraising practices, both operationally and in terms of financial reporting.

Before any donations can be solicited, any NPO must file with the state of incorporation. In the state of South Carolina, all 501(c)(3) NPOs must register with the South Carolina Secretary of State Division of Public Charities. This registration allows NPOs to solicit contributions from the residents of the State of South Carolina as stated in the South Carolina Code of Laws Section 33-56-30. After the original filing, an annual renewal registration must be submitted every year thereafter within four-and-half months after the close of the fiscal year. There is a $50 registration fee that is required with the original filing only. A financial report, a copy of the preceding years Form 990, must accompany the registration every year as well. There is $2,000.00 fine for filing the registrations forms late (South Carolina Code of Laws - Title 33 - Chapter 56 - Solicitation Of Charitable Funds, 2015b).

In addition to the legal requirements for solicitation, there are several standards of accountability that an NPO must adopt or continue to use in order to ensure accountability to donors.

At the time a gift is received from a donor, a receipt should be given. The receipt should contain a statement acknowledging GSHS is a charity recognized as tax-exempt by the IRS under Section 501(c)(3). It should also include the amount donated, or a description of the property if the donation is not monetary. If goods or services were provided in exchange for a gift of $75 or more, the statement must include a "good faith estimate of the value of the goods/services provided" (National Council of Nonprofits, 2015b).

At the time of the gift, the GSHS must record those donations in their records. In order to accurately report revenues on the financial statements and IRS documents, strong record-keeping of

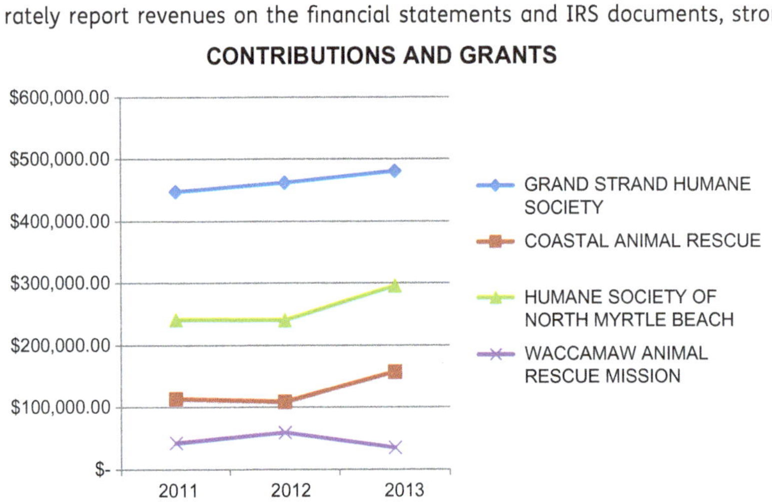

Figure 16. Contributions and grants, local animal welfare organizations.

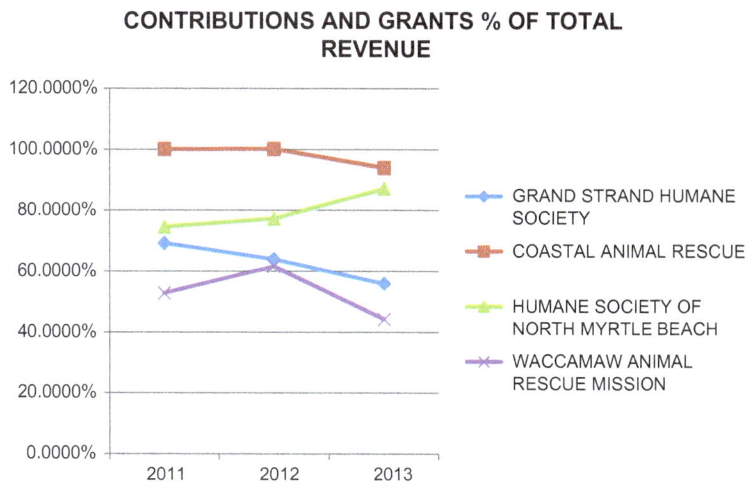

Figure 17. Contributions and grants as a percentage of total revenue, local animal welfare organizations.

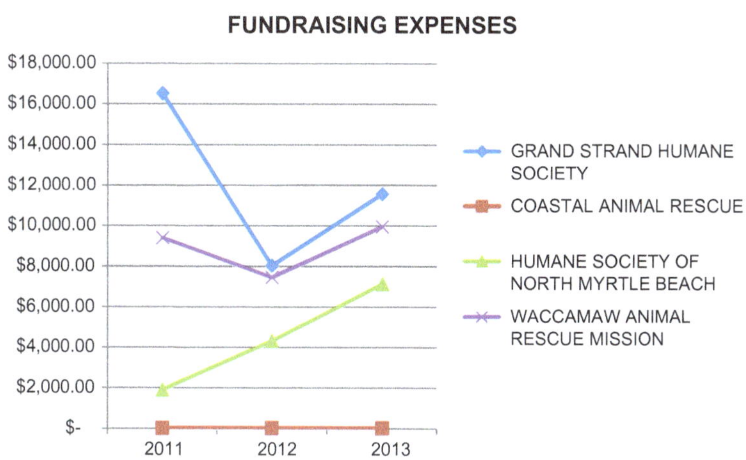

Figure 18. Fundraising expenses, local animal welfare organizations.

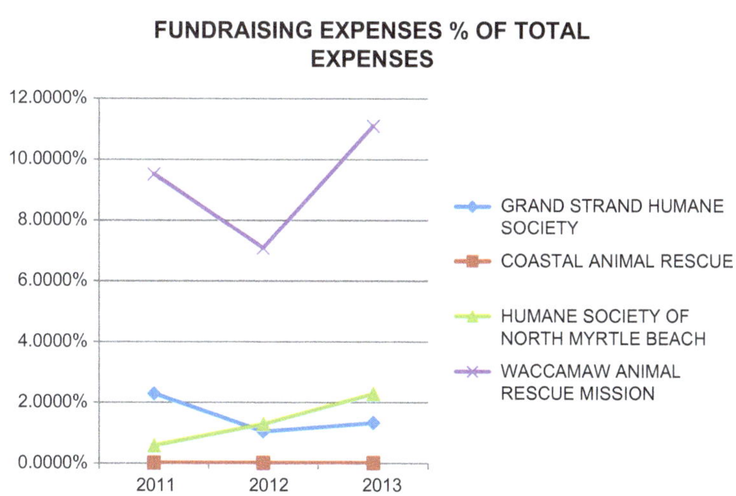

Figure 19. Fundraising expenses as a percentage of total expenses, local animal welfare organizations.

revenue generation must be maintained. Form 990 provides several columns to report fundraising events. Revenues generated through fundraising should follow this model. The revenues and expenses of all events held by the GSHS should be recorded in the GSHS system separately (IRS, 2015b).

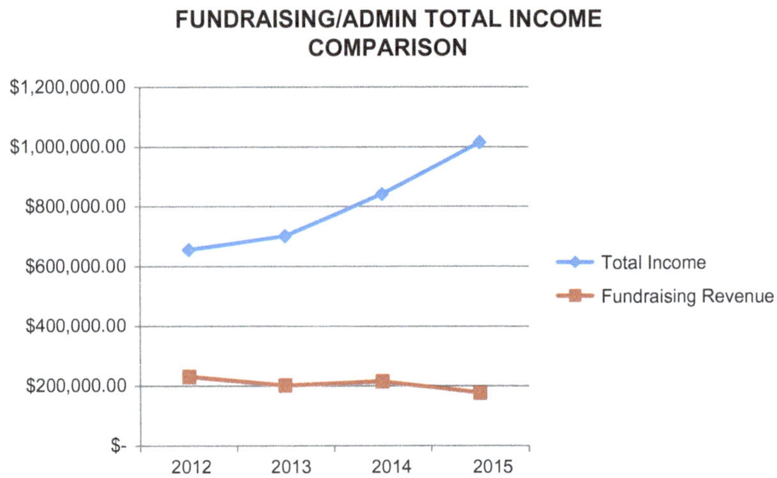

Figure 20. GSHS comparison of total and fundraising unit income.

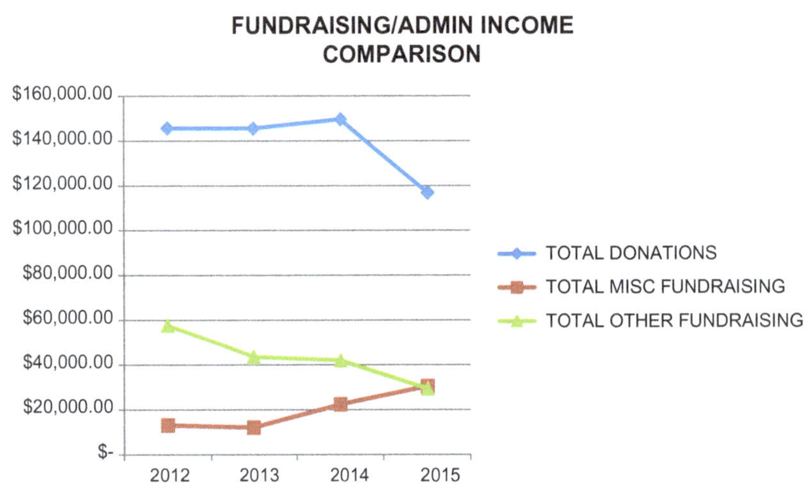

Figure 21. GSHS fundraising unit income.

Equally as important as record-keeping and donation tracking are the issues of donor anonymity and donor intent. If a donor wishes to remain anonymous or provide a contribution that is restricted to a specific use, this is a request that an NPO must respect. In order to curtail concerns related to donor anonymity and use of restricted gifts, the Association of Financial Professionals (2015a) has established a Donor's Bill of Rights which delineates the rights of anyone making a contribution (National Council of Nonprofits, 2015a).

Modern technology has provided an invaluable resource for fundraising in the form of solicitation over the Internet and through social media. However, these forms of fundraising come with their own set of rules and regulations. In South Carolina, charitable fundraising is administered by the Division of Public Charities in the office of the South Carolina Secretary of State (2015). The required documentation for Internet solicitation in the State of South Carolina is covered by the original and renewal registration requirements mentioned previously.

The Charleston Principles are nonbinding Internet fundraising guidelines for soliciting donations in states where an NPO is not registered (National Council of Nonprofits, 2015a). In order to actively solicit donations from multiple states, an NPO must be registered in the state from which they are soliciting donations. However, in terms of social media and NPO websites, simply having the ability to receive donations from out of state sources does not qualify as soliciting donations. A donor can be out of state and make a donation without the NPO having to be registered in that state. The laws in place regarding multi-state solicitation simply deter organizations from actively targeting out of state donor contributions (Law For Change, 2015).

Currently, South Carolina NPOs are not eligible for the Unified Registration Statement, which seeks to provide standardized reporting and data requirements for NPOs registered in multiple, eligible states (The Multi-State Filer Project, 2015). IRS Publication 1771 explains the federal tax law for NPOs that received contributions that are tax deductible for the donor (IRS, 2015c).

An NPO must be diligent in recording expenses related to fundraising. In order to achieve the transparency required to instill donor confidence and qualify for federal grants, segregation of expenses must be sustained. Transparency of expense reporting achieves two goals. First, it allows the financial statements to provide useful financial information to its users. Second, transparency helps make donors expectations more realistic. Expenses related to fundraising can include postage and printing, Internet charges, the special costs related to certain events held to generate donations, and all the indirect costs related to fundraising. The indirect costs related to fundraising are comprised mainly of the salaries and wages of the associates performing the fundraising functions (Association of Financial Professionals, 2015b).

The short-term recommendation for the fundraising segment of GSHS again involves the immediate utilization of Pet Point for fundraising. Performance Measurements available via Pet Point for fundraising include:

- Donations and Mailing Lists
- Flexible Reports
- Pet Requests
- Receipts (Pet Point, 2015).

The first short-term recommendation for the administrative segment of the GSHS is the utilization of the Pet Point system. The second short-term recommendation is to obtain Pet Point training for the new Director of Operations. All available Pet Point packages provide:

- Free setup/training
- Free user support
- Data conversions available
- Fully customizable Pet Point Data Management System
- Integration with 24PetWatch, Petango, and Happy Tails (Pet Point, 2015).

In addition, given that the Director of Operations recently earned a promotion based on merit, leadership training is also recommended. The unscheduled facilities walkthroughs suggest that employees behave differently when management is present versus absent. While the employee issues observed during the informal issue were not the result of actions by the new Director, it is our opinion that they are issues that the new Director must deal with on an ongoing basis. Leadership training would provide the Director with knowledge on how to motivate, oversee, and at times discipline employees.

The third short-term recommendation is to utilize the existing cameras at the GSHS to remotely monitor facilities operations. Cameras can identify employees in the case of theft, reduce employees' perception of their ability to steal or shirk their duties, and most importantly can identify employees that excel in their duties (Fox, 2015). South Carolina allows visible cameras, such as those in the GSHS facilities, to be used for video surveillance. It is not recommended, and an attorney should be consulted, if the GSHS wants to extend its camera coverage to include places where employees may have an expectation of privacy, such as in the restroom. South Carolina is a “one party consent” state with respect to audio recording (South Carolina Code of Laws - Title 16 - Chapter 17 - Offenses Against Public Policy, 2015a).

10. Summary of recommendations

The objective of this project is to evaluate the current financial and compliance status of an animal welfare NPO and present recommendations for improving operational efficiency and achieving best practices. The following recommendations are given based on the findings detailed above for the Grand Strand Humane Society. In addition, the long-term recommendations provide a framework for compliance that can be adopted by any animal welfare organization.

The recommendations presented in this project are divided into two categories. Short-term recommendations are those intended to be implemented within the next 60 days. Long-term recommendations are those that are intended to be implemented over time in order to work toward achieving best practices and building capacity. With both categories of recommendations, the objective is to enable the GSHS and other animal welfare NPOs to:

- Obtain affordable audits and reviews
- Develop and utilize cost-effective techniques
- Improve the internal control process
- Adhere to the grant compliance requirements
- Promote leadership and governance
- Enhance community engagement

10.1. Short-term recommendations

In terms of recommendations to be implemented within the next 60 days, this project has determined three items that can be immediately addressed.

- Full utilization of Pet Point Software
- Obtain Pet Point and leadership training for the new Director of Operations
- Utilize the existing webcam system

The GSHS should begin using Pet Point immediately for pets currently residing and being treated at the facility. Pet Point is an application designed specifically for animal welfare organizations. It contains features intended to track and streamline all aspects of animal welfare. The GSHS already has purchased and has access to the Pet Point application. It is our opinion that immediate utilization of the software would address several issues. Specifically, Pet Point provides record-keeping and reporting services that will enable the GSHS to track operations within the clinic and shelter. In addition, Pet Point provides donation and mailing list services that would enable the GSHS to actively track donations and maintain contact with previous donors.

The different services that the Pet Point application can provide are available on the Pet Point website (www.petpoint.com). In addition, Pet Point offers monthly statistics based on the results obtained from users of the Pet Point application. These statistics provide a basis for comparing an organization's results and are provided regarding the intake, outcomes, and adoptions of both cats and dogs. Adoptions are further broken down by the age of the animal (Pet Point, 2015).

The training recommended for the new Director of Operations directly coincides with the utilization of the Pet Point application. Pet Point offers free training and user support to all users. This training would give the Director the ability to fully utilize the data provided by the Pet Point system. In addition, it is recommended that the Director be provided with some level of organizational leadership training. While the employee issues observed during the informal issue were not the result of actions by the new Director, it is our opinion that they are issues that the new Director must deal with on an ongoing basis. Leadership training would provide the Director with knowledge on how to motivate, oversee, and at times discipline employees.

Directly related to the training for the new Director of Operations is the utilization of the existing webcam system. During the walkthrough, a number of webcams were observed throughout the facility and it was indicated that the webcams were fully operational. This provides an opportunity for the Director of Operations to observe the situation and conduct of employees within the facility without being physically present. If it is not currently available, the webcam system should be set up for remote access. Also, a periodic review of the cameras and footage should be conducted at unannounced and random intervals.

10.2. Long-term recommendations

For long-term recommendations, those intended to be implemented over time in order to work toward achieving best practices and building capacity, this project has identified six categories of recommendations:

- Utilize Pet Point
- Adequate Record-Keeping
- Inventory Tracking
- Adherence to established standards
- Proper Cost Allocation
- Fundraising

The utilization of Pet Point is a duplication of the short-term goal with the added recommendation that the full capacity of the software be explored and utilized. This would require the completion of the training indicated in the short-term goals. Following the training, a review of the capabilities of the software and an assessment of the best uses of the provided services should be conducted.

Adequate record-keeping is in part related to the utilization of Pet Point. The Pet Point software provides a system of electronic record-keeping that should be utilized. The primary goal of record-keeping is to satisfy the requirements of the Internal Revenue Service. The IRS requires that an organization keep books and records that are relevant to its tax exemption and filings (IRS, 2015b). This is just a minimum requirement, however, and the IRS further encourages an organization to adopt a written policy establishing standards for document integrity, retention, and destruction that should cover:

- Electronic records
- Backup procedures
- Archiving of documents
- Regular check-ups of the reliability of the system (IRS, 2015b).

It is therefore recommended that the GSHS develop a written policy that includes the utilization of Pet Point which adheres to the recommendations set forth by the IRS.

Inventory tracking is once again related to the utilization of Pet Point. The Pet Point system contains the ability to manage and track inventory and orders. In addition, it is recommended that the GSHS create an inventory policy that contains:

- A min/max inventory threshold for each item
- Discontinuation procedure for rarely used medications
- Increased security on high risk items such as controlled medications
- Procedures for the storage, handling, and preparation of vaccines

Adhering to established standards involves compliance in both governance and day-to-day operations. We recommend that the GSHS begin the process of complying with the following:

- Internal Control Policy requirements of the Sarbanes–Oxley Act of 2002 (Independent Sector, 2003)
- Occupational Safety Directives of OSHA (Occupational Safety & Health Administration, 2015)
- Outbreak Containment Protocol of the University of Florida College of Veterinary Medicine (The University of Florida, 2015).

It is recommended that the GSHS undertake a project to examine and modify the current system of cost allocations. Analysis of financial statements and tax filings indicated that the current system of cost allocation does not provide the level of transparency required for the reporting of fundraising proceeds and expenses, charitable contributions, medical expenses, and administrative expenses. Further basis for the allocation of income and expenses between the Clinic and the Shelter needs to be examined and a proper driver for the allocation should be determined. Note that in a previous graduate research service learning project conducted by Dr. Maguire's class with GSHS, the NPO's current chart of accounts was mapped to the Unified Chart of Accounts (UCOA), which is compatible with multiple nonprofit requirements, including those mandated by the IRS, FASB, and the Office of Management and Budget for federal grant reporting (National Center for Charitable Statistics: Unified Chart of Accounts, 2015). Pet Point is fully customizable and is compatible with accounting software that includes the Unified Chart of Accounts (Pet Point, 2015).

In order to increase the amount of fundraising and donation income, it is recommended that the GSHS examine the current state of their fundraising efforts. Once current efforts have been examined, a plan should be created to both increase the effectiveness of current fundraising activities and to provide additional fundraising opportunities. Specifically, it is recommended that the GSHS utilize social media to expand their presence and name recognition. Evidence that the new Director of Operations has begun this process is apparent on the GSHS's website and Facebook page.

As previously mentioned, the tracking of fundraising specific income and expenses along with proper documentation of donations is recommended. While the system for tracking fundraising income and expenses will have to be adopted, the system for tracking donations is already available within the Pet Point application.

Pet Point is already in place at GSHS, and further education on how to operate that system can immediately improve GSHS's fundraising compliance. The service provides the ability to record cash donations, noncash donations, and allows an organization to send receipts and thank you letters to donors. The system allows you to record noncash donations in inventory as a donation, instead of a purchase. The program allows you to separate events, and enter the revenues and expenses related to those events accordingly. Once these values are properly recorded, the transition to UCOA-based financial statements and required IRS forms will be facilitated. Those correct, consistent financial statements and IRS documents will provide the transparency necessary in increasing donor confidence in GSHS, likely increasing donations. In the long term, that transparency and accurate reporting will make obtaining federal grants feasible and federal grant reporting possible. This leads to achieving best practices and building capacity.

11. Charity navigator

Adoption of the recommendations presented in the previous section will have benefits extending beyond the stated goals of the project. An example of one such benefit is the ability to be profiled by the Charity Navigator Organization and obtain a rating that will attract more donations. Charity Navigator is a trusted resource that works to provide an easily accessible profile of charity organizations to possible donors.

Currently, the Grand Strand Humane Society does not qualify for a Charity Navigator profile, but this project undertook the creation of a profile based on the guidelines set forth by Charity Navigator. These guidelines, along with the information for those organizations being compared to the Grand Strand Humane Society, are the property of Charity Navigator and are located on the web at www.charitynavigator.org (Charity Navigator, 2015).

Charity Navigator was created as a resource for potential donors to evaluate charities that are grouped in the same category and participate in similar causes in order to facilitate more informed philanthropic decisions based on a standardized set of qualities and calculations (Charity Navigator, 2015).

To be eligible for Charity Navigator to rate the organization, it must be:

(1) A 501(c)(3) organization.
(2) Revenue generated from public donations must be more than $500,000 and the total revenue produced must be more than $1,000,000.
(3) The charity must be in existence for seven years and be able to produce an IRS Form 990 for each of those years.
(4) The charity must be based in the U.S but can have international causes.
(5) The charity must be registered with the IRS.
(6) The charity must incur fundraising expenses and be actively soliciting public donations (Charity Navigator, 2015).

Charities are evaluated in two categories—their Financial Health and their Accountability & Transparency—which are then used to calculate an overall score and assign a one- to four-star rating, with four stars being the best rating. These charities can then be compared to the results of other charities and an overall average for the industry (Charity Navigator, 2015).

For a demonstrative comparison, the four-rated animal welfare charities located in South Carolina and a restricted industry sector, to the southern region only, are utilized in this paper. These charities are as follows:

- Charleston Animal Society
- Pet Helpers
- Greenville Humane Society and
- Spartanburg Humane Society

To prepare the Grand Strand Humane Society, 2015 financial statements to be utilized in computing the financial health in accordance with Charity Navigator guidelines (2015), the following modifications were required:

(1) A revenue-based driver was calculated to allocate, both indirect costs and overhead, to each of the cost centers. The results of the total $1,014,395.17 generated in revenue were as follows:

- Shelter produced $598,559.77 or 59.01% of the revenue.
- Clinic produced $239,913.23 or 23.65% of the revenue.
- Fundraising produced $175,922.17 or 17.34% of the revenue.

(2) "Gray accounts" and errors were revised in the following ways:

- 6300-01 Reception Allocation of $30,732, originally subtracted from shelter COGS and added to clinic COGS, was moved to indirect costs/overhead and was allocated to each cost center based on the percentage of revenue produced by each cost center.
- 5090-00 Veterinarian Services—shelter and 4010-09 Services to Shelter—Clinic, originally subtracted $156,684 from the Clinic COGS—Personnel and expensed it to the shelter's COGS—Personnel accounts. The expense was reassigned to the clinic.
- 6350-00 Administrative Allocation-Fundraising was reported at a negative amount of ($65,796) and was deleted.
- Moved 5140-00 Pet Walk Expenses ($387.50) and 5165-00 Golf Tournament Expenses ($4,031.40) from Administrative expenses to Fundraising expenses.

Once the adjustments are made, the financial statements can be evaluated to assess GSHS's performance in seven different performance metrics which measures, both financial efficiency and financial capacity.

11.1. Charity navigator GSHS's financial health score

The first four performance metrics measure the financial efficiency of an organization and illustrate how the charity manages its daily operational finances (Charity Navigator, 2015).

Performance Metric 1: Program Expenses

This metric reveals how much of the total functional expenses are used on a charity's programs and services (Charity Navigator, 2015). For the GSHS calculations, the shelter expenses $478,060.29 and $ 396,180.42 are added together to equal $ 874,240.71. These total expenditures were then divided by the total expenses reported by the charity in the amount of $1,182,274.71.

The result and comparison by program is:

- Shelter 40.44% and Clinic 34%
- Charleston Animal Society—animal services—74.2%
- Pet Helpers—Spay and Neuter services—60%
- Spartanburg Humane Society

(a) Shelter and basic care—51.7%
(b) Veterinary Clinic—38%

The overall was calculated earlier as the program expenses divided by total expenses (Table 2).

Compared to:

- Charleston Animal Society 84.6%
- Pet Helpers 84.5%
- Greenville Humane Society 95.8%
- Spartanburg Humane Society 84.0%
- Industry average 82.2%

Table 2. GSHS program efficiency ratio

Year	Program services expenses	Total expenses	Program efficiency ratio
FY 2015	$874,240.71	$1,182,274.71	73.95%

Performance Metric 2: Administrative Expenses

This metric shows the percentage of total functional expenses devoted to management and general costs. GSHS had a total of $251,640.70 in administrative and general expenses, which when divided into its total functional expenses of $1,182,274.704 yielded a 21.28% result.

Compared to:

- Charleston Animal Society 4.5%
- Pet Helpers 10.5%
- Greenville Humane Society 3.5%
- Spartanburg Humane Society 5.3%
- Industry average 9.1%

Performance Metric 3: Fundraising Expenses

GSHS had a total of $5,675.80 in fundraising expenses and when it is divided by the total functional expenses of $1,182,274.74 shows that 0.48% of the expenses are incurred by fundraising.

Compared to:

- Charleston Animal Society 10.8%
- Pet Helpers 10.5%
- Greenville Humane Society 0.5%
- Spartanburg Humane Society 10.6%
- Industry average 8.6%

Performance Metric 4: Fundraising Efficiency

This was calculated earlier by dividing the total fundraising expenses by the total fundraising income (Table 3).

This means for every dollar GSHS raises, it spends $0.50.

Compared to:

- Charleston Animal Society $0.05
- Pet Helpers $0.07
- Greenville Humane Society $0.00
- Spartanburg Humane Society $0.19
- Industry average $0.14

The next three metrics measure financial capacity to determine if the charity possesses enough resources to both increase their programs and services over time and to respond to outside economic threats without the disruption of its daily operations (Charity Navigator, 2015).

Performance Metric 5: Primary Revenue Growth

To determine GSHS's primary revenue growth, the total income derived from revenues and other income sources was calculated for the years 2012–2015 (Table 4).

Table 3. GSHS fundraising efficiency ratio			
Year	Total fundraising expenses	Total functional income	Fundraising efficiency ratio
FY 2015	5,675.80	175,922.17	.50

The standard formula for calculating annualized growth:

$[(Y_n/Y_0) \wedge (1/n)]-1$

is then utilized where: Y_n = the total income for 2015, Y_0 = the total income for 2012, and n = the interval length in years (3).

GSHS has been increasing its revenue by 16.26% annually.

Compared to:

- Charleston Animal Society 57.7%
- Pet Helpers 20.5%
- Greenville Humane Society 38.5%
- Spartanburg Humane Society (6.1)%
- Industry average 9.3% (Charity Navigator, 2015).

Performance Metric 6: Program Expenses Growth

To determine GSHS's program expenses growth, the total amount of expenses derived from COGS and other expenditures was calculated for the years 2012–2015 (Table 5).

The standard formula for annualized growth was applied to program expenses where: Y_n = the total expenses for 2015, Y_0 = the total expenses for 2012, and $n = 3$.

GSHS has been increasing its expenses by 17.6% annually.

Compared to:

- Charleston Animal Society 13.5%
- Pet Helpers 12.9%
- Greenville Humane Society 22.9%
- Spartanburg Humane Society (4.9)%
- Industry average 7.7% (Charity Navigator, 2015).

Performance Metric 7: Working Capital Ratio

Table 4. GSHS primary revenue growth

	2012	2013	2014	2015
Revenue	$665,115.10	$700,673.37	$841,298.36	$1,014,395.17
Other income	$8,233.24	$22,032.84	$18,659.34	$2,070.98
Total	$646,881.86	$722,706.21	$859,957.70	$1,016,466.15

The working capital ratio is used to determine how long a charity can sustain its current operations without generating new revenue. The amount of working capital was calculated previously by subtracting the total current liabilities from the total current assets (Table 6).

GSHS's amount of working capital is then divided by its total functional expenses for 2015 of $1,182,274.74 to disclose a ratio of 0.093 years or 34 days.

Compared to:

- Charleston Animal Society 3.56 years
- Pet Helpers 2.21 years
- Greenville Humane Society 1.44 years
- Spartanburg Humane Society .9 years or 328.5 days
- Industry average 2.8 years (Charity Navigator, 2015).

Once all the performance metrics are analyzed, each of their raw scores are multiplied by 10 and the resulting amount is either accumulated as is or adjusted by a score conversion table; then, the score amount is increased by 30 points to convert the total to a 100-point scale (Charity Navigator, 2015).

Final assigned financial score for GSHS equals 77.3 and receives a two-star rating (Table 7).

Compared to:

- Charleston Animal Society has a score of 95.97 and a four-star financial health rating.
- Pet Helpers has a score of 98.45 and a four-star financial health rating.
- Greenville Humane Society has a score of 99.58 and a four-star financial health rating.
- Spartanburg Humane Society has a score of 70.20 and a two-star financial health rating (Charity Navigator, 2015).

Table 5. GSHS program expenses growth

	2012	2013	2014	2015
Calculated previously				$1,182,274.74
COGS	$534,039.14	$589,731.28	$667,733.93	
Expenses	$192,042.38	$181,562.84	$204,418.64	
Other	$864.49	$1,431.38	$1,333.07	
Total	$726,946.01	$772,725.50	$873,485.64	$1,182,274.74

Table 6. GSHS working capital

Year	Total current assets	Total current liabilities	Working capital
FY 2015	$138,518.09	$28,352.35	$110,165.74

Table 7. GSHS charity navigator financial score calculation		
Performance metrics	**Raw score**	**Raw score × 10 or conversion**
Program expenses	.733	7.3
Administrative expenses	.2128	5 (converted)
Fundraising expenses	.0048	10 (converted)
Fundraising efficiency	.5	2.5 (converted)
Primary revenue growth	.1626	10 (converted)
Program expense growth	.176	10 (converted)
Working capital ratio	.09	2.5 (converted)
Total score	+30 points	47.3

Conversion Tables used in the assigning of financial scores and financial health scores are available from the author.

11.2. Charity navigator GSHS's accountability and transparency score

The second category which Charity Navigator uses to evaluate charities is on their accountability and transparency. This illustrates the organization's willingness to explain and justify its actions and the efforts it exerts to ensure that its vital information is accessible to its stakeholders (Charity Navigator, 2015).

The data for GSHS retrieved from IRS Form 990 were utilized to answer the following questions (Table 8).

The information about GSHS contained on its website (Table 9):

GSHS's accountability and transparency score is 51 and it has a rating of 0-stars.

Compared to:

- Charleston Animal Society—96 score and four-star rating.
- Pet Helpers—88 score and three-star rating.
- Greenville Humane Society—80 score and three-star rating.
- Spartanburg Humane Society—82 score and three-star rating (Charity Navigator, 2015).

Finally, Charity Navigator computes the overall score using the following formula (Charity Navigator, 2015).

$$100 - \sqrt{\frac{(100 - \text{Financial})^2 + (100 - \text{A\&T})^2}{2}}$$

GSHS has an overall all score of 61.81 and receives a one-star rating (Table 10).

Compared to:

- Charleston Animal Society—95.97 score and a four-star rating.
- Pet Helpers—91.44 score and a four-star rating.
- Greenville Humane Society—85.85 score and a three-star rating.

Table 8. GSHS charity navigator accountability and transparency form 990 data

Data needed	Is the answer provided on Form 990?	Deducted from score of 100
Is the Board independent, a voting majority, and consist of at least five members?	Yes	
Is there a material diversion of assets in the last two years?	None	
Audited financials prepared by an independent accountant with an audit oversight committee?	No	15 points
Loan(s) to or from related parties?	No	
Are board meeting minutes documented?	Yes	
Is the board provided a copy of Form 990 prior to filling?	Yes	
Is there a conflict of interest policy?	No	4 points
Is there a whistleblower policy?	No	4 points
Is there a records retention and destruction policy?	No	4 points
Is the CEO listed with salary information?	No	4 points
Is there a documented method for determining the salary of the CEO, as well as reviewing and updating it?	No	4 points
Are the board members and their compensation disclosed?	Yes	

Table 9. GSHS charity navigator accountability and transparency website data

Data needed:	Is the answer posted on website?	Deduction from score
Are the board members listed?	Yes	
Is key staff listed?	Yes	
Is the audited financials published?	No	4 points
Is the Form 990 published?	No	3 points
Is there a published donor privacy policy?	No	4 points
Is there an opt-out donor privacy policy?	No	3 points

Table 10. Charity navigator scoring system

Overall rating:	★★★★	★★★	★★	★	0 Stars	Donor advisory
Overall score:	≥ 90	80–90	70–80	55–70	< 55	N/A

- Spartanburg Humane Society—75.38 score and a two-star rating (Charity Navigator, 2015).

Comparing the overall scores (Figure 22):

Recommendations

(1) Create a Standard Operating Procedures (SOP) manual that includes:

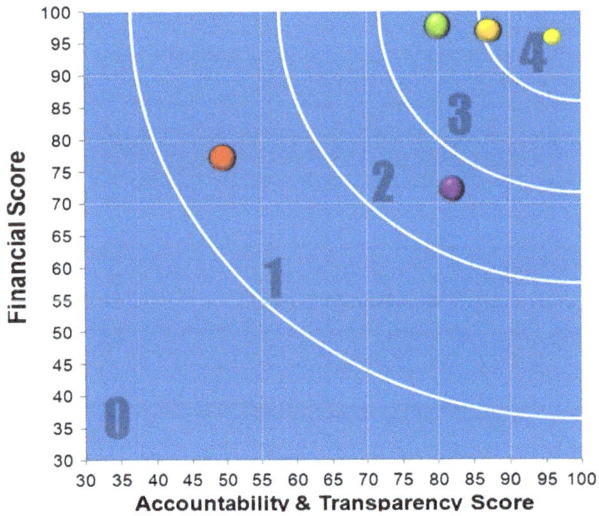

Figure 22. GSHS charity navigator score mapping.

Legend: GSHS—Red; Charleston Animal Society—Yellow; Pet Helpers—Orange; Greenville Humane Society—Green; and Spartanburg Humane Society—Purple.

- A conflict of interest policy
- A whistleblowers policy
- A records retention and destruction policy, and
- A standardized process for establishing CEO salary, as well as, a review process

(2) Update the GSHS website to include:

- Form 990
- A donor privacy policy
- A Opt-out donor policy

12. Conclusion

Working in collaboration with The Chapin Foundation, the output of these multi-stage research projects will assist NPOs achieve best practices in their "back room operations" now and as they grow. Achieving compliance with best practices for financial accountability, transparency, and board governance, the output of these projects facilitate the link between philanthropic leadership, charitable resources, and civic influence with community needs and opportunities.

The recommendation for the future is to continue to conduct research for NPOs that will provide education on how to achieve best practices. Research with the participation of Master of Accountancy graduate students at Coastal Carolina University provides the opportunity to assist the NPOs in several areas. Through the research, assistance can be provided to help NPOs achieve best practices for corporate governance, accounting, and auditing, and reduce the costs of attaining these goals.

This research process is intended to assist South Carolina NPOs achieve compliance with best practices for financial accountability, fundraising, and board governance. Essentially, by strengthening the financial knowledge and practices of South Carolina NPOs: donors will have more confidence; NPOs will have the ability to obtain the funding needed to reach their goals; achieving efficiency in "back-room operations" will increase effectiveness in "front-room operations;" NPOs can build capacity; and NPOs can continue providing charitable services to our communities. This research provides a mutual benefit to both Coastal Carolina University and the South Carolina NPO community.

Acknowledgments

It is both an honor and a privilege to work with the Master of Accountancy students on these research service learning projects. I cannot thank them enough for their dedication in helping nonprofits, teamwork, leadership, and sense of humor.

Funding

The author received no direct funding for this research.

Author details

Karen A. Maguire[1]

E-mail: KMaguire@coastal.edu

[1] Department of Accounting, Coastal Carolina University, PO Box 261954, Conway, SC 29528, USA.

References

American Society for the Prevention of Cruelty to Animals. (2015a). *ASPCA professional calculating your humane capacity*. Retrieved from http://aspcapro.org/resource/shelter-health-animal-care/calculating-your-humane-capacity

American Society for the Prevention of Cruelty to Animals. (2015b). *ASPCA professional live release rate and animals at risk*. Retrieved from http://aspcapro.org/live-release-rate-and-animals-risk

Asilomar Accords. (2004). Retrieved from http://www.asilomaraccords.org/

Association of Financial Professionals. (2015a). *Donor Bill of Rights*. Retrieved from http://www.afpnet.org/Ethics/EnforcementDetail.cfm?ItemNumber=3359

Association of Financial Professionals. (2015b). *New Accounting Standards on Reporting Fundraising Expenses*. Retrieved from http://www.afpnet.org/Ethics/EmergingIssuesDetail.cfm?itemnumber=4227

Bousfield,B., & Brown, R. (2010). *Animal Welfare*. Retrieved from https://www.afcd.gov.hk/english/quarantine/qua_vb/files/AW8.pdf

Charity Navigator. (2015). *Methodology*. Retrieved from http://www.charitynavigator.org/index.cfm/bay/content.view/cpid/33.htm#.VjB4eVNdEdU

Drug Enforcement Administration. (2015). Retrieved from http://www.dea.gov/index.shtml

Financial Accounting Standards Board. (2015). Retrieved from http://www.fasb.org/home

Foundation Center. (2015). Retrieved from http://foundationcenter.org/findfunders/990finder/

Fox, V. (2015). *Security Cameras vs. Employee Rights*. Retrieved from http://smallbusiness.chron.com/security-cameras-vs-employee-rights-13147.html.

Grand Strand Humane Society. (2015). Retrieved from http://www.grandstrandhumanesociety.com/

Guidestar. (2004). *Why ratios aren't the last word*. Retrieved from http://www.guidestar.org/Articles.aspx?path=/rxa/news/articles/2004/why-ratios-arent-the-last-word.aspx#calculate

Independent Sector. (2003). *Publication The Sarbanes-Oxley Act and Implications for Nonprofit Organizations*. Retrieved from https://www.independentsector.org/sarbanes_oxley

Internal Revenue Service. (2015a). *How to Figure Cost of Goods Sold*. Retrieved from https://www.irs.gov/publications/p334/ch06.html

Internal Revenue Service. (2015b). *Instructions for Form 990*. Retrieved from https://www.irs.gov/pub/irs-pdf/i990.pdf

Internal Revenue Service. (2015c). *Substantiating charitable contributions*. Retrieved from https://www.irs.gov/Charities-&-Non-Profits/Substantiating-Charitable-Contributions

Law For Change. (2015). *South Carolina fundraising registration and regulation*. Retrieved from http://www.lawforchange.org/images/lfc/SouthCarolinaFundraising.pdf

The Multi-State Filer Project. (2015). *The unified registration statement*. Retrieved from http://multistatefiling.org/index.html

National Center for Charitable Statistics. (2015). Retrieved from http://nccs.urban.org/resources/faq.cfm

National Center for Charitable Statistics: Unified Chart of Accounts. (2015). Retrieved from www.ncss.urban.org:http://nccs.urban.org/projects/ucoa.cfm

National Council of Nonprofits. (2015a). *Ethical fundraising*. Retrieved from https://www.councilofnonprofits.org/tools-resources/ethical-fundraising

National Council of Nonprofits. (2015b). *Saying 'thank you' to donors*. Retrieved from http://www.councilofnonprofits.org/tools-resources/saying-thank-you-to-donors

Occupational Safety and Health Administration. (2015). Retrieved from https://www.osha.gov:https://www.osha.gov/

Pet Point. (2015). Retrieved from http://www.petpoint.com/

South Carolina Code of Laws – Title 16 – Chapter 17 – Offenses Against Public Policy. (2015a). Retrieved from http://www.scstatehouse.gov/code/t16c017.php

South Carolina Code of Laws - Title 33 - Chapter 56 - Solicitation Of Charitable Funds. (2015b). Retrieved from http://scstatehouse.gov/code/t33c056.php

South Carolina Department of Health and Environmental Control. (2015). Retrieved from http://www.scdhec.gov/

South Carolina Secretary of State. (2015). Retrieved from http://www.scsos.com/

The University of Florida. (2015). *Maddie's shelter medicine program*. Retrieved from http://sheltermedicine.vetmed.ufl.edu/shelter-services/

The World Organisation for Animal Health, OIE. (2015). Retrieved from http://www.oie.int/

Permissions

All chapters in this book were first published in CBM, by Cogent OA; hereby published with permission under the Creative Commons Attribution License or equivalent. Every chapter published in this book has been scrutinized by our experts. Their significance has been extensively debated. The topics covered herein carry significant findings which will fuel the growth of the discipline. They may even be implemented as practical applications or may be referred to as a beginning point for another development.

The contributors of this book come from diverse backgrounds, making this book a truly international effort. This book will bring forth new frontiers with its revolutionizing research information and detailed analysis of the nascent developments around the world.

We would like to thank all the contributing authors for lending their expertise to make the book truly unique. They have played a crucial role in the development of this book. Without their invaluable contributions this book wouldn't have been possible. They have made vital efforts to compile up to date information on the varied aspects of this subject to make this book a valuable addition to the collection of many professionals and students.

This book was conceptualized with the vision of imparting up-to-date information and advanced data in this field. To ensure the same, a matchless editorial board was set up. Every individual on the board went through rigorous rounds of assessment to prove their worth. After which they invested a large part of their time researching and compiling the most relevant data for our readers.

The editorial board has been involved in producing this book since its inception. They have spent rigorous hours researching and exploring the diverse topics which have resulted in the successful publishing of this book. They have passed on their knowledge of decades through this book. To expedite this challenging task, the publisher supported the team at every step. A small team of assistant editors was also appointed to further simplify the editing procedure and attain best results for the readers.

Apart from the editorial board, the designing team has also invested a significant amount of their time in understanding the subject and creating the most relevant covers. They scrutinized every image to scout for the most suitable representation of the subject and create an appropriate cover for the book.

The publishing team has been an ardent support to the editorial, designing and production team. Their endless efforts to recruit the best for this project, has resulted in the accomplishment of this book. They are a veteran in the field of academics and their pool of knowledge is as vast as their experience in printing. Their expertise and guidance has proved useful at every step. Their uncompromising quality standards have made this book an exceptional effort. Their encouragement from time to time has been an inspiration for everyone.

The publisher and the editorial board hope that this book will prove to be a valuable piece of knowledge for researchers, students, practitioners and scholars across the globe.

List of Contributors

Imen Fakhfakh Sakka
Faculty of Economics and Management of Sfax (FSEGS), Department of Finance and Accounting, Sfax, Tunisia

Anis Jarboui
Department of Finance and Accounting, Higher Institute of Business Administration (ISAAS), Sfax, Tunisia

Mouna Abdelhedi-Zouch and Achraf Ghorbel
Laboratory URECA, Faculty of Economics and Management of Sfax, Universite de Sfax, Sfax, Tunisia

Geeta Rani Duppati
Department of Finance, Waikato Management School, University of Waikato, Hamilton, New Zealand

Narendar V. Rao
Department of Finance, College of Business and Management, Northeastern Illinois University, Chicago, IL, USA

Michael Adusei
Department of Accounting and Finance, Kwame Nkrumah University of Science and Technology, Kumasi, Ghana

Amanjot Singh and Manjit Singh
University School of Applied Management, Punjabi University, Patiala 147002, Punjab, India

Hakan Karaosman, Gustavo Morales-Alonso and Mercedes Grijalvo
Department of Industrial Management, Business Administration and Statistics; School of Industrial Engineering, Universidad Politécnica de Madrid (UPM), Calle de José Gutiérrez Abascal, 2, 28006 Madrid, Spain

Muhammad Ali Nasir, Junjie Wu, Milton Yago and Alaa M. Soliman
Faculty of Business & Law, Leeds Beckett University, Leeds, UK

Anwar Ammar
Faculty of Management, Multimedia University, Cyberjaya, Malaysia

Elsadig Musa Ahmed
Faculty of Business, Multimedia University, Melaka 75450, Malaysia

Abdelkader Derbali
Department of Finance, Higher Institute of Management of Sousse, University of Sousse, 22 Street Zarkaa Al Yamama, Sousse Erriadh 4023, Tunisia

Slaheddine Hallara
Department of Finance, Higher Institute of Management of Tunis, University of Tunis, Tunis, Tunisia

Marcelo Eduardo and Brooks Poole
Mississippi College School of Business, Clinton, MS, USA

Karen A. Maguire
Department of Accounting, Coastal Carolina University, PO Box 261954, Conway, SC 29528, USA

Imen Fakhfakh Sakka
Faculty of Economics and Management of Sfax (FSEGS), Department of Finance and Accounting, Sfax, Tunisia

Anis Jarboui
Department of Finance and Accounting, Higher Institute of Business Administration (ISAAS), Sfax, Tunisia

Mouna Abdelhedi-Zouch and Achraf Ghorbel
Laboratory URECA, Faculty of Economics and Management of Sfax, Universite de Sfax, Sfax, Tunisia

Geeta Rani Duppati
Department of Finance, Waikato Management School, University of Waikato, Hamilton, New Zealand

Narendar V. Rao
Department of Finance, College of Business and Management, Northeastern Illinois University, Chicago, IL, USA

Michael Adusei
Department of Accounting and Finance, Kwame Nkrumah University of Science and Technology, Kumasi, Ghana

Amanjot Singh and Manjit Singh
University School of Applied Management, Punjabi University, Patiala 147002, Punjab, India

Hakan Karaosman, Gustavo Morales-Alonso and Mercedes Grijalvo
Department of Industrial Management, Business Administration and Statistics; School of Industrial Engineering, Universidad Politécnica de Madrid (UPM), Calle de José Gutiérrez Abascal, 2, 28006 Madrid, Spain

Muhammad Ali Nasir, Junjie Wu, Milton Yago and Alaa M. Soliman
Faculty of Business & Law, Leeds Beckett University, Leeds, UK

Anwar Ammar
Faculty of Management, Multimedia University, Cyberjaya, Malaysia

Elsadig Musa Ahmed
Faculty of Business, Multimedia University, Melaka 75450, Malaysia

Abdelkader Derbali
Department of Finance, Higher Institute of Management of Sousse, University of Sousse, 22 Street Zarkaa Al Yamama, Sousse Erriadh 4023, Tunisia

Slaheddine Hallara
Department of Finance, Higher Institute of Management of Tunis, University of Tunis, Tunis, Tunisia

Marcelo Eduardo and Brooks Poole
Mississippi College School of Business, Clinton, MS, USA

Karen A. Maguire
Department of Accounting, Coastal Carolina University, PO Box 261954, Conway, SC 29528, USA

Index